*structural
functions
in music*

structural
functions
in music

WALLACE BERRY

Professor of Music
University of British Columbia

DOVER PUBLICATIONS, INC., NEW YORK

Published in Canada by General Publishing Company, Ltd., 30
Lesmill Road, Don Mills, Toronto, Ontario.

This Dover edition, first published in 1987, is an unabridged and
corrected republication of the work originally published by Prentice-
Hall, Inc., Englewood Cliffs, New Jersey, in 1976. Corrections have been
made by the author specially for this Dover edition.

Manufactured in the United States of America
Dover Publications, Inc., 31 East 2nd Street, Mineola, N.Y. 11501

Library of Congress Cataloging-in-Publication Data

Berry, Wallace.
   Structural functions in music.

   Reprint. Originally published: Englewood Cliffs, N.J. : Prentice-Hall,
1976. With corrections by the author.
   Includes bibliographical references and index.
   1. Musical analysis.   I. Title.
MT6.B465S8   1987   781   86-31912
ISBN 0-486-25384-8 (pbk.)

to Maxine

contents

CHAPTER TWO

texture, 184

CHAPTER THREE

rhythm and meter, 301

APPENDIX ONE
editorial notes, 425

APPENDIX TWO
translations, 427

index of musical examples and citations, 433

index of subjects, names, and terms, 437

preface to the dover edition

It has been more than a decade since *Structural Functions in Music* was first published. Thus, I should perhaps affirm at the outset of this new edition—which is not a revision—that although my views and particular correlative analytical approaches have undergone certain refinements and redirections of formulation evident in a number of publications during the intervening years, the fundamental ideas and methods explored in this book remain, for me, valid and useful. These include the important concept of musical structure and significative shaping as (in one critical sense) an undulation between tendencies of progression and recession.

This book's three essays constitute one testimony among many to the deepening preoccupation in the professional community of music theory with allied and often parallel questions about structural unities, organic substance, and modes of expressively directed fluctuation in *all* of music's cofunctioning elements. Since its appearance in 1976, *Structural Functions* has been a factor in, and has directly stimulated, abundant discussion of various and frequently innovative approaches to studies of the shaped elements of music. Such proliferating studies—complementary or refutative, and often speculative—have appeared in the form of conference papers, unpublished research by young professionals, including many student theses, and a substantial stream of published work. Indeed, probing inquiries into music's melodic and harmonic dimensions, texture, rhythm, and other elements continue, as they must, without end. The complexities of preliminary and derivative questions about the expressive and intellectually provocative properties of music are such that the theorist's quest is assuredly not for final answers, whose unattainability we know enough to know, but rather for deepened channels of understanding consistent with our responses to music as sensitive musicians.

I wish in this brief prefatory statement to express the hope that this book will continue to be a basis for respondent and pursuant investigations, as one of a growing number of theoretical works treating related issues in disparate ways, yet always to the end of better understanding of structure and effect in music. It is, to be sure, a matter of gratification to me that the general accessibility of *Structural Functions in Music* will be significantly broadened as a result of its republication as a Dover paperback.

WALLACE BERRY

Vancouver, 1987

preface to the first edition

Major premises and objectives which are the basis for these studies are fully set forth in the Introduction; the work can be characterized, simply and in summary, as an inquiry into *tonal, textural, and rhythmic structures in music,* and into conceptual and analytical systems for the study of these fundamental elements. While assuming the reader's understanding of basic principles of tonal form and analysis, this book carries ideas concerning tonality, texture, and rhythm—their processive functions and structural configurations—into the analytical discussion of many works and extracts ranging from early modal styles to recent times.

Much important theoretical work that has provided foundation for my thinking about tonality (conceived as a principle relevant far beyond the conventions of the eighteenth and nineteenth centuries), and by which I have been informed and motivated, will be evident to readers who are familiar with traditions, and with certain recent procedures of inquiry, in music theory. Such sources and points of departure (which include the theoretical works of Schoenberg as well as important literatures embodying and reflecting concepts of hierarchically ordered structural elements) are cited at appropriate stages in this book. At the same time, I have sought to bring about a presentation of ideas in conformity with certain essential underlying premises and in the interest of consistent exposition of a pervasive point of view which is, essentially, mine. The studies in texture and rhythm have few if any significant, direct antecedents; the work in those two areas (Chapters 2 and 3) is largely in original formulation.

Many of the ideas and approaches set forth in this book have been the bases for graduate and to some extent undergraduate courses and seminars in music theory in which, at the Universities of Michigan and British Columbia, I have been privileged to explore with inquiring and highly committed student collaborators the lexical, methodological, and conceptual systems and problems of the three areas of concern. The responsiveness, but more the challenges and initiatives, of students in these studies, and in research stemming from them, has been of the greatest benefit to me in the preparations for this book and the cultivation of ideas central to its content.

A seminar on texture proved to be the source of at least three extensive research studies of which I am aware, and that on rhythm and meter the source of others at early and advanced levels of graduate study, not to mention numerous searching papers of more limited scope. The dissertation of Dr. Anne Hall (*Texture in the Violin Concertos of Stravinsky, Berg, Schoenberg, and Bartók;* Ann Arbor: University Microfilms, 1971) brought to impressive refinement theoretical and practical systems in the realm of texture, applying them in probing analysis of significant extracts from the four subject works. I wish it were possible to list the names of other student contributors, some of them engaged in important research at this time.

During crucial stages in this work (the longer periods of its inception and conclusion) I have enjoyed access to the resources and facilities of the Music Division of the San Francisco Public Library and the Music Library of the University of California; my indebtedness to the staffs of both is very substantial indeed. And I owe special thanks to Ilene Silverman, of the Music Library at the University of Michigan, who helped me in many ways during the year in which the book was completed.

My colleagues, Professors Ilene Olken, John D'Arms, and Otto Graf, advised me with respect to translations of texts in certain works cited as examples.

A number of publishers have kindly granted authorization for the reprinting of copyrighted materials, and while these are acknowledged in on-page citations in the text I should also take this opportunity to express my appreciation to all of them, and especially to Boosey and Hawkes, Inc., and Theodore Presser Company, for permissions to quote from restricted works. Obviously, a book like this is quite literally impossible without such permissions.

My wife, to whom this book is dedicated, has helped in many ways, even in such tiresome chores as proofreading, but particularly, and critically, in her quiet encouragement through pressured times, and in her everlasting patience with my brooding preoccupations during such times. I thank her for a companionate, sustaining presence, and for sharing with me so overtly the exhilaration of achievement, whatever its measure, as this work has evolved in many places to which we have travelled, and where we have found composure in memorable natural ambiences, during these past seven years.

Finally, I am grateful to have learned a great deal, through much reading, discussion, and analysis preliminary to and concurrent with the preparation of this book, especially about Josquin, Beethoven, and Webern, and thereby about what I think to be broadly relevant factors in the experience of music.

WALLACE BERRY

1975

structural
functions
in music

introduction

Outside of simplest genres, it is unlikely that we ever attain full understanding of a particular musical experience, so complex are its elements, their actions, and interactions. This book seeks to move toward a better understanding of structure and experience; it does so in systematic exploration of the elements of structure and their important interrelations, laying out a variety of approaches to the analysis of directed successions of events involving tonality, melody, harmony, texture, and rhythm—each of these treated throughout much of its range of potential operations.

These four studies thus seek to give comprehensive exposition to particular syntactic processes in which music can be said to have meaning, and to illuminate in penetrating analyses of works of many kinds the procedures by which structural elements in nearly all music function expressively. A major concern is the consideration of relations between specific formulations and expressive effect in significant works, and a number of concerns are treated in conceptual, methodological, terminological, and analytical systems relevant to such particular structural formulations.

One sets out in a project of this kind in the hope, to use Edmund Wilson's haunting words, of being "cured of some ache of disorder, relieved of some oppressive burden of uncomprehended events." I cite these words not because I can hope to have achieved with consistency so elusive an objective, but because they reflect so eloquently the intensity of purpose and commitment to which a writer on serious matters is dedicated who seeks to put forth systems of analysis and thought by which understanding can be induced.

To a large extent, explorative emphasis centers here in theories of rhythm and texture, structural parameters to which relatively little attention is given in the existing literature of music theory. A large-scale scholarly, philosophical, analytical, and systematic penetration of these two vital factors in musical structure and experience is an undertaking of awesome difficulty; yet, any broad, probing effort toward systems by which rhythmic and textural processes can be investigated constitutes, to the extent that it is successful, a needed and useful step in the direction of better understanding of these and related critical factors in the musical experience.

Although concerns with rhythm and texture are, in the somewhat more pioneering efforts they represent, of central importance in this work, related and interactive tonal, harmonic, and melodic systems are examined as parallel shaping factors in musical structure. Moreover, by recurrent reference to interrelations among element-systems, reciprocal and analogical correspondences are indicated in which the actions of individual elements are seen to project expressive shapes of progressive, recessive, static, or erratic tendencies. Progressive and recessive (intensifying and resolving) processes are seen as basic to musical effect and experience.

In the effort to subject to theoretical exposition and analytical explication a consistent, fundamental view of *syntactic* relations in music, a strongly permeative value is, by implication, embraced: a belief in the importance and necessity of logical analysis of the musical experience, of the study of objective data derived in the analysis of structure and experience. That experience can be regarded as the sum of responses attributable to particular musical processes, the action-reaction complex set up whenever there is perception (and enhanced when there is cognition[1]) of musical stimuli issuing in contexts in which syntactic relations are cultivated and controlled as the result of disciplined creative acts. I strongly affirm that belief in logical analysis, and in the necessity and worth of the pursuit of rational inquiry into the musical experience. At the same time, I see that mode of inquiry as one in which conjectural hypothesis and intuition (where intuition is the creative fusion of acquired knowledge and experience) are vital in triggering necessary questions and answers, and in suggesting interpretations which can be examined for plausibility and, at times, susceptibility to empirical verification.

Thus, the many analyses in which theoretical premises are throughout this book brought into focus are directed to consideration of the vital question: How does music speak, and what is the nature of its language? Or, *to what specific inflections can we be said to respond with understanding and feeling?* The study of particular syntactic techniques and procedures, however tentative its conclusions, can render the expressive communication of musical meaning less mysterious than it is often thought (and sometimes wistfully hoped) to be;

---

[1]The distinction intended is that between two levels of awareness in the experience of music, two levels going beyond simple hearing: the cognitive level is regarded as that involving understanding as opposed to that of simpler affective sensory apprehension. This distinction is related to that between knowing and feeling, insight and innocent reaction; both kinds of factors are critical in the musical experience.

indeed, the belief that logical insights can be had into relations between structure and effect underlies all productive aesthetic inquiry. It is a belief proudly affirmed in this book. The business of musical analysis is to consider the nature of *functions and expressive effect* in the tones and rhythms of which music is made.

Surely it is clear that any serious investigation of structure and effect, to the extent of its validity, must significantly inform the critical evaluation, stylistic understanding, and interpretation of music, while laying important bases for decision in musical creativity. Beyond this general statement[2] one can do little more than affirm with the most positive emphasis that the understanding of structure and effect in all musical elements and in their interactions is of very decisive importance in all serious, professional endeavor in music, and to the listener-participant as well. Moreover, a theoretical system which affords useful comment on the relation of structure to expressive effect will suggest many significant and necessary parallels linking music with other, especially temporal, art forms.

The performer, for his special part, must fully understand the functional-expressive basis and significance of *energizing and subsident element-processes* which it is his challenge to portray and project. However, I believe the path from analytical insight to interpretive decision is one of considerable complexity. Conclusions drawn from the analytical undertaking do not lead directly and unequivocally to particular interpretive decisions; rather, the performer must often—perhaps usually—make difficult judgments within a range of plausible solutions (for example, whether in performance to underscore by the slight adjustment of tempo an essential recessive process). For now, in the interest of achieving a rigidly defined, circumscribed fundamental purpose, I have had to be content with a restricted number of suggestive references to problems of interpretive decision in the examples to which this book refers. Nonetheless, such references occur, especially in Chapter 3.

I believe a great deal of understanding of musical process, in its essential terms, to be accessible to the involved layman or amateur. Indeed, many of the most persuasive factors in musical effect and function are delineative of shapes and processes that can be demonstrated, given necessary theoretical and analytical calculations, relatively simply. A related view holds that many of music's most immediate and compelling strengths derive from the shaped actions of elements of primitive substance and effect (e.g., those of dynamic changes, or timbral differences). Nevertheless, the thorough analysis of all the elements of structure in their confluent and con-

---

[2]See also relevant statements in the Preface to the author's *Form in Music*, 2nd ed. (Englewood Cliffs, N.J.: Prentice-Hall, Inc., 1986).

tiguous operations at all relevant hierarchic levels is an issue of sophistication and complexity—and one that must constitute a significant and essential part of the competence and experience of the professional musician.

In an important sense, this book is concerned with *grouping* of many kinds and at diverse levels—event-groupings going beyond those of *form*, the articulation of units by "formal" (cadential, thematic) procedures. In general, structure is discussed as to its functional and expressive consequences within an "intensity curve" delineated by groupings and controlled associations of events underlying nearly all composed music.

In music that is composed (as opposed to music of random operations or random consequences), actions (changes, events) involving various elements (lines of pitch change, tonal and harmonic succession, rhythm and meter, texture, and coloration) are so conceived and controlled that they *function* at hierarchically ordered levels *in processes by which intensities develop and decline,* and by which analogous feeling is induced. Element-actions may converge in collaborative, directed lines of change; or, probably more commonly, certain prevailing lines of change function toward a particular expressive end while others, subordinate to the essential functional tendency, are counteractive.

Examples of universal musical processes can be indicated in observations of the sort: "the music is coming to a close," or "the music is advancing toward a peak of intensity," or "the music is in a tentative state, with something of special consequence about to emerge," and comparable cognitions. In the first of these instances, the process of closure, predominant element-actions of necessity follow a course of decline but at the same time others may and often do resist that essential structural tendency. For example, *crescendo,* or increase in textural density, or, in cases of tentative internal closure, even increased textural diversity, may result in relatively "active" cadential process:

Essential to this concept is the principle that the sense of "motion" in music ("passage" from one event or state to another) largely, although not exclusively, depends on *change* within one or more element-successions. From this premise, it follows that where there is not change there is in critical respects "immobility." For example, in the fixed repetitions of an ostinato pattern at the same pitch level there is "motion" at only the lowest level of structure—that of profiled configuration within the pattern itself. Eventfulness in music demands that iteration without change, at any specified level, occur only within limits: to the point of such limits iteration can be intensifying, while beyond these limits, difficult to define, tedium and tautology result.[3]

Motion in music may, in principle, be erratic, but its usual condition is one of directed activity—courses of change—in lines of *growth or decline* at various levels. (A line of decline at one level may be observed to be subsumed within a broader line of growth at another.) The punctuation and proportionalization of such lines of change constitute an important aspect of rhythm (i.e., are expressive of element-rhythms and meters which may or may not converge). The successions of element-events trace shaped, controlled "profiles"—a concept arising analogously in the sense of temporal "paths" and, where lines of action cross fields of pitch, of "shapes" in "space." Musical structure may be said to be *the punctuated shaping of time and "space" into lines of growth, decline, and stasis hierarchically ordered.*

Of course, not all elements act in commensurate significance, or even act at all, in given instances of such concurrent lines of change. For example, it is clear that the process of digression from and resolution into a primary tonal system will have little or no significance in certain styles; or the action of melodic line in rising and falling, conjunct and disjunct, pitch successions may in particular instances be in part irrelevant or utterly inapplicable. In the analysis of the interactive (and hierarchically related) element-actions in expression of particular functional processes the initial question is, thus, that which seeks to determine *within which parameters contributive actions occur.*

As to general relative importances of such actions in perception and cognition of functional-expressive effect, we will make conjecture from time to time—speculating, for example, that such immediate, direct, and primitive actions as changes in dynamic intensity or textural density have more palpable persuasive force than a relatively elusive factor like that of tonal fluctuation. But, in general, the question of relative significances of correlative actions in cognitive experience is a difficult issue which this book does not attempt to explore.

Element-actions in music function in certain basic formal processes or activities which can be rather simply stated, assuming it is understood that there is an infinite range of possible and palpable degrees of change, rates of change, and specific configurations of interrelations among contributive elements—and hence of expressive effect conceivable and potential within such formal processes. Such fundamental classifications of formal process are those of (1) introduction—often involving dissonant prolongation as a primary factor of expectant intensity in precarious balance with quiescent,

---

[3]Presumably, the limited capacity of pure iteration for intensification is accountable to the rising expectation of inevitable digression.

tentative conditions such as relative textural sparsity and slow tempo; (2) statement—normally in a context of relative stability; (3) restatement—often involving variation, but again in relatively stable conditions; (4) transition and development—both normally relatively fluctuant; and (5) cadence—in an environment of relative decline and deceleration. Some aspects of formal technique are characteristic of particular styles and, of course, particular systems; those most representative of broadly prototypical formal procedures are explored in many existing works.[4]

The present work addresses itself to theoretical discussion and analysis of certain (growth-connected and decline-connected) intensity-activity shapes in which functional and expressive lines of change are very commonly conveyed. Although certain formal processes are by definition associated with particular functional tendencies (e.g., that of the cadential process with recessive action), in general, progressive and recessive lines of change occur variously in diverse formal contexts. Indeed, music is constantly involved (in both concurrent and contiguous event-relations) in a *dialectic* in which opposing tendencies of growth and decline (and their correlatives up-down, far-near, dense-sparse, simple-complex, etc.) are in continual interplay at different hierarchic levels.

Formal processes and element-actions of growth and decline are thus both discretely identifiable and interdependent as aspects of form and structure, and the study of lines of changing intensities yields significant understanding of particular compositional techniques by which formal processes are carried out. The primary concern of this book is the analysis of structure apart from formal process as such, but it cannot fail at the same time to note that particular functional tendencies are critically allied to essential and universal techniques of form.

The idea of music as *dialectically* in balance between intensifying and resolving tendencies, and involving complementary or counteractive relations, brings to mind a moving, terse statement by Pousseur on the third of Webern's Three Pieces, Op. 11, for cello and piano (discussed as to metric structure on pp. 397–400 of this book).

> ... it is through the positioning of well-defined and clearly perceptible units, articulating themselves by means of reciprocal effect, each one limiting and defining the nature of its fellows. Thus an available space is established among the units, an emptiness within which they may reign calmly in all their abundance.
>
> Symmetry and asymmetry, determination and indetermination, equality and inequality, are thus more than simply contradictory principles excluding each other in an absolute manner; rather, they are complementary properties, each conditioning the other and mutually dependent. An excess in one sense

---

[4]These include the author's *Form in Music,* cited earlier.

or the other leads to the same pathological disorder. Only a correct proportion, a balanced tension (which may be realized in an infinitely varied manner) can engender a free order, vital and significant, representing multiplicity and communication, individuality and recognition.[5]

Pousseur is talking about relations of units; yet, the remarkable spectrum of expressive possibilities within the range of musical techniques is immediately apparent when one-thinks of further potential relations *among units of different (but concurrently functional) elements*, and of the cofunctioning, complementary or counteractive, relations of such element-units *at diverse hierarchic levels of structure*. The musical situation and its experience pose in this light a challenge of great complexity, yet one of beguiling interest and inescapable significance.

To see structural function in music as it concerns lines of intensity change is to see, in general, three possibilities: that of increasing intensity (to which we apply the term *progression*), that of subsiding intensity (to which the term *recession* is applied), and that of event-succession involving unchanging degrees of intensity (*stasis*).[6]

Of the latter, it is noted that true immobility is probably inconceivable at the lowest structural level; even a succession of sound events of "equal" qualities can be viewed as consisting of attack-decay "shapes" in each of which it may be reasonable to postulate recession in theory and experience. At the same time, the principle of stasis, even while it cannot be said to have absolute applicability throughout a leveled structure, is of practical importance. For example, repetition of a motivic unit in which parametric factors by which the motive is characterized remain unchanging (to the extent that this is possible in performance which is not mechanical) is, for all practical purposes, static at levels beyond that of the motive itself.

The concept of musical *motion* is critically allied to the concept of progressive, recessive, and static events and event-complexes. To the extent that motion is a useful concept in musical experience, it may be said to reside in factors of three kinds, of which the most important is that involving changing qualities in contiguous sonorous events.

---

[5]Henri Pousseur, "The Question of Order in New Music," in *Perspectives of New Music,* V, 1 (1966), pp. 104–5; translation by David Behrman.

[6]It is assumed that certain structural conditions generally (but in random contexts only accidentally) are expressive of intensity, others of release. Such conditions are evocative of feeling—of anxiety, of calm, of exhaltation, etc., not really explored here as such, but implied.

This underlying assumption is in some degree subject to conditions of probability, predictability, and familiarity within the respondent's relation to a particular style, system, or rhetoric. Thus, any assumed intensity scale or state within a given structural parameter depends in part both as to kind and degree on the understanding or intuition of probabilities within the terms of a particular style and system.

First, in a purely temporal sense a succession of (even equal) sound events, such as one that consists of evenly spaced strokes on a drum lacking dynamic or other changes, is felt as "moving" in time. Thus, "passage" through a temporal "field" is felt as a kind of motion—a stream of eventfulness which courses through time. Even when a stretch of time is "vacant" (unpunctuated by events, as in 🎵), it is bounded by events at its extremities whose "connection"—a relation reaching across the vacant temporal field—denotes passage as "motion" of a kind.

A second and far more critical factor of motion in musical experience is that associated with successions of sound events *having changing qualities*. As suggested, such change in element-actions is normally traceable in, at given levels, consistent directions of increasing or receding intensity, but it may, at given levels, be (or seem) arbitrary and erratic too. In any event, the succession of a sound event by another *of different quality or qualities* (say, two events of different degrees of loudness) conveys an analogical impression of motion— of a "distance" between disparate qualitative states having been "traversed." Thus, in a sense, in music, change *is* motion.

A third factor has to do with the illusion of a "spatial" field in music delineated by the pitch ambitus inherent in the spectrum of perceptible frequencies; this of course can be viewed, within the scope of the second factor described above, as motion implicit in change within the element of pitchline, of melody. But obviously it has special significance and is usefully regarded as a distinct factor. To the extent that succeeding sound events of changing pitches are felt as coursing "over" an analogical spatial field (a "broad" leap between two pitches is felt as going "farther" than a succession linked by a conjunct intervallic relation), the events can reasonably be said to describe "motion" within that field. Thus it is that lines actively "cross" or are related "diagonally" or "triangularly" in musical texture.

With reference to all of these factors, this book embraces a concept of motion in music presupposing, in its direction and control, a value which inheres in significant musical expression of all times.

It was earlier stated that directed, functional-expressive element-successions have three conceivable tendencies: progression, recession, and stasis (that of "aimless" or arbitrary lines of change in some music would constitute a fourth, although its consequence is likely to be one of relative stasis at given levels). In any real musical situation several elements are likely to be active, and these do not necessarily—in fact are not likely to—correspond with consistency in delineating progressive, recessive, or static concurrent lines of change. Moreover, when element-successions move in parallel, or complementary, directions, they often do so, as some analyses in this book will show, at differing rates of "ascent" or "descent" in the intensity line— at differing "rhythms" of element-change.

Within these concepts, musical structure (if "form" is seen as the thematic-developmental "scenario") can be regarded as the *confluence of shaped lines of element-succession* which either agree (are complementary) in intensity direction or disagree (are mutually counteractive, or compensatory) in direction. Within the range of musical elements subject to control within these procedures, some are of course of greater relevance to certain styles than others; but the underlying concept of the confluence of functional element-actions as fundamental to musical structure and effect is of crucial significance in all styles.

We may posit, for example, certain common kinds of element-action having function analogous to that which is clearly pertinent within the loud-soft (⎯⎯⎯⎯ ⎯⎯⎯⎯) spectrum of effect. Some seem relatively clearly demonstrated in identifiable musical experience; others are of more conjectural functional significance. One thinks of rising pitch, shrinking units (acceleration), increased textural quantity, increased compression of texture, *crescendo*, harmonic succession of increasing tonal distance, increase in the overall spatial field, fluctuation toward more penetrating coloration, increased rate of attack, and dissonance, among other musical states commonly associated with increased intensity.

Such a tentative and preliminary discussion takes no account, of course, of the question of *rates* of change, which may be gradual or sudden, or anything within these extremes, with profound consequences for expressive effect. And it has been noted that confluent actions often differ in rates of change—in "angles" of descent or ascent. The factor of rate of change in element-successions, of the degree of "incline" or "decline" in the angle of ascent or descent, is a highly important and pervasive aspect of rhythm in music, one of the most telling factors in the perception of motion and eventfulness. As a matter of fact, temporal segments in music are identifiable, in one sense, as discrete stages in lines of element-change, as rhythmic units of one kind, their progressive or recessive shortening or lengthening (acceleration, deceleration) expressing intensification and release of further functional significance within the rhythmic parameter.

Implicit in all of this is the thesis that contiguous sound events manifesting change within any parameter and in any degree result in functional-expressive effect of, to that extent, intensity change. Put another way, the premise is that no change distinguishing contiguous sound events can be neutral with respect to intensity.[7] Thus, pitch change, however slight, is suggestive of modification in the degree of intensity, as are any and all changes in tonal reference, harmonic content, rhythmic activity, textural complexity

---

[7] It is by now clear that "intensity" is regarded as a product of qualities or states involving usually many concurrently operative parameters; as such "intensity" can only be defined in the listing, conjectural or demonstrable, of such qualities. Particular intensifying conditions of melodic, harmonic, tonal, textural, and rhythmic structures are recurrently discussed as a fundamental, continuing concern in this book.

and quantity, metric structure, and coloration. Of course, in accord with the necessary concept of hierarchic levels of structure, it can be stated that change at a relatively low level is of inferior structural significance (relatively neutral) in contexts of a higher level—i.e., in broader implications. Thus, the pitch succession a-b-a is in a sense, at the level of the total unit, "unchanging"; the progression to b, in the total context, is in a sense "neutral"— subsidiary to an underlying, "fixed" pitch event. But at the circumscribed level short of resolution (a-b-) the modest ascent in pitch (and minute tonal departure) has identifiable functional-expressive significance which can be felt as important in a "leveled" structure and experience.

A theoretical formulation in which vital factors of musical meaning are attributed to controlled directions of growth and decline in lines of element-change requires, as suggested above, hypothesis and observation with respect to the connotations of various qualties in the dialectical intensity-release scale of "values."

Further such assumptions are stated, in a summary way, in the following outline; a number of them will be regarded as having a kind of "common-sense" logic (e.g., complexity = intensity, or the *forte-piano* dialectic), others have the support of traditional acceptance (e.g., dissonance = intensity), while others emerge as of more tentative significance. At the same time, the theory of functional-expressive significance in controlled lines of change within structural element-actions with shaped tendencies to and from points of intensity at different levels has intrinsic importance apart from any specific formulation of connotative values within the intensity-release scale.

While any premature statement in the direction of classification of intensity values within elements of music is inevitably too simple, it can be useful if read as suggestive only, and of very restricted scope of concern. These ideas are extensively developed in the three studies to follow. In Fig. 0-1 specific manifestations of recessive tendency are not indicated but are of course opposite to the kinds of events characterized as progressive.

Reasoned premises concerning the functional-expressive connotations of events (and kinds of events) and concerning their interrelations and confluent parallel or resistant tendencies and interactions are indispensable in analysis.[8] And since in the complexity of real music the likelihood of comprehensive verification, or even susceptibility to verification, is uncertain, analytical judgment is commonly one of carefully reasoned, interpretive

---

[8]The question of *ambiguity* in particular element-qualities requires distinct, special consideration. In ambiguous conditions, by definition, the cognition of structure must be considered uncertain, and functional-expressive significance would depend on that cognition. Where *apparently* ambiguous conditions are *understood* as ambiguous, in a context in which ambiguity is not a "normal" state, the effect is presumably intensifying. This problem is treated further, but not extensively, in Chapter 3.

Fig. 0-1. *Some premises respecting intensity values within the spectrum of qualities pertaining to each of certain fundamental elements of musical structure.*

Element	Progressive action: ———————
Melody, a line of contiguous pitches	*Up*; leap expecting closure, especially when dissonant; instability of tonal or other felt tendency
Harmony, the line of harmonic succession	*Away from tonic*; dissonant; inverted; complex forms; chromatic (deviation from primary diatonic resource)
Tonality, the line of tonal reference	*Away from primary system*, in relation to tonal "distance" and assuming referential adherence of primary I; chromatic succession and expansion
Meter, the succession of accent-delineated units	*Toward shorter units*; asymmetry and fluctuation; clarity of more frequent accent (acceleration); toward instability, departure from relational unit norm
Tempo, or rhythmic "pace"	*Acceleration* in rate of occurrence at given level
Texture, the line of changes in numbers and interactions of components	*Greater interlinear diversity* and conflict; increased density; wider spatial field
Timbre, events involving coloration, dynamic level, registral change, articulation	*Increased sonorous weight and penetration* (strings ——▶ woodwinds ——▶ brass?); louder; higher registers—sharper "focus" of intense color; more percussive, stressed articulation

choice. Within any association of partly counteractive confluent element-actions, the analytical judgment of prevalence—i.e., what tendency dominates and is germane to broad structural effect and intent, is of course extremely critical.

Stasis is nonaction, to whatever extent this can pertain, within any parameter at any given level. We have noted that stasis, being "unnatural" and expecting the intervention of change, is short of the point of tautology intensifying, and usually counteracted by eventfulness within some opposing parameter.

Within tonal structure, for example, stasis does not necessarily denote neutrality of intensity: indeed, prolongation (e.g., of V) is common as intensifying technique. But intensifying stasis of tonal condition almost invariably involves dissonance, often gradually *increasing* levels of dissonance, as a distinct factor significantly complicating an apparent condition of tonal immobility. Dissonance is, by definition, active and mobile and must be regarded, in one sense, in its discrete significance.

One serious aspect of the oversimplicity of Fig. 0-1 is its incompleteness in the listing of parameters of potential action; at each stage in this book primary attention is given to the fullest possible statement and illustration of areas of potential functional-expressive action within each broad element classification. This is carried out with exhaustive attention to quoted examples, and to the presentation, development, and illustration of many techniques of analysis applied to these examples at all stages of discussion.

Lines of element-change controlled and directed along profiles of appreciably increasing or decreasing intensity are common to all music except that limited literature of very recent time in which concurrences and confluences of sound events are unforeseen, and of purely or significantly arbitrary association.

Of course, the association of tonal distance with intensity would have radically diminished relevance to the extent that a style is "atonal"; dynamic progression and recession in loudness levels are of unlikely significance in fifteenth-century polyphony; or, in twelve-tone music, the predetermination of pitch-class (PC) content in simultaneous aggregates *may* (although it does not necessarily) result in diminished significance in functional-expressive contextual control of, say, dissonance-consonance values within that parameter and, correlatively, increased significance in other element-structures. Moreover, that the *manner* in which elements are articulated (i.e., the *techniques* of element-change) differs among stylistic approaches can be noted, for example, in strikingly different applications of the rhythmic factor of tempo change in Baroque as opposed to Romantic styles, or of melodic and textural change in vocal as opposed to instrumental polyphony. These are only a few examples of *particular* relevances of *particular* actions in *particular* styles.[9] Still, it is a sound basic premise that the shaping of lines of element-change is an all but universal factor in musical function and expression; and certain elements are applicable across virtually all historical-stylistic boundaries, notably those of texture and rhythm.

Techniques of progression and recession in lines of change are, then, in different ways significant in the relation between structure and expressive function in some important degree in all music in which controlled contextual function is a compositional objective and aesthetic desideratum. With this assumption, analytical effort must be directed to those elements which are functional in the particular style or medium, or particular work in question.

The concept of progressive and recessive actions within confluent element-structures suggests the useful basic principle that, in an important

[9]It is clear, too, that the particular medium of expression significantly conditions the prevalence of certain elements over others, or to the exclusion of others. Thus, for example, in solo media the timbral spectrum is limited to registral, dynamic, and articulative differences, in addition to such devices as muting or other "preparations" of the particular medium —a fundamental distinction as compared with the broad spectra of more heterogeneous media.

sense, *there are "dissonances" and "resolutions" within all of music's parameters.* The clear relevance of this idea is apparent with even a little thought: thus, for example, an upward leap in the pitch-line, a highly active (perhaps imitative) texture of competing lines, relative ambiguity or (in relation to a referential norm) asymmetry of metric relations—any of these can, like other, comparable conditions of instability and expectancy of restoration of "simpler" states, be conceived as "dissonant," as evocative of intense feeling and subjective involvement in potently absorbing actions and interactions taking place within the projected medium of sound events. These actions and interactions, pertinent to the elements of tonality, harmony, melody, texture, and rhythm, as to further parameters within each of these, are a principal substance of function and expression in music.

Levels of pitch structure, as of other element-structures, can perhaps usefully be conceived as analogically of relative "distance": the most fundamental as "background" in an imagined three-dimensional field, the most immediate as "foreground," in "focus" as one regards the structure at close range. The metaphoric conceit of relative focus is helpful in engendering the image of structural "depth" in this sense, and in conceiving of various "middlegrounds" coming into increasingly sharp exposure as details "blur," and as increasingly comprehensive events are the objects of attention.

The idea of referring to (identifying) such levels as to *spans of context* is at times also useful: "half" of a bipartite form thus can "represent" that level at which its own inherent, delimiting fundamental elements are in focused exposure—that broadly "middle" level which *is "nearer" than superior element-functions extending into contexts beyond that of reference,* in this case one of two major divisions. More "foreground" levels are thus identifiable as to more limited temporal units, or spans. In this sense, "the level of the phrase" would mean "that level at which those events of primary structural basis *in the phrase* are in exposure"—that level whose primary events go "out of focus" in favor of elements of broader significance as one regards broader contexts (more basic levels) "through" events of the relative foreground. Or, "the level of the phrase" is the level of those events which *delimit the phrase as to its most basic content* while more fundamental levels—extending ultimately to that of the whole—are comprised of events whose implications reach beyond that of, in this case, the phrase, or other, limited referential context. In the succession of two phrases having harmonic content I, IV, V - I, IV, V, I, the phrase-level action (structure at the level of the phrase) is I, V - I, while the action at the broader, two-phrase level is I-I, the comprehensive tonic prolongation. It is my belief that levels of depth, providing the basis for important analytical constructs, have experiential validity within all elements of musical structure.

The idea of "level" also arises in other connections: for example, as to the abstracted, leveled hierarchy by which a tonal system, particular or generalized, can be represented, or the "multilateral" leveling of pitch events as noted in Chapter 1. Moreover, a conceptual basis for identifying structural levels in meter as to temporal spans (one of which is taken as the referential metric unit) is discussed in Chapter 3; in that respect, metric structure "at the level of the phrase" is that whose metric unit is the phrase.

The concept of hierarchic levels of structure is of great importance. To put it in the light of the above formulations: every individual element-event has immediate (local, foreground) implications; those that are more fundamental have broader implications as well. Hence, the concept of hierarchic levels in *all* element-structures arises naturally and inevitably, and it must be seen as applicable to the functioning of events within any given confluence of action.

The theory of hierarchic levels is not only of very critical importance in the study and analysis of functional-expressive effects of element-formulations, but it also has important implications for theoretical treatment of individual structural elements, especially in matters of classification and terminology.[10] Thus, for example, the difficulty of "modulation" as it concerns the extent and perceptual significance of tonal reference (tonicization) is greatly attenuated when it becomes possible to speak of tonal shift having referential significance *at a given level* and not at others. The problem of tonal shift remains one of complexity and, at times, ambiguity; but in at least many instances it proves to be of significant clarification to see the tonicization of secondary pitch factors as *relevant to particular levels* (e.g., those of the phrase and smaller units) but not to higher levels.

A like approach to the discussion of "fluctuation" as manifest at given, identifiable levels of structure can be found useful in the theoretical treatment of other structural parameters too—for example, meter, coloration, and texture. (Consider, for example, broad potential implications within the symmetry-asymmetry polarity in metric structure, as opposed to purely local effects of subordinate fluctuation within this particular parameter; and a comparable polarity within the realm of texture is that of the homorhythm-

---

[10]The concept of "leveled" structure derives preeminently from the analytical approaches of Schenker to pitch structures in tonal music, but from the work of other theorists too—for example, that of Hindemith in his concept of "step progression" or Schoenberg in his important concept of "monotonality."

"Schenkerian" approaches have no strict or direct representation in this book, but see Felix Salzer, *Structural Hearing: Tonal Coherence in Music* (New York: C. Boni, 1952) or Salzer and Carl Schachter, *Counterpoint in Composition* (New York: McGraw-Hill, 1969), in addition to many other sources in an expanding literature, some of them cited at appropriate later stages in this book (see page 113). Hindemith's concept of step progression is set forth in *The Craft of Musical Composition* (New York: Associated Music Publishers, 1937), Book I; Schoenberg's theory of monotonality is presented in *Structural Functions of Harmony* (London: Williams and Norgate, Ltd., 1954). Other sources of comparable interest are noted in appropriate, later contexts.

polyrhythm dialectic, with its varying levels of significance.) In analyses which make up much of the substance of this book, the issue of hierarchic structure is recurrent and of fundamental importance.

We have noted the importance of hierarchy in such qualitative distinctions as that which observes stasis at one level (e.g., the level delineated by a pedal point) and activity at a lower level (e.g., that of fluctuation over a fixed or elaborated, prolonged pitch event). Similarly, application of the concept of hierarchic level can bring about decisive and critical refinement of a theoretical idea like dissonance: in comparison, for example, of dissonance function of purely local importance (e.g., the foreground melodic event in conflict with surrounding pitch factors) and that of broader importance (e.g., the expansive dissonance prolongation that often prepares a stable area of thematic statement). And the underlying concept of hierarchic levels serves to inform and establish certain functional distinctions between elements themselves: note, for example, the clear significance of the concept of hierarchic level in the frequently differing implications of harmonic as opposed to tonal events, the latter a hierarchically "superior" extension or amplification of the former.

It thus follows that recessive and progressive lines of element-change must finally be evaluated as to *level of functional significance;* within this necessary approach, broadly viewed actions of one classification will be seen commonly to "contain" lower-level actions of an opposing (or corresponding, but subordinate) classification.

Let the reader contemplate briefly some of the element-structures in which the extension of implications to the broadest structural level can most easily be grasped—conceptually and often perceptually. Thus, in any multimovement work the succession of primary tempi constitutes a broad line of change which is the highest manifestation of the tempo-structure. Or, the broadest level of metric structure in any work of such major formal divisions (i.e., movements or comparable units) is evident in the proportional differences and interrelations manifest among such divisions. And the coloration of a multimovement work constitutes, at broadest level, a line of color change in differences (involving *areas* more than *details* of spectrum) of critical functional-expressive effect. More difficult is the fact that the broadest lines of tonal succession can be seen in many instances to correspond to (to be an "augmentation" of) those of relatively local tonal or harmonic (and melodic) successions.

It seems to me that there is no reason to doubt the *perceptual*, experiential as well as conceptual, significance of these broadest configurations in element-structures, especially those functioning within element-structures of most immediate and uncomplicated apprehension—within the soft-loud, dark-brilliant, slow-fast, long-short, and comparably apprehensible lines of change. In carrying out expositions and analytical illustrations of major categories of element-structure and element-content I have at times been compelled to stop short of discussion and application at broader (in a sense simpler) levels, those for example of intermovement relations. But it is my assumption that these concepts are applicable and apprehensible throughout the structural hierarchy, especially where they concern music's most direct and palpable areas of action and interaction.

In any concern with the functional consequences of contextual associations and interrelations, there arises the issue of randomness, whether overt or the result of the "blind" predetermination of musical events. Křenek embraces unpredictability as a premised value underlying total serialism; in a somewhat ambivalent statement about "inspiration" (*Einfall*) as spontaneous and uncontrolled (therefore of "random" consequences), Křenek correctly notes that it is in fact conditioned by prior understanding and experience. In that light, he says of the composer of totally serialized music:

> In order to avoid the dictations of such ghosts (i. e., recollection, tradition, training, and experience), he prefers to set up an impersonal mechanism which will furnish, according to premeditated patterns, unpredictable situations.[11]

But the surprise which is thus assured is one in which no contextual norm of probability is demonstrable or relevant; hence, an environment is established in which *all events, and no events, are surprising*. (The affective value of surprise, important to any composer, must derive from a context in which a particular event is not what the percipient is conditioned to expect.)

Roger Sessions asks of total serialism:

> . . . what is being organized, and according to what criterion? Is it not rather a matter of organizing, not music itself, but various facets of music, *each independently* and on its own terms or at best according to a set of arbitrarily conceived and *ultimately quite irrelevant* rules of association?[12]

The affective value which inheres in isolated (from contextual relations) sonorous events should not be overlooked or discounted in any comprehensive view of musical expression and experience. Whether isolated sonorous qualities can properly be said to convey "meaning,"[13] there seems no doubt that

---

[11]"Extents and Limits of Serial Techniques," in *The Musical Quarterly*, XLVI, 2 (1960), p. 228.

[12]"Problems and Issues Facing the Composer Today," in *The Musical Quarterly*, XLVI, 2 (1960), p. 169. Italics added.

[13]This depends on whether "meaning" is considered to require syntactic relations, or whether a kind of "meaning" inheres in any single event or element-complex eliciting (affective or other) response. Meaning in the experience of art is commonly considered to depend on controlled contextual interactions of elements: once two events occur in temporal

phenomenal-perceptual attestation and experience speak persuasively of the affective force implicit in such events quite apart from contextual interactions of the kind which are the prevalent concern of this book. The primitive impact of the naked musical event—its intensity, its timbral quality, its general pitch locus, its density (if it is a tone complex), and the like, divorced from syntax, must be regarded as an aspect of musical effect which is far from adequately understood, yet of a level and substance surely inadequate to full experience of a temporal art form in cognitive, intellectual dimensions.

Implicit throughout these studies, and from time to time made explicit in them, is the belief that *controlled contextual function* of element-events is of fundamental value and, even, of necessity in musical communication where the respondent is engaged in apprehensions of *functional ordered relations* as aspects of experience. The view that purely superficial sound qualities in individual isolation—*or in adventitious association*—have a primitive communicative potential suggests some kind of noncontextual significance, even though an important aspect of any "meaning" in the isolated event (say, a big tutti attack in the orchestra) is normally the *expectation it arouses* with respect to likely subsequent events. At the same time, however, the most important aspect of musical experience derives from the *interactions and interrelations* of contiguous and concurrent events of differing qualities *within contextual procedures determined by controlled lines* of progressive and recessive successions. Such a concept of meaning is not applicable where event-confluences are random and arbitrary.

A subtle factor in this area of critical judgment is the problem of element-change of a *rate and degree* so extreme as to, in effect, nullify the effect and perception of controlled change, even of change itself. (A useful analogy here is in the rapid spinning of a color wheel, which becomes white beyond a certain speed of rotation.) Where change (e.g., of register) is fast, constant, and extreme, many percipients testify to the dulling *effect of uneventfulness* which is the ironic consequence of such action. This point is quite independent of whether element-successions in a situation of this kind are, in compositional intent, random or arbitrary, but it is a related question because the phenomenon of "uneventful" change is in fact characteristic of many products of total serialism.

This book includes within its range of musical illustrations several instances of random and highly serialized (i.e., serialized beyond the single

---

contiguity, the percipient assumes a contextual "syntax" to be the basis for their association, and for their further role in a larger context. Told that such functional contextual interrelations are beside the point, he is left to the limited experience of individual events whose association has no appreciable rationale—events cooccurring in an apparently contradictory situation in which they have no appreciable functional interaction or interrelation but are nevertheless run together.

element of pitch) operations in order to provide some exposition of specimen techniques and in order to provide the basis for analytical comment. But it is important to concede at the outset the bias by which successions of events having no controlled or even foreseen contextual associations, relations, and interactions are regarded as antithetic to systems of meaning upon which the musical experience, in virtually the entire history of the art, critically depends. (The issue might be characterized as one of starting-going-stopping in a given musical structure as opposed to beginning-progressing-receding-ending.) When a sound event succeeds another purely fortuitously, contextual interrelation is precluded (unless it is accidental, or unless preselection is within a narrow range of planned consequences); and change which leaps far across a spectrum of possibilities in rapid succession often tends to nullify the effect (and the effectiveness) of change.

It is an interesting fact, too, that music in which important decisions are left to the performer is guided, and often contextually directed, by *whatever creative gifts and intuitive experience the performer may bring to his participation.* But music in which major elements are prescribed in predetermined serial operations (i.e., in which few if any significant elements are left for determination on the basis of the needs of context) is the most "random" of all, in that contextual relations are little if at all foreseen, much less a basis by which events are determined. The highly serialized piece is thus in a critical sense more "random" than the overtly "random" piece in which fundamental decisions are left to the performer.

Of course it is recognized that the intentions and creative purposes of the total serialist may have nothing to do with determined-in-context associations of events, nor can he be censured for failure in an aesthetic desideratum and objective he does not embrace. On the other hand, it must be stated that two common protestations—that performer-directed "chance" music is simply an extension and further manifestation of historical improvisatory procedures, and that extreme serialism is merely another systemic basis for controls analogous to those of modality or tonality—are decisively rejected. In no traditional system are contextual associations adventitious or predetermined in any critical degree: in traditional improvisation, structure is rigidly planned and specified in crucial, prevalent parameters; and in historical systems of modality and tonality creative choices as to contextual affiliations of rhythmic, textural, and relatively foreground pitch events and event-complexes are of broad and decisive latitude, with functional consequences in context, rather than predetermining systemic influences, the considerable basis for creative choice and the determinants of content in the particular piece.

Tonality as a system thus predetermines the content of the particular musical instance in only the most general terms (within which expectations are aroused and fulfilled), and only with respect to certain structural elements; and contextual associations in tonal music are determined as to the functional-expressive needs of specific contiguous and concurrent conditions, not predetermined.

Even while an underlying assumption of the value of contextual determination is conceded, the presentation of specific works and extracts in which this value is called into question will inform the reader of disparate compositional practices, while calling attention to works and ideas that may by their own persuasion lead him to conclusions very different from those stated in the foregoing commentary, with respect to an area of concern fraught with heavily contentious and controversial issues.

It is important to emphasize that the serialization of *some* elements in no way precludes the contextual determination of others. Moreover, any predetermination in classical twelve-tone procedures is commonly of PC (pitch-class) rather than of specific pitch, so that, for example, melody is preconditioned in only one of its aspects. The serialization of PC content in classical procedures in which rhythms and other element-actions are left for contextual determination has produced a vital literature, even at times with tonal bases, as examples in this book demonstrate. Important twelve-tone works are cited and discussed in illustration of this book's fundamental premises and in documentation of the values it espouses.[14]

To the extent that the composer does not determine or significantly condition (or even foresee) the concurrences and contiguities of events in planned contextual relations, analysis can only describe procedures and show their applications. It can, in theory, attempt to describe expressive-functional consequences of random procedures, but any effort to do so, in critical comment based upon premises of value likely to be contradictory to those underlying such works, is irrelevant to the extent that the contextual confluences of events are arbitrary and uncontrolled.

---

[14]The problem of the apprehension of significances of events whose association in particular contexts is purely or essentially adventitious is sometimes discussed as a problem of "overload" in the "channel" of communication of "information," with reference to the concepts of information theory: ". . . the absence of a *stable* stylistic *syntax*, archetypal *schema, audible* compositional *order,* and patent 'natural' patterning results in a level of redundancy so low that communication is virtually precluded." (Leonard Meyer, *Music, The Arts, and Ideas*; © 1967 by The University of Chicago Press; p. 290; all rights reserved. Emphases added.)

See too Edward Cone's discussion of the problem of what he refers to as "synoptic comprehension" in the musical experience (*Musical Form and Musical Performance*; New York: W. W. Norton and Company, Inc., 1968; pp. 88–98). At one point in this excellent essay (pp. 95–96), Cone makes the statement that ". . . 'non-determined' music, whether the sequence of events is left up to the performer or to pure chance, may imply a continuum that often seems to combine the purely musical with the quasi-dramatic. The two determinisms of formula and fortune lead to the same result: the arbitrary way in which such products begin and end and the *fortuitous nature of their inner connections* ensure that they can at best be experienced only as surfaces." (Emphasis added.)

This book's discussions of structure and analysis in harmonic and melodic successions are less extensive than one might wish, but there are many sources, reflecting a variety of approaches and points of view, to which the reader can refer in these connections, and it has seemed important to concentrate heavily on problems of structure not widely treated in the existing theoretical literature, especially those of texture and rhythm.

Moreover, the treatment of quasi-serial cellular associations of pitch and PC complexes is limited, and the treatment of this aspect of structure centers primarily in complexes having tonal or quasi-tonal significance; again, the reader is referred to supplementary resources.[15]

And it has proved impossible to extend this book to the point of including a discrete study of structural functions of coloration (of timbral differences, of orchestration, etc.), although there are many parenthetical references to these factors in connection with central issues of concern and treatment, especially that of texture. In view of this, it seems well to make a point of the fact that one vital aspect of coloration, that expressed in dynamic levels, often goes very far indeed in accounting for the nature of musical experience and meaning. If its attention in these chapters is not equal to its importance, it is largely because its function is direct and obvious, and because of its comparative accessibility of function and significance.

In the organization of this book, it is true that the treatment of "discrete" elements in individual chapters imposes somewhat arbitrary lines of distinction. But overlapping concerns are explicit, for example, in the book's concept of rhythm as including the rhythms of all element-changes (e.g., tonal rhythm), or in the obvious relation of texture and harmony, and in many other instances and connections. With the understanding that this book is about *music*, none of whose structural elements often assumes independent manifestation, it will be acknowledged that there is a methodological advantage and common didactic purpose in individuating at provisional stages identifiable and classifiable element-actions for singular emphasis and for explication of conceptual and practical ideas relating to each such element-structure in turn.

On the other hand, a very important manifestation of the conceptual unity and interdependence of this entire range of studies can be noted in the conscious effort *to treat in analysis certain recurrent examples from chapter to chapter*, and to refer as often as possible to associated events involving cofunctioning elements other than those of immediate concern. To some examples an effort is made to apply comprehensive, although summary, treatment at various stages; each chapter cites examples of substantial scope treated in full at least as to operations of the particular element under primary consideration.

---

[15]The most important of these having broad applicability is George Perle, *Serial Composition and Atonality: An Introduction to the Music of Schoenberg, Berg, and Webern*, 3rd ed. (Berkeley and Los Angeles: University of California Press, 1972).

The procedure by which a basic, highly diverse, set of musical references was established for analytical (at times recurrent) treatment had been an essential premise from the earliest stages of this study. In fact, the selection of works to which to devote attention was the first problem undertaken. Implicit in that initial undertaking was the challenging assumption that a thesis of broad importance in the structure of music had to be, and must be shown to be, applicable to an ample sampling of works representing a great breadth of chronology, medium, system, and stylistic disparity.

Only occasionally has it been necessary to omit the quotation of music to which significant reference is made; usually this is because of necessary reference to lengthy excerpts whose quotation has proved impractical, or because of restrictions of copyright. On the other hand, reference is often to music readily available in widely circulated, published anthologies.[16]

While there are within the range of twentieth-century practice some illustrations of "new" techniques, this book would be highly untrue to itself if it conveyed an impression of special advocacy of contemporary or recent music in which novel means are evident at the expense of twentieth-century music of, in the particular element of concern, more traditional persuasion. It is somehow a particular mark of the present time that musicians tend to devote disproportionate attention to works that constitute manifestoes, or are in some sense apparently trailblazing, when in fact there is much of great interest, force, and resourcefulness in music of traditional bents and assured confidence within conventional means—music that is unfortunately less studied in view of its relative accessibility. Again, one can only plead the limitations of space. What is of interest is the discovery of relations pertaining between structure and expressive effect in all music that is strong and interesting; indeed, the restless assertion of novelty often finds its outlet in mere notational appearances.

Notational problems are a primary reason for the lack of attention to electronic music—not only the problem of the accessibility of scores, but the absence of any generally intelligible mode of graphic representation of specific elements of structure. But I wish to state at the same time my conviction that the principles of contextual shaping to which this book is devoted are fully applicable, within a context of vastly expanded resources not yet well understood in perceptual and cognitive implications, to electronic music.

Analyses of musical extracts and pieces take many forms in these studies, and that breadth of technique of application is altogether intentional. I

---

[16]These include Burkhart, *Anthology for Musical Analysis*, 2nd ed. (New York: Holt, Rinehart and Winston, Inc., 1972); Davison and Apel, *Historical Anthology of Music*, 2 Vols. (Cambridge: Harvard University Press, 1949); Starr and Devine, *Music Scores Omnibus* (Englewood Cliffs, N. J.: Prentice-Hall, Inc., 1964); Parrish, *A Treasury of Early Music* (New York: W. W. Norton and Co., 1958); and Berry and Chudacoff, *Eighteenth-Century Imitative Counterpoint: Music for Analysis* (Englewood Cliffs, N. J.: Prentice-Hall, Inc., 1969).

strongly reject the concept of any fixed orthodoxy of analytical procedure and representation, believing that the approach depends on the nature and basis of inquiry, and may in specific areas take, equally, any of a number of forms. Thus, some of the analyses in this book take form in descriptive statements of an expository nature; others are graphic or symbological within a substantial range of possibilities—some innovative, arising necessarily out of newly formulated concepts. Throughout this work I have sought to fulfill the analyst's obligation to make clear all lexical and symbological bases for graphic, expository, and other methods.

Analytical sketches, of which there are many and many kinds, go beyond the text in analytical comment and statement and must be reviewed in necessary supplement to the text. The question of how to prepare synoptic sketches of pitch structures is often treated informally, again within the intent of latitude and flexibility of specific mode of execution; there is, however, an abundance of illustrations, and suggestions of symbols and procedures are given. In general, it should be kept in mind that sketches of pitch (or PC) content represent *for each example*, sometimes within a limited, specified context and restricted realm of inquiry, an interpretation of structure and functional process and affiliation. This applies not just to pitch structures but to all the elements examined; in Chapter 3, too, the hierarchy of metric functions is represented with careful explication of devices employed.

In any study of this kind, the problem of terminology is a difficult and considerable one. It has been my hope to counter this problem at least in significant degree by the best possible consistency and clarity of terminological selection and definition.

The index lists all crucial and problematic terms together with numbers of pages on which their definitions can be found. In many instances signification is probably self-evident, given a few stated, underlying terminological assumptions, but I have tried to give the reader the benefit of any conceivable doubt.

Brief exposition of certain most essential and recurrent terms and usages might be given here in passing, but it should be read as tentative and preliminary. I use the term *element* with reference to any of that set of primary structural parameters within which events of like significance and character take place in music; thus, the element of *tonality* is projected in *tonicizations;* that of harmony in *chords* (or vertical *simultaneities*) ; that of *melody* in *contiguous pitches* or attacks occurring within an identifiably continuous linear stream, voice, or stratum; that of *color* in *timbres or sonorous qualities*[17] within a given

---

[17]These are determined by physical characteristics of the (sometimes altered or manipulated) sounding medium, by registral locus, by articulative mode of production of sound, and by degree of loudness.

vocal or instrumental spectrum; these are for the greater part conventional usages.

The element of *texture* might be said to consist in *events by which the interrelations of lines or other cofunctioning components are conditioned*, but the textural element is also regarded as including such factors as *density* and *space*. The most complex element of all, that of *rhythm*, is in a sense the product of actions of all other elements; constituent parameters of *tempo* and *meter* are seen as of great importance. Naturally, all of these terms and concepts have full presentation in the chapters which follow.

The terminological premises noted briefly above, and given full explication at later stages in this book, yield certain derivative terms which I have adopted or devised in accord with underlying theoretical concepts. A hyphenated term like *element-structure* refers to the shape delineated by changing qualities and intensity levels (assuming there is change) within a given element, or to the "flat" shape of unchanging events within that element. Terms like *tonal structure* are simply specifications of the generic form, element-structure; but comparable specifications are also used to denote structures arising within constituent parameters. Thus, *tempo structure*, and related terms, are employed from time to time. Similarly, terms like *element-action*, *element-event*, *element-change* yield the more specific forms of which *metric event* and *harmonic action* might be cited as instances. [The hyphen occurs in generic forms, and in terms, especially noun-noun forms, which I have devised (e.g., *pulse-tempo*), and where the association of component terms might not be self-evident.]

Equally fundamental are the terms *progression, recession, succession*, and to a lesser extent *stasis*; in fact, these terms represent in the simplest consolidation a primary conceptual basis for this book, as we have seen. Forms like *element-succession, harmonic progression, tonal recession*, and the like, are in constant use.

I use the term *function* to refer to the processive, structural role of an event or succession (*succession* denoting a generic concept subsuming *progression* and *recession*). If the concept of structural *function* is in terminological reference commonly allied to that of *expression*, it is because I cannot regard them as distinguishable in the object-subject relation of actual musical experience: function is the role, or nature of participation, of an event in the import of expressive content and significance; element-function is the basis for (source of) expression; the functional-expressive meaning and substance of the event are its perceived, cognized characteristics (or those presumably intended) and relations to affiliated events in a given work at a given level.

It is my view that every musical event in contexts to which these theories are applicable (i.e., all except those in which contextual contiguities and simultaneities are fortuitous and arbitrary) has discernible, rationally interpretable, functional and expressive significance. The expressive content or potential of any musical event rests very decisively on its functional role within a contextual process; an event's functional significance (in the structure) is indissolubly allied to, and the primary basis for, its expressive impact (in the experience).

It seems to me that the only sense in which these are experientially separable concepts (assuming consideration not merely of objects, but of experience) is that in which the isolated musical event (whether it *is* in isolation, or is *construed* in isolation in the absence of apprehension of contextual relations) might be said to have purely expressive as opposed to *functional-*expressive import.[18] Since this book is concerned with the analysis of contextual relations in shaped combinations of events, it employs commonly the hyphenated form *functional-expressive* in addition to didactic use of the individual terminological components.

When I wish to refer to the event without necessary regard to its expressive content or functional role I often use the term *projection*, denoting simply that which issues from source to percipient in the musical experience—the stimulus itself, whatever its functional-expressive content and significance, and apart from such significance.

Finally, with respect to the confluent successions of concurrent element-actions, I employ fundamentally the terms *complementary* and *compensatory* (sometimes such associated terms as *parallel* and *counteractive*) to denote relations between element-actions which have, respectively, allied or resistant functional tendency at some level. Within this concept, the term *neutral* is at times necessary, having to do with stasis or nonparticipation—nonfunction *within a given element-structure, with respect to a given directional tendency, at a given level*. In description of situations characterized by the confluence of several element-successions, multiple terms such as *tonal-harmonic succession* or *textural-metric intensification* are useful, even unavoidable.

The above summary of some basic terminological propositions is, to be sure, not intended as a glossary; for explicit discussions of these and many other terms the reader is referred to the text of the book itself and to the index. The foregoing is intended simply to call attention to lexical items of most general importance.

While discussing particular structural elements and consequences in a very broad selection of works, this book points out and illustrates many approaches to analysis. It should pose no unusual difficulty for the reader equipped with understanding of fundamental concepts of music theory, and it is my hope that these studies succeed in laying out in theory and in application some vital ideas and methods in supplement to the work of many others

---

[18]Compare Cone's "immediate apprehension" as opposed to "synoptic comprehension" in the source cited earlier (footnote 14).

along distinct but often complementary lines of inquiry. Important, relevant theoretical sources are cited from time to time.

By no means do I regard extramusical systems and communicative structures, applied analogously or adopted as sources of theoretical models, as lacking important usefulness in the study of music.[19] But the present studies by and large follow from direct encounters with musical works themselves, from which observations are drawn with respect to functional elements and expressive effect, without recourse to parallels in extramusical systems and without employment of systemic analogs and models of other kinds. Understanding is sought in direct discourse with the object itself—the score page and the sound images of which it is the symbol, and in exploration of the experience of what psychologists call the "stimulus object," the musical work transpiring in time.

Of course much work remains to be carried further; the problem of logical consideration of paths from analytical insight to decisions of performance is only one area of need that comes quickly to mind.

I have also implied that, in my view, thorough study of subject response to the single musical event in isolation (in the widest possible range of combinations of parameters) must ultimately play its part in the understanding of the musical experience; for, if the syntactic operations and relations of confluent events are expressive of meaning at the most sophisticated levels of apprehension and comprehension, the naked qualities which inhere in the single event (unconfused by contextual disorder) presumably have evocative powers in themselves in some "pure" and "primitive" sense. (A dancer will respond with "related" movement triggered by the affective content of a single sound.) The qualitative impact of the individual event is intrinsic rather than syntactic—with this I mean not just the event out of context, but the event for which no plausible functional relation to surrounding events can be felt or deduced, or those aspects of the event, contributing to its import and impact, heard and felt apart from contextual associations. Thus, the qualities of single events (e.g., articulation, density, loudness) often have in themselves unusual affective importance at low levels of structure. I have the feeling that purely "surface" qualities—those divorced from (or regarded and felt apart from) contextual implications—are underestimated in the study of musical experience, probably because of the apparently unintellectual nature (absence of the intuitive or deliberate, cognitive act of *relating*) of the appreciation of affective values in isolated events of pure, local surface.

Of further areas of potential exploration, one feels that, for example, subjective association of musical events with extramusical experience—association triggered by analogical parallels of various kinds—may have greater

[19]Perhaps the most important current sources of such analogs are set theory, probability and information theory, Gestalt psychology, and linguistics.

significance and may be more capable of broad categorization than we tend
to think.

But the development of the three studies in this book, all of them involving theoretical and practical discourse and illustration, moves with considerable singularity of purpose in investigation of a pervasive concept of
techniques by which in nearly all musical styles lines of element-change are
caused to "mean" changing levels of intensity in controlled, shaped configurations which hold opposing tendencies in balance. *Virtually every aspect of musical
structure is engaged in this effort,* and I do not hesitate to claim for the underlying
concepts material significance for ordered inquiry into musical function and
expressive effect. The chief, potential practical adaptability of these studies
is in their incorporation of a *very large number of demonstrative analyses and
illustrations of a multitude of kinds.*

Perhaps the basic intent of this book can be expressed, finally and in
summary, as that of exploring a mode of musical meaning expressed in
relations in contextually shaped processes of mounting and receding intensity,
processes and relations involving the entire spectrum of elements. The capacity of related musical events to convey the sense of intensity (dissonance,
complexity, instability) and release (resolution, stability) is of fundamental
importance in the musical experience, at least in that stimulating kind of
experience in which *thought and feeling* are cofunctionally engaged. The
inquiry parallels and is an extension of the experience: one feels the impact
and import of the event and of its associations with other events; by that
stimulus one is led to a searching of the structure and the experience for
identifiable qualities to which the functional-expressive effect can rationally
be ascribed.

Inevitably, this work is in some of its aspects more tentative than in
others, but it is my hope that readers, many of whom will be students, will
find among the many approaches to analysis and views of structure presented
and developed here some that prove useful, and that special interest may be
found in encounters with some new ways of inquiring into important parameters of structure not widely investigated in other works.

CHAPTER ONE

tonality

Introductory notes

The concept of the hierarchic ordering of pitch content has in one manifestation or another served as a basis for musical structure since the earliest
stages in the Western tradition. It is the intent of this chapter to introduce
some ideas about tonal order in music and to illustrate and discuss certain
approaches in the analysis of tonality and tonal successions according to the
concepts presented.

The practice of hierarchic systems of tonal order, by which the concept
of tonality is engendered, is of truly monumental significance. Man's cultural
history is marked by few achievements of comparable magnitude; indeed, it
can be argued persuasively that nearly all music of the Western tradition is
structurally conditioned by some kind of expression of tonality. The discussion that follows rests upon the broad definition of tonality necessary to such
an argument.

Tonality may be thus broadly conceived as *a formal system in which pitch
content is perceived as functionally related to a specific pitch-class or pitch-class-complex
of resolution*,[1] often preestablished and preconditioned, as a basis for structure
at some understood level of perception. The foregoing definition of tonality
is applicable not just to the "tonal period" in which the most familiar conventions of tonal function are practiced (roughly the eighteenth and the
nineteenth centuries), but through earlier modality and more recent freer
tonal applications as well.

The *tonal system* consists of a hierarchic ordering of PC factors, with the
tonic (final, axis, center, etc.) the ultimate point of relationship which tonal
successions are contrived to "expect." In the tonal period of conventional
"common practice" the primary system consists of hierarchically oriented
degrees of the diatonic scale and the tertian harmonies erected on these

---

[1]The terms *pitch-class* and *pitch-class-complex* (symbolized PC and PCC) are used to
denote pitch independent of specific registral occurrence, or a complex of such pitches generically understood.

degrees. In modal styles, corresponding systems are the modes, with normative points of tentative and final cadential repose. In more recent styles in
which tonality is relevant a system may (but need not) consist of specific
scalar formulations (PC collections) of these or other kinds, with derivative
melodic and harmonic configurations disposed in such a way as to express
and give primacy to a particular "tonic" or, in fluctuant contexts, particular
"tonics." Often such tonal content is reminiscent of conventions of the tonal
period, and its validity in experience may in significant part be based on
powerful conditioning in the all but universal practice of systems of tonal
order in Western music.

There are of course musical idioms, especially of the current period, in
which tonality as a formalized system is less relevant—or irrelevant, and the
less relevant tonality in a particular style the more musical structure must
depend on other factors, even extramusical factors, except where considerations of structure are put aside altogether, as in some aleatoric music. Moreover, styles in which tonal fluctuation is constant and extreme in latitude may
find the structural function of tonality impaired, resulting in a changed
experiential significance for the sense of tonic or vacillating tonic.

Although no amount of argument can settle the question of relevance of
tonality in music described as "atonal," it is important that the question be
raised in the light of specific musical instances. The many examples of
twentieth-century sources in the following series of analytical presentations,
and the discussion of tonal references or allusions affirmed to be implicit in
them, will amplify the question and suggest possible interpretations. These
analyses thus include reference to music later than (as well as earlier than)
that in which *conventions* of tonal-harmonic order prevail.[2]

Questions of the establishment of tonal reference by harmonic-melodic
succession, and of the nature of tonal fluctuation, like that of conjectured
tonal allusion in antitonal styles, are necessarily somewhat subjective, and
the concern in the analyses which follow will be to cite methods arising from
theoretical propositions stated, and to present plausible conclusions arising
from such methods and hypotheses, rather than to achieve any kind of
inflexible "truth" about the examples and ideas explored. Effort is directed
here to an understanding of the techniques by which tonality is expressed and
to formulation of interpretations of tonal implications which are demonstra-

---

[2]The terms *convention* and *conventional* will refer specifically to triadic and other tertian
harmonies, and melodic successions having these as their framing bases, as well as predictable
successions of harmonies by which others are seen as "exceptional" or "deceptive" in the
period of major-minor tonality. "Conventions" of tonal expression are thus *particular* means
of affirming the tonal hierarchy in practice as opposed to the *broad principle of hierarchic order*
in the sense in which it can be seen to be generally applicable.

ble in the circumstances discoverable in the analysis of a given work. In discussion of "tonicizing" factors (those which support the emergence or existence of a particular tonal center, or central PCC) primary interest resides in techniques by which the *basic tonal order is affirmed and established.*

Introductory comments concerning tonal and linear functions

Melodic and harmonic functions are of two kinds: the first of these has to do with position, identity, and hierarchic status in each of the system components of the particular tonality in question (*tonal function*); the second is the role of the event in the melodic-harmonic linear stream (*linear function*), also hierarchically defined with respect to a given level of reference. Linear function is the relation of an event to the structural (relatively "essential") linear frame or basis, or its auxiliary (subsidiary, elaborative, embellishing, prolonging) relation to an event of higher order. We shall suggest that these functions are multidimensional—tonal function as to relatively deep or superficial levels of tonality, and linear function in a comparable sense but also in the fact that a given event is associated often with more than one other event in different ways, even at the same structural level of reference.

Of linear functions, the *neighbor auxiliary* embellishes a structural point in harmonic or melodic succession and is often derived in voice-leading of one or more stepwise adjacencies, common-tone associations, or other proximate relations. Often a neighbor separates two appearances of the structural harmony it elaborates. A second type is the *passing auxiliary* (often a succession of passing events) in which movement, up or down, links two harmonic or melodic points in an action filling space beyond that which is normative in the neighbor association. In a passing configuration, implicit in one or more voices will be relatively conjunct descent or ascent in a passing stream normally filling intervals of a 3rd or greater. Distinction between neighbor

(e.g., $\wedge$ or $\vee$) and passing (e.g., ⎯⎯⎯) configurations involving linear auxiliary functions is, then, a matter of voice-leading; where harmonic as opposed to monophonic textures are concerned, *the consideration of voice-leading gives primary attention to outer voices, and especially to the bass.*

An event may be auxiliary at a broad level, essential at a more immediate level; or a neighbor auxiliary at a very local level may be seen as part of a broadly passing stream at a higher level. For example, a V cadence with $\hat{2}$ (second scale degree) in the upper voice is the essential structural aim of succession at the level of the phrase it concludes; at a broader level the cadence is perceived as auxiliary to its I (and $\hat{1}$) consequent. Thus emerges the concept of *multileveled linear function* paralleling that of multileveled tonal function.[3]

Example 1-1 points up the issue of *linear function* as related and compared to *tonal function*, and it argues that the two kinds of function do not reflect, as is sometimes supposed, mutually contradictory or exclusive concepts. The analysis is based on the premise that except in relatively rare tonally "nonfunctional" elaborations, tonal function is of significance and in evidence (and an experiential reality) in foreground, immediate contexts at the same time that the series of harmonies may be of significance as a "space-filling linear stream" of passing or neighbor auxiliaries. The example is a severe reduction and abstraction of harmonic content in mm. 303–12 of the fourth movement of Beethoven's second symphony. The essential succession is iv-V, the former appearing in two positions linked by a complex succession of passing auxiliaries *related by tonal function as well as by chromatic succession in the lower voice* (and other, comparable linear successions). Following the process of subdominant elaboration, V undergoes prolongation by neighbor auxiliaries, chromatically related, above and below.

This sketch, vividly illustrating the two aspects of harmonic (and melodic) function which are a principal premise for this study, is indicative of the fact that *linear and tonal functions nearly always appear in complementary conjunction in tonal music.* In the Beethoven the linear force of chromatic ascent is of course inescapable, but at the same time the tonal functions indicated are plausible, perceptible, and never far removed from the primary system;

---

[3]The concept of *multileveled linear function* is unavoidable, and its comparability to that of multileveled tonal function will be readily apparent. The multileveled aspect of linear function has to do, as would be expected, with the *differing functions* of pitch events at various levels of structure—a multiplicity of function crossing structural levels. For example, a pitch event which is of central (essential) function within a phrase is seen to be auxiliary to more fundamental factors at broader levels, as in the instance described above; or an event which is a neighbor auxiliary at a very immediate level is seen to be a factor in a larger, passing complex of events. The concept of multileveled linear function thus concerns *the nature of the function itself* as viewed (or heard) within differing levels of perspective.

Linear function has a further aspect of multiplicity, or ambivalence: that in which a particular event is affiliated with more than one related event. For example, a particular pitch might function as upper neighbor auxiliary to another and at the same time anticipate (be a factor in the prolongation of) an essential point which follows. Or a particular pitch event might function as auxiliary to two related pitches (in the succession g-a-f-g-a, the f is part of the neighbor encirclement of g and at the same time a lower auxiliary of a). This kind of dual, or multiple, functional relation may be operative *at a single level* of structure; it has to do with the fact that an event in a linear succession can be many-sided in its roles. This might be termed *multilateral linear function* in keeping with its character, as described. Multilateral linear function thus concerns *the different events of affiliation* of a given factor *at a given level.* The multiplicity of linear function is, then, of two dimensions.

See pp. 37–40 for further reference to these concepts; added treatment of these issues is also to be found in discussion of examples to follow.

Ex. 1-1. Beethoven, Symphony No. 2 in D, Op. 36.
Abstraction of a passage in the fourth movement.

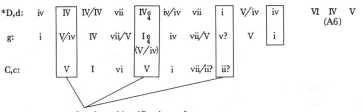

Specimen identifications of
multileveled tonal function (see page 52).

*Some roman numeral symbols are simplified.

Ex. 1-1 continued.

they include brief, but felt, local tonicizations of iv/iv (c) and V (A), in addition to that of iv (g) itself, the primary harmonic basis for the entire ascending passage. Roman numeral analyses are given at several tonal levels, including tonic and subdominant, the former of broad significance, the latter of significance at the immediate level of the passage itself, reflecting the principle of *multileveled tonal function*. The example demonstrates two fundamental classes of harmonic (and melodic) activity: that of *prolongation* (of iv, IV⁴, then of V)

[4]The conjunction of two like symbols of upper- and lowercase, separated by the comma, denotes a situation in which major and minor forms or systems are conjoined, and in which both are relevant.

and that of *movement* (in this case, recessive succession, overall, from iv to V), as well as linear functions both *passing* and *neighboring*. The reader may wish to make comparable study of other passages from the same movement, harmonic fluctuations of comparable features—for example, mm. 220–21, 317–21, or 240–44.

A further example of harmonic abstraction is given in Ex. 1-2 in resumé (unfortunately without quotation of the too extended extract on which it is based) of the reaffirmation of T: I⁵ and V following developmental fluctua-

Ex. 1-2. Beethoven, Symphony No. 3 in E♭, Op. 55.
Synoptic harmonic abstraction of an extract from the fourth movement.

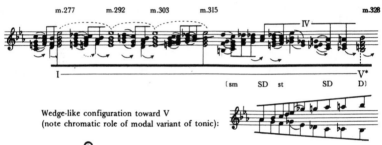

Wedge-like configuration toward V
(note chromatic role of modal variant of tonic):

*Undergoes 21 measures of unbroken prolongation.

tion in the final movement of Beethoven's "Eroica" Symphony. T: I is stated powerfully in a series of utterances, given in the one-staff sketch, elaborated by neighbor auxiliaries some of which tonicize the diatonic harmonies ii, IV, and vi, with ultimately a more extended reference to A♭, the subdominant—normal medium for direct reintroduction of T: V—and with linking, passing auxiliary harmonies embellishing the recessive harmonic movement from IV to V. All of this is summarized in the sketch, *to make the essential harmonic directions and functions visible,* and there is added a brief synoptic representation of the contrapuntally potent, largely chromatic, wedge-like configuration toward the V. Although it is not represented except by an inserted note, the V undergoes no fewer than 21 measures of insistent prolongation (plus fermata) in a typical atmosphere of growing intensity before the I is reaffirmed in thematic statement.

The Beethoven extract shows a primary tonal system on E♭ expanded by references to the diatonic tonics f, A♭, and c. Again, purely linear factors are obvious and extremely persuasive (and they are accounted for); but *tonal*

⁵I. e., I of the tonic (T) system, here E♭.

function is in no sense superseded by linear function, and tonal function is strongly felt, even very locally, in expansion of the tonal-harmonic resources of PC content. Tonics of reference can be seen as a characteristic "inflation" (through tonicization and establishment of secondary tonal regions) of a very prototypical harmonic succession to V.

An excerpt from a Chopin Prelude is investigated in Ex. 1-3 in consideration of some of the same problems. The primary dominant is here

Ex. 1-3. Chopin, Prelude in E♭, Op. 28, No. 19.

Ex. 1-3 continued.

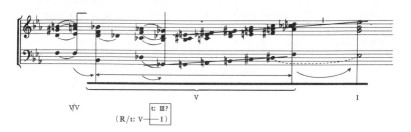

prolonged and embellished by a series of chromatic auxiliaries. They become, in mm. 29–32, virtually nonfunctional,[6]—i.e., their positions as passing chromatic harmonies in embellishment of the structural harmony *does*, in this context, eclipse any potential inference of tonal meaning in the stream of diminished 7th-chords. This is because of the parallel succession in which any inherent potential for contrapuntal interaction and affiliation, or leading-tone action in support of potential tonics of reference, is avoided. (This is very different from the Beethoven examples, in which despite the force of consistent linear succession in elaboration of essential harmonic content, tonal tendencies *are fulfilled or suggested in foreground actions* at immediate levels of structure.)

If relative significances of linear as opposed to tonal functions are a matter of degree, it is nonetheless a valid analytical judgment that at some point tonal function is superseded in experiential effect by the force of relatively "straight" linear function in which potential leading-tone relations are unfulfilled at any structural level of perceptible connection, and not at other points, where such relations are contextually demonstrable. The juxtaposition of the Beethoven and Chopin examples is useful in illustrating this distinction.

The Chopin analysis must also give attention to the root succession at a more essential level: B♭-G♭-E♭—a triadic formulation with its own logic. The sequential relation at the outset of the succession (F-B♭, D♭-G♭) imparts

[6]Again, with respect to *tonal* significance; thus, in mm. 29–32, despite the pattern of tonal shifts (D?-G?-A?-D?-E?) inferable from and inherently potential in the succession of diminished 7th-chords, and the logic of 5th movement in that succession, the passage involves *direct, parallel chromatic succession* from one diminished 7th-chord to the next. The chords are of as purely linear function as it is possible to imagine, lacking tonal significance of even immediate functional value. Thus, the parallelism of voice-leading preempts and precludes expression or suggestion of tonal function inherently, if ambiguously, potential in the chords. Such pure parallelism of voice-leading is a primary technique of *tonally nonfunctional harmonic usage*; it is to be found in examples, especially of "fantasy" or improvisational style, in the eighteenth century, and of course becomes common as an elaborative device in late-nineteenth-century impressionism.

a further underlying, logical unity.[7] The chromaticism of the vocabulary of the example is enhanced by chromatic succession at a number of points.

In Ex.1-3, to set the stage for the series of passing diminished 7th-chords, the primary tonic is impaired by cancellation of its leading-tone in the intriguing, repeated allusion to the G♭ passing tonic (t: III?). Compensatory reaffirmation of the primary tonic at m. 33 is consequently of enhanced, strongly resolving effect.

The concept of multileveled function further explored

The concept of tonal functions as ambivalent, in accord with that of tonics of reference of various levels of structural significance having relatively local or broad implications, is of continuing necessity in the analysis of tonal-harmonic function.

Similarly, the linear interpretation of functions of pitch materials (their dispositions in lines—their "horizontalness" and contiguity in time) concerns a leveled structure except in the most microcosmic contexts. Often many levels can be characterized, ranging from the extreme background (the total form as an all-encompassing impulse)—the broadest and highest hierarchic architectonic level, through numerous intermediate grounds, to the most immediate, local context of reference treated in traditional theory as foreground, the actual surface of music.

It is vital in the consideration of leveled structure in music that the surface, or foreground, be kept always in view, while regarded in its proper hierarchic status. The reference to hierarchic status as "low" in level bears no implication of relative importance. Indeed, one might well observe that in music of normative stylistic terms (i.e., music in which norms can be identified—nearly all music), *background structure is of more generic content the more broadly it is viewed;* the flavor, character, and unique expressive consequence of the particular work resides in very important respects in the particularities of elaboration in the foreground by which broader structural factors are realized and amplified. Analysis is far too often content with delineation of broad structure as THE structure, leaving untreated the vital, arresting patterns by which the great work of music projects and extends in time the prototypical basis. We have been concerned in discussions of pitch structure to this point, and continue to be concerned, with functions—including tonal functions and identities—of pitch complexes within very local areas of reference *as well as more essential functions*, insisting that immediate tonal implication is very critically a part of the experience of music.

---

[7]Consider as well the horizontalizations F-B♭-D♭, B♭-D♭-G♭, and G♭-B♭ (implied root of the primary dominant at the end of the passing stream of diminished 7ths)-E♭.

The concept of multileveled, or multiple, tonal function is the basis for discussion of the concept of tonal fluctuation (modulation), in which it is asserted that the *significance* of fluctuation in any given instance corresponds to the breadth of structural level over which an emergent referential tonic "prevails." Similarly, the concept of chromaticism, as it concerns alteration of the factors of the diatonic scale in melody and harmony, depends for definition on the concept of multiplicity of level and of tonal reference: thus, a particular PC may be "chromatic" in relation to the tonal system at one level (e.g., the primary system C, where an F♯ appears in tonicization of the V) but not at another level (in the same hypothetical situation, not at the secondary level represented as the immediate context of the tonicization of G, where the F♯ is diatonic).

Important, then, is a procedure of analysis which examines a particular harmonic or melodic line in stages ranging from the particulars of its appearance on the score page to the general structure described by its most essential[8] points.

For example, even a small unit of melody can be viewed varyingly so that at one level a particular factor appears relatively essential while at another level relatively auxiliary (subsidiary, elaborative). (The differing conclusions derived in this way are not of course contradictory; rather, they are complementary and interdependent views.) To put it another way, a melodic line of several formal units reveals, in analysis, an increasingly complex hierarchy of functional significances: an essential point within a phrase may appear to have an auxiliary relation to a more basic point when the phrase is viewed in a larger context, and the high point in pitch within a single phrase is likely to be interpreted as a subsidiary high point in the analysis of that phrase in combination with others.

Two examples follow, each involving a kind of linear analysis of pitch functions having "leveled" significances. The high point of the first phrase of Ex. 1-4 is subsidiary to that of the second phrase of the group. This (the expansion of spatial compass) is, along with motive mirror, the chief means by which the content of the opening phrase is varied in the second. There is thus a conjunction of formal units into a larger unity by relative superiority (here of pitch, but often of duration, stress, density, etc.) of one event over a related event in a linear sequence. *The significance of both points in tonal function* ($\hat{1}$, $\hat{3}$) *should also be emphasized;* and a high-level conjunct succession of high points and structurally important cadential pitches, clearly implied despite registral variance, is shown as part of the representation in Ex. 1-4.

---

[8]In all references to linear function of pitch materials, the term "essential" is of course to be understood as meaning "of the essence" and not in the more restricted sense of "necessary."

Ex. 1-4. Brahms, Trio in C minor for piano, violin, and cello, Op. 101, third movement.

The phrase from the *Sequenza II* for harp by Luciano Berio[9] (Ex. 1-5) is a concise melodic unit, its cadence achieved in part by rhythmic means.[10] The example illustrates a further aspect of hierarchic relations among melodic units within a single phrase. The structural basis is felt in the succession of principal and subsidiary high and low points toward the cadential D, which can be interpreted as analogous to the traditional tonic.

Ex. 1-5. Berio, *Sequenza II* for harp.

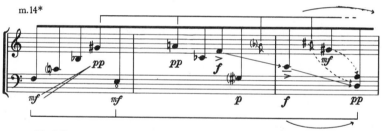

*Each "measure" is a fixed durational unit at 40MM.

The quotation, with supplementary explanatory symbols, makes these functional interrelations visible. The melodic line assumes a kind of wedge-like character seen in this light, its course very purposefully controlled. Several observations need to be made in extension of the analysis: both

[9]In the index will be found a listing of cited composers and their years.

[10]Each vertical "bar-line" corresponds to one metronomic pulsation at 40MM. Time distributions within the unit are represented spatially, and approximately, in the notation of pitch events. Berio uses accidentals only to indicate pedal change. Accidentals given in parentheses in the quotation are those applicable by virtue of already established pedal settings.

cadence PCs (D, A) are immediately preceded by "leading-tones" whose resolutions are fulfilled in octave displacement; the recession of low points is diatonic, the sequence of high points chromatic; the stressed notes, marked *forte*, constitute in a middle register a descent (diatonic) toward D, complementing that of the succession of low points; each subsidiary high point is preceded by a rest and/or upward leap; and a rest precedes the precipitate cadential succession. It is of course vital that these relations, functions, and interactions be understood in performance.

Some of the examples of recent music to be presented in later analytical discussion in this chapter will be concerned with instances of hierarchic linear arrangement and order in which tonality is not, or is less, relevant.

The ideas of primacy and hierarchy among pitch-classes and pitch-class-complexes; generic and particular tonal systems

The discussion and analytical exploration of tonality, however broadly conceived, tends to center in those particular conventions by which the tonal period is identified. Propositions respecting expressions of tonal order in earlier and later styles are often introduced in analogous relation to that most immediately understood conventional practice.

In the projection of a primary factor within the PC content of a musical work (or style) much of the weight of historical practice suggests the chief importance of its relation to the pitch a semitone below (and, in some styles, above) and the pitch a 4th below or 5th above. The "leading" or "leaning" force of the proximate pitch in semitonal relation, and the strong "natural" relation of the 5th and its inversion, emerge throughout tonal practice of all kinds as preeminent affiliations by which the central factor in the hierarchic order is approached and understood. The primacy of the tonic[11] is a function too of its role as the ultimate point of cadential arrival.

The hierarchic *tonal system* can be referred to as one of *generic* applicability—i.e., the tonal system of a style might be conceived as that embracing, for example, a diatonic set together with vertical PCC derivatives of common usage and expanded by subsidiary collections of chromatic affiliates usual in such a given style. Thus, the "tonal system of a style" would represent *the normal range and ordering of PC material* reasonably to be expected. In the same way, the tonal system of any class of works might be theoretically conceived.

Of more immediate concern is the concept of tonal system as it applies to a particular musical instance, a particular work and the experience of that

---

[11]The word *tonic* will be freely used to denote the PC or PCC at the center of the hierarchic order in all styles in which such order is a relevant principle, including those which predate and postdate the period of major-minor tonal conventions.

work, as opposed to the theoretical system generic to the class of which the work is a member. The generic system might be, for example, the phrygian scale together with predictable secondary leading-tones attending (and inflating, or tonicizing) certain of its degrees, or the diatonic scale of C comparably expanded. The tonal system specific to a composition represents the total resource of PC content basic to that work, and the hierarchic ordering of the content *as expressed in the formulations of that particular work.*

We will see of course that particular tonal systems reflect stylistic norms; but at the same time the analysis of the tonal system of a composition will illuminate its tonal structure by making visible the *particular directions, range, and (by implication) rates of fluctuation* by which its primary system is expanded and enriched. Such a *particular system* may include chromatic factors (e.g., Neapolitan harmony) as significantly projected secondary centers, may be seen to extend a particular modal ambitus beyond the norm, may be seen to have some kind of anomalous second-order component (e.g., recurrent cadential G within the phrygian context, or predominantly plagal action within the framework of eighteenth-century tonal structure), or may be seen as, for example, a primary system consisting of a trichordal or tetrachordal collection rather than the more extended resource common to a given generic system. Methods will be suggested here for the analytical representation of tonal systems, methods by which the tonal "image" of a work can be portrayed and its latitude and directions of fluctuation shown. In the representation of a particular tonal system the rate of fluctuation may be inferred in a general way; but the rate of fluctuation is a rhythmic factor to be treated precisely in subsequent portions of this book.

Tonal systems of compositions: regions and interrelations

The *specific tonal system* may be defined as the collection of tonics (tonicized PCs and PCCs) and the supportive (encircling, leading, preparing) pitch factors oriented toward each of these.[12]

Example 1-6a is a graphic representation of the tonal system underlying the exposition and development in the first movement of Mozart's Sonata in F for piano, K. 332. It shows a *primary system* on F, and *secondary* (expanding, auxiliary, inflating, embellishing) *systems* on C, (B♭), d, E♭, (G), and (a); those shown as "parenthetical" are of distinctly inferior status. The *tonal range* (expanse, scope, latitude) is immediately evident. Although the ascending order of the chart represents the *chronology of tonal reference* in the piece, it could also be arranged to represent a *hierarchic ordering* based on such factors

[12]See pp. 134–38 for several representations of the tonal system of the fourth movement of Beethoven's second symphony.

Ex. 1-6a. Mozart, Sonata in F for piano, K. 332, first movement.
Representation of the tonal system and extracted key tonal events in exposition and
development.

m. 28

m. 41

m. 60

m. 84

m. 113

Ex. 1-6a continued.

as frequencies and durations of tonic occurrence and cadential prominences of such occurrences. Curved arrows represent directions and paths of (especially dominant-tonic) tonal affiliation within the system. The whole is a visible, synoptic image of the tonal resource; it could of course be extended to represent the total harmonic resource as well.

Example 1-6b is a further kind of representation of the same example and its tonal system. While relative importances of tonics are suggested by note values, specific durations of tonal reference are not represented. It is important to emphasize in a graphic exercise of this kind that the notation represents PCs only, not specific pitches, and should of course not be read as a pitch-line.

The underlying tonic and dominant components[13] are of first-order and second-order significance, respectively, as might well be expected in the style of which the example is an instance. A tentative representation of fluctuation to and from points of relative distance is given below the example as further indication of the structural importance of fluctuation within the expanded tonal system. Specific types of tonal function (embellishing, passing) are in evidence here and will be discussed further later. Of course, the relative superiority of any given tonic of reference is a question of *structural level:* the central tonic, F, is thus preeminent at the broadest level; C, the dominant, is

---

[13]The term *component* or *system component* refers to a level within the total system—a related system, itself hierarchically ordered and capable of expansion by superimposed inferior system components. Thus, in the Mozart (Ex. 1-6), d is a system component of relatively inferior status.

Ex. 1-6b. Mozart, Sonata in F for piano, K. 332, first movement.
Further representation of the tonal system of exposition and development.

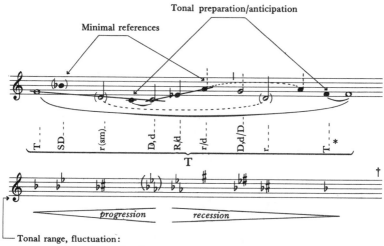

— Tonal range, fluctuation:
an aspect of structure and style.

*See pp. 48–50 for explanation of symbols.
†Signatures reflect the tonicizing raised $\hat{7}$ of the minor mode.

an *embellishing* component at the broadest level but of *primary significance within the local area of its emergence.*

An example of Josquin, which can be seen in Vol. I of the *Historical Anthology of Music*,[14] is the striking *Tu pauperum refugium*, Part 2 of the motet, *Magnus es tu, Domine*. It is a phrygian piece whose general form involves digression—very pronounced in textural contrast—and homorhythmic return in metric and other variation (m. 34). Several extracts are quoted in Ex. 2-16, pp. 238–40.

Points of cadential arrival are in accord with phrygian usage: E, A, C (final, plagal cofinal, and authentic cofinal) and individual phrases can be analyzed as embellishments and prolongations of central "harmonic" factors. The first, for example, centers on "i" in plagal embellishment with the bass moving e-A-a-e in encirclement of the final, e; phrase 2 contrasts with the "closed" prolongation of the first in its progression from "i" to "iv."

[14]Archibald T. Davison and Willi Apel, eds., *Historical Anthology of Music*, Vol. I (Cambridge: Harvard University Press, 1949), p. 92.

The concept of an emergent secondary tonal system can be seen in a representation of the modestly expanded primary system as shown in Ex. 1-7a. It indicates a tonicized "iv" as second-order system component and

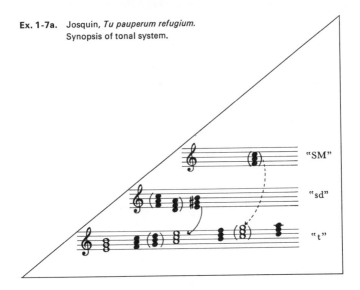

Ex. 1-7a.   Josquin, *Tu pauperum refugium.*
Synopsis of tonal system.

suggests the mildly tonicizing effect of the plagal approaches to the cadential "VI" as well. The secondary region on A is tonicized in the second phrase and elsewhere by application of the G♯ leading-tone. The applicability of the principle of tonal expansion bringing about limited excursion beyond the fundamental, primary system is obvious, and its representation as shown provides an image of hierarchic tonal order which can properly be viewed as a foreshadowing of complex tonal structures of later music.[a]

In *Tu pauperum refugium*, tonal structure is of course also evident in cadential functions, and the hierarchic order of cadential functions is of fundamental significance in study of the tonality of the piece (Ex. 1-7b).

Examples in this chapter reflect *the concept of tonality broadly defined*, as is evident in the most cursory examination of sources. That concept applies to early music (predating the tonal period) no less than to tonal music of the twentieth century: it is implicit and essential in the idea of a scalar or other PC resource hierarchically disposed in cadential and other focal applications. Indeed, in that sense it is evident in liturgical chant no less than in sixteenth-century polyphony. Beyond that general concept, much music of modal systems can be seen to foreshadow the conventions of later tonality as well: the functions of root relations of "chords" and of primary and secondary

Ex. 1-7b. Josquin, *Tu pauperum refugium.*
Succession and hierarchic order of cadential centers.

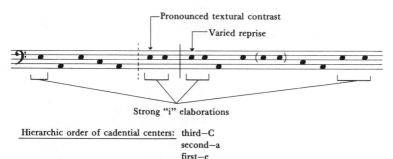

Hierarchic order of cadential centers: third—C
second—a
first—e

leading-tones in the applications of *musica ficta*, which show in incipience the means of later, broad tonal expansions by chromatic extensions of fundamental diatonic collections. And the tonal principle of opposition of areas of fluctuation with stability, and of ambiguity with focus of tonal orientation, is evident in many highly provocative sixteenth-century works.[15]

The concept of a generic tonal system explored in theory

Since the intent of this chapter is chiefly to explore tonal principles and specific tonal systems manifest in individual works, the concept of a generic tonal system pertinent to a class of compositions is discussed only limitedly in a forthcoming illustration. The deduced norm-defining tonal system of a class of works, while not a major concern here, can constitute a useful point of reference in the study of stylistic trends, terms, and evolutions.[16]

[15]Two relevant, interesting sources might be mentioned, one concerned with early manifestations of tonality, the other with later manifestations. Edward Lowinsky's paper, *Tonality and Atonality in the Sixteenth Century* (Berkeley: University of California Press, 1961) illuminates aspects of tonal order, as well as what the author calls "atonality" and "floating tonality" in sixteenth-century works, in provocative studies in which tonality is conceived as "a tonally centered organization" (p. xii). Examples of sixteenth-century tonality are discussed often in the light of emergent devices common to later major-minor conventions. At one point Lowinsky notes that "a net of cadences *on varying degrees related to the tonic* and organizing a whole work into various sections comes closer to defining tonality" (p. 15; emphasis added). Another source of substantial interest and relevance to the concept of tonality broadly viewed is Roy Travis, "Towards a New Concept of Tonality?" in *Journal of Music Theory*, III, No. 2 (1959), pp. 257–84.

[16]The theoretical presentation which follows is related to, but significantly distinct from, the "chart of the regions" suggested by Arnold Schoenberg in *Structural Functions of Harmony* (London: Williams and Norgate, Ltd., 1954), Ch. III. The reader is referred to Schoenberg's theory as a statement of major importance promulgating a theoretical, generic concept of tonal system applicable to derivative representations of the tonal systems of individual works.

What follows (Ex. 1-10) is a theoretical representation of a chromatic, panmodal tonal system on C, capable of course of transposition throughout the equal-tempered pitch resource.[17] It is a theoretical system of proposed *generic* significance as opposed to one (Ex. 1-6) in which systemic content derives from a *particular* context.

A symbology of *tonic* designation akin to Schoenberg's is adopted here. It represents *tonicized* factors within an expanded tonal system by symbols which go beyond the usual letter designation of PC to indicate the relation of a secondary tonic to the primary tonic. Thus, such symbols as T (tonic), ST (supertonic), M (mediant), R (relative), and like symbols, as well as lower-case correspondents to represent minor system components, will be used. The affix /T or /t will be used where confusion might result (as in uses of the symbol D as dominant to distinguish it from that standard letter designation of pitch or PC); otherwise it is understood that the symbol is one of direct reference to the primary tonic (e.g., st is understood as st/T). The slash also shows other kinds and levels of affiliation within the system: e.g., r/D (relative minor of the dominant), etc., as well as relations farther removed: e.g., r/D/st, etc. Again, /t or /T is understood as the concluding term, explicit only when necessary to preclude ambiguity. (The symbol r/T or r = relative minor of the primary major tonic; R/t or R = relative major of the primary minor tonic. M or M/T = E, G♯, B in C major; M/t = E♭, G, B♭ in C minor; etc.)

It is important to recognize that in a representation of this kind these symbols represent *tonics*—actual or potential centers of system components or (in Schoenberg's term) "regions" of tonality, not merely harmonic factors. In that sense, SD can be viewed as an extension of the principle of IV and a succession T-SD-D *an extension or inflation of the succession I-IV-V.*

Similarly, to indicate relations as well as simple PC identities, symbols like sm:iv (in C, iv/vi or a:iv) or D/T:ii (in C, ii/V or G:ii) are sometimes used. Relations of considerable removal from the primary system (SD/SD/N, where N denotes the Neapolitan) are sometimes shown; although such relations can be adduced within an infinite breadth of systemic possibilities, it is important to make distinction between relations of a theoretical nature (like those adduced in the following chart, Ex. 1-10) and those of a contextual, or practical, basis (which are the chief concern of particular analyses).

Example 1-10 includes a listing of relations by which all PCs within the chromatic primary system can be relatively closely identified with the central tonic, C. These are listed as nearest relations, i.e., *relations of fewest terms.* Although the N is noted occasionally, in view of its common membership in many practical individual systems, the relations given are otherwise *through diatonic links.* Thus, for example, the identification of f♯ as st/D/r or m/D/D

[17]Other, related generic systems could be adduced as pertinent to phases of stylistic experience within the tonal period: e.g., that of the unexpanded diatonic major or minor collection and its derivative harmonies, or that of the bimodal collection without further chromatic expansion.

suggests that its nearest relation to C (easiest diatonic accessibility) is as seen in Ex. 1-8. Again, note that Ex. 1-10 *represents tonal, not merely harmonic factors;* the summary given as Ex. 1-8 should similarly be read as consisting of tonics—tonicized harmonies, rather than simple harmonic successions within a diatonic system.

Ex. 1-8.

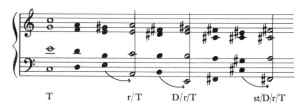

T   r/T   D/r/T   st/D/r/T

T   D/T   D/D/T   m/D/D/T

    Key signatures are listed as including the tonally vital leading-tone of the minor system (a practice shown in Ex. 1-6b). Although key signatures are one indicator of tonal distance, this factor alone can be deceptive, as is noted in the discussion of tonal distance which follows later in this chapter. A very critical factor in tonal distance (or proximity) is the immediate adaptability of a major triad as dominant to T or t—what Schoenberg called the interchangeability of mode[18]—a principle responsible in very significant degree for the expansibility of tonal systems in conventional tonality. Implicit in Ex. 1-10 are a *theory of chromatic harmonic succession* and a *theory of multileveled (or multiple) harmonic function*, both of these treated further as this chapter unfolds.

    Since the concept is involved with questions of *tonal* rather than purely harmonic range, all degrees in the primary chromatic system are regarded as of tonic function; hence, each is considered the root of a major or minor triad and its theoretical significances and accessibility derived from that assumption. The minor triad has such potential significances as r, sd, st, m, or sm. The major triad may have tonic significance as R, D, SD, or SM. Where potential system components are hypothesized, *diminished and augmented triads*

---

[18]Schoenberg, *Structural Functions*, Ch. VII.

are not considered to be of potential tonic function, i.e., to be capable of functioning as system centers.

Analyses of tonal fluctuation, as suggested in the chart, might well show
the particulars of relation demonstrated in specific contexts; the symbology
proposed has the advantage of showing ultimate relations to the primary
tonic as well as immediate functions within secondary tonal systems. Such a
representation might be as in Ex. 1-9, which includes a branched diagram in
which the dominant system component (region) appears as an outgrowth (in
the given context) of the primary system, and the third component as an
outgrowth (again, in the given context) of the second. The first-order system
(primary) is shown at the base as T. The designation of relations by this
principle avoids the often dubious identification of, say, a B♭ triad in expansion of the system of C as lowered "subtonic" and suggests for it such a
plausible, precise contextual relation as SD/SD.

Ex. 1-9.

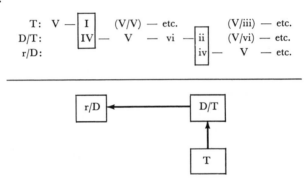

Finally, in extension of a chart of this kind (Ex. 1-10), or in representation of any modification or qualification of this hypothetical, generic,
tonal system, further relations—relations of greater complexity, of greater
distance, of more terms—could of course be adduced. For example, one
might go further, in theory and without reference to any particular contextual derivation, to note such potential relations as r/SD/SD for the minor
triad on G, or SM/r/D/r for the major triad on A, etc.—*all such relations potential
and plausible in functional tonal contexts.*

Implicit in the functional chromatic system is the principle that the
chromatic factors have a diatonic basis, i.e., derive as alterations of factors
in the basic diatonic collection on T or t.

Ex. 1-10. A view of a theoretical, generic tonal system, and hypothetical, proximate *diatonic relations* linking each of its potentially tonicized degrees with C,c.

Mode of Tonic Triad	Tonic Degree	Signature	Examples of Close Relations of Diatonic Succession	
m			m/R/t, st/SD/T	–i. e.,
M			D/T	
m			m/T	
M			D/sm(r)/T	–i. e.,
M			R/t	
m			sd/sd/sd/t	–i. e.,
m			st/T	
M			D/D/T	
m			r/D/r/T	–i. e.,
M			SM/sd/t (+N)	
m			t	
M			T	
m			m/D/T	
M			D/D/r/T	
M			SD/SD/T, D/R/t	
m			sd/sd/t	
m			r(sm)/T	–i. e.,
M			D/st/T, D/D/D/T	
m			m/D/r/T	
M			SM/t	
m			st/D/r/T, m/D/D/T	–i. e.,
M			SM/sd/sd/t	
m			sd/t	
M			SD/T	

Primary and secondary tonics and their structural and
auxiliary functions; multileveled (multiple) tonal-harmonic
function; tonic and dominant forms

As implied in Ex. 1-6b, tonics can be represented in much the same way that structural and auxiliary embellishing harmonies (and, in melody, individual pitches) are represented in common techniques of linear, reductive analysis. A fundamental difference must, of course, be kept in mind: a stream of tonics in such a graphic, hierarchic representation can in no sense be interpreted as a sounding line of actual pitch events.

Vital to this consideration is the concept of *structural level*. The primary, or central, tonic is of course always of first-order importance (as the term "primary" suggests). At the same time, secondary tonics of reference may be *structural* in implications *within low-level contexts over which they prevail* (e.g., F at the level of a single phrase over which it has tonal predominance). But the idea of low-level predominance does not pertain to the cadential tonic representing *within the same unit of reference* a tentative departure from the primary or other superior tonic, where departure expects return and conditions the interpretation of the tonic of departure, if hierarchically inferior, as submissive, and the superior tonic as governing.[19]

The concept of level of tonal structure yields that of *multiple tonal-harmonic function*, or *multileveled tonal-harmonic function*, a concept by which it is proposed that the "true" analytical interpretation of tonal function in any given harmonic (or melodic) event is often one of numerous terms.

The multiple function of tonal harmony is suggestive of an ambivalence (not necessarily ambiguity) in the significance of any single harmonic event or succession influenced by the emergence of a secondary tonic or complex of such tonics. At one level, tonal meaning is traceable to the most immediate tonic of reference; other functional meanings derive from references to other systems operational in the given context. A number of the examples analyzed in the following pages will illustrate this concept. The full explanation of a secondary tonal factor involves a range of tonal functions which, with experience and understanding, can be felt in a way that lends harmonic events within multileveled systems *an extraordinary depth of significance*, and consequent expectation of ultimate, sometimes very remote, fulfillment within the primary, expanded system.

If in a specific tonal structure there is one, and only one, primary system (Schoenberg's "monotonality"),[20] it follows that there is among

---

[19]Some of the examples to follow will demonstrate, however, particular contexts in which the tonic of departure ultimately prevails—tonal structures, that is, which set out initially in subordinate regions ultimately "absorbed" within a culminating, different system (e.g., some songs of Wolf).

[20]Schoenberg, *Structural Functions*, Ch. III, especially p. 19.

secondary system components a hierarchic arrangement particular to the musical instance (see Ex. 1-7). Given the terms or norms of a particular style it can be predicted that, for example, the dominant or relative might well emerge as second-order system component. In certain tonal styles other orders are somewhat predictable, often occurring at intervallic distances of the 5th (or in other idioms the 3rd), just as in modal systems PCs of likely cadential prominence can be preinferred. But beyond such norms the particulars of tonal system are a vital factor in the character of the individual work and its expressive potential.

The concept of secondary tonal levels is of course the basis for identification of specific harmonic events as "secondary dominants," "secondary subdominants," etc., and for such a term as "secondary leading-tone." All of these have their counterparts: primary subdominant, primary leading-tone, etc. We have already made use of the terms *primary tonal system, primary tonic, secondary system* and *system component*, etc., as well as *expanded tonal system*, the latter denoting all primary and secondary system components particular to a given composition (or class of compositions), the system components collectively viewed.

Those triads of the diatonic system most likely to assume the role of secondary tonic in music of the tonal period are of course the consonances— the major and minor triad forms. Such functions as T:vii°, t:vii°, or t:ii° and III⁺ [21] will function as secondary tonics only when modified to appear as major or minor triads.

When t:vii° and t:III⁺ are tonicized as major triads they normally involve the lowered $\hat{7}$, a violation of the primary leading-tone, and have a consequent weakening effect on the primary tonic. It is for that reason especially that tonal-harmonic functions of the minor mode commonly derive from the harmonic form of the scale. (I. e., the evolution of major-minor tonality out of modality involved more than any other single factor the inflection of the $\hat{7}$ as a leading-tone.) For the same reason tonal change toward the minor tonic's relative major (R/t) can be regarded as far more disruptive of the primary tonic and its predominance than fluctuation into the dominant region, whose tonic triad (unless t:v) has solid diatonic status within the primary system. [22]

[21]The leading-tone triad in the major and minor modes, respectively, and the supertonic and mediant in the minor mode.

[22]In other words, fluctuation in the direction of R/t (t:III tonicized), exceedingly common in tonal forms, is considered here to pose the particular problem of unusual disruption of the primary system (in cancellation of the primary leading-tone) as compared with the equally common fluctuation in the direction of D/t or D/T, whose tonic is diatonic, and highly supportive, in relation to the primary center. This will be discussed later as one manifestation of "distance" between "relative" systems as compared with others of greater apparent distance. Prevalence in the tonal period of fluctuation and tonal expansion in the

Just as particular chord forms function as tonics (*tonic forms*: major and minor triads), so particular chord forms function as dominants. *Dominant forms* are those in which the two chief factors of dominant action and potential relation are in evidence or clearly implied: (1) the leading-tone and (2) the potential for root relation a 5th above the affiliate tonic form. (It must be recognized that when the leading-tone, i.e., the note a semitone below the tonic affiliate, is the apparent "root" of the chord, the particular dominant form in question is a variant of the very closely related form built on the note

a major 3rd below that leading-tone. Thus, [chord] is virtually indis-

tinguishable from and interchangeable in function with [chord] .)

A resumé of the group of dominant forms is given in Ex. 1-11, arbitrarily relating to a potential tonic affiliate D. All have potential dominant function, primary or secondary. Listed forms of III⁺ and I_6^4 are of course understood as highly dependent chords—tentatively delaying the usual dominant major triad of resolution and, in fact, inseparable from (auxiliary anticipations of) the dominant triad. To these forms could be added still

Ex. 1-11.   A resumé of common dominant forms.

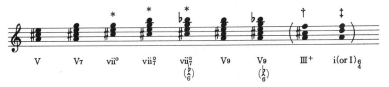

$$V \qquad V_7 \qquad vii° \qquad vii°_7 \qquad vii°_7 \atop (♮_6^♭) \qquad V_9 \qquad V_9 \atop (♮_6^♭) \qquad III⁺ \qquad i(or\ I)_6^4$$

*Often considered to have the dominant degree as implied root, thus analogous to the corresponding V_7 and V_9 forms.
†Usually in first inversion, the dominant degree as lowest note.
‡In second inversion: delaying, dependent on, succeeded by the V.

others: for example, the dominant 7th-chord with its 5th raised or the dominant triad with the same alteration—a favored device of the later nineteenth century, especially of Brahms. Of the following dominant forms, the dominant 7th-chord and the diminished 7th-chord on the leading-tone must be recognized as the most important; it is understandable that such dissonant forms would have priority over the simpler dominant triad because of their strong drive toward tonal resolution. The diminished 7th-chord is favored over the half-diminished because of its versatility in

direction of R/t may well be a residual tendency remaining from modal traditions of cadential fluctuation lacking dependence on the later leading-tone function by which major-minor tonality is largely defined.

resolution to both major and minor triads; other aspects of its versatility are treated later.

In Ex. 1-12 certain factors of apparent tonal significance are quickly evident: there is reiteration of the major triad on C at the outset; there is fluctuation from the diatonic system (F♯ in m. 2, B♭ in m. 5); both of the accidentals introduced in the fluctuant portions are soon cancelled; and the original C is reaffirmed in these cancellations and by appearance of its dominant in m. 9.

Ex. 1-12. Beethoven, Sonata in C for piano, Op. 53, first movement.

Tonal fluctuation thus occurs precipitately, and the early threat to the primary tonic, C, is one of the factors conveying a sense of unrest in the opening passages of this work.

The first accidental, F♯, is *in a very local sense* a leading-tone, resolving to G, its tonic, as can be seen clearly if mm. 2–3 are, solely for analysis, considered in the context of the secondary system of G. Since the primary system is C, not G (as examination of the entire movement would confirm), the F♯ must be interpreted as a secondary leading-tone, the G as a secondary tonic;

thus, these events *have tonal import in some degree.* The primary tonal system, on C, is thus expanded and embellished by the inflated significance attached to its dominant (i.e., by the presence of a secondary dominant, by the tonicizing of C:V).

The above analysis of mm. 2–3 as expressing a secondary tonic, auxiliary to C, suggests that the opening harmony, the tonic of C, has an ambivalent, dual function—again, in a very local sense (making possible by simple diatonic means the reference to the secondary level, G); it is also a subdominant in the secondary system on G, hence a secondary subdominant.

The progression following m. 5 is analogous in important ways: it is a sequential repetition of the opening, a step lower; it is a reference to the secondary tonic, F, involving the same secondary functions (IV, V). There is an important difference, however: it is not derived diatonically. That is, the introduction of B♭ involves chromatic succession (mm. 4–5, B♮ becoming B♭), expanding the system beyond the preceding tonicized V. The consistent chromatic line in the bass within and surrounding this succession "eases" the approach, indeed makes it seem inevitable.

In broad analysis of the Waldstein opening, these processes might well be capsulated as momentary deviants swiftly brought into focus as *embellishments of the primary tonic.*[23] An analysis of the tonal structure and system unique to this work accounts for the inflation of that system by system components auxiliary (neighboring, encircling) in relation to it—D/T and SD/T, *symmetrically ordered around the primary C*, each prepared by a secondary IV (the SD/T:IV alien to the primary diatonic system, more distant, and chromatically derived). The entire process leads to an unequivocal T:V₇ by persuasive and inexorable chromatic descent in the bass linking $\hat{1}$ and $\hat{5}$.

Example 1-12 illustrates *auxiliary secondary tonal systems* in expansion and embellishment of a *primary system.* Secondary systems can be seen in general to have functions of two discernible principal classes: some embellish the primary system, with such *embellishing secondary systems* succeeded by reaffirmation of the primary tonic; others can be seen to link disparate systems. Such *passing* or *transitional* secondary tonics also embellish and expand, of course, but they have the particular function of participating as connective links in transitional, fluctuant successions. A *parenthetical system*, which can have either function, is one which has a tentative presence within the procedural relations of tonal expansion, but which does not have more than a very nebulous, implied manifestation (e.g., B♭ in Ex. 1-6). (A parenthetical system can often be identified as important in defining the relations by which tonal fluctuation occurs, while its perceptual signficance is uncertain or clearly negligible; see, among others, Exx. 1-39 and 1-47.)

---

[23]The A♭ of m. 8 has no tonal significance; it simply alters the mode of the secondary tonic, F, continuing the bass's chromatic descent to the dominant by which the primary tonic is powerfully reaffirmed.

In the Beethoven, G and F appear as embellishing secondary systems symmetrically neighboring the primary C. The issue of the *level* of structure taken as referential is essential to the characterization of function of a system component: thus, for example, in the Beethoven, G is passing at one level, embellishing—neighboring, surrounding, encircling—at a broader level. *At the broadest level of structure all secondary system components can be interpreted as expanding the primary system and elaborating the primary tonic.*

The third of Liszt's *Transcendental Etudes* contains, just before its conclusion, a provocative expansion of the primary tonality conditioned by a largely chromatic descent in the bass linking F:I with F:V (Ex. 1-13a).

Ex. 1-13a.   Liszt, *Transcendental Etudes,* No. 3 in F (*Landscape*).

Ex. 1-13a continued.

The F:I is given a dissonant 7th, making it a potential V_7 of IV (it has been long established as a consonant tonic), the E♭ then assuming the augmented-6th function, D♯, for resolution to A:I$_6^4$. A:V$_7$ acts similarly enharmonically as an augmented-6th into A♭:I$_6^4$. At this point there is an elision in which the expected sequential reference to the passing tonic G is omitted (see Ex. 1-13b); the progression from A♭:V$_7$ directly to G♭:I$_6^4$ is chromatic and deceptive. The G♭ dominant is now prolonged for six measures, finally acting as augmented-6th into F:I$_6^4$ for restoration of the primary dominant—the enharmonic factor being the C♭/B♮.

Ex. 1-13b.

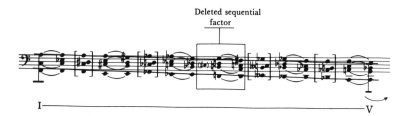

Deleted sequential
factor

I ——————————————————————————————————————— V

In the Liszt succession references are remote from the primary system and the means of tonal fluctuation extreme. There are firm primary tonal pillars framing the passage (I, V) and the fluctuation is swift and brief; yet the auxiliary tonics emerge as distinct secondary passing functions, enriching the primary system chromatically in the work's final developmental episodes.[b]

As examples for analysis reflect progressively late styles in the tonal period, increasingly provocative questions may arise, since extremes of range and fluctuation are more common in later nineteenth-century music. The parameters are those of *frequency of tonal change* (the quantitative facet of tonal rhythm) and *distance and volume of change*—both vital questions of style. Tonal expansion, especially as it concerns the second of these considerations, might be symbolized as in Fig. 1-1.

Fig. 1-1. Symbolic representation of tonal expansion.

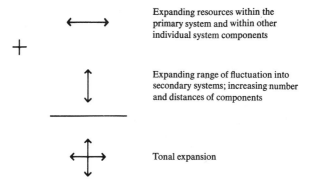

Expanding resources within the primary system and within other individual system components

Expanding range of fluctuation into secondary systems; increasing number and distances of components

Tonal expansion

In more fluctuant styles of highly chromatic idioms there are sometimes extremely remote and rapidly driven fluctuations in the tonal structure—even at such critical stages as the beginnings of works, creating tonal forms which might be represented graphically as in Fig. 1-2, the level portion showing the ultimate stable expressions (relative focus) of tonality after widely ranging fluctuation at the outset. Indeed, this is a shaping principle by which a great deal of later tonal music is conceived.

Fig. 1-2. Symbolic representation of tonal structure broadly receding toward final point of relative focus.

It is in severe fluctuations, those to remote tonal systems taking up sometimes vast proportions of a given structure, that the significance of the primary system seems, or may seem, radically diminished in its shaping effect.

In Ex. 1-14, after the most insubstantial reference to the primary tonic (C), there is immediate extreme fluctuation, violating the primary leading-tone in the second bar, *coming into focus with dominant references to the primary tonic several measures later.* The passing tonics, following chromatically, include not only B♭, in cancellation of the leading-tone of C, but D♭, the Neapolitan degree, as well. The passage is conditioned in part by text[24]; yet, it is not

Ex. 1-14. Brahms, *Alto Rhapsody,* Op. 53 (reduction from the orchestral score).

[24]The text includes the words "... verliert sich sein Pfad" (... loses his way).

unlike many instrumental as well as vocal works of highly chromatic idiom (less common and generally less severe Classical precedents of course exist) in which the primary tonic is very richly expanded—its prevalence even impaired—at such crucial points, or at great length in the form's internal stages.[c]

It must be emphasized that the sketch below the Brahms quotation is contrived to show tonal, not merely harmonic, succession.

Essential and auxiliary linear functions of pitches and pitch-complexes, their hierarchic basis often determined by tonal and cadential factors

A central premise of the present study is evident: harmonic and melodic analysis is, in an aspect complementary to that of concern with tonal function, the interpretive identification and evaluation of auxiliary and essential linear functions which make up the stream of successions.

While of course not the only approach to harmonic and melodic analysis, nor its only important aim (we might note, for example, the importance of study of style characterization), the identification and evaluation of linear functions are nevertheless basic.

The identification of some harmonic or melodic factors as essential (basic) and others as auxiliary (elaborative) is not a matter of absolutes. The conclusions reached, based upon a complex of factors less objective than those by which tonal function is determined, constitute an "interpretation" of linear functions. Linear function is strongly conditioned by tonal function as well as, at lower levels or in nontonal contexts, rhythmic prominence, reiteration, stress, cadential position, and like characteristics of events. There are, of course, some interpretations which are readily seen to be ill-founded while others derive from persuasive logic. And in the midst of such extremes many analytical interpretations represent a range in which "right" and "wrong" are in some degree inapplicable concepts. Only in some instances is there reason for insistence upon a "right" interpretation to the exclusion of others.

In the identification and analysis of essential harmonic functions we are inevitably much concerned with the analysis of cadences and their relative strengths. Cadential events are invariably of fundamental, essential function at some level, the level of significance depending on the strength of the cadence in relation to others, its strength a product of such subtle cadential qualities as registral placement, distribution of harmonic factors, metric prominence, linear approach to the cadence point, and especially *the positions of the cadential harmony in relevant primary and secondary tonal systems* and the place of the cadence in form (conclusive as opposed to preliminary). A predominant preoccupation of harmonic analysis is thus the analysis of cadence—its functional identity and character, the motions toward it, its relation (relatively affirmative, tentative, etc.) to cadences which precede and succeed it. These are vital, crucial considerations in all harmonic analysis of whatever nature or premises, and with respect to whatever musical styles.

In very much conventionally tonal music, harmonic analysis will reveal a broad prevalence of the primary (often triadic) harmonies: tonic, dominant, and subdominant (i. e., I and its chief auxiliaries a 5th removed), and especially of the first two of these. In such tonal music the vast majority of harmonies designated as "essential" in the basic frame of structure must be I and V—the latter, *when tonal music is viewed in broadest terms*, an auxiliary support and embellishment of the former, for which it is the principal medium of tonicization. Conventional tonal composition thus generally manifests the central structural functions of I, IV, and V; in fact, we tend to regard others as tentative or allied forms of these. Thus, we think of (and hear) II as functionally interchangeable with IV (having considerable overlap of PC content, and often occurring in first inversion with $\hat{4}$ as bass note); we regard VI, preceded by V, as a tentative "substitute" for I—a delaying action which brings about resolution of the leading-tone and introduces $\hat{1}$ but otherwise suggests further motion toward more conclusive resolution. And we consider VII analogous in function to V—almost indistinguishable from V_7, and III, often III_6, as V-like in function because of an overlap of PC content which duplicates the leading-tone and the $\hat{5}$ itself. The centrality of I, IV, V in conventional tonal composition is necessarily a crucial basis for distinctions among relatively essential and relatively auxiliary harmonic events in the linear stream; and the discussions which make up much of this chapter are concerned with this underlying premise.

While any and all dimensions and parameters of musical articulation are potentially significant in the interpretation and effect of essential and auxiliary functional distinctions, precluding any simple, general ranking and accounting of such factors, the following broad observations can be useful if they are not read as absolute and universal in their implications.

(1) Cadential harmonies are essential in the linear functional hierarchy, although at relatively broad levels of structure weaker cadences are auxiliary to more affirmative, tonally and formally more decisive cadences to which they are related.

(2) The primary tonic and dominant are very often, in conventionally tonal music, the essential substance of the structural frame. However, individual tonic and dominant harmonies can, in low-level rhythmic formulations analogous to those in Ex. 1-15, function as highly subordinate auxiliary events.

Ex. 1-15.

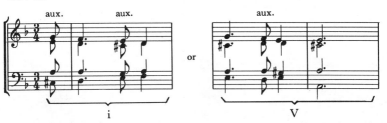

(3) Many factors extrinsic to actual, specific PC content can at lower levels affect, even determine, the structural value of a harmonic or melodic event: e.g., stress, reiteration, duration, etc. (Ex. 1-15 is pertinent to this point.)

(4) In nontonal styles, such factors extrinsic to actual PC content, and the factor of cadential occurrence, are of increased significance.

The general superiority of tonal primacy, where tonality is relevant, to other manifestations of structural value can be illustrated and empirically demonstrated in the imagination or in improvisation of a frequent situation in tonal music: that in which a dissonant factor (a dominant 7th-chord, an appoggiatura, a dominant triad over tonic pedal, etc.) is of great relative duration (i. e., of decisive agogic superiority) in comparison with its cadential resolution. No ear would deny the superior structural value of the higher-level resolution, the ultimate aim of motion, the medium of "absorption" of preceding dissonant energy and intensity.[25]

Finally, *all evaluation of linear (like tonal) function must rest upon evidence intrinsic to the particular context in question.*

The first prelude of Bach's *Well-Tempered Clavier*, Vol. I (Ex. 1-16) illustrates harmonic prolongations and auxiliary embellishments.

[25]The issue of distinction between superiority of tonal and linear function and metric (accentual) value must be introduced very tentatively at this point, to be developed further in Chapter 3. We are not, in the present context, saying that *metric or accentual value* necessarily inheres in the chord of cadential resolution by virtue of its tonal primacy. In Chapter 3 we shall wish to make a firm distinction between *metric* structure, in which units are delineated by *accent* (dissonance, density, duration, stress, etc.) and the kind of structural basis which is our concern in the present chapter. In the present frame of reference, the superseding cadential event (ultimately I) is the supreme tonal-harmonic-melodic factor upon which all other events of pitch and pitch-complex are suspended in elaborating, prolonging actions. But it is not necessarily a medium of metric "accent," or a delineator (initiator) of metric unit. Indeed, within the elements of pitch content the primary tonal event (I, or Î) is the *object of recessive action*. We shall take the position in Chapter 3 that articulations in which elaborating PC and pitch events are seen as grouped in functional associations around more basic, structural events interact, as do purely formal-cadential groupings of events, interestingly and vitally in musical structure with often counteractive delineations of *metric (accentually projected) units and unit relations.*

Ex. 1-16. Bach, Prelude No. 1 in C (*Well-Tempered Clavier,* Vol. 1).
Representation of linear and tonal functions.

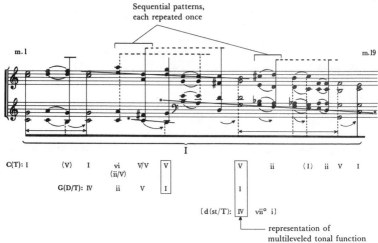

*Note bass descending diatonic scale (c¹-c).

Ex. 1-16 continued.

m.17

m.19

The function of ii$_2^4$ and V$_5^6$ in the prolongation-embellishment of the opening I is particularly clear in the voice-leading, in the easy adjacency of pitches of the two auxiliaries. Reading ahead from this relatively brief prolongation (which serves to establish the primary tonic), we can see that the ultimate aim of the ensuing succession is the tonic of m. 19, toward which there is general descent, made visible in the analytical sketch. (The fact of linear descent suggests a melodic recession complementary to that of the tonal-harmonic course toward I.)

The diagonal lines drawn through the bass of the sketch indicate the succession of passing auxiliary harmonies *linking the essential points* at either extremity in this overall succession. (Auxiliary elements of rhythmic-metric emphasis might be indicated by the symbol ▼ , used in other, comparable situations.) Two sequences in the descending, passing stream are bracketed and they of course represent a highly standardized convention of the style. (Harmonic content beyond m. 19 consists of an expansive affirmation of I by a broad cadential formula encircling I with its primary harmonic supports: I(V/IV)-IV-V/V-V(prolonged for nine measures, 23–31, eight of these over the $\hat{5}$ pedal)-I.

There are two secondary tonal references, one to the dominant, the other to the supertonic, the latter derived chromatically. (There are also subsequent, ephemeral secondary references to the subdominant region, e.g., mm. 20–21, and again to the dominant, m. 22.)

The roman numeral symbols show what has emerged as a most important factor in the theories of analysis developed here: the deep tonal significance (multiple, or multileveled, function) of harmonies. For example, the minor triad on A, followed by the C:V/V, is shown as vi in the primary system, as ii in the secondary system, and as ii/V in the primary system; indeed, *it has all of these significances within a leveled perspective.* The later D minor triad is both i in the secondary system and ii in the primary system—a tonicized primary supertonic.

The dual or multiple meanings of harmonies in tonal contexts are thus here reemphasized as a fundamental premise. The designation by roman numeral symbol of a harmony in two or three lights (e.g., the C:vi, ii/V, G:ii) is not an inconsistency; it is a realistic representation of the range of functional significances attending a harmony of both primary and secondary contexts of tonal reference. The identification of such multiple functions is a reflection of the *depth* of tonal-harmonic meaning and of the way harmony is heard in tonal music. *The concept of multiple function is necessary in the full explication of tonal-harmonic significance.*

Tonal order as an inflation of harmonic order and succession

It is well to pause here to make explicit the concept of tonal order and hierarchy as directly analogous to, and an inflation of, harmonic order, hierarchy, and succession. Harmonic rhythm thus has its counterpart in tonal rhythm and all parameters of harmonic structure their counterparts in tonal structure. The inflationary process by which IV or

$$\underbrace{\qquad\qquad}_{\text{IV}}$$

becomes SD is one of tonicization; $\hat{4}$ becomes the basis not merely for a harmonic factor, but for a secondary tonal system expanding the primary tonal system.

Thus, there is an important sense in which, as a hypothetical example, a five-part rondo might be seen as an inflation (extension, prolongation) of the contrived harmonic structure illustrated in Ex. 1-17.

Ex. 1-17.

An example of tonal expansion is given in Ex. 1-18a. In Ex. 1-18b, the succession of tonicized factors (*tonal* events) can be seen as a broadly, richly inflated underlying harmonic succession.

Ex. 1-18a. Chopin, Prelude No. 9 in E.

The tonicized C is a member of the parallel diatonic minor and A♭ (first major, then minor) is identifiable as the diatonic mediant, enharmonically notated, but the substantial reference to F (Neapolitan?) projects a secondary tonic of distinctly chromatic origin. Strong linear influences are at work as in the forceful drawing apart of outer voices. The expansion of the primary tonality is extreme for a work of modest dimensions (but consider the tempo); there is a series of enriching tonal shifts, all chromatic in process except that of m. 6, in which C:I is taken as F:V.

Curiously, although the reference to F is substantial, that tonic does not appear (it does later, in a following deviation into m. 10). Thus, the numerous F dominants have deceptive resolutions. The A♭ region is strong, although briefer, in view of its broadly paced functions and its position at the peak of a climactic drive. The triad on A, at m. 7, has no emphasis or supportive dominant and is best considered in its immediate relations a simple (nonfunctional[26]) chromatic neighboring auxiliary to two positions of F:V; never-

---

[26]A harmony, often but not necessarily a dominant form, failing to act even very locally in support of a primary or secondary tonic, structural or ornamental, is often described as *nonfunctional*—a concept negatively concerned with tonal, not linear function. Thus, a poten-

theless, it *is* IV of the primary system. The restoration of the primary tonic is accomplished by enharmonic-diatonic succession (see p. 73) in which a♭:i acts pivotally as E:iii. Example 1-18b shows (without fidelity to original voice-leading) the entire passage as an elaboration of E:I (again with linear expression of the factors of the prolonged tonic—its root, 3rd, 5th). The passing secondary tonics are identified as embellishing tonal functions.

Ex. 1-18b.

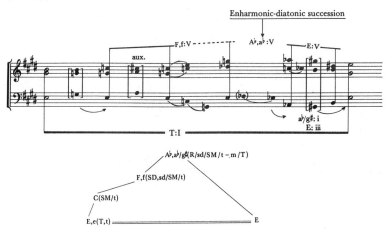

The "vagrant" diminished 7th-chord is important in the progression: the harmony at the end of m. 7, notated with E♮, looks back to the tonicized F through which the music has passed; notated with F♭, it looks ahead as a dominant to A♭.

Tonal fluctuation and techniques of immediate succession by which it is effected

Tonal fluctuation is, of course, denoted by the appearance of accidentals, whether they represent shifts to primary, embellishing, or passing systems.

---

tially tonic or dominant harmony may occur purely as a sonorous linear factor having no significant tonal function. On the other hand, if a dominant form is suggestive of a tonic prevalent in local or broad context, or if it has sufficient durational or other emphasis, it may have functional effect without association in the immediate context with the expected tonic of resolution or its deceptive substitute, i. e., without normal root movement or expected resolution of the leading-tone. The concept of nonfunctionality is applicable to only low levels of structure, and the judgment that a particular factor is "nonfunctional" is, inevitably, often interpretive.

(In theory, T:IV can be tonicized by I without accidentals, but this is rare and, without $\hat{7}$, not really convincing.[27]) Accidentals may, of course, appear without tonal significance, as when the normal raised $\hat{7}$ of the harmonic minor scale appears, when purely modal changes occur, when altered non-harmonic tones are used, or when there are cancellations of any of these alterations lacking tonal significance. The special concern of tonal analysis is the change or set of changes introduced in the harmony so as to have the effect of making reference to a "new" tonic.[28]

Alterations through which the primary system persists unimpaired in its hegemony (i.e., those of no tonal significance) will be cancelled shortly after appearance except when the change is one of more or less lasting modal shift.

The identification of specific places where tonal reference shifts is based upon objective criteria, while again the force of the shift is often a considerably subjective question (to some listeners even the most elusive change may upset an established tonal sense). To put the issue another way, the question of the existence of tonicization relevant *at some level* is one of substantially objective determination; the question of a *hierarchic ordering of system components*, like the judgment that a tonic emerges only "parenthetically," is one in which determination is in some part subjective.

Our definition of *tonal fluctuation* will be simple and inclusive: it is a change of tonal reference, secondary or primary in its implications, and however immediate in its significance. We will consider that a secondary tonic is as a rule supported by the appearance of its leading-tone (i.e., is tonicized by a dominant form) or, occasionally, by other means[29], normally including but conceivably without the expected tonic resolution or its substitute, since the dominant alone may have strong tonal implications. *Tonal fluctuation involves tonal events—harmonic successions inflated by tonicization;* every tonicization is of tonal significance in some degree.

Tonal fluctuation is thus significant with respect to a level of function: for example, a secondary leading-tone may have purely foreground impact. Moreover, the significance of a particular event in the tonal structure depends in part on the environment in which it occurs. Thus, if a tonicization occurs

---

[27] $\hat{7}$ denotes the lowered seventh scale degree.

[28] The theoretical problem of "modulation" is, again, entirely one of the *level* of analysis (perception, observation). Any change of tonal significance—any tonicization other than that of prior incipience or prevalence—is "modulation" in some degree ranging from purely parenthetical to very substantial expansions of the primary system. The significance of tonal shift is thus measurable in accord with the level of structure over which its effect is relevant; it is true of course that the retentive influence of a prior system, like the extent of its supersession by an entering one, is a partly subjective issue.

[29] Tonicization can of course, although less commonly, be brought about by plagal action and even, in theory, by durational or other insistence on a particular tonic form without support of attendant harmonic functions.

within an atmosphere of fluctuation (e. g., during the course of what we shall refer to as *accelerated tonal rhythm*), it has more persuasive effect *as tonal change* than one that occurs within a stable (closed) context in the tonal structure (e. g., one that occurs over a pedal point, or one surrounded by persuasive references to an underlying system having predominance over a broader structural level). For example, the tonicization of D/T at the end of an antecedent phrase will have significance in its cadential affirmation *at the level of that phrase*, while at the level of the entire period of which it is part the function of D/T will be seen to be tonal embellishment of the prevailing T which the consequent reaffirms. Finally, this study continues to make the point that the analysis of harmony, including tonicized harmony, is ideally comprehensive and multileveled, with the multiple interpretation and identification of harmonic function a necessary consequence of the fact of structural levels in music.

Secondary (or renewed primary) tonal references (shifts, fluctuations, modulations) involve *particular techniques of derivation*. While such techniques are of less interest to many theorists than are the broad outlines of tonal structure, we would argue for their importance, like the importance of many sharply felt events that are of primarily local impact, in the expressive effect of the musical surface. *How* a tonal inflection takes place—the process—can be decisive in the quality of its expressive impact. Processes, or techniques, of tonal change can be classified in a way that provides a basis for useful inferences and conjectures respecting such effect.

A *diatonic succession* occurs between two pitch factors (pitches, PCs or PCCs) which coexist in a single diatonic tonal system[30]—not necessarily the primary system in whose context the succession occurs, possibly even a parenthetical system. A *diatonic tonal fluctuation* occurs through a diatonic succession (Ex. 1-19).

Ex. 1-19.

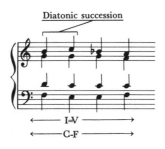

Diatonic succession

I–V

C–F

[30]For these definitions, "diatonic tonal system" in the minor mode is considered to be the harmonic scale, with the raised $\hat{7}$, since it is this scale form which expresses tonal function. The lowered $\hat{7}$ is a melodic factor tending to subvert the tonal sense by a leaning toward the relative major.

A *chromatic succession* occurs between two pitch factors which do not coexist in any single diatonic tonal system (Ex. 1-20). It often involves a chromatic inflection (G-G♯, B-B♭, D♭-D♮, etc.), but this is not necessarily true (consider an augmented-6th chord and its resolution). A·*chromatic tonal fluctuation* occurs through a chromatic succession.

Ex. 1-20.

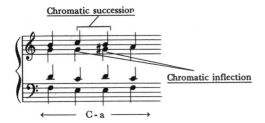

The hypothetical generic tonal system discussed earlier implies a possible, interesting theory of chromatic succession germane to its apparent experiential effect. That is the theory that chromatic succession, when of tonal significance, is in effect *tonal elision* (Ex. 1-21). Thus, for example, the

Ex. 1-21.

modulatory process by which SM/T(= D/st/T, etc.) is derived, when one of direct chromatic succession, may be regarded as an elision of the process T-D-D/D-D/D/D(= SM). This theory of chromatic fluctuation proposes that the fact of omission of stages (terms) in a potential diatonic series of underlying relations in some degree accounts for the effect of apparently wide tonal thrust in relatively little time. Whether relatively distant regions emerge directly (chromatically) or gradually from T is an important facet of style.[31]

[31]Since very nearby regions can be derived chromatically (e. g., approach to the SD of C by the inflection B-B♭), the presence of chromatic succession does not of course in itself imply tonal distance.

An *enharmonic succession* is one in which enharmonic equivalence pertains and enharmonic change occurs, explicitly or implicitly. It (the succession) may be diatonic or chromatic, so that it is proper to distinguish between an *enharmonic-diatonic succession* and an *enharmonic-chromatic succession.* Where tonal significance is involved, these are further techniques of tonal shift.[32]

In Ex. 1-22a, diatonic relation pertains between the two harmonies, assuming the necessary enharmonic interpretation; in Ex. 1-22b, a chromatic (nondiatonic) relation pertains.

Ex. 1-22a, b.

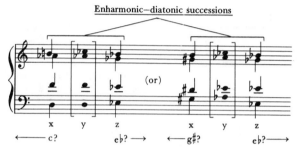

Enharmonic—diatonic successions

Note: $x - y$ an enharmonic relation;
$y - z$ a diatonic relation.

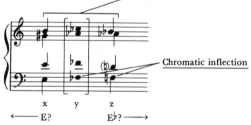

Enharmonic—chromatic succession

Chromatic inflection

Note: $x - y$ an enharmonic relation;
$y - z$ a chromatic relation.

[32]Analysts sometimes speak of an "abrupt modulation" as a classification of technique, but it must be seen that if the term is construed to denote an "unprepared" entry into a new tonal region, the concept is contradictory and illusory. While a modulation can (when associated with the entry of a new formal unit, or when approached by—especially radical—chromatic and/or enharmonic change) appear relatively "abrupt," there is always at the point of tonicization a discoverable relation which forms a link between the two systems involved. Moreover, the concept of "common tone" as a technique of shift overlooks the fact of harmonic *implication.* Thus, when a particular note is said to "imply" a certain harmony, it is meant that if that note were harmonized appropriately a certain harmony would be most

Example 1-23, from the second movement of Beethoven's Sonata for piano, Op. 13, illustrates *enharmonic-diatonic process*. The movement's fundamental primary tonic is A♭. If the shift is regarded as from G♯ minor to E, or from A♭ minor to F♭ major, it assumes a conventional appearance. The progression from m. 41 to m. 42, from a♭:i to E:V₇, is clearly diatonic; the two harmonies coexist in E, the first of them a common chord ($\longleftarrow$ a♭:i = E:iii $\longrightarrow$). The change of tonic is thus by enharmonic-diatonic process.

Ex. 1-23. Beethoven, Sonata in C minor for piano, Op. 13, second movement.

A final example in this series (Ex. 1-24) is taken from Schubert's Quartet in D minor, D. 810. Here, the process involves enharmonic change (E/F♭, G♯/A♭, B/C♭) and a chromatic relation as well. The F♭ appearing in the cello must, in view of relevant tonal systems preceding (F is the most immediate tonic, a the tonic of slightly broader level), be seen as "E becoming F♭." The augmented-6th chord thus enharmonically derived has, with the succeeding a♭ dominant, a chromatic relation. (I. e., although there is no chromatic inflection, the augmented-6th chord and its resolution lack diatonic relation; the process is *enharmonic-chromatic*.) The a♭ reference is extremely brief.

---

likely; this is the harmonic "implication." In many instances a particular implication will be inescapable, in others a matter of interpretation. Actually, in most cases, the harmony said to be "implied" will be explicit in an immediately surrounding context as harmonic basis for the isolated tone.

Ex. 1-24. Schubert, Quartet in D minor for strings ("Death and the Maiden"), D. 810, first movement.

*The "German" augmented 6th (on iv) in g♯/a♭ is enharmonically equivalent to a:V_7 (more locally derived as a diminished 7th on $\hat{2}$ in F); the augmented 6th, with its resolution, always constitutes a chromatic succession.

Tonal organization as a pattern of relative stability opposed to relative flux

While it may be obvious both in principle and in application, it is well to make a particular issue of the importance of the concept of tonal structure as alternating between, and opposing in various ways, areas of relative stability and areas of relative fluctuation. It is vital too that the concept be extended beyond developmental as opposed to expository practices of the tonal period, despite the significance of these practices. Thus, applications in earlier and later practices are relevant: in a modal form, a series of phrases culminating on the final, as compared with others expressing fluctuation to other degrees; and in late styles of the tonal period and in the twentieth century, the delineation of tonal structure by projection of, quite apart from *specific* tonics, areas of relative instability (ambiguity, lack of clarity, nonresolution) contrasted with areas of relative stability (focus, clarity of tonal direction, resolution).

Some examples in this chapter (pp. 59–60, 142–47) illustrate procedures in which tonal structure derives very importantly from the ordering of successions whose overall function is gradually to bring the tonality into focus, or the reverse of this, with the final cadence left undecided in opposition to clear tonal orientation at the beginning. Of course, we must also be concerned with the comparable opposition of stability and instability as a critical shaping element in the music of Classical tonality.

Consider, for example, a traditional form in which the principle of alternating stability and fluctuation is a fundamental point: the eighteenth-century imitative invention or fugue. It is in the nature of the episode in the invention-fugue genre that it is fluctuant (see Exx. 1-25a,b), often serving to bring about transitional tonal references in preparation for the level of a following, stable thematic statement (and, usually, its imitation). That an entire form can be conceived as deriving in an important sense from this principle (as well as from the principle of ultimate tonal "rounding" or reaffirmation of the initial, primary system) is evident in examination of any instance of fugal procedure.

One has only to consider a work of this kind as auditory experience to be vividly aware of the fundamental significance of the alternation of tonal *conditions*, and a further look into the areas of fluctuation normally reveals a number of elements functioning in *complementary support* of the organic principle of tonal fluctuation: for example, an acceleration in surface rhythmic activity, or the complementary activating force of imitations at relatively brief intervals of time.

An example of Classical tonal procedure will serve as a basis for further techniques of analysis and representation of tonal structure and system, and tonal processes of expansion, elaboration, and fluctuation.

It has been noted that the fugal episode, like transitional and developmental passages in tonal forms, can be conceived as an area of *accelerated tonal fluctuation*. Tonal succession and the fluctuative process are illustrated in two episodes from the Mozart Fugue in C for piano, K. 394 (Exx. 1-25a,b).

The episode quoted and summarized in Ex. 1-25a reveals a passing stream of harmonic successions involving chromatic relations—transitional and auxiliary in linear function but nevertheless of *locally significant tonal reference*. The analysis shows the operation of a trileveled tonal structure in which system components are represented by symbols indicating their relations to T—relations not merely theoretical but of demonstrable contextual validity. Although it is not carried out thoroughly, a multileveled harmonic analysis is indicated, one in which it is suggested that, for example, the D major sonority

Ex. 1-25a. Mozart, Fantasy and Fugue in C for piano, K. 394.

Passing, locally functional, chromatically related harmonic events:

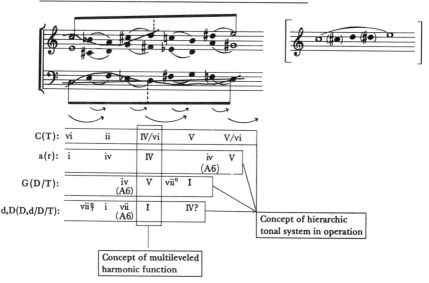

C(T):	vi	ii	IV/vi	V	V/vi
a(r):	i	iv	IV	iv V	
				(A6)	
G(D/T):		iv	V	vii° I	
		(A6)			
d,D(D,d/D/T):	vii⁷	i vii	I	IV?	
		(A6)			

Concept of hierarchic tonal system in operation

Concept of multileveled harmonic function

can be (and must be) heard *in varying functional implications as it is related more broadly or locally to hierarchically ordered operational systems relevant to the example.*

A second quotation from the Mozart Fugue (Ex. 1-25b) reveals a comparably fluctuant environment reflecting again a multileveled tonal system. But here the process is entirely diatonic: i. e., the successions are diatonic first in SD, then in SD/SD. (At the same time there is an element of chromaticism in evidence in the function and relative distance of one *nondiatonic tonic*: B♭, SD/SD.) As in Ex. 1-25a, the tonal references are of swift and ephemeral effect, serving primarily to fill "tonal space" and achieve forward linear motion with factors of harmonic richness beyond the primary tonal

Ex. 1-25b. Mozart, Fugue, K. 394.

m. 19

Passing, locally functional, diatonically related harmonic events:

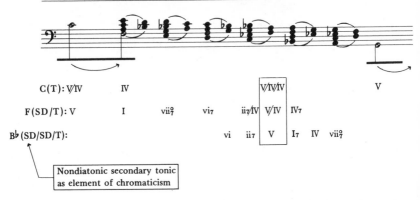

resource; yet, their implications are locally felt as expansions of that tonal resource, and thus an important subject of inquiry. Without such inquiry neither the directions of expansion of the primary system nor the means of such expansion would be apparent.

Tonal rhythm

What we have stated in the preceding section, put another way, is that it is fundamental to tonal structures that they are characterized by controlled distributions of changing tonal reference, that the time intervals separating tonicizations contract and expand in functional ways. This control of the rate of tonal change constitutes an aspect of the rhythm, and rhythmic life, of a composition. *Tonal rhythm*, characterized at active, developmental stages by substantial acceleration (with surface rhythmic drive and other elements often accelerated and intensified in complementary actions), is an important part of organic substance in music.[33] In this sense, we can see the traditional principle of development (transition, episode, etc.) as, in an important respect, one of tonal rhythm. (See Ex. 1-45 and the attendant discussion.)

The strength (definiteness, clarity) of a tonicization is certainly an aspect of its rhythmic function; in other words, if a tonal reference is a rhythmic event, it must be true that the degree of insistence in that event, what one might call its accentual force, is a necessary factor in *tonal rhythmic effect*. Again, one has only to think of the acceleration in tonal fluctuation as experience, and of the extent to which that experience is enforced in circumstances in which tonal changes are strong and emphatic. A tonicization is relatively strong if it is effected by devices that lend clarity (that carry the ear along without equivocation into an emergent tonal region); other factors in the accentual strength of tonicization are the degree of distance traversed (the extent of change represented by a given tonal event) and the duration of the predominance of a system component. Of course, emphasis of any kind (of timbre, of texture, etc.) is relevant here.

The questions of tonal intersection, direction, and distance; intervals of fluctuation; high-level chromatic successions and nondiatonic tonics; the interchangeability of modes and the "equivalence" of parallel tonics

We have reached, with the need to discuss *tonal distance and direction*, a particularly critical and difficult stage in the theoretical treatment of tonality. For while a concept of tonal distance is at least inferential in much of our thinking about tonality (we speak of two systems as "closely" related—e. g., C and G), the evaluation of distances between tonal systems is a very complex problem.

The tonal distances traversed in a given musical form are surely of great significance in structure and style, and in expressive effect. While it is doubtful that any absolute scale of relative tonal distances (e.g., list of systems related to any given system in the order of distance from that system) can be achieved, we can make some useful observations of certain criteria by which a theory of tonal distance would be informed.

One problem, of course, is: What does one measure? For instance, if accessibility of one system to another through diatonic harmonic succession is a reasonable criterion, we must recognize that the outline given in Ex. 1-10 (a theoretical chromatic tonal system of hypothetical, diatonically nearest,

---

[33]Tonal rhythm is comparable to but not to be equated with harmonic rhythm, which may or may not be parallel.

relations) shows that all of the chromatic degrees, even as roots of major and minor triads, are fairly readily approachable in tonicizations by diatonic succession.

But that has to do only with process—i. e., *how* do you derive a second system without recourse to direct chromatic succession? Another basis of criterion must be the question of *where* you are—the extent of difference between two systems. This question is probably more crucial in the experience of fluctuation, since no distance is significantly inaccessible even diatonically, and especially allowing such common nondiatonic devices as the Neapolitan harmony. The criterion of *extent of change* between two systems is probably decisive in the "effect" of being at a given point tonally "remote" from another point.

The following is an outline of some bases of criterion and measurement of tonal distance, letting *system*, for the present purpose, mean *diatonic system* in exclusion of even very common chromatic factors. Obviously, *tonal distance is in some sense a function of the extent of intersection between diatonic PC collections of tonal systems.* What is problematic is that tonal distance cannot be conceived merely as the extent of such intersection; the *particular factors which intersect* (since some are more crucial to tonal expression than others) are of necessary consideration.

(1) *The extent of intersection between two systems: key signature.* Correspondence of key signature is one indicator often cited. If the key signature indicator is to be of use, it must account for the raised $\hat{7}$ of the harmonic minor scale, since this is vital to tonal function. Moreover, the "distance" of three flats or sharps between signatures of parallel keys (e.g., C and c) is surely in an important sense illusory.

(2) *The extent of intersection: scale and primary degrees.* One easily measurable factor is the extent of intersection between two diatonic scalar sets of PCs; yet, it must be that the lack of intersection involving such fundamental degrees as $\hat{1}$, $\hat{5}$, and $\hat{7}$ would have especially significant tonal consequences.

(3) *The extent of intersection: triadic diatonic systems, and primary triadic functions.* Again, the intersection of diatonic triads coexisting in two systems is easily measurable; but the intersection involving those of primary tonal significance is certainly more critical. The intersection ◄——— IV = V ———►linking, say, C and B♭, would presumably constitute in this sense a "closer" relation than would the intersection ◄——— iv = vi ———► linking, say, e and C.

The foregoing considerations suggest that T and t are very closely related systems, despite the considerable difference of signature. In fact, the crucial correspondence of fundamental functional harmonic content (I,i; IV,iv; and especially V) suggests that in practice it is reasonable to consider

T and t as distinct modal forms of the *same tonal system* and to distinguish sharply and fundamentally between *tonal change* and *modal change.*

These observations also lead to intriguing reconsideration of the issue of distance between so-called "relative" keys in practice of the tonal period, a problem to which reference was made earlier. Thus, T and r are very similar in signature (there is one important difference if the inflection of $\hat{7}$ is taken into account), and an analogous situation pertains in the relation between t and R, whose signatures are alike but for the crucial question of $\hat{7}$ in the minor mode. This is the basis for earlier comment that T and D are significantly more closely allied than the pairs T, r or t, R. Fluctuation in the direction of R from t, a commonplace in conventional tonal practice perhaps deriving from modal traditions,[34] has far more drastic or emphatic effect as tonal change *than does the easily interchangeable succession T-D.*

In summary, the issue of intersection *is* fundamental, provided accounting is made of the *particular factors* which do and do not intersect. One such factor is of course V; and the importance of harmonic intersection in evaluation of tonal distance is further evident in the likelihood that we experience greater remoteness from a system when there is fluctuation to another tonic having nondiatonic relation to the first—i.e., when there occurs a *"high-level chromatic succession"* between two tonics, even though the second may be derived in a low-level, step-by-step diatonic process.

(4) *Diatonic accessibility of the second V, or a V preparation in the second system,* a particular, vital aspect of the question of intersection. Tonal distance might be conceived in terms of the capacity of one system to yield diatonically (without recourse to direct chromatic succession) the V of another, or the V preparation. That is, when V of one system is contained in another, an especially significant kind of relation pertains; and the intersection involving a potential V preparation (commonly I, IV, or II) is a significant relation not much removed. Chromatic necessity in derivation of the critical V implies and conveys a sense of distance. The issue of diatonic intersections involving V, or common V preparation, is summarized in Fig. 1-3. Here, the summary takes as an assumption the equivalence of enharmonic relations and tonal

---

[34]The problem more acutely concerns T-r (R-t) than t-R (r-T) since in the latter process R:V is immediately accessible from t:i (e. g., a:i, being equivalent to C:vi, can introduce C:V without chromatic inflection). No doubt a better understanding of the evolution of major-minor tonality (especially of seventeenth-century music) would illuminate bases and origins of the conventional, standardized practice of fluctuation between "relative keys." Three factors must certainly be (1) the ambivalence of $\hat{7}$ in evolution of the minor mode (its lowering inclining t in the direction of R), (2) the prevalence of $\hat{7}_{\flat}$—with the same result— in avoidance of the awkward melodic interval of the augmented 2nd, and (3) the attraction toward potential tonal function in the relation of ii°-III (as secondary vii°-I) inherent in the diatonic aeolian mode.

Fig. 1-3. Summary of accessibility of V and V preparation in relations between systems.

	FIRST ORDER (V occurs in T, t)	*SECOND ORDER* (V preparation— I,i and/or II,ii and/or IV,iv— in T, t)	*THIRD ORDER* (Neither V nor V preparation in T, t)
c,C ⟶ C♯/D♭, c♯	✓		
c,C ⟶ D, d		✓ (e. g., V = IV, iii = ii, ii = i)	
c,C ⟶ E♭, d♯/e♭		✓	
c,C ⟶ E, e		✓	
c,C ⟶ F, f	✓		
c,C ⟶ F♯/G♭, f♯			✓
c,C ⟶ G, g		✓	
c,C ⟶ A♭, a♭/g♯		✓	
c,C ⟶ A, a		✓	
c,C ⟶ B♭, b♭/a♯	✓ (i. e., IV = V)		
c,C ⟶ B/C♭, b		✓	

identity of parallel systems of modal difference. In this presentation, the *direction* of fluctuation within a given IC (interval-class) of separation is a factor of distinction (e.g., cf. C ⟶ F and C ⟶ G).

(5) *Intervallic distance between tonic PCs.* This factor constitutes a basis of measurement in itself;[35] but a partly inverse relation is seen to pertain when extent of intersection is also taken into account.

In Fig. 1-4, taking for simplicity systems of *major mode only*, a relation is

---

[35]Two possible parameters might be mentioned: that of the size of the interval and that of its "natural" basis, to which the proximity of T and D is often attributed.

Fig. 1-4. Relations between interval separating tonic PCs of major mode systems and tonal distance as to intersections of $\hat{1}$, $\hat{5}$, and $\hat{7}$.

Interval Class (IC)	Comment	Number of intersecting relations: proximity = high value	Key signature difference: proximity = low value
1 (m2)	Difference of ⑤ flats or sharps; intersections: $\hat{1}$ ⟶, $\hat{7}$ ⟶.	2	5*
2 (M2)	Difference of ② flats or sharps; intersections: $\hat{1}$ ⟶, $\hat{7}$ ⟶, ⟵ $\hat{5}$ ⟶.	4	2
3 (m3)	Difference of ③ flats or sharps; intersections: $\hat{1}$ ⟶, $\hat{7}$ ⟶, $\hat{5}$ ⟶.	3	3
4 (M3)	Difference of ④ flats or sharps; intersections: $\hat{1}$ ⟶, $\hat{7}$ ⟶, $\hat{5}$ ⟶.	3	4
5 (P4/5)	Difference of ① flat or sharp; intersections: ⟵ $\hat{1}$ ⟶, $\hat{7}$ ⟶, ⟵ $\hat{5}$ ⟶.	5	1
6 (A4)	Difference of ⑥ flats or sharps; intersection (allowing enharmonic interpretation): ⟵ $\hat{7}$ ⟶.	2	6

Most distant?

Closest?

*The lower value (e.g., as to C and B or D♭) is given rather than 7 (e.g., as to C and C♯ or C♭).

suggested between the interval of tonic PC separation and the apparent tonal distance as to intersections of $\hat{1}$, $\hat{5}$, and $\hat{7}$.

The inadequacy of Fig. 1-4, as to establishing a generally valid scale of tonal distance, is particularly evident when one considers the vastly more complex problem of intersection when it takes into account the correspondence of *chords* (even diatonic) rather than simple degrees. Moreover, the issue of intersection as it concerns the V, and especially the leading-tone, is probably more critical than questions of other intersections (including the tonic note itself). Thus, intersection of *both $\hat{5}$ and $\hat{7}$* in one or two directions at intervallic distances of IC2 and IC5 is a further vital factor in the apparent relative proximity characterizing these relations. In the relation IC3, $\hat{5}$ intersects in one direction (e. g., C-E♭) and $\hat{7}$ in the reverse direction (e. g., E♭-C), but they do not jointly intersect in the same direction.

The special proximity of systems whose tonics are separated by IC5 is evident on a number of significant bases. Indeed, it is well known that tonal fluctuation in conventional styles often proceeds in 4ths and 5ths. When that happens, it is useful to distinguish further between *plagal actions* (those in which succession is a 5th down or a 4th up—i. e., in which one tonic is, at least in this important sense, dominant to the succeeding tonic) and the reverse. That is another way of referring to the critical V intersection (cf. C → F and C → G in Fig. 1-3).

(6) *The number of terms in any harmonic diatonic succession leading into the second system.* Here, reference is again made to Ex. 1-10. For example, the relation of T to D or SD might be conceived as one of two terms (there is an immediate diatonic relation between them), but T to SM of three terms [as in the diatonic succession T-st-SM (in which st = sd/SM)]. In the discussion attending Ex. 1-10 a number of variables are noted, including the fact that this basis of measuring tonal distance accounts neither for relative frequencies of diatonic triadic functions nor for possibilities of succession including such common nondiatonic functions as the Neapolitan.

All of the above must be understood as a set of observations germane to (perhaps in the direction of, but far from constituting) a theory of tonal distance. The concept of *tonal direction* is related: theorists speak of the "flat direction" (counter-clockwise in the circle of 5ths) and "sharp direction" (clockwise); as suggested, for example, in connection with fluctuation in 4ths and 5ths, reversals of "direction" have significant implication in structural function in music and, often, in the perception of tonal distance as well (i. e., the nature and extent of intersection, and the severity of change).

Concepts of tonal progression and tonal recession

To the extent that distance and direction can be inferred on the basis of stated principles, we shall regard tonal fluctuation away from the primary tonic as *progressive* and fluctuation toward the primary tonic as *recessive*. The concepts of *tonal progression* and *tonal recession* are thus opposed (*tonal succession* applies to both tendencies, denoting change without accounting for relative distance). These concepts are in keeping with a fundamental idea of this book: the idea of *progressive fluctuation in the direction of intensifying conditions expecting resolution* (dissonance, complexity, ambiguity, instability, distance, acceleration, etc.) opposed to that of *recessive fluctuation in the direction of conditions achieving or tending toward resolution* (consonance, simplicity, clarity, stability, proximity, deceleration, etc.). These concepts require the assumption that in any particular tonal structure, if there is fluctuation,[36] there are points of maximal tonal distance and "best" tonal stability (the latter, at broadest

---

[36]Where tonal fluctuation is lacking, there is harmonic fluctuation of restricted but analogous effect. The concept of *harmonic distance* (from I) within a single diatonic system or

levels, usually terminating) against which tonal progressions and recessions are evaluated. A tonal structure is thus seen as fluctuant between conditions of tonal "dissonance" and "resolution"—distance from and proximity to the primary system. The progressive and recessive actions within the tonal structure may conform to (have complementary relation to) those of other elements, but the tendencies of concurrent elements are often opposed (in compensatory, counteractive relation). These tendencies and interrelations of element-actions, of which tonal fluctuation is one, are regarded as fundamental to structural function and expressive effect in music.

While space does not permit their quotation, we may refer in passing illustration of these concepts to two songs of Wolf, both characterized by the unusual condition of *tonal fluctuation at the broadest level*. One of these, to which reference must be made without quotation, is *Selig ihr Blinden* (No. V of the *Italienisches Liederbuch*, Vol. I), which begins in E♭ and concludes in A♭. Surely the tonal relations so described constitute a *tonal recession* overall from D to T (rather than, say, a progression from T to SD); but the tonal structure is complicated by the fact that E♭ yields to more distant regions (G♭—R/d?, and B♭—D/D/T) before its role as D/T is directly fulfilled. Thus, the tonal structure is first progressive, then recessive; the path of recession must by any reasonable estimate of tonal distance be seen to begin with the reference to B♭, m. 16. The function of E♭ as D/T is first clearly suggested in the appearance of E♭:I as a dominant form (with D♭) in m. 19, after which it undergoes elaborate and extended prolongation before T arrives in m. 27, itself then prolonged and embellished in a fourteen-measure, strong verification.

A Wolf song of comparably recessive, active tonal form is *Der Mond hat eine schwere Klag' erhoben*, No. VII of the same volume, also unfortunately discussed without reprinting. Its three tonal system components (whose centers comprise the notes of T:I!) are shown in Fig. 1-5 with their relations to T

Fig. 1-5. Outline of recessive tonal structure in Wolf, *Der Mond hat eine schwere Klag' erhoben* (No. VII of *Italienisches Liederbuch*, Vol. I).

Recessive tonal succession: e♭ $\overparen{\text{G♭, g♭/f♯, G♭}}$ C♭ = components of C♭:I

m———⟶ D, d, D ———⟶T
(r/D)

expanded system is of course related to the issue of tonal distance, and is implicit in standard theories of common practice harmonic succession (e. g., VI-IV-V-I) as well as in observed probabilities of succession and cadential formulation in modal systems. The inflation of such a principle of harmonic distance could provide a further basis for measuring tonal distance (note the proximity of V, I as compared with that of D, T).

adduced on the basis of plausible contextual function. In describing the overall structure as recessive, the system on G♭ is, in view of the tonally powerful I = V intersection, regarded as closer to C♭ than is e♭.

Concepts of harmonic and melodic progression and recession; complementarities and counteractions of element-successions

Melodic and harmonic successions are likewise capable of classification as to progressive and recessive (or static) action. It follows that an attempt at such classification, on a theoretical basis subject to empirical verification, is a vital necessity once a premise is undertaken to the effect that *harmonic and melodic changes are generally not neutral with respect to the intensity-release scale of expressive effect.*

Of the following observations, some are relatively conjectural, some are easily demonstrable, and a few are manifestly reasonable and even self-evident.

(1) *Progressive harmonic action*, action in the direction of increased intensity, might be summarized as:

> (a) *Action away from I* (to V, thence at some level to II, IV); the succession I-V-II (IV)-VI-III can be regarded as one of increasing progressive tendency provided the close associations of VI and I, and II and IV, as well as in certain contexts III and V, are taken into account whenever pertinent; a general consideration of progressive action away from I, in the sense in which it is noted here, would of course be of relevance particular to conventional tonal systems, and the concept "away from I" in freer, or other particularized, tonal systems requires adaptation to the terms unique to such systems or individual works.
>
> (b) *Action in the direction of increased dissonance of an implicit kind* (increased dissonance of a tonal kind would presumably be synonomous with increased distance from I).
>
> (c) *Action in the direction of increased density and of increased spatial field* (a concern of texture explored in Chapter 2).
>
> (d) *Action in the direction of acceleration of harmonic rhythm* (noted in Chapter 3).
>
> (e) *Action in the direction of more intense coloration*, or of relative intensity within other cofunctioning elements.

(2) *Progressive melodic action*, action in the direction of increased intensity, might be summarized as:

> (a) *Upward succession*, in which intensity is increased by the extent of leap (i.e., rate of ascent) and by the duration-span of continued local or essential ascent.

(b) *Action away from* $\hat{1}$—a consideration of tonal bases (cf. the above criterion of harmonic action away from I).

(c) *Action in the direction of increased dissonance of intervallic relations* between pitch events at a given level of structure.

(d) *Action in the direction of acceleration of melodic rhythms or more intense coloration*, etc.

The conjectural observations listed above have to do with the specific structural parameters (dimensions) of harmony and melody, respectively, or with related, cofunctioning element-actions. In the characterization of certain successions as progressive and others (opposite to those listed) as recessive, various relevant factors must at some point be regarded independently. Factors such as those listed do, in fact, *often function in parallel (complementary) effect*—i.e., a melodic succession may move away from $\hat{1}$ and up at the same time; but it is obvious that a line *may be recessive in tonal fulfillment and progressive in intensifying upward movement at the same time*, and *such counteractive tendencies are in fact very common in music* and of important paradoxical effect. Similarly, for example, in a harmonic succession there may be concurrent, complementary effect in parallel actions toward increased dissonance and away from I; but the reverse is common—e.g., harmonic action toward I but involving intense, implicit dissonance in (often prolonged) V on the "brink" of (in very close proximity to) I. In such a situation, the counteractive relations of coincident element-actions *are of very powerful effect indeed*, and dissonance often increases progressively (e.g., $V\text{-}V_7\text{-}V_9$) in the course of prolongation. What we are talking about is of course tightly related to concepts of tonal progression and recession noted earlier, except that considerations here have to do with possibilities inherent in a purely diatonic, unexpanded tonal system.

One can readily hypothesize or cite further situations in which distinct melodic and harmonic actions which are coincident are of *complementary* effect or of *counteractive* effect: for example, one might imagine, cite in music, or improvise an ascending melody over static harmony, or any comparable or reverse situation. While observations in these studies are not always made specific with respect to progressive and recessive tendencies, the implications of such expressive actions should always be kept in mind.

Some examples of quasi-tonal order in melodic and composite functions

Melodic analysis of initiating subject statements is shown in extract from a setting of the *De profundis* text by Josquin (Ex. 1-26a). Three of the statements are seen to fluctuate, essentially, between the final and cofinal of the mode, as would be expected, while one of them—that of the altus—is comparably structured at the level of the 5th above, the cofinal G its most essential point.

Ex. 1-26a.   Josquin, *De profundis clamavi* (Motet).

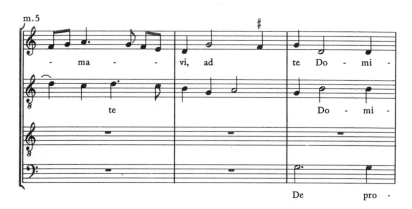

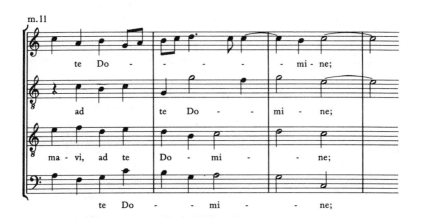

Reprinted from the Smijers edition, published by G. Alsbach and Co., Amsterdam, by permission of Creyghton Musicology-Musica Antiqua, Bilthoven, Netherlands.

The relatively tentative character of the superius statement is evident in the primacy, within its own terms, of G. The other three statements have, in comparative melodic structures, relatively stronger affirmations of C, the final, as essential basis. They can be seen in a composite sketch as reflecting very clearly the "V"-"I" motion (Ex. 1-26b) which further underlies the entire

Ex. 1-26b.   Josquin, *De profundis*.
Composite sketch of initial entries showing essential motion toward C ("I").

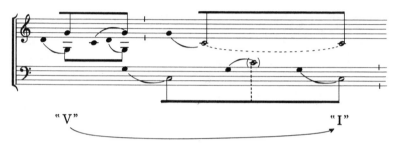

"V"   "I"

composition. In the composite sketch only essentials, degrees $\hat{1}$, $\hat{5}$, and $\hat{2}$, are represented, with the auxiliary neighbor and passing indications of the melodic reductions of individual subjects omitted for a more fundamental view.

In the Berg melody (Ex. 1-27a) certain notes, by virtue of tonal conditioning, actual resolving motion, and/or subordinate status in relation to more essential melodic points to which they are proximate and rhythmically oriented, are of clearly auxiliary function. Some are of especially strong tendency. The second note, $d\flat^2$, is approached like and resolves like the classical appoggiatura. The subordinate g^2 at the end of m. 2 is a neighbor auxiliary to the prominent $a\flat^2$ preceding; it has resolution in the following measure, but then reappears, lacking resolution except as part of a descending passing group. The $f\flat^2$ of m. 3 expects $e\flat^2$ (which does occur in the piano), but it is released unfulfilled (an important aspect of expressive effect), even in its second appearance at the end of the same bar, where the sense of nonresolution is intensified. Its felt relation to $E\flat$ has to do with the prior appearance of $e\flat^2$ in the line, and the impact of an $A\flat$ "tonic" expressed in the clarinet's first measure.

Although rhythm as such is not at this point a matter of attention, we can briefly note how ideally rhythmic effect complements the melodic structure. Essential points have agogic emphasis ($a\flat^2$, m. 2; $e\flat^3$, m. 5) as well as emphasis by repetition (mm. 3–4). As the line ascends to its high point the

Ex. 1-27a. Berg, Four Pieces for clarinet and piano, Op. 5; No. 2.
(Clarinet line transposed to sounding pitch.)

Copyright 1924, Universal Edition. Used by permission of the publisher. Theodore Presser Company, sole representative United States, Canada and Mexico.

motion is hesitant (frequent pauses, *sehr langsam, etwas langsamer,* then *ritardando*). But the descent, which traverses half again the melodic distance in about the same time, is characterized by increased rhythmic motion (m. 5)—gradual—suddenly drawn back (the *marcato* of the end of m. 5, the longer values and *ritardando* of mm. 6–8) to the conditions of the beginning.

There is palpably balanced control of the distribution of conjunct-disjunct motion. Leaps are prominent in the first half of the line, but they are invariably balanced by steps, usually in opposing directions. (A curiously exposed pitch is the a¹, or b♭♭¹, of m. 4, projected as a subsidiary low point of some prominence, awaiting resolution.) The descent of the line finds compensation for greater distance and faster motion in more conjunct succession in which even 3rds and 4ths give the impression of "steps" in a sequence of motion-stasis-motion or descent-plateau-descent.

Ex. 1-27b.

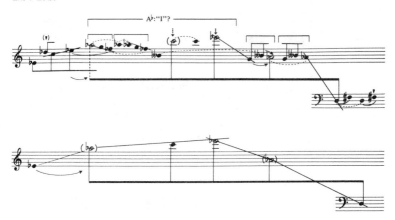

A synoptic sketch of the Berg melody, with auxiliary notes oriented toward the basic outline, reveals some persuasive factors of unity and ambiguity (Ex. 1-27b). What emerges most strikingly is a triadic basis on A♭, with a two-octave ascent (to e♭³), the high point occurring almost exactly at midpoint, then a descent of approximately three octaves in accelerated, recessive motion of line. Ambiguity is expressed in the conclusion, which is ironically contradictory to the established tonal implication, arriving at the structural d, manifesting a tritonal relation with the otherwise fundamental A♭.[37] The tonal structure of the line is thus open.

The sketch suggests a relation between that isolated a¹ (b♭♭¹) of the clarinet (m. 4) shortly before the high point and the pitch (notated as b♭♭¹ in Ex. 1-27a) appearing later as upper neighbor to the essential a♭¹; the earlier is interpreted as an "anticipation" of the upper auxiliary, unresolved until the subsequent motion to the a♭¹ "tonic." That is its effect. The characteristic

---

[37]The piano too has an open tonal structure, insistent (on D) but contrasting to that of the clarinet, moving, in chromatic bass descent, from the D "tonic" of the opening to a concluding B♭. In this light, a composite alignment of bitonal tendencies can be seen to intersect, for the apparently deviant outcome of the clarinet line achieves D, the "tonic" of the piano's initial repetitions. In fact, those repetitions consist of the major 3rd, d and f♯, duplicated in the final utterances of the clarinet on the same pitches exactly.

anacrustic material of the opening, lending strong accentual value to the immediate goal of the line, a♭², is represented as associated with the a♭², but with slurs and arrows suggesting lower-level orientations within the anacrustic group. Essential prolongations, high points, and other factors are represented as in other examples, and a second sketch shows a further reduced resumé in which the most essential motions and directions are extracted.[d]

The Webern example (Ex. 1-28) is perhaps an exaggerated instance of melodic tonal expression, as the sketched analysis makes abundantly clear, showing auxiliaries of strong leading-tone function in affiliation with a structural "tonic." The lower leading-tone, G♯, provides in addition to strong support of A the needed low point in a line whose curve is beautifully molded, moving in its most basic outline from a to a¹, with the range of the line extending slightly above and below these points. The motivic unity of the melody, involving sequence, is represented in the analysis in a limited way.

Ex. 1-28. Webern, Four Pieces for violin and piano, Op. 7; No. 3.

Melodic curve

The curve (pitch-profile) of a melodic line can be represented in many ways, showing upward and downward directions with whatever specificity or generality seems appropriate in accord with the aim of inquiry, and revealing the graphic image of its tonal succession or basis. For example, in a sense and at one level of consideration, Ex. 1-29 reveals a series of up and down movements; in another sense it is a static melodic element.

Ex. 1-29.   Brahms, Intermezzo in A, Op. 118, No. 2, for piano.

The graphic representation of the melodic curve would show clearly where the melodic activity is concentrated in the range of the line and temporal durations of its active and static stages, illustrating the comparative breadth or narrowness of its pitch compass (range, ambitus). Such a representation could be designed to illustrate the symmetry or asymmetry of its units, and the disjunctness or conjunctness of its intervallic successions, and the balance and distribution of skips and steps. A very important part of the analysis of curve must derive from the particulars of melodic movement the broader strokes of which are described by the essential points of the line.

Example 1-30a shows the graphic representation of a melodic curve in a period theme. The essential direction of the first phrase is down, that of the second both down and up. The second phrase reaches beyond any point established in the first—thus, while built upon the same motives, establishing a new high point. In the graphic picture of the line, vertical units on the left represent divisions of pitch (each having the value of a semitone) while those across the top represent divisions of time (in this instance, each representing an eighth-note or eighth-rest).

The diagram shows where the melody moves, where it is stationary, and in what directions and by what distances it moves; it shows whether the melody moves in large or small intervals, and where the activity is slow, where accelerated—all important factors in its effect. High and low points in pitch are immediately apparent and it is clear whether or not they are repeated and how they are approached through subsidiary high and low points. It

Ex. 1-30a. Haydn, Symphony No. 102 in B♭, first movement.
Graphic representation of curve of opening period melody.

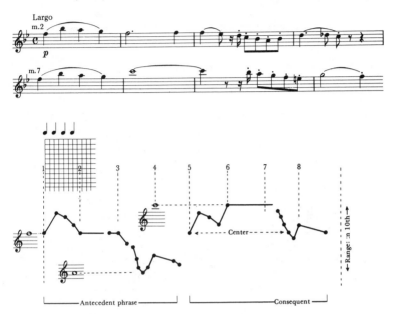

is apparent whether the line is one of extensive or restricted range, and how its separate units (in this case, phrases) compare in this and other respects.

Particular centers of activity within the range and within the durational span can be seen. One can see that short time divisions are usually concurrent with short spatial (intervallic) divisions, and that, in the example, a considerable leap is followed by shorter movement in the opposite direction. In short, one can see much of the melody's character, and the general effect of its linear functions is made apparent.

The curve shows that the high point (second bar, second phrase) is established only once. Frequently this is true, for repetition except when fairly immediate can weaken its effect. The high point is only a step higher than the b♭^{2} of the first phrase, a subsidiary high point, *thus manifesting a common principle of step relation between high points* and preserving the relatively modest range of the line. The high point is prominent not only because it ascends to a pitch not touched earlier; it is approached by the largest leap, it is the longest note, it is metrically strong, and it is of essential tonal significance. The climax note often appears late, as in this example, where it extends into the seventh of eight measures.

If we isolate the essential notes of each phrase of the melody to which Ex. 1-30a refers, we arrive at a *reduced curve,* that of a more basic dimension. The analysis of curve will thus be simplified in a way that is useful for perceiving the *most essential directions of the line*—a higher level of structure (Ex. 1-30b).

Ex. 1-30b. Syncptic representation of curve in the Haydn melody.

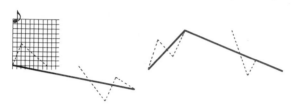

This process is analogous to that in which structural points are identified and outlined—those most strongly asserted and/or fundamental (i.e., in tonal and linear function) as opposed to those which are ornamental and auxiliary—as a means of getting at the most fundamental basis.

The principal notes of the melody in the interpretation suggested are f^2, with which the first phrase begins and with which it continues after brief digression through more than half of its length; c^2, with which the first phrase ends and toward which the movement of the line is aimed after the initial f^2 is abandoned; the f^2 with which the second phrase begins (the same pitch as that with which the first opened, thus manifesting a *prolongation* of that note); the c^3 at mm. 8–9, climax note of the entire melody; and the f^2 with which the second phrase ends, still another manifestation of a pitch central to the entire period at the broadest level. These points have special significance with respect to one or more of the following factors: formal articulative function (e.g., initiating or cadential), durational value by repetition or sustained length, metric prominence, dynamic projection, prominence by virtue of high or low pitch, relatively emphatic manner of approach (i.e., by leap, and by interval of leap), and most important of all, *centrality of function in the tonality,* a decisive criterion in all tonal music.

It is of interest that the principal notes are the dominant and supertonic (dominant of dominant) degrees. *The essential tones of the melody are factors in dominant harmony.* The eschewing of any point of tonic repose in the melody quite befits its introductory role. The intensity occasioned by the prevalence of dominant feeling in the introductory theme ($\hat{5}$, $\hat{2}$ or $\hat{5}/\hat{5}$) is ultimately resolved only in the *Allegro* which it prepares, and the melodic line of the two-phrase theme of the *Allegro* carries out this intent.[38]

---

[38]Identification of structural points in the consequent *allegro* theme would show that its melody is an expression of tonic harmony just as that of the introduction is an expression of dominant.

A melody of Boulez, radically different in character and substance, and atonal, appears as the final subject in this series; it is useful in illustrating analytical representation of a melodic "curve" of extreme fluctuations posing particular questions (see Ex. 1-31a).

Ex. 1-31a. Boulez, *Structures* for two pianos, part Ia.

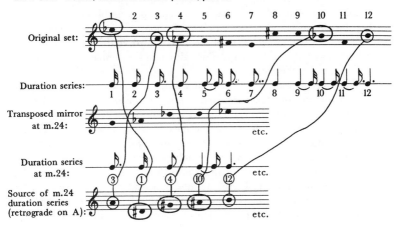

The melody in Ex. 1-31a is sounded without counterpoint or accompanying voices. Its curve is one of great extremes of range (in a single phrase it encompasses almost the entire piano keyboard) and angularity of movement. The leaps are of such extreme distance that smaller relations of intervallic succession (d-E♭, e²-f♯, or the concluding F-b) appear almost conjunct in the established context. In general, changes are quick and of radical scope. The high and low points are temporally adjacent, occurring just beyond the middle of the phrase. It is possible to imagine discretely perceptible groups or units within the phrase—the first three notes, four notes, or five notes, defined by the inherently punctuative effect of the longer third, fourth, and fifth notes, as well as any comparable formulation, although the composer prescribes a *legato* execution of the entire phrase.

The sheer extremes of movement within the line impart, certainly, a sense of drive, and the absence of tonal function contributes to an effect of unpredictability (and mobility). Lacking repetitions of any kind—of motive, of rhythmic value, of pitch or PC, the melody is one of constant renewal.

The example, like others of its kind, poses problems of coherence and apprehension, despite such unities as achieved by the shape of line [the wedge-like succession and interrelation of high and low points, clear in the graphic representation (Ex. 1-31b), settling at a relatively middle ground at the end of the phrase], or the consistency of dynamic level, like other elements a product of serial control. The problems are not merely of the absence of any sense of divisibility in the phrase into smaller units that can be grasped as such and of which any point is made, or of the absence of hierarchic function lending any kind of tonal order. More basic still is the fact that in its disposition of pitch and rhythmic differentiation—the primary factors by which melodic form is perceived—*contrasts are so extreme and so constant that the effect of contrast is, ironically, radically attenuated.*[39] There is a paradoxical feeling of randomness in the melody—paradoxical in view of the thorough predetermination of all its elements.

Henri Pousseur discusses the Boulez, referring to this same phrase along with another from the same work:[40]

[39]One recognizes that these judgments, in which some degree of conjecture must be acknowledged, are based on values which can be declared irrelevant to the aesthetic of the work in question. But the aesthetic itself is the subject of the questions posed. The issue of more or less "total" serialization of elements and element-events and the comparable question of random operations in musical composition are treated in this book's introductory section, where the importance (functional, expressive) of *the determination of events and event-relations on the basis of contextual interaction* is argued.

[40]Henri Pousseur, "The Question of Order in New Music," in *Perspectives of New Music*, V, 1 (1966), pp. 93–111; translation by David Behrman. There is no assertion, in the quotation of these passages from Pousseur's excellent article, that his concerns necessarily parallel those of this writer. The second melodic example to which Pousseur refers is that of Piano I, mm. 57–64 (*Très modéré*), in *Structures*, Part Ia.

Ex. 1-31b. Graphic representation of the Boulez melodic phrase.

Note: Each graph unit represents one semitone vertically and one ♪ horizontally.

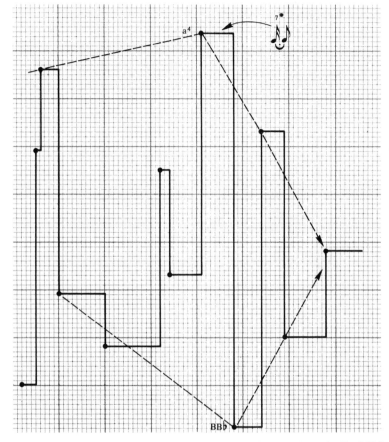

*Anomalous: a unit of 11 would be expected (see derived duration series, Ex. 1-31a).

Our difficulty in making a precise comparison between the two figures when we listen to them is caused, among other things, by the fact that each one is organized in the most irregular, least periodic fashion possible. Both passages might be likened to what are called "Brownian movements," i.e., movements lacking (from the observer's viewpoint) in all individual signification and therefore offering a high degree of resistance to unified over-all apprehension and to distinct memorization.

Thus the rigorous serial procedures which determine all the detail do not seem to have a positive function. Far from establishing perceptible symmetries and periodicities, regularity in similarity and in differentiation—in other words, an effective and recognizable ordering of diverse figures—they seem instead to *hinder* all repetition and all symmetry: or to put it another way (insofar as order and symmetry may be assimilated one with the other), all true *order*. The effect of statistical disposition (differentiation of dynamics, tempo, and attack . . . , or differentiation in density between the two and other moments of the piece) upon the "over-all form" is to guarantee a *permanent renewal*, and an absolute degree of unpredictability, at this higher structural level.

Some further observations concerning melodic analysis

The foregoing discussions of methods of melodic analysis are concerned chiefly with melodic curve and linear functions. We find that any example of melody has a certain *essential structure*—not an objective absolute, but something of presumed empirical validity that analysis seeks to discover and interpret. The basic structure consists of points in the line which we have classified as *essential*, these points elaborated and prolonged by points classified as *auxiliary*—some dissonant and nonharmonic, others consonant with immediate harmony, some stressed, some themselves embellished by auxiliaries of a less fundamental level. The perception and understanding of such melodic functions are of importance in how a melody is heard, and of course in interpretive performance.

In modal examples, underlying, essential structure is determined largely by systemic functions in significant ways analogous to those of later tonal systems. In modal melody the final and cofinal are primary degrees (often $\hat{1}$, $\hat{5}$) on which the melody is conceived and on which it most often comes to rest, in graduated stages of finality.

Underlying structure in tonal music is, of course, similarly conditioned by the hegemony of the tonic and its main support, the dominant. We have observed that tonal melody *is often the horizontalization of harmonies*, and that structural points often express the primary triads and other tonal harmonies.

We have noted other qualities by which low-level (and nontonal) essential structure is projected, by which in analysis certain points are regarded as essential, others as auxiliary, both classifications relevant to hierarchic level. These have to do with such factors as duration, prolongation by subsidiary embellishments, dynamic stress, metric prominence, cadential function—any characteristic imparting significance to particular points in the line and greater relative significance to certain melodic events. Still, *the factor of high-level primacy of tonal function surpasses all others*, where it is relevant to the style in question, so that, for example, a dissonant appoggiatura $\hat{2}$, however long or intense (however "accented"), is structurally subordinate to the $\hat{1}$ of its resolution. This is a consideration that becomes particularly important in later tonal styles, in which dissonances are sometimes of great agogic value.[41]

Many examples studied in this chapter reveal that even when tonal expression is unorthodox, in comparison with norms of established systems, tonal function can be a decisive factor in establishing and projecting essential structure.

Some features of melodic structure and form (motivic unity, sequence, inherent contrapuntal implications in compound line, balance of conjunct-disjunct movement, and others) are treated only peripherally in these studies, although they are discussed extensively in many existing books on form, counterpoint, thematic process, and comparable subjects. Factors which lend motivic unity to a line, or which motivically relate the various formal units of melody, are sometimes elusive (yet significant in effect) and discovered only when analysis penetrates beneath the surface. In Ex. 1-32, the es-

Ex. 1-32. Brahms, Trio in E♭, Op. 40, for piano, violin, and horn, third movement.

---

[41]An aspect of this problem is the necessary distinction between significance in the sense of linear and tonal functional primacy as opposed to metric accent, often counteractive

sential succession of tonally structural points is seen to involve important relations expressing significant deep unity between the two formal segments shown. (Certain repetitions are deleted in the analysis.) These two units are, in fact, identical in essential succession, while importantly varied in color (register, etc.) and embellishing configurations.

To go only slightly further in these supplementary comments concerning *underlying motivic and procedural unities* in melody—factors revealed only in the analysis of structural bases—we might well note the very general relevance of underlying step succession in melody of all times. Some theorists believe this a virtually universal condition having implications of "necessity" and value.[42] This characteristic can be observed in Ex. 1-33.

Ex. 1-33. Boulez, *Le Marteau sans Maître* ("The Hammer without a Master"), on texts of René Char; third movement, for alto voice and alto flute.

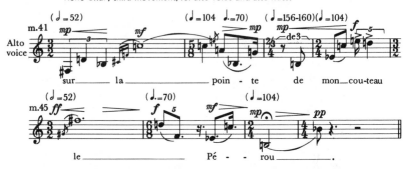

This example is the conclusion of the third movement of the Boulez work (flute part omitted). The ear is very likely, especially with familiarity, to hear the conjunct or nearly conjunct succession of high and subsidiary high

points:  —particularly those of

to the structural significance of tonal "absorption" of the kind characteristic of the authentic cadence. Of course, in styles in which tonality is diminished in importance, other factors of primacy of projection, including many which are external to specific PC content as well as registral superiorities of some pitches over others, become especially important in delineating essential linear structure. In these circumstances, linear and metric functions are more likely to coincide. (See Chapter 3 for further treatment of these issues.)

[42]Among these is Hindemith. See *The Craft of Musical Composition*, Vol. I, translated by A. Mendel (New York: Associated Music Publishers, Inc., and London: Schott and Co., Ltd., 1937), Chap. V, especially pp. 193–96.

the final cadence, and perhaps to interpret them as supportive of B♭ as something analogous to "tonic," or point of tonal objective and quasi-tonal resolution.[43]

Some particular issues of harmonic analysis in later styles

While basic procedures and aims of harmonic analysis are appropriate to many twentieth-century idioms, it is obvious that the harmonic analysis of some works of the recent period dictate or suggest special premises, objectives, and approaches. We reject any assertion or implication that harmony, properly and comprehensively defined, is fortuitous or irrelevant except in certain extreme instances of randomness.

We have already seen, for example, that tonal functions, quite apart from other manifestations of harmonic progression, are of vital importance and relevance in many twentieth-century styles. Where tonal function is less relevant, or irrelevant, as a significant organizing principle, the fluctuation in degrees of harmonic dissonance as a means toward motion and punctuation, and progressive or recessive action, may be an important object of analysis. (See the discussion of a cadential extract from Schoenberg's Op. 23, p. 107ff.)

In other idioms the textures of chords, the quantitative factor of texture often referred to as *density*, may be an important object of harmonic analysis, with harmonic intensity and release achieved significantly by fluctuations in harmonic density. (Factors of textural fluctuation are treated in Chapter 2.)

In some instances harmonic succession has a basis of logic in voice-leading itself (i.e., of individual strata); voice-leading (the persuasions of linear function) can be very important as a governing factor apart from, or in some degree apart from, considerations of specific tonal function or dissonance or density fluctuation. Voice-leading is thus an important harmonic determinant in all styles, with such considerations as adjacencies or proximities linking harmonic events, textural resistance of opposing directions (a "progressive" tendency), and semitonal and quasi-leading motion, as the bases for harmonic content and major conditioners of harmonic substance and control. *Voice-leading can emerge as a truly critical factor in contexts of pronounced tonal ambiguity.*

Such a succession as in Ex. 1-34 must be considered to derive in significant degree from the pure logic of voice-leading. Although the example is contrived, it points up the doubt that semitonal voice-leading can achieve harmonic succession independent of quasi-tonal allusion; this is because of

[43]Quasi-tonal effect is enhanced by the penultimate B♮ (the same PC begins the final phrase, m. 43, voice part), constituting a chromatic, leading-tone factor in octave displacement, enforcing B♭, as well as by the prominence of the C-B♭ relation in the penultimate phrase (mm. 41–42).

Ex. 1-34.

the relation of semitonal succession to leading-tone function, as in the D♯-E succession or, to a lesser degree, the G♯-A relation.

Other factors extrinsic to specific PC content can be of great significance in the sense of harmonic progression and resolution. For example, a harmony whose content is not of appreciably changed dissonance or density can convey the sense of cadential release by virtue of its registral location (e.g., the culmination of descent), its dynamic level (e.g., the culmination of *diminuendo*), or rhythmic factors like duration, often the indefinite duration of the fermata.

The operation of factors extrinsic to specific tonal or linear function, and specific PC content, can be demonstrated with reference to Ex. 1-35.

Ex. 1-35.

If the dissonant harmony notated in half-notes is played with any of the bass notes played after, the entire sonority held as though with fermata, it will be perceived that the total complex assumes cadential feeling because of agogic value and textural isolation of the final note, and despite severe dissonance and considerable overall density. Moreover, the bass note, whichever it is, may assume the character of "root," even "tonic," because of its temporally and registrally isolated, final appearance and consequent cadential prominence.[44,e]

[44]Perhaps the "best" root-tonic should be said to be F♯, forming a lowest perfect 5th and a major 3rd with the top note of the chord. A comparable situation is the subject of reference (footnote e) with respect to the piano piece, *Accenti*, from Dallapiccola's *Quaderno Musicale di Annalibera*, in which dense, dissonant harmonies find "resolution" in single tones which often take on the effects of quasi-tonics by virtue of the emphasis inherent in their cadential isolation and in the "recession" into so radically reduced textures after heavy density.

Traditional or quasi-functional harmonies, embellished by linear harmonic functions, are often concealed by irregularity of position, notation, or resolution. The augmented 6th to the primary dominant of mm. 29–30, in Debussy's *l'Ombre des arbres*, is an example of this (Ex. 1-36a); its function as a passing auxiliary is readily apparent, but its tonal relation (like that of the V/V following it) to the dominant at the end of m. 30, while significant, is less evident.

Ex. 1-36a. Debussy, *l'Ombre des Arbres* ("The Reflection of Trees"), No. 3 of *Ariettes Oubliées* ("Forgotten Melodies"), on poems of Paul Verlaine. See Ex. 1-36b for relevant excerpt.

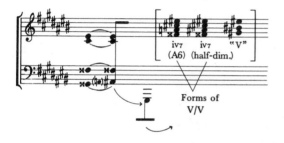

Copyright 1888, Jean Jobert. Used by permission of the publisher, Jean Jobert, and Elkan-Vogel, Inc., sole representative for the United States.

Voice-leading is essential to the understanding of the series of passing chords starting at m. 24. This succession, representative of some of the features and problems of harmonic analysis in impressionist styles, is worth extracting for special focus. Two half-diminished 7th-chords occur in the direct parallelism of succession which is one of the style's best known techniques, constituting the most severe denial of traditional contrapuntal interaction and an extreme negation of *immediate* tonal function in the passing, potentially functional, individual chords. The harmony following the two half-diminished 7th-chords retains three of four pitches to form a diminished 7th-chord (seeming thereby to move in the direction of clearer tonal focus and function, yet still obscure). This harmony, on A♯, takes on the feeling of altered submediant to a parenthetical secondary tonic C, in view of the dominant 7th on G which follows in m. 27. But the reference is slight indeed and the "dominant" on G (mm. 27–28) is of course a reminiscence of the recurrent harmony of m. 2 in a changed, passing context which prepares the primary dominant of m. 29 (Ex. 1-36c). In the abstraction (Ex. 1-36b), elements of pure parallelism and of common tone retention are encircled.

Example 1-36c is a sketch of these closing bars in two distinct representations; in both, the strong and simple functional basis is evident.

Ex. 1-36b.

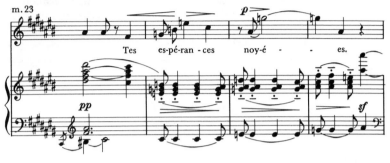

m. 23

Tes   es-pé-ran - ces   noy-é -   - es.

m. 27

Très retenu   *sempre dolcissimo e morendo*

(C: vi°   V₇ ?)

Ex. 1-36c.

C♯(T):   IV——————————————— V ———— V I

vii₇/V   ii

—— F♯(SD): vii₇/V | I₆/₄ (V)

*Originally (m. 2) auxiliary to I, now to V.

i. e.—

*The horizontalized diminished 7th-chord is identical to that recurring in the passing series.

The chief concern of this chapter is the presentation of analyses of diverse extracts in which interpretations of tonal and linear functions can be suggested. And it has been noted that aspects of harmonic process extrinsic to specific PC content—questions of harmonic rhythm, and textural-spatial fluctuation—are reserved for treatment in more appropriate contexts.

We might well, however, digress from central purposes briefly to consider the issue of dissonance fluctuation. The question of dissonance is of course difficult and problematic, and little understood in connection with expressive process in music. Nevertheless, few would deny that it is a very vital factor in musical expression; we are inhibited in the theoretical exploration of dissonance fluctuation as a controlled, purposeful process because of the difficulty of objective understanding of dissonance "values"—degrees of severity in dissonance as experienced. We are certain that any scale of dissonance value must relate to the stylistic context in question, but studies have been inadequate and inconclusive in dealing with the problem of relative dissonance values. Nor is it clear how far techniques of scientific inquiry can ultimately lead in the direction of objective understanding of dissonance effect in the musical experience. Still, something can be learned in the exploration of the issue of controlled dissonance fluctuation on the basis even of selected (not, perhaps, implausible) premises; let us consider, for example, *questions and possible techniques of inquiry* with respect to dissonance fluctuation in a brief extract from Schoenberg, the final six bars of the second of Five Pieces for piano, Op. 23 (Ex. 1-37a).

Our concern here is with evaluation of the final cadence, particularly in the matter of dissonance fluctuation.[45] Before turning to consideration of the harmony, it would be good to enumerate a number of other elements serving the effect of cadential release: decline in pitch, clearly recessive in general tendency toward the very low descent of the final, bass motive; deceleration in the qualities of rhythmic motion (see Chapter 3, p. 309) which, while not within the range of immediate concern, is probably the most persuasive single factor in the achievement of cadence; reduction in textural density

[45]The consideration of dissonance here is dependent in part upon an interpretation of norms associated with the tonal period out of which Schoenberg's style evolves.

Ex. 1-37a. Schoenberg, Five Pieces for piano, Op. 23; No. 2 (*Sehr rasch*).

Reprinted by permission of G. Schirmer, Inc., agent for Wilhelm Hansen Edition.

toward the final counterpoint of two voices; the recessive *diminuendo*. *Each of the foregoing is of enormous importance in complementary relation to the harmonic element.*

A factor in dissonance and its fluctuation is the predominance of diminished triads, in some degree of dissonant effect, in the first two measures quoted, extending into m. 20, and their gradual abandonment. In this process of release, the major triad emerging at the beginning of m. 20 (right hand), and such increasingly consonant melodic motives as the three-note units appearing in the bass of mm. 20–21 following the initial diminished triad outline, are of importance.

Example 1-37b is an abstraction of the intervallic relations occurring in the last four bars. Enharmonic equivalents are treated as interchangeable.

Ex. 1-37b.

*Intervals of disparate sizes of the same class (IC)—e.g., M2 and m7—are distinguished on the assumption of different dissonance intensities. However, and arbitrarily, compound intervals are distinguished from those within the octave only to the extent of the 9th, although more refined distinctions would undoubtedly be pertinent on the same basis of assumed milder intensity for larger intervals.

In any evaluation of dissonance fluctuation it must be borne in mind that intervallic content is not alone decisive. Such factors as the extent of simultaneity of pitch events, the registral levels at which they occur, the distances between coincident pitches, the relative timbres, the dynamic levels, the manner of articulation, the rhythmic values of the notes—all of these, and the list could be extended, *have to do with the relative severity of dissonance effect.* The evaluation of dissonance fluctuation is thus a vastly complex question, of which the comparison of intervallic differences is only an important part.

Even the single question of relative dissonance severity (intensity) is itself highly complex, and agreement is difficult concerning any proposed scale for intervals and chords.[46] There *is* agreement, however, with respect

[46]Efforts to understand the experience of relative dissonance intensities go back to Plato and Euclid, extending to Helmholtz in the nineteenth century, Hindemith in our own, and many other musicians, philosophers, and physicists; in the twentieth century dissonance is a fundamental concern of the psychology of music (in which one concept of dissonance intensity would trace it to relative degrees of "fusion" of tones in the phenomenological

to the existence of significant functional differences in dissonance severity (and consequent fluctuations in most musical contexts) and as to the importance in most music of the consideration of dissonance qualities and functions. The profile emerging from controlled dissonance fluctuation is especially vital in twentieth-century music in which tonal functions are diminished, although the conclusion may at times seem inescapable that dissonance fluctuation is arbitrary, with form deriving, presumably, from purposeful fluctuations in other element-changes.

The following attempt to evaluate dissonance relations takes into account none of the extrinsic elements enumerated above, and it is intended to suggest only a further dimension in the analysis of Schoenberg's cadence, and a methodology for its consideration within one parameter of harmony. At the left is a scale of hypothetical values, with those intervals of assumed greater intensity listed at the top of the scale (Ex. 1-37c). (The tritone, listed as an interval of considerable intensity because of what are regarded as inescapable traditional implications of ambiguity, is sometimes considered of "neutral" dissonance quality.)

The graphic representation of the "dissonance curve" shows a line of detailed changes which is a jagged one with frequent fluctuations often among extremes. Superimposed over this line are two "essential" curves showing relatively low dissonance intensity at the start, relatively severe dissonance in the middle of the succession, relative release at the end—a profile which, in complementation to other factors noted earlier, must be regarded as of harmonic significance in the process of conclusion of the piece.

Whatever the value of conclusions derived in a study of this kind, there is useful exercise in the exploration of premises, questions, and procedures for

experience of intervals and chords). An important, if not widely accepted, effort to establish a physical basis for generally applicable theoretical approaches to the analysis (and compositional usage) of dissonance fluctuation, as well as a scale of dissonance values and broadly encompassing theory of interval and chord roots, can be reviewed in Hindemith's *Craft of Musical Composition*, Vol. I. The question of dissonance values is also treated by Ernst Křenek in *Studies in Counterpoint* (New York: G. Schirmer, Inc., 1940). Křenek suggests no physical basis for his conclusions, listing the unison, m3, M3, P5, m6, M6, and 8 as consonances; the M2, m7 as "dissonances of lower tension;" and the m2 and M7 as "dissonances of higher tension." He states that the "degree of tension may be explained by vibration-ratios, combination-tones, or other acoustical phenomena; yet, the decision of what shall be considered a dissonance and how it should be handled is an *arbitrary assumption* (emphasis added) inherent in a particular musical style, for it depends exclusively on aesthetic concepts." He suggests that the P4 is consonant or dissonant depending on its context (a traditional view), consonant when the preceding intervals are of higher tension, dissonant when the preceding intervals are of lower tension. He regards the tritone as "a neutral interval, dividing the octave in two equal parts." Křenek goes on to discuss the "tension-degrees of chords" on the basis of their interval components (e.g., chords of three consonances, of two consonances and one mild dissonance, etc.). Hindemith's concepts of dissonance and dissonance fluctuation are far more elaborately stated, taking into account physical factors and complex theories of the effects of spacings and vertical alignments in chords, and more absolute in conclusions.

inquiry into dissonance fluctuation. Such a procedure could presumably be extended and refined to account for relative dissonance durations, dynamic intensities, registral intensities, and other factors proposed as significant in affecting dissonance properties.[f]

Ex. 1-37c. Graphic representation of dissonance fluctuation in the cadential recession concluding Schoenberg's Op. 23, No. 2.

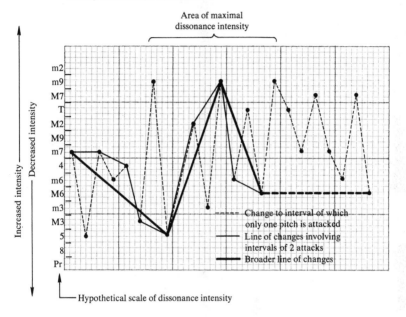

It would be well at this point to make an effort to summarize some of the important principles of and approaches to consideration of harmonic succession (progression and recession, where relevant) in twentieth-century music in which harmonic functions of one kind or another are *controlled structural factors*.

(1) There are, of course, instances of harmonic succession and content of traditional orientation and of relatively clear tonal significance: quasi-tonics, quasi-dominants, and other quasi-functional events, but strictly orthodox tonal-harmonic and modal functions as well.[g, h]

(2) Fluctuations in textural density are often controlled in such a way as to create profiles of mounting intensity and release, of ebb and flow, in the relative densities of harmonies (Chapter 2).

(3) Even where there are not appreciable or perceptible tonal-harmonic functions, orthodox or unorthodox, there may be controlled profiles of dissonance fluctuation, of relative intensity of dissonance and relative consonance, creating a sense of harmonic progression and recession within this parameter.

(4) Harmonic successions may have significant logical basis in principles of voice-leading (even "pure" linear function in adjacencies and other factors of approach and departure), in supplement to or independent of other harmonic principles.

(5) The harmonic qualities may be vitally conditioned by factors (rhythm, dynamic intensity, and others mentioned) extrinsic to specific PC content of harmony. The control of harmonic rhythm is often in itself a critical shaping factor.

(6) Particular harmonic factors, by virtue of structurally essential status underscored in agogic, iterative, dynamic, cadential, or other modes of emphatic projection, may be heard as basic, embellished by surrounding auxiliary (neighbor, passing, elaborative) harmonies, apart from tonal significance.

(7) Harmonic techniques of any of these, or of other kinds, may conceivably prove irrelevant, or of no significant relevance, in the particular instance in question. [In many musical situations, structure must be seen as shaped decisively by certain element-actions which predominate while others are not of shaping relevance to structure; in serial music, for example, PC content of harmonic and melodic events *may* be determined largely by factors external to immediate contextual function and process within recessive and progressive tendencies, while other elements (rhythm, registral distributions, densities, etc.) are contextually determined and of decisive importance.]

Procedures of analysis; symbolic representations of melodic and harmonic functions and affiliations

In the application of the following symbols and methods to analysis of tonal music, *tonal order (including modal and other systems of quasi-tonal order) significantly governs the structural hierarchy*. Pronounced agogic superiority of an event in a nontonal style might well be decisive in establishing its hierarchic first-order status, while in a tonal order emphasis of that kind is submissive to the predominance of tonal considerations at higher levels. The procedures outlined in these pages are applicable to lines of both melodic and harmonic events.

The systems of symbolic representation of linear functions and affiliations are useful *where reductive graphic sketches are relevant to particular analytical purposes and objects of inquiry.* Many of the symbols and procedures given here are related to those of existing studies (especially of Schenkerian tradition); others are not.[47]

Since the relation of symbology given here to those systems allied to Schenkerian tradition and thought will be evident, it should be noted that there are important conceptual differences between analytical approaches pursued in this chapter and those of orthodox Schenkerian procedure. A chief difference is visible in the mere *diversity* of sketching procedures employed in these pages, and the underlying premise that works and styles of music suggest (and require) varying modes of inquiry and procedure even within the consideration of hierarchy of pitch materials. Thus, for example, in many instances harmony is abstracted and represented as an element apart from its specific applications in voice-leading and textural distribution —a procedure that is legitimate and useful *when tonal apart from linear function is the primary object of inquiry.*

Other procedures, or procedural modifications, are adopted in line with other modes and purposes of inquiry. Moreover, a number of conceptual interpretive departures from traditional Schenkerian method (including the interpretation of hierarchic structure in contexts other than those of conventional tonality) will be apparent to the reader who is aware of that tradition, by which at the same time the present study is significantly affected. Naturally, an important aim in this context is the presentation of concepts and procedures which are deemed vital and which do not significantly duplicate those of widely available existing sources.

One hesitates to add yet another system of symbology to the many which exist (some of them cited in the note printed below); yet, the "system" presented here is innovative where particular approaches are thought useful as representing conceptual points of departure basic to this study. No dogma is intended, no universally applicable assertion of a *number of levels* common to music, nor is there insistence or even necessary consistency in the modes of treatment of various subjects, methodology subject rather to particular contextual problems of different kinds and different demands. Our purpose is to explore a range of questions and possibilities of useful analytical approach. At the same time, many of these analytical representations do employ the

---

[47]Despite differences of conceptual substance and emphasis, one is reluctant to offer a redundant and necessarily superficial review of techniques of analysis of voice-leading and directed motion associated with the now firmly established theoretical literature deriving from Schenker and allied analytical systems; that expanding literature speaks powerfully, if often within unfortunately narrow biases, for itself. Schenker's most important treatise, *Der freie Satz*, is available in a translation by Ernst Oster, published under the title *Free Composition* (New York: Longman, 1979). And a comprehensive and systematic presentation of Schenker's theories and methodology of analytical representation is *Introduction to Schenkerian Analysis* by Allen Forte and Steven E. Gilbert (New York: W.W. Norton and Co., 1982).

technique of sketching harmonic and melodic essentials; where that is true, the following symbols are often used and will be useful in carrying out further analyses of like purpose and comparable basis.

(1) Representations of pitch factors in general, where hierarchy of structural function is germane to the analysis, are notated in the following, descending order of significance (*within the perspective of the example itself*):

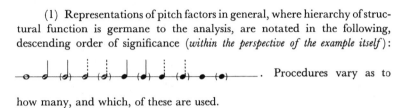 . Procedures vary as to

how many, and which, of these are used.

(2) Beams by which pitch events are linked represent hierarchic status and prolonging affiliations by various means: at times, an outermost beam is representative of higher-level structure while inner beams represent progressively lower structural levels:

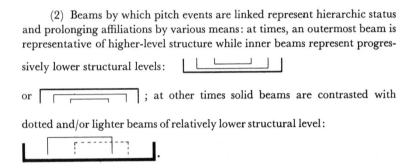

or ⌐ ⌐ ⌐ ⌐ ⌐ ¬ ¬ ; at other times solid beams are contrasted with

dotted and/or lighter beams of relatively lower structural level:

(3) An event's notation may be enclosed in a rectangular form for any stated reason on the basis of which attention is drawn to it: .

(4) Emphasis extrinsic to specific PC content (dynamic stress, duration, etc.) may be indicated by an accent symbol over the notation of the event: .

(5) Passing configurations are often shown in summary by a diagonal line, with actual pitches omitted: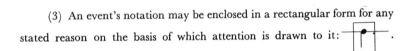

(6) Formal punctuations of relative significance are indicated by one, two, or more vertical dashes through the top line of the staff: .

(7) Attention is drawn to particular events, often high and low points in melodic line, by arrows over or under the event in question: the representation of such points by dotted or parenthetical arrows denotes hierarchic leveling of significance comparable to the devices given in item 1 above:

(8) Brackets over or under a sketched example are often used to draw attention to comparable (often sequential or iterative) groupings of events, or for other purposes indicated with the particular example:

(9) A wavy line may indicate excision of material which is redundant or extraneous to the particular purpose of the illustration in question:

 or , etc.

(10) As with passing configurations (item 5, above), particular very local elaborative contours may be represented without inclusion of specific pitches:  .

(11) Arrows linking pitch events indicate dominant relations, the arrow pointing to the tonic of reference at an appropriate level of representa-

tion:  or .

(12) As in numerous examples already given, harmonic alignments of multiple tonal implication (functional significance at different levels of tonal reference) are shown by vertical rectangular enclosure, by vertical brackets, or by braces:

$$V \quad \begin{array}{|c|} \hline I \\ IV \\ \hline \end{array} \quad \text{or} \quad] \quad \text{or} \quad \} \quad .$$

(13) Upper- and lowercase distinctions (G, g; VI, vi; M, m; SD, sd; etc.) are generally observed to distinguish between major and minor elements in conventional tonal situations. But these distinctions are abandoned (a) where the reference is to an abstract concept apart from any specificity of application—e. g., V as a concept apart from any particular form or manifesta-

tion, and (b) where, in freer tonal styles, the major-minor distinction is of diminished or negligible significance—e.g., where there is free and constant interchange, or where the issue of mode, as in a quasi-functional "I" or "V", is subordinated to the free application of PC complexes resembling but departing from conventional models.

(14) Other adaptations of roman numeral symbols and tonal system symbols (letter designations of keys) are by now familiar: the use of quotation marks to qualify the symbol as an adaptation of the conventional model or as preliminary to the systematization of tonal conventions ("I", "IV", etc.); the use of a question mark where identification is speculative and uncertain (V?, or g?); superpositions of symbols in vertical alignment separated by a horizontal bar, where a harmonic element occurs with and over another $\left(\dfrac{V}{I}\right)$ as in pedal situations; and use of the plus sign or comma to join elements in which there is a mixture of conventional factors (I + V, or I,V), i.e., as a symbol for "and."

(15) Functional connections between pitch and PC events, connections of various kinds having, as necessary, explanation in particular representations, are shown by conventional slurs, ties, lines, beams, or other modes of grouping; where these are tenuous, or applicable over considerable durational spans, they may be dotted. Elaborative affiliations of neighbor and passing factors may also be shown by inclination in the direction of a notated

beam: .

(16) A horizontal brace (or other device given explanation in a particular context) may denote and embrace a succession of local harmonies essentially prolonging and embellishing one of broader significance:

⌒
V . This is also shown by horizontal arrows within the

notated beam: |⟵———— I ————⟶| .

(17) Octave displacement (or other registral displacement), the continuation of a linear tendency in a changed registral locus, is shown by inclusion of the octave duplication in parentheses in the originating registral placement: .

(18) Parentheses may occur around a pitch or harmony expected but omitted, and parentheses are used for other purposes (e.g., notation of enharmonic equivalents) presumably self-evident in given contexts.

An event's representation as to hierarchic level of linear function often *changes as the level of reference changes*—the broader the level of reference the fewer "essential" factors, locally "essential" events subsumed and seen as auxiliary in the more comprehensive view. We have described this aspect of linear function as *multileveled*.

With enumeration of the foregoing suggestions of symbology for representation of tonal and linear (essential or auxiliary) function of harmonic and melodic events, it should be repeated that in many of the graphic sketches given in this chapter actual voice-leading among harmonic events is not given, nor is every pitch of a given harmonic complex necessarily represented. Where emphasis of attention is on tonal identity and function—usually multileveled—it is often useful to abstract harmonic factors without consideration of linear alignment and distribution; no single illustrative representation can portray every functional significance, and there is value in isolating for analytical attention single aspects of such functional significance. At times, too, voice-leading is faithfully represented with respect to one voice, or two (often bass, or outer voices), while inner voices are represented in summary abstractions, or not at all. At the same time, we should make very explicit the desirable, ideal end of comprehensive analysis which takes all pertinent factors into account.

Certain of the proposed techniques are in evidence in examples already given. The analysis of a melodic conception of Corelli (Ex. 1-38) will further illustrate some of the methods outlined.

Typically, the melody outlines the primary notes of the tonality. The line is particularly striking for a number of reasons: its wide range for so few bars, the melodic dissonances (diminished 4th, diminished 7th), the sequential repetition suggested but not fulfilled,[48] and the failure of certain tendencies to resolve as expected—the g^2 of m. 4 and the e^1 of m. 6.

The prolonged $\hat{1}$ with which the melody begins might otherwise have

been indicated by connection to the underlying beam ♩   ♩ ,

or by other, comparable devices. Affiliated embellishing groups appear beamed and oriented to structural pitches to which they refer; they might also be represented by slurs or by other techniques of self-evident significance.

---

[48]Melodic analyses in this chapter are devoted primarily to considerations of pitch relations within the linear structure and tonality and do not usually treat questions of motivic connections and processes; that is again only because choices have to be made in assigning limited space. Nothing is of greater importance in the experience of melodic unities than motivic relations and permutations, but these issues are treated extensively in existing sources and to a marked degree in standard music pedagogy. [See, for example, Rudolph Reti, *The Thematic Process in Music* (New York: MacMillan and Co., 1951).]

Notes attached to the underlying beam are here selected to show essential pitches which have superior projection and *which comprise the i harmony* of which the melody is, as often within tonal conventions, a linear expression or "horizontalization." The sketch includes most of the actual pitches (except for symbolized passing groups). Further excision or symbolization (e.g.,

) would yield a broader view—a more "essential" image. Tendency tones having accentual emphasis are indicated as , but their resolutions and more primary pitch affiliations are represented as tonally-structurally superior, as are points of cadential arrival. Were the analysis extended to include subsequent phrases, further reduction would be of increased significance in showing essential melodic functions (in the illustrated bars, from f^{1-2} to c^{2-1}, expecting long-range resolution on the tonic degree).

Ex. 1-38. Corelli, Concerto Grosso in F minor, Op. 6, No. 3, third movement.

*The f^2 is represented as "expected" because of (1) the precedent in the initial five-note motive, (2) the unfulfilled leading-tone e^2 preceding (cf. the e^1 of the second phrase), and (3) the otherwise consistent conjunct descent from the high point, $a\flat^2$, to c^2.

Example 1-39, also from the eighteenth century, is a four-measure extract from the binary first part of a dance movement by Couperin, that portion in which the secondary tonic, b, emerges. The relative major of the secondary tonic (D major, R/d/t) appears as a brief parenthetical reference linking the two chief tonics. The essential progression, from e:i (also b:iv) to b:V (also e:V/V), is through a passing formulation of roots a 5th apart, in sequence. The aim of the progression, b:V, has prolongation and embellishment well beyond the point quoted before its resolution in b:i at the conclusion of the section. The strong tonal allusions are fortified by the fact that the underlying, structural progression goes to b:V from its subdominant, a further, important functional meaning of e:i. This broad view is included in the representation of roman numeral symbols of multileveled harmonic function.

Example 1-40 is an extract from the twentieth century, a piano piece of Křenek of which the final cadence, instructive in a number of ways, is shown. The factor of voice-leading adjacencies is clearly of decisive importance in the derivation of auxiliary harmonies, and the strong sense of E♭ as root and "tonic" at the end imparts to the penultimate bass D the sense of leading-tone in a quasi-dominant. There are at the same time functional dispositions of both dissonance and density in the direction of release.[i] The example serves, in a limited context, to illustrate further some of the techniques of analytical representation outlined.

Ex. 1-39. Couperin, *La Bondissante* (from *Ordre* 21) ; ornaments omitted.

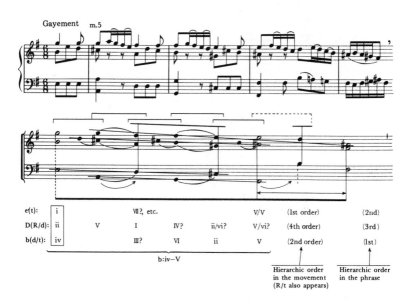

Ex. 1-40. Křenek, Eight Piano Pieces; No. 4, *Toccata.*

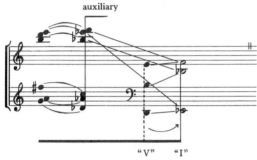

© *1956, Mercury Music, Inc. Used by permission.*

Gregorian chant, *Veni creator spiritus*

The chant, *Veni creator spiritus* (a hymn for the Second Vespers of Whit-sunday), one of the most beautiful of the literature, is quoted as a complete example for melodic analysis (Ex. 1-41a). It is given (in part) in the notation of the *Liber Usualis*[49] as well as in a free modern notation. Only the first stanza is given.

While it would represent an unmanageable digression from present purposes to discuss modal systems in general, it should be pointed out that the chant is in Mode 8 (hypomixolydian), with G as final and C as cofinal.[50]

[49]The reader will find the example in the *Liber Usualis,* traditional modern repository of liturgical Roman rites and their music (Tournai, Belgium: Desclée and Company, 1938), on p. 885; and he may wish to inquire into problems of notation, transcription, rendition, modes, and like matters, in the *Liber*'s "Rules for Interpretation," p. xviiff.

[50]Three sources on modal theory and tradition might be cited: Willi Apel, *Harvard Dictionary of Music,* 2nd ed. (Cambridge, Mass.: Harvard University Press, 1969), p. 165ff.; Apel, *Gregorian Chant* (Bloomington, Ind.: Indiana University Press, 1958), p. 133ff.; and F. S. Andrews, *Medieval Modal Theory* (Unpublished Ph. D. Dissertation, Cornell University,

Ex. 1-41a. Chant, *Veni creator spiritus* (authorship uncertain).

These pitches are, of course, of central importance in the melodic structure and we regard them as analogous in importance to primary degrees in later tonal systems.

[The first phrase makes it abundantly apparent that premises of tonal conventions of major-minor usage must be put aside in understanding and perceiving the relation between modal final and cofinal. Heard in the terms of later practices of Classical tonality, the progression from G to C, describing the interval of a 4th, suggests dominant to tonic. Similarly, the cadence of the second phrase, in the sense of later tonal usage, has the effect of a domi-

1935). A discussion of the history and traditions of *Veni creator spiritus,* and a translation of its text, will be found in Carl Parrish, *A Treasury of Early Music* (New York: W. W. Norton, 1958), pp. 16–18.

nant cadence in C, with the final cadence, if we submit to the conditioning of later conventions, seeming inconclusive. The confusion that can arise in the conflict between modality (in the Medieval-Renaissance sense) and tonality (in the eighteenth- and nineteenth-century sense) has largely to do with the conditioning of modern ears to regard the leading-tone to tonic succession ($\hat{7}$-$\hat{1}$) as a necessarily semitonal relation, so that in the example of chant given here the succession F-G requires deliberate acceptance as having conclusive function to the modal final ("tonic"). Thus, a deliberate effort must be made (how "deliberate" depends on the listener's experience and understanding) to hear the chant in modal terms and in accord with modal functions. Although the foregoing is somewhat digressive, it seems important to urge upon the reader a conscious dismissal of the norms of Classical tonality in approaching the problems of analysis of the example.]

Certain general conventions illustrated in the chant should be noted briefly: the overall curve of the melody consists of a rise to the high point e¹, *at almost the exact middle*, and a return to the starting note, the modal final, thus describing an arched profile of wonderful grace. The first phrase consists of an essentially ascending progression, from g to c¹ (with d¹ as auxiliary neighbor); the second describes a further essential ascent to d¹; the third moves down and up again—an inverted arc within the established pitch range; and the final phrase, with its more affirmative function, is essentially a recessive descent from c¹ (or b?) to g (the latter having an auxiliary lower neighbor, f), *the opposite of the first phrase.*

Part of the perfect unity of the melody is inherent in the musical "rhyme" of phrases 1, 2, and 4, which employ the same cadential motive, mirrored in the final phrase. The cadential degrees are dominant (cofinal) for phrases 1 and 3, and final, as expected, for phrase 4, while the second phrase concludes on d¹, the cofinal of the authentic form of the mixolydian, functioning here as, at the broadest structural level, an auxiliary to c¹.

Example 1-41b is an interpretation of melodic functions. Some passing notes are omitted, and hierarchic levels are represented by "leveled" beams running below the sketch. It shows the essential progression of the first

Ex. 1-41b. Sketch of linear functions in *Veni creator spiritus.*

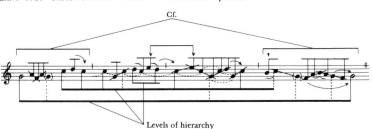

phrase from final to cofinal, g to c^1. Each of these points is seen as embellished by auxiliaries: the g is embellished by upper and lower neighbors, the c^1 by its upper neighbor. The final is established with considerably greater prominence in the first phrase, having four appearances; on the other hand, the cofinal emerges strongly in its cadential placement.

The analysis of phrase 2 exposes a primary essential progression from c^1 (there is a subsidiary, elaborating deviation to g and back during the prolongation of c^1) to d^1, the latter embellished by its upper and lower neighbors (the final, C, thus having an auxiliary function in the second part of the phrase) and identified as a significant structural point because of its cadential role, yet more broadly of auxiliary function in its strong leaning toward the more basic c^1 which surrounds it.[51] Indeed, the d^1 resolves to c^1 in direct succession into phrase 3.

While C, the cofinal, is clearly the primary structural basis for the third phrase, there are several embellishing deviations—passing formulations up to auxiliaries e^1 (an early repetition of the high point) and d^1, and twice down to g.[52] The vacillation of the line throughout between g and c^1 is of course conventional in the application of the mode, with the expected structural primacy accorded the final and cofinal.

The fourth is the only phrase not beginning with final or cofinal; it has a particularly striking effect, starting as it does with the leaning, lower neighbor of c^1. The analysis shows this auxiliary to have emphasis. It is of course not actually stressed, but its position as the first note of the phrase does mark it for attention. Phrase 4 is shown to have an essential structure mirroring that of the first phrase. Again, each of the two essential points has embellishment. The note b appears for the first time as auxiliary to a degree other than the cofinal—in this case auxiliary to a, which in turn is auxiliary to the final, manifesting again the "dimensional" implications of linear

---

[51]I.e., d^1 is clearly of greater hierarchic value *at the level of phrase 2* in view of its cadential role than at the broader (higher) level of phrases 2 and 3 conjoined; in the larger context it is seen and felt as clearly dependent on c^1. There is, here, as in numerous other references self-evidently comparable, an instance of the multileveled significance of linear functions (d^1 of phrase 2 is of different significances at different levels). The first d^1 of phrase 2 can be seen in ambivalent *multilateral* function at the same time: it is upper neighbor auxiliary to the essential c^1, as well as anticipation of the cadential d^1 (part of the prolongation of

that pitch). It might be symbolized thus: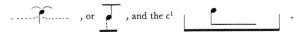

[52]One can see again at this point the interdependence of structural *level* and linear *function*: in the local context of phrase 3, the final G is clearly subsidiary to the cofinal C; at the more basic level of the total melody the reverse hierarchic relation is evident; the linear functions of both pitches in phrase 3 are thus multileveled. The g might be symbolized

function. (The contrasting tendencies of b in these two environments— ⌐ and ⌐—is a striking factor here.) The final cadence repeats, at a much removed point in time, the melody's low point, f.

It scarcely needs to be said that it is of the utmost importance in the execution of a melody of this, or any, kind to be aware of these essential directions and linear functions, of the degrees of repose or lack of it in the cadences (tentative, more tentative, tentative, conclusive), of the nearly contiguous reiteration of the high point, suggesting a slight difference of inflection. (This will be affected in some degree by the text setting; the first e¹ has its own syllable, while the second, except in the sixth stanza, continues the syllable of the preceding note; on the other hand, the more dependent auxiliary role of the first e¹, and the exposure of the second in its échappée-like departure by leap, suggest further criteria of interpretive decision making.)

Having observed in careful analysis both the overall and individual curves of the melodic units, and hierarchy of functions at a level in which all notes are represented, we may characterize the melodic structure at more fundamental levels.

Example 1-41c summarizes, in a more fundamental analytical interpretation, the two primary structural points, the modal final the more basic of the two, with d¹, the cadential note of phrase 2, shown in this more basic sense as an auxiliary of c¹, the elaborating and supportive cofinal.

Ex. 1-41c.

Carrying the implications implicit in this procedure to their proper conclusion, Ex. 1-41d shows the most fundamental essence of the melody as an extensive prolongation of the modal final, G, with the two other most important pitches, in a hierarchic ordering, shown as auxiliaries: C as auxiliary to G, D as auxiliary to C.

Ex. 1-41d.

Two Preludes from Fischer, *Ariadne Musica*

Two of the preludes of the *Ariadne Musica* of Fischer (1715, a forerun-
ner of Bach's *Well-Tempered Clavier*) are treated next in reductive analyses of
two different kinds and purposes. The Prelude in E (phrygian) is seen as, at its
broadest level, a prolongation of the "tonic" in elaboration with A, an important cadence point in conventional applications of the phrygian mode. The
sketch (Ex. 1-42) is conceived to represent, primarily, the interior manifesta-

Ex. 1-42. Fischer, Prelude in E (phrygian) from *Ariadne Musica* for organ.

Interior manifestations of "iv" ("sd/t") in broad "plagal" elaboration

Twice-tonicized G ("R,M/t") —
lower neighbor of second-order a

Reprinted from Liber Organi: Deutsche Meister des 16. und 17. Jahrhunderts, *E.
Kaller, editor, published by Schott's Söhne, Mainz. Used by permission of Belwin-Mills Publishing
Corporation.*

tions of the repeatedly tonicized "iv" as the chief neighbor auxiliary of the
prolonged "i", in a *broad plagal action of embellishment*. Third-order manifestations of G (in later tonal evolution the R/t) are also represented; G can be
seen in multileveled function both as lower neighbor auxiliary of A and, more
broadly, as a passing linear factor linking the elaborative A with E. The

broadly elaborative A is represented by the upper beam and upward stems, as indicated. The example includes a complete sketch, but omits the concluding three bars ("i" prolongation) of the piece itself.[53]

The Prelude in D minor from the same work is sketched (Ex. 1-43) to represent, over a broad harmonic fundament, entries of the persistent motive 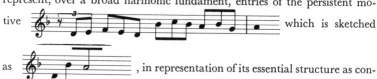 which is sketched as  , in representation of its essential structure as consisting of an anacrustic "wind-up" from the 5th below (the anacrusis note embellished) and extending to the upper neighbor auxiliary (also embellished), both of these elaborative of the arrival note, which has agogic, cadential, tonal, and metric prominence. Seen in this reduced sketch, an interesting V-expressing relation of essential factors in the top voice and those of the tenor emerges: the former rests on the PC succession A-E-A-E-C♯, the latter on the succession A-E-C♯-E-A. The bass, absolutely without elaboration, underscores in a series of pedal points the fundamental I-V-I structure. Typical elaboration of the concluding I (with the auxiliary iv, of which it is dominant) is again in evidence. In Ex. 1-43 the quotation of the piece itself is necessarily abbreviated; however, the sketch is complete.

Ex. 1-43.   Fischer, Prelude in D minor from *Ariadne Musica.*

Reprinted from Liber Organi: Deutsche Meister des 16. und 17. Jahrhunderts, *E. Kaller, editor, published by Schott's Söhne, Mainz. Reprinted by permission of Belwin-Mills Publishing Corporation.*

[53]Both preludes, with others, are included in Wallace Berry and Edward Chudacoff, *Eighteenth-Century Imitative Counterpoint: Music for Analysis* (Englewood Cliffs, N. J.: Prentice-Hall, Inc., 1969).

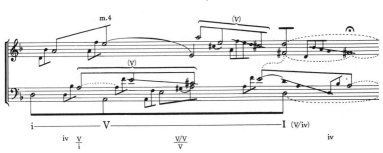

Bach, "Drauf schliess ich mich in deine Hände" from Motet, *Komm, Jesu, komm*

In the quotation of a choral movement from Bach's Motet, *Komm, Jesu, komm* (Ex. 1-44a), parts for two choruses are compressed into notation on two staves, with the text[54] given above the staves except where necessary to show a different setting for the bass voice.

Ex. 1-44a. Bach, Choral aria "Drauf schliess ich mich in deine Hände" from Motet, *Komm, Jesu, komm.*

[54]For a translation of the text, see p. 428.

Ex. 1-44a continued.

In as conventional and ordered a tonal style as this the essential harmonies are those of primary tonal importance—the tonic and dominant (cadential harmonies are one or the other, although of course frequently at other than the primary tonal level). These are the harmonies of most frequent prolongation, reiteration, rhythmic-metric prominence, and key positions in the articulation of form. Auxiliary harmonies are, logically enough, very often those one step back in the tonal order: dominant auxiliary to tonic, subdominant and supertonic to dominant, submediant to subdominant, etc., and the intensity of relation is frequently underscored by chromatic alteration (Ex. 1-44b).

Ex. 1-44b.

The following series of analyses takes each phrase in turn, sketching some linear and tonal functions and relations. Roman numeral analyses are included to show many (not all) of the tonal functions in primary and secondary tonal systems. Finally, under each of the sketches the analysis is carried to a more fundamental level.

The sketch of the first phrase (Ex. 1-44c) reveals a linear expression of i, one in which the background of the soprano pitches outlines that harmony (as does the bass) and in which i occurs at critical points including the beginning and end. As i has an "outer prolongation," there is "inner prolongation"

Ex. 1-44c.

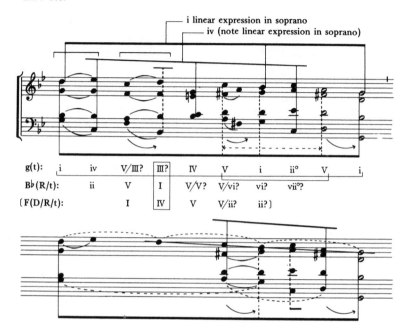

of iv, also underscored by upper voice factors, as represented. Most individual harmonies are symbolized in accord with the concept of multileveled tonal significance. Primary i and V are linked, in hierarchic order, to an underlying beam, and harmonic recurrences are shown in association by established means. Where necessary, actual explanatory or identifying notes are inserted. The value in this procedure is in the analytical reasoning by which it is derived as well as in the image of structure which it immediately affords. In the further reduction given below the first sketch, the essential harmonic factor is seen as i, supported by its chief auxiliary, V.

In the second phrase analysis (Ex. 1-44d), it is shown that, especially in reference to a secondary tonic, the primary tonic has auxiliary function in a context of its tonal and rhythmic subordination.[55] It is incidental *at the level*

[55]At the same time that it points toward the cadential B♭:I, the g:i contributes to prolongation of the preceding cadential harmony (a *multilateral* implication) and asserts a more tenuous link with the underlying tonal basis even while it participates in the linear encirclement of B♭:V (a *multileveled* implication). (Functions of the harmony which begins phrase 3 are comparable.) This analysis of the Bach movement is not sufficiently detailed and exhaustive to account for all such *multidimensional* implications.

Ex. 1-44d.

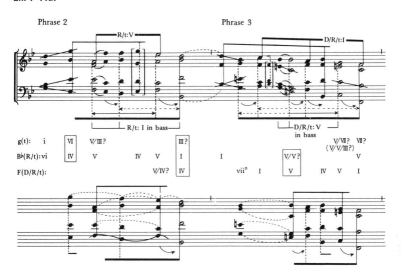

of the second phrase, functioning as part of the embellishmental group in the secondary tonal expression of B♭. In the analysis of phrase 3 (Ex. 1-44d) a number of harmonies (and a few in the second phrase) are given questioned interpretation in the primary tonal system. Because both III and VII, as secondary tonics, involve the cancelled primary leading-tone, it is considered that their effect as functions *in the primary system* is substantially attenuated. In phrase 3, the harmony containing E♮ is reasonably interpreted as vii°/V in B♭; the question refers to the fact that the tonic of reference is in dissolution, submitting to F.

Phrase 4 (Ex. 1-44e) is directed toward the tonicized primary dominant.[56] Its first appearance as a minor triad is the natural result of the preceding secondary tonics, both of which involve F♮, but the phrase concludes with the triad in major form; with this, its reference to the primary tonic is of course sharpened in affirmative effect.

In phrase 5 (Ex. 1-44e), directed toward the primary subdominant, there is a single deceptive succession in which c:V moves to vi°, indicated in the functional analysis as a provisional, extremely local tonic substitute. Questioned functional interpretations have the same bases as those in preceding phrases. They are included because the tonics of reference, while in

---

[56]Certainly this event abridges the distance from the primary tonal system, despite the apparent proximity of B♭ to g (R to t).

Ex. 1-44e.

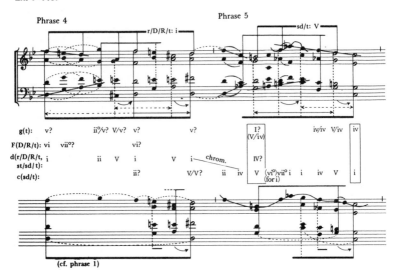

(cf. phrase 1)

dissolution or uncertain in effect, are nonetheless demonstrably relevant in the large or immediate context of the harmony concerned.[57]

The sixth phrase (Ex. 1-44f) takes up the secondary tonic, c, as primary subdominant for a very persuasive statement built on the prolonged and embellished primary iv, V, and i. The structural importance of $\left.\begin{array}{c} c:i \\ g:iv \end{array}\right]$ at the outset of the phrase is a product both of its prolongation and reiteration and its tonicization in the phrase just preceding. Here, as throughout, chromatic successions (of which there are few) are indicated. In all six phrases, many additional linear and tonal functions and relations could be noted.

A condensation of the essential harmonic stream of the entire movement is illuminating in a number of ways. It is a picture of tonal order of relations and functional events extremely characteristic of the tonal period: essential harmonic movements between harmonies whose roots are a 5th apart, often in dominant-tonic relation; secondary tonics of conventional "distances" from the primary system—the mediant (relative major, R/t), the dominant (D, d/t), the dominant of the relative (D/R/t), and the subdominant (sd/t). Attention is drawn in the summary (Ex. 1-44g) to successions of

---

[57]The "retrogressive" movement of phrase 5 to the sd/t, after the D/t of the preceding cadence, is a momentary denial of expected continued movement toward t:i—an increase in tonal and harmonic distance from t:i, a progression temporarily delaying the expected recession from D/t (of phrase 4) to t (of phrase 6).

Ex. 1-44f.

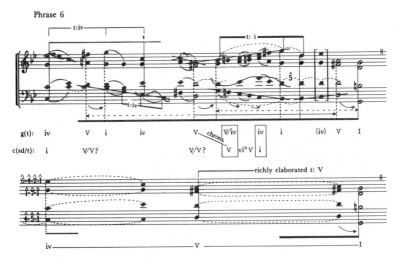

Phrase 6

| g(t): | iv | V | i | iv | V | V/iv | iv | i | (iv) | V | I |
| c(sd/t): | i | V/V? | | | V/V? | V | vi°V | i | | | |

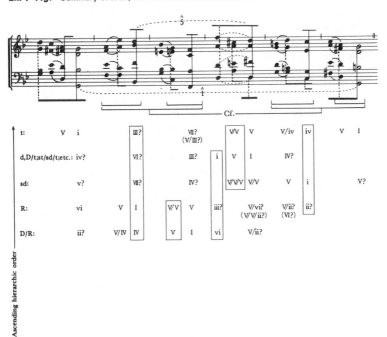

Ex. 1-44g. Summary of total, essential harmonic stream in the Bach movement.

t:		V	i		III?		VII?(V/III?)		V/V	V	V/iv	iv		V	I
d,D/t;st/sd/t;etc.:	iv?				VI?		III?	i	V	I	IV?				
sd:	v?				VII?		IV?		V/V/V	V/V	V	i			V?
R:	vi		V	I		V/V	V	iii?	V/vi?(V/V/ii?)	V/ii?(VI?)	ii?				
D/R:	ii?		V/IV	IV		V	I	vi	V/ii?						

Ascending hierarchic order

analogous content between phrases 1 and 4, and between the pairs 2–3 and 5–6.

Beethoven, Symphony No. 2 in D, Op. 36, fourth movement
Representations of the tonal system and tonal rhythm

Figures 1-6a and 1-6b and Ex. 1-45 show varied representations of tonal structure in the fourth movement of Beethoven's second symphony, the music of which is not reprinted but might well be consulted. Figure 1-6a is an abstract view of the entire tonal system, a view generally of a kind suggested earlier. In this case the system components are not hierarchically ordered, and they are not in chronology of appearance (other versions of the chart could show these or other arrangements); rather, the systems are arranged in an order of increasing sharps in one direction and increasing flats in the other. However, there is limited implication of hierarchic significance in the enclosure in horizontal rectangles of the most important primary systems (they are D, f♯, A—the factors of the tonic triad). Important intersecting relations linking the systems in contextual operations are shown by vertically aligned rectangular enclosures. Roman numeral symbols not so enclosed simply list harmonies which occur significantly as part of the tonal resource but do not participate in intersecting relations. The indication of modal variants in the listing of tonal system components suggests, as does the inclusion of roman numeral symbols of both upper- and lowercase at certain intersections, the importance of modal variation in facilitating the intersections by which tonal fluctuation is often achieved.

Some minor mode tonics emerge as variants within major contexts, while others appear independently (e.g., f♯, g, and c). Although the chart does not give symbols identifying specific practical relations of secondary systems to the primary system, such relations can be inferred on the basis of actual contextual functions and derivations as in Fig. 1-6b.

Example 1-45, a further representation of the Beethoven movement, is the result of a difficult and tedious exercise which is at the same time extremely revealing as a digest of *actual tonal rhythm*. (Again, it must be remembered that the digest is not to be read as a pitch-line in any sense at all; the notes are staff representations of PC tonics in the order in which *and in the durations for which* they emerge and, even momentarily, prevail before a superseding fluctuation.)

Structural and auxiliary distinctions, i.e., relative importances of systems, are evident in some degree in relative durations, but a continuous beam is used to link all occurrences of T, and subsidiary beams to link the important tonal systems D/T and r/D (= m/T). Items in parentheses are of most fleeting

Fig. 1-6a. Beethoven, Symphony No. 2 in D, fourth movement. A representation of the tonal system.

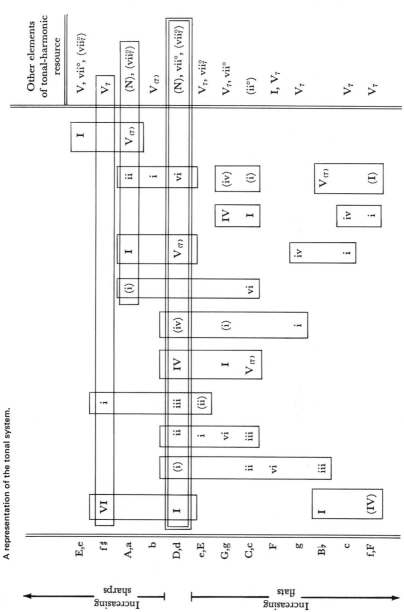

Fig. 1-6b. Beethoven, Symphony No. 2 in D, fourth movement.
Secondary system components and their contextually implied relations to the
primary tonic D,d.

Second-, third-order systems {	A	D/T
	f♯	m, or r/D/T/

Decreasing sharps,	E	D/D
increasing flats	b	sm(r), or st/D
	e	st, or sm/SD
	G	SD
	C	SD/SD
	a	r/SD/SD
	F	R/t
	g	sd/t
	B♭	SD/R/t
	c	sd/sd/t
	f	sd/sd/sd/t

effect; the accent symbol ▼ is here used to indicate emphasis not necessarily
of duration; arrows denote dominant affiliations; the symbol ? indicates
uncertainty of tonicization effect; and a wavy line indicates an excision of
repeated material. The circled numbers over the sketch are for reference to
the list of notes following. In this list of notes PC letter names are used in
addition to symbols of relation to T; where D might otherwise be unclear,
it is shown as D/T if the dominant system component is meant. Finally,
a list of durational note-values arbitrarily employed in the sketch, but precise
in their applied relations, is given at the left in Ex. 1-45.

1. Note within the first stable area very slight tonicizations of f♯ and b, perhaps
   predictive of subsequent strong tonicizations of these factors. Typical symmetry
   of tonal reference, here in 3rds.
2. Transitional phase characterized here by D-A vacillation: highly significant
   tonal-rhythmic ordering in increasing values of A.
3. Passing secondary tonics in movement in 5ths.
4. Symmetries within D/T area: E-A-D, C-A-F. Note again a rhythmic ordering
   in the tonal form—*decreasing values of A tonicizations.*
5. As predictable in conventional tonal practice, D/T has emerged as structural
   tonic of second-order importance (of course auxiliary to T at broadest level),
   and is in decline as noted above.
6. Longest pure manifestation of primary tonic.
7. Note passing tonics in symmetrical formulations.
8. Emergence of strong reference to mediant (m/T—f♯). [Note embellishing,
   mild tonicization of D/m (C♯?).]
9. Compare the beginning of the exposition, but here the primary tonic is reaffirmed as expected in single-movement sonata form.

Ex. 1-45. Beethoven, Symphony No. 2 in D, fourth movement.
Actual tonal rhythm expressed in indicated note-value relations.

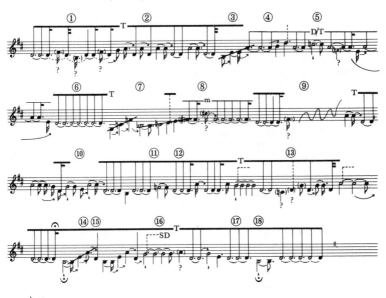

1 = ♪ (⅛ bar)

2 = ♪

3 = ♪.

4 = ♪

6 = ♪.

8 = ♪ (1 bar)

16 = ♩

32 = ♩

48 = ♩. (6 bars)

10. Note G-A emphases as surrounding, embellishing tonics in symmetrical relation to D. *First strong reference to G, SD/T.*

11. B-F encircling elaboration of primary tonic, again a symmetrical arrangement.

12. Note radically diminishing values of T (D) references in another *rhythmic ordering in the tonal structure.*

13. G-D (SD, T) ambiguities; cf. G-D ambivalences of second thematic element
in first group.

14. Fermatas have important effect in balancing references to b (r). Again, symmetrical formulations around T (SD, D/T) as well as around st (r, D/T).

15. In repeated tonal pattern (b-e-A-D, b-e-A-D), note important variation in
tonal rhythm.

16. Note traditional, almost universal *emphasis on SD* (seen in incipience in six-teenth-century examples) in coda as in elaborations of authentic cadence in general; very strong here.

17. Note changes in values of G and D (SD and T) in the coda: again, rhythmic ascent in values of T, descent in values of SD—*controlled changes in the tonal rhythm* having clearly functional implications.

18. Note final tonics as outline of SD:I; cf. 16, above.

19. While relative prominences as represented here would clearly be a factor in any broad, hierarchic ordering of system components, other factors would qualify any mere computation of relative rhythmic values: e.g., degree of *uninterrupted* prevalence (as of m, f♯, at 8); and degree of *independence* of mani-festation of secondary system (cf. m, f♯, at 8, with SD, G, at end of movement, which has much stronger dependence on the primary tonic undergoing elabo-ration); and, among other factors, the *position* of occurrence of the tonicization in the form.

Particularly important is the *controlled change of tonal-rhythmic values*, mentioned a number of times in the above notes.

Wolf, "Das verlassene Mägdlein" from *Gedichte von Mörike*

A further example of striking tonal expansion is extracted from a song of Wolf, one that is much discussed. Its tonal structure is "closed" (tonally "rounded"), unlike the "open" tonal structures of the two Wolf songs cited earlier (pp. 85–86).

The point at which the extract begins[58] rests upon the tonic PC ex-pressed at the beginning of the song, A. It is followed by a series of successions, some of them chromatic, referring ephemerally to passing tonics.

A number of the dominant harmonies have the form of the augmented triad. As a dominant form, the augmented triad has a particular wayward-ness in view of its ambiguity of root. It can resolve (as might t: III_6^+ or V^+)

$$\begin{smallmatrix} \sharp \\ 2 \end{smallmatrix}$$

to a "normal" tonic consequent (Ex. 1.46a, mm. 20–21, 26–27, 28–29), but it can also act in deviant ways. In mm. 22–23 there is evasive, nonfunctional (i.e., tonally nonfunctional) chromatic succession from one augmented triad (A♭: V^+?) to another a semitone below. While the notation of the augmented triad of m. 23, on G♭, would suggest it might function as a dominant to C♭, there is no realization of that potential. Rather, there is a further chromatic succession to still another augmented triad, notated as a dominant to B♭. This time the suggested tonal direction is confirmed by the resolution at m. 27, repeated at m. 29. Analogous processes continue until, at m. 34, an augmented triad on G (which could function as a dominant of C)

[58]The entire song is included in Burkhart, *Anthology for Musical Analysis,* 2nd ed. (New York: Holt, Rinehart and Winston, Inc., 1972).

Ex. 1-46a.   Wolf, "Das Verlassene Mägdlein" from *Gedichte von Mörike.*

Ex. 1-46a continued.

assumes the function of mediant (as dominant) to e. The e of its resolution is then inflected to become a dominant, then a dominant 7th-chord, for reaffirmation of the primary tonic.

The above has perhaps seemed somewhat digressive for the immediate purpose of description of tonal structure and fluctuation, but the ambivalence of the ubiquitous augmented triad between tonal function and nonfunction is an important aspect of tonal structure in the song. What is presented here, between m. 17 and the clear restoration of the primary tonic at m. 37, is an extended passage of characteristic tonal fluctuation and uncertainty. One is almost tempted to assert that the tonal structure is best characterized not in terms of specific tonics but, rather, in terms of the pattern (tripartite) *stability-fluctuation-stability*. Still, one approach does not exclude the other, and both A♭ and B♭, in one sense *embellishing neighbors of A*, are tonicized in significant actions.

The passage of fluctuation is extreme in a number of ways: (1) in the recurrence of the vagrant augmented triad (sometimes a V+, sometimes

III_6^+, sometimes nonfunctional), (2) in the complete denial of functional expectation aroused by the dominant 7th of m. 18 ($\text{A}:\text{V}_7$ of vi?), which gives way to seemingly irrelevant chromatic succession to start the stream of fluctuation, and (3) in the tonal *distances* traversed: there are references to A♭, B♭, and finally e, which becomes the primary dominant in function. Especially the relatively longer references to A♭ (a semitone below the original tonic) and B♭ (a semitone above) seem to impair, yet in a purely linear sense so logically elaborate, the initial tonic A. The A♭ and B♭ references thus have a persuasive linear logic as semitonal neighbors of A, and thus act as tightly related linear compensations to the errant tonal progression to remote regions of which they are centers. In summary, *two "leading-tones," B♭ and A♭, act as encircling tonal (not merely harmonic) embellishments.*

A fundamental view of the entire passage, illuminating the chromatic derivations of two passing tonics, functional and nonfunctional augmented triads, and implicit chromatic linear successions of the voice-leading, is given in Ex. 1-46b. A telescopic view reveals a stepwise succession of augmented triads linking two structural appearances of A,a:I,i.

Ex. 1-46b. Synoptic sketch of the Wolf example.

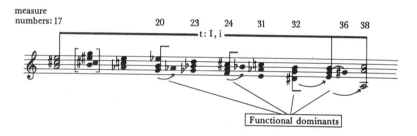

As complement to the foregoing discussion of pitch structure in an extract from Wolf's song, "Das Verlassene Mägdlein," there is given in Ex. 1-46c a reduced sketch of the entire harmonic structure *in abstraction*. (Successions in and profiles of individual voices are not represented except for some fidelity to essential movements in outer voices.) Again, an exceedingly simple basis (V-I) underlies an elaborate superstructure in which there is chromaticism of immediate succession as well as of tonal expansion. A synopsis is given on a single staff above the example, representing in the midsection the tonicized chromatic neighbors—A♭ and B♭—of the primary A. This provocative material is seen in a further light in the one-staff representation below the example: the plausible interpretation of bass factors as expressing, horizontally, the primary dominant, with the primary leading-tone represented enharmonically.

Ex. 1-46c. Wolf, "Das Verlassene Mägdlein."
A reduced sketch of abstracted tonal-harmonic structure.

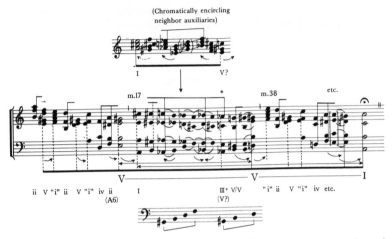

*Substitution of augmented for major triad on "A♭" to provide enharmonic form of primary dominant (III⁺)?

Ravel, "Le Martin-Pêcheur" from *Histoires Naturelles*

A Ravel song is the subject of reference in the following discussion.[j] In the song (Ex. 1-47a), a primary tonal system on F♯ is expressed, richly colored, and confirmed at its conclusion. Example 1-47b is a synoptic rendering of the entire structure, only a few details of which can be discussed.

The final six bars (see Ex. 1-47b, where key measure numbers are given) are a prolongation and embellishment of F♯:I (even in its final appearance activated by static dissonances, G♯ and D♯); prior to this there is modulation from the principal secondary tonic, E, to F♯.

Measure 15 affords an excellently clear illustration of the prolongation and embellishment of a structural harmony (here, $E:V_{13}$) by parallel auxiliary chords of similar (here, identical) intervallic content. While these are for the most part represented only symbolically in the sketch, the dominant on B is embellished by an auxiliary dominant on A and these are, at a more immediate level, linked by chromatic passage among nonfunctional parallel chords, the root of each yielding an ornamenting bass note.

The process of parallel embellishments continues in m. 16. That bar begins with the same $E:V_{13}$ and the same auxiliaries but instead of returning to the E:V they continue a step farther to a dominant 13th-chord on G (shown in the sketch). The shift toward the primary tonic now takes place by

Ex. 1-47a. Ravel, "Le Martin-Pêcheur," No. 4 of *Histoires Naturelles.*

Ex. 1-47a continued.

m. 20

- lé de peur, mais qu'il a cru qu'il ne fai-sait que pas-ser d'une

m. 22

branche à une autre.

Ex. 1-47b. Synopsis of tonal structure in the Ravel.

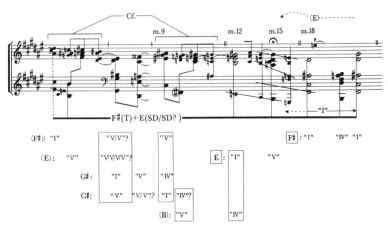

chromatic succession to F♯: "I". It is interesting that the harmony of m. 18 is a shadowy reflection of those of the preceding bars; it is thus of somewhat dominant character, although its minor 7th, E, is delayed to give the harmony relatively greater stability. After a series of auxiliary harmonies (on E, D, B in a descending stream) the F♯ harmony is returned as the ultimate tonal resolution.

The technique of tonal shift which had earlier introduced the secondary tonic E (mm. 9–12) is related and should be compared. Measure 9 begins with a quasi-dominant of F♯. This harmony is "horizontalized"—note the bass notes C♯, G♯, B (not shown in the sketch)—until at the second half of the same bar the bass settles on the primary tonic note; but the chromatic succession of parallel auxiliary chords above the bass now settles into an harmonic complex making of that F♯ a dominant 9th-chord. The dominant 9th on F♯ becomes a minor 9th-chord in m. 10, the F𝄪 (so it is notated in the voice part) resolving into E:I after tantalizing delay, and the C serving as a chromatic link to the B of E:I. Despite these passing, nonharmonic factors, the progression at its basis is diatonic, the two essential harmonies having diatonic relation in B, represented as a *parenthetical system* in the structure.

One further element in the succession described above must be noted: it is an harmonic elision of a sort typical of the style. The dominant on F♯ "expects" B, which would in turn be a potential dominant of E. But the movement here omits the B harmony which would resolve the one and prepare the other. Viewing the succession in this light helps to clarify its nature as a diatonic rather than chromatic succession, and further accounts for the "parenthetical" function of B.

Finally, attention is called to some summary concluding notes which have direct reference to the sketch in Ex. 1-47b. The reader should note: the extent of chromatic relation in contiguous harmonies, functional and nonfunctional, especially in embellishing successions; stylistically characteristic resistance to semitonal successions in the voice-leading (reflected in the overall tonal successions F♯-E-F♯); the significance of an underlying motive, 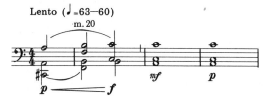 , as bass line determinant; the types of embellishing chords (e.g., major dominant 9th-chords and derivative half-diminished 7th-chords); means of tonal stabilization opposing the activating power of dissonance—the broad F♯-E-F♯ succession of prolongation and neighbor auxiliary; comparison of the "I" of m. 1 and its recurrence at the end; m. 15 as a very visible prolongation and embellishment of surrounding, functional, structural harmonies (e. g., retention of g♯^{1}); mm. 18–22 as prolongation of F♯: "I"; the recurring e^2 of mm. 18–20 as a backward look toward the secondary tonic E; and most fundamentally the underlying "closed" and explicit manifestation of the primary system, whose expansions are unorthodox in the quasi-modal prominence of the system on E, but nevertheless, in their secondary tonics, entirely diatonic (more strictly, pentatonic) in their relation to F♯.[59]

Bartók, String Quartet No. 2, Op. 17, third movement

The Bartók movement poses some relatively complex problems of tonal analysis, but its approaches to tonal structure are stringent and definite: it is a structure whose chief foci are diatonic to A. Consider, for example, the tonal implications of the succession in Ex. 1-48a, which constitutes a recurring

Ex. 1-48a. Bartók, String Quartet No. 2, Op. 17, third movement.

Lento (♩=63—60)

[59]The collection of secondary tonics, together with the primary, have a very characteristic formulation when rendered in a chordal configuration as PCs superimposed over E: . (Compare the form taken by F♯:"I" in opening and concluding appearances.)

harmonic motive in the movement. (While some fragments of Bartók's music are quoted in connection with the following discussion, the reader should, ideally, have the score at hand.)

The succession is strongly affirmative of A,a,[60] the tritone F,B acting as a quasi-dominant of the sort discussed earlier.

With the tonic A in mind (it is established early in the movement), consider the tonal implications of the lines in Ex. 1-48b, each of them directed toward or otherwise giving prominence to leading-tones of A, the tonic "resolution" explicit in the bass following in each instance.

Ex. 1-48b.

Like other freely tonal music (and this work is part of a vast body of music of comparable aesthetic in the twentieth century), that of Bartók relies upon some of the techniques of tonal expression noted earlier, especially the following: emphasis upon the tonal center and its supportive functions by iteration, prolongation, stress, etc.; affirmation by quasi-functional harmonic and melodic elements resembling conventions of the tonal period (the quasi-dominant action continues to rely heavily upon the concept of leading-tone tendency and accustomed root movement); and by linear direction toward and indirect or direct encirclement of the tonic PC, especially at points of formal punctuation.

[60] In the Bartók movement, the tonal system is typically one in which modal differences are freely exploited. Symbological distinctions between A and a (despite the movement's conclusion on the minor 3rd sonority), or between "I" and "i", etc., are not observed in the discussion of this example.

The initial two motives in the cello form, with the viola's E, a kind of evasive tonic ($+$ dominant) sonority in which the root, A, is tentatively suggested by encircling motions above and below: B-B♭ and G♯ are pivotal in these movements (cf. A: V_{13}). Thereafter, the cello phrases consistently conclude on A, which is always a longer note (mm. 11–12, 15–16, 21–22) and often directly supported by leading-tones above and below. Its descending triad of mm. 18–19 may be said, moreover, to act as "V" to the "I" (minor 6th, C♯ and A) which follows.

At the same time, the long major 6th in the viola (mm. 9–12, then 15–17) resolves as a "V" to the later octave C, eventually absorbed into A: "I". Note that this major 6th is also part of the traditional A: V_7, just as the tritone of m. 20 is both suggestive of C and an element in the traditional dominant 9th of A, which of course prevails at the cadence.

One of the most compelling of the melodic formulations of quasi-dominant character is the first violin motive of mm. 11–12, beginning on one leading-tone of A, ending on the other, strongly expectant of the tonic PC, which is held in reserve. The same is true of the second violin motive, mm. 1–2, which accompanies the tonic note.

The opening measure thus both establishes A and sets against it a V-like motive (primary dominant "augmented 6th"?) in the second violin. Thereafter, within the first section, the melodic units often are projective of and/or directed to G♯ and B♭ (leading-tones to A, sometimes, as a reflection of ambivalent tendencies, notated enharmonically) and D♯/E♭ (E is established early by emphasis in the viola, and quasi-leading auxiliaries are strongly felt in the recurring E♭ of viola, mm. 13–14, and second violin thereafter; in the first violin's active tritonal succession of mm. 1–2; in the major 2nd of m. 5, etc.; and especially at the release of the first violin, m. 19). While these interrogative leading-tone gestures and motives occur, the cello part continues to be directed consistently and repeatedly toward the A of the cadence.

The longest notes in these opening 22 measures are E, D, C, B, *and* A, their functions in the tonality obvious. It is interesting that despite suggestive leaning toward E, and early emphasis on E in the viola, that PC fails to emerge cadentially, omitted from the quasi-tonic sonority at m. 22, perhaps because of its subsequent prominence in the tonally contrasting section to follow.

Immediately before the cadence, there are two tentative suggestions of quasi-tonic harmony: the end of m. 20, where the harmony is activated by a suspended B in the bass, delaying the root; and the second half of m. 19, where the lower instruments express the tonic at the same time that the upper instruments express the inconclusive "dominant."[61] Preceding this is a quasi-

---

[61]Quite possibly, the C♯, D♯, G♯ sonority is predictive of the C♯ secondary tonic to come.

dominant (which includes the upper leading-tone, B♭, notated as A♯) of exactly the kind referred to in theory earlier in this chapter.

In Ex. 1-48c are some of the melodic and harmonic materials to which we have referred, as well as others that are supportive of the tonality of these opening bars.

Measures 23–27 repeat the cadential formula, reestablishing the A tonic, coincident with the now familiar G♯-B♭ leading-tones, then to lead into and prepare the contrasting *lento* which follows. It is impossible to examine every detail, but let us at least point out further manifestations of the cited techniques of tonal expression.

Again there are clear examples of tonal direction and orientation. The first violin of mm. 23–27 articulates a phrase beginning and ending with the two A leading-tones, strongly emphasizing B♭. Later it comes to rest on G♯ (mm. 33–36), which resolves to A, then conjunctly climbs to and insistently reiterates E, as part of the cadence at m. 46.

The final harmonies of this section are ambivalent in tonal meaning. The violins, one sustaining E, the other reiterating A and its upper leading-tone, are supportive of A, and the F of the inner voices seems not to have departed far from the primary tonal system. But the ultimate thrust of the cello toward c^2 and $c♯^1$ foreshadows, in the environment of an inconclusive cadence, the C♯ tonality to follow. The more intense outer voices (*piano*, as opposed to the *pianissimo* of second violin and viola) project the C♯,E *secondary quasi-tonic* sonority.

The C♯ has been suggested harmonically, of course, much earlier. The sustained, motivic harmonies at the beginning of this section first reiterate and reconfirm the quasi-dominant and quasi-tonic functions in A (mm. 25–27). But at mm. 29–31 they effect a tonal shift pointing to C♯, the latter "tonic" sonority having the same form as that of A which preceded. From here to m. 46 the melodic lines are in essence expressive of A and C♯, sometimes ambivalent between the two tonics, like the first violin from m. 31, which has quasi-dominant suggestiveness of C♯ at the same time that the resolution of the long G♯ to A is reminiscent of earlier tonal reference.

The second violin from m. 27 also tends to expect C♯; it prepares perfectly the eventual C♯,E resolution at m. 31. In the climactic, essentially rising passage leading up to the cadence, the subtle hints of C♯ combined with its careful evasion are of enormous importance in the effectiveness of its ultimate arrival in the cello. Consider, for example, *the "substitution" of B♯ for C♯ in the otherwise diatonic rise of the first violin from $g♯^2$ to e^3*.

The transitional passage to which we refer above is sketched in Ex. 1-48d in a manner intended to show (in larger notes, by enclosures, by arrows, by connecting lines, and by other symbols) some of the expressions of tonality we have noted as well as others of importance and comparable function and technique.

Ex. 1-48c.

Quoted melodic fragments of quasi-dominant character and function:

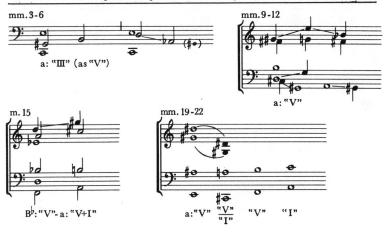

Sketched harmonic fragments of quasi-dominant and quasi-tonic character and function:

Ex. 1-48d.

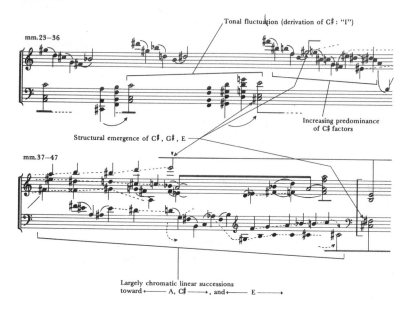

It is necessary from here on to limit discussion to the most essential points, leaving for the reader's independent investigation a number of elements of tonal expression comparable to those already identified in earlier portions of the movement.

The close relationship of C♯ to A, the fact that G♯ is both the dominant root of one and the leading-tone to the other, and the coincidence of the notes C♯ and E in both tonic triads, make it possible for Bartók to express a certain ambivalence in the contrasting material following m. 47, to establish tonal variety (by functions suggestive of C♯) without relinquishing implications of the original tonality. Note too the interrelations explicit in the forms the quasi-tonic harmonies take: the occurrence of A:"I_6", with C♯ as its lowest pitch, in the motivic harmonic succession, as well as the implicit relation between the two "tonics" in the M,m triad on A, consisting of superimposed minor 3rds which are the basic ingredients of the two chief harmonies of resolution: .

Melodic analysis of the first violin part from m. 47 to m. 67 would show very clearly that it is built around E at the beginning (a member of the C♯:"I" and at the same time a dominant preparation for the ultimate destination of the line, A): its first nine measures, in fact, are a prolongation of e¹, after which it prolongs e³. Following this high point (in a broader sense, a resumption of the e³ of mm. 41–46), the line descends (emphasizing B♯, the C♯ leading-tone) in a quasi-dominant formulation from m. 60 to m. 63. The descent of the line after this point, sequential, is a condensed, abrupt, reaffirmation of A, the note of its cadence, through an intriguing diversity of modal implications.

The second violin part also requires examination in similar connections. It is, of course, conceived to a considerable extent as a parallel doubling of the first violin; much of it is a prolongation of the note B (lending a modal quality to the tonic C♯). Shortly before its final resolution, on an emphasized A, there are reiterations of the upper leading-tone (B♭, notated as A♯, in the repeated succession B-A♯), and the lower leading-tone, G♯, has a single tentative appearance in m. 64, important nonetheless in its propinquity to the arrival point.

The strongest affirmation of C♯ is in the cello, fundament of the harmonic structure, whose melodic analysis would show a prolongation of c♯ in the first several measures, then describing an octave descent to C♯, through G♯ and F♯. With the cancellations of sharps (except for the bass note of A: "I⁶" in its familiar form and context at m. 65) at mm. 64–67, the cello comes into agreement with the other voices in the shift which restores the primary tonic. We do not take space for the melodic analyses suggested, although the reader may wish to do so in confirmation of the tonal expressions of the individual lines in this passage; perhaps the consequences of such analysis are, in general, preevident.

The harmony is, of course, conditioned to a considerable extent, like the individual lines, by Bartók's technique of mirroring the outer voices and filling the texture with the parallel 4ths which accompany them in the opening bars of the *Lento assai*. Nevertheless, harmonic functions, especially quasi-dominants and quasi-tonics, are of decisive importance in the expression of tonal feeling and coherence. The first harmony of m. 47 is a recurring C♯ : "I". Some of the auxiliary chords by which it is embellished, incorporating one or more leading-tones, act as quasi-dominants (e. g., very potently at m. 50, third beat); these are marked in the sketch in Ex. 1-48e. The cadence of mm. 54–55 prolongs the "I" (approached through a quasi-dominant in mm. 52–53) by alternating the root position with the first inversion. Elided with this, the violin quintole figures describe triadic functions suggestive of A, alluding to the later restoration of that primary tonic.

The sketch indicates essential quasi-tonal functions in the modulatory section of mm. 56–67 (Ex. 1-48e). The C♯ : "I" is seen to persist in upper voices and there is a C♯ : "V" on G♯ following. (The G♯, as suggested before, has an ambivalence in the tonal dichotomy of this passage— leading-tone of A, dominant root of C♯.) The cello reiteration of F♯ denotes a prolongation of harmony on D♯, coincident with the prolonged leading-

Ex. 1-48e.

tone of C♯ in the top voice; the A♯ of this C♯: "II", as we have seen, later turns, as B♭, toward the cadential A, so that the D♯ triad also has something of an ambivalent function. The final cadential harmonies in the primary tonality are by now familiar, although in this instance the viola F of m. 66 makes of the A: "I₆" a "I" + "VI", the F anticipating the recurring quasi-dominant of m. 66.

The developmental section which follows (mm. 68–87) is of great interest tonally, and of considerable fluctuation and some ambiguity, ultimately directed toward the SD level, D (see mm. 84–85). It should be regarded from two viewpoints.

In the beginning of this section the two violins reiterate a motive derived from m. 47; except in m. 85 consistently a 3rd apart. At first, the 3rds move twice to a D root, forecasting the PC of culmination at m. 85. The pattern is as shown in Ex. 1-48f; the points designated by accent are those which are repeated or, in the case of the conclusion, stressed dynamically and otherwise prominent as high points in the rise of pitch. (Note that the sketch notates the upper note of the penultimate interval, the only tritone, as E♭; it does indeed act as an upper leading-tone of D in a harmonic complex which is a strong quasi-dominant consisting of the normal dominant root, A, and the upper leading-tone, E♭.) Also striking is the relation of adjacent interval pairs *as compared with that of the movement's two chief tonic sonorities.*

The second stratum of tonal progression (the two are initially in a kind of antiphonal relation, but come increasingly into confluence as the develop-

Ex. 1-48f.

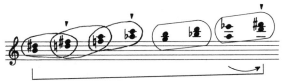

Progression of upper tessitura toward
D tonicization culminating at m. 85

ment progresses) is that of the viola and cello, in which the second violin also participates. This series of harmonic successions begins (mm. 69–70) with the familiar cadential formula in A, with its familiar resolution. The progression is then repeated four times, with extension and variation, deceptively moving to harmonic sonorities of changing tonal implications. The A:"V" by this time in the movement *clearly "expects" the A:"I"*, realized only in the first succession of the series. The deceptive resolutions create a sense of fluctuating tonal direction: each is a dissonance, each has one or more specific tonal implications (see Ex. 1-48g; possibly they are quasi-functional in C♯ and A), but the sum total is one of considerable, uncertain fluctuation until the final clarification at m. 85.

If the flats (like those of mm. 74 and 77) are heard enharmonically, the range of tonal fluctuation is less wide than it seems. Against the precedents established earlier the second harmony of m. 74 is interpretable as C♯:"IV" and that of m. 77 as C♯:"V". The sketch in Ex. 1-48g shows that the second

Ex. 1-48g.

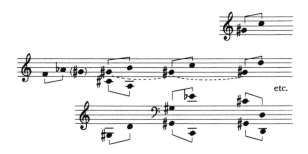

of these, the A♭/G♯ harmony of m. 77, now recurs as consistent penultimate harmony in the motivic recurrences which follow. While it has the effect of recalling earlier quasi-dominants of A and C♯, it "resolves" indecisively to deceptive dissonances until finally, abruptly on D. In the course of this the expansion of the motivic interval is of course deliberate and intensifying, and the tonal implications of its placements are visible with the extraction in Ex. 1-43g.

Example 1-48h is a sketch, like those seen earlier, intended to represent schematically some of the observations of the above discussion. The *piano* appearance of the motive in mm. 86–87, somewhat whimsical, tends to subvert any tonal decision achieved by the strong succession preceding it. It serves both to establish inconclusiveness of cadence and to recall in a subtle inflection the primary tonic, at the same time easily interpretable within the secondary tonal system on D, just affirmed, neither of which is supported in the measures which follow.

Ex. 1-48h.

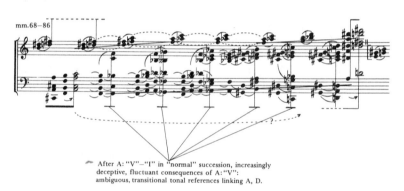

mm. 68–86

After A: "V"–"I" in "normal" succession, increasingly deceptive, fluctuant consequences of A: "V": ambiguous, transitional tonal references linking A, D.

The Bartók movement approaches now a second stage in developmental procedures which will lead back to clear reaffirmation of the primary tonality. The source of the materials developed after m. 88 will be found in the movement's first bars (first violin takes the cello motive of mm. 3–4 as its point of departure, as of course does the viola; the opposite voices—second violin and cello—take for extension and variation the top voice of mm. 15–16, which in turn relates to that of mm. 11–12, or the second violin of mm. 7–8).

The tonal fluctuation of the section following m. 88 begins with a strong allusion to F, F and C♯ symmetrically related to A; it is a tonal reference in which both voices join.

Following the first few bars of this section (Ex. 1-48i) tonal meanings are again relatively ambiguous. The B♭,E tritone so suggestive of F in the above-mentioned extract gives way now to rapidly changing tritonal relations (in which the lines do not concur)—each of them having certain tonal implications but none of these realized, as tonal allusion shifts from dissonance to dissonance. In the brief sketch in Ex. 1-48j (mm. 92–97) the

Ex. 1-48i.

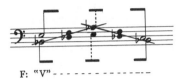

F: "V" - - - - - - - - - - - - - -

Ex. 1-48j.

indeterminate tritonal fluctuations are bracketed; the sketch also makes very apparent the essential chromatic descent of the bass from the B♭ of the initial F reference down to F♯, a point of brief prolongation.

It must be acknowledged in passing that the above-noted passage can be broken down into more explicit tonal allusions if the individual lines are examined. For example, the top voice of mm. 93–94 (expressing E♭) is sequentially related to that of mm. 89–90 (expressing F). But the difference is that in the case of mm. 89–90 the lower voice supported the reference to F; in mm. 93–94 the lower voice is more independent, although the E♭: "VII" is briefly formulated in the bass notes D, C♭, A♭ at mm. 94–95. Another significant difference is in the fact that in the earlier passage the prolonged E (leading-tone of F) moved down to C (F: "V"), while in the latter the E♭,D succession moves to A (in one of the tritonal movements), tending to disrupt any sense of E♭ which may have been fleetingly conveyed.

Again, the passages treated above *have* tonal implications which can be felt; that they constitute an interval of *relative* tonal flux and obscurity at the same time is a necessary conclusion of analysis, revealing an important aspect of the idiom and the form. What is evident here is the shaping opposition of relative ambiguity with relative clarity of tonal reference, a principle probably applicable to all idioms of tonal music despite differences in the means and extent of ambiguity.

In mm. 97–99₁ the lower voice traces the leading-tone harmony of C♯ and the upper voice underscores that reference in an elaboration of the quasitonic harmony; here, C♯ is a clear passing tonic in which the voices concur. It is broken up with the bass G of m. 101 and the tritonal leap from G♯ to D in the upper voice of the same bar. Either note could of course function ornamentally in the C♯ tonal system, but they signal a tonal departure at this point.

Measures 101–11., in which the materials are developed climactically, are the sort of passage sometimes described as *pantonal*, although tonal specificity and unanimity become relatively more pronounced in the approaches to the cadence. As the climax develops there are brief tonal allusions within the lines but the general tonal effect is largely indeterminate. At one point a suggestion of bitonality arises, when the bass expresses a quasi-dominant, then tonic, formulation in imitation of a similar configuration in the upper voice expressing G♭. The tensely dissonant clash of tonal references (Ex. 1-48k) is calculated to serve the rising intensity.

Ex. 1-48k.

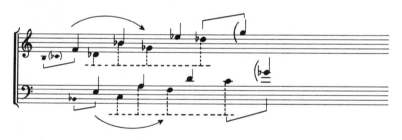

The approach to the cadence at m. 111₁ is also bitonal, the first violin persuasively affirmative of A♭ (primary leading-tone?), the lower voices joining in quasi-dominants and quasi-tonics suggestive of B. At the cadence, interestingly, the upper voice ends with a quasi-dominant formulation in A♭, the lower voices stating the first inversion of the B tonic. All of this is shown in the sketch (Ex. 1-48m) of mm. 104–111.

Finally, it should be noted that while the cadential successions into the B: "I" are underway the bass voice is itself of extraordinary fidelity in the

Ex. 1-48m.

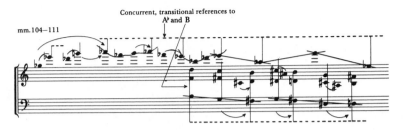

expression of that harmony in a linear succession which includes a complex of leading-tones (mm. 107–11; see Ex. 1-48m).

Bartók has manifested in the above passages the traditional tendency to establish in developmental areas a pattern of tonal fluctuation. Following m. 114 the primary tonic is restored in harmonic and melodic functions of greater stability, recollective of those of the first part.

The fluctuation into the primary tonal system (retonicization of A) is brought about in a number of ways. The first violin part of mm. 112–13, the only voice occupied with significant melodic motive, is itself revealing, as indicated in Ex. 1-48n.

Ex. 1-48n.

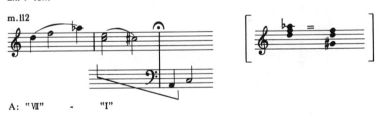

At the same time, the harmony is a quasi-dominant (m. 113) which is an expectant preparation of the A of the cello. That harmony is built on B, which has throughout the movement been a vital factor in quasi-dominant functions within the primary tonal region. The "V" contains the upper and lower leading-tones (the latter notated as A♭), and it is anticipated in the first violin of the measure preceding. The D of the viola might be said to have its premature "resolution" in the C-C♯ of the first violin motive. This quasi-dominant (see Ex. 1-48o) is itself introduced by a harmony of semitonally related auxiliaries (except for the bass, which is tied)—suggesting again the kind of linear determinant of harmonic auxiliaries which is so crucial in this and other late tonal styles. The "V" and its prior auxiliary harmonic complex are shown at the outset of the concluding sketch (Ex. 1-48o) of tonal functions and affiliations in the Bartók movement.

Ex. 1-48o.

mm.112–125

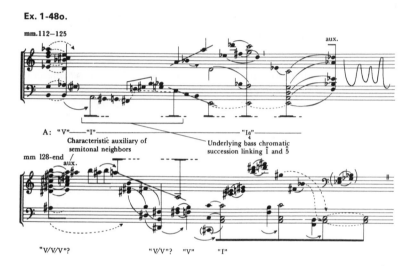

The phrase which begins at m. 114, with the first violin imitating the cello abortively, provides in the unaccompanied A the resolution of the preceding quasi-dominant. The diminished triad motive thereafter occurs at various levels: on A and A♯, on G and G♯ (a momentary sounding of A: "VII"), on F and F♯. The tonal references are thus free and fluctuant but two factors are of particular importance: the ultimate quasi-tonic "six-four" over the bass "dominant" E, toward which the entire succession is directed, and the chromatic descent of the bass melody (with two register shifts) from the "tonic" A to the "dominant" E—the latter sustained for three bars. Both factors are represented in Ex. 1-48o. The quartal "I_6^4" has considerable prolongation, embellished by quartal auxiliary chords again consisting of semitonally related neighbors (i.e., leading-tones) in a rising sequence of pitches. The prolongation of the "I_6^4" (traditionally a dominant auxiliary) *is a striking functional preparation for the final resolution.*

One of the embellishing auxiliary chords, an enharmonic notation of those preceding, is itself prolonged as a quasi-dominant—the harmony built on the bass A♯ at mm. 127–29; this harmony is embellished by auxiliary neighbors of its upper members, but the bass A♯ remains constant. That A♯ can again be understood as the upper leading-tone of the tonic A and, in accord with its notation, *as the ambivalent lower leading-tone to the B prolonged with it*, the B also resolving to A (mm. 128–29 and 131 in first violin, and mm. 130–32 in cello) in a functional recession which has been recurrent (Ex. 1-48p). The harmony is, like the preceding "I$_6$", fully quartal in construction.

Ex. 1-48p.

In a quartal harmony the identification of root is problematic; the analysis suggested here gives tonal, functional precedence to the bass note of the harmony on A♯ (as does any reasonable tonal assessment of the traditional I$_6$). The harmony occurring over A♯ can be construed as quasi-dominant *twice removed* ("V/V/V"), introducing the "V/V" on B, the A♯ acting *in its ultimate course* as an upper leading-tone to A (see Exx. 1-48o, p, q). The cadence is consummated by the motivic quasi-dominant tritonal sonority (F, B) and the quasi-tonic harmony (A, C), preceded by a dissonant anticipation of "I" combining C with C♯ in characteristic modal ambivalence. The entire succession might be conceived as analogous to the following traditional sequence of tonal harmonies, a hypothesis best examined *in actual, attentive listening* to Bartók's cadence in comparison with the conjectured prototype, which is reprinted in Ex. 1-48q in explicit demonstration of the significance of the concept of quasi-functional tonal harmony.

Ex. 1-48q.

While the cadential formulation is underway there is a most important manifestation of tonal expression in the first and second violin parts. The earlier prolonged B in the former, with its A♯ auxiliary embellishment, now descends to A (a²), after which the line falls two octaves into a cadential resolution on a. The second violin, moving in parallel 3rds down to G, a "modal" auxiliary, underscores the arrival on the tonic in a concurring resolution.

The primary tonic is now well reestablished; the rest is its prolongation for conclusive finality. The sketch in Ex. 1.48o shows the motive of rising 3rds, only mildly evasive in tonal allusion, subtly animating that concluding tonic elaboration. These motivic iterations supply A: "V" once (m. 132) and otherwise recall the secondary tonics C♯ and D, as well as the B of the cadential function just realized. The motive occurs once again, on E♭, in a slight stir of tonal evasiveness immediately preceding the final two tonic statements, this time lacking the quasi-dominant tritone.[k]

Further enhancing the sense of tonal resolution is a melodic tonal reference—that of the first violin in its phrase at m. 135, again beginning on G♯ and ending on B♭ (compare mm. 11–12 or 23–27).

We have sought in the above discussions to explain the overall and specific directions of Bartók's tonal structure in this movement, identifying tonal functions in melodic and harmonic extracts, and pointing out areas of relative tonal stability and relative activity as delineating structural factors and giving analysis of the means by which tonal reference and tonal fluctuation are carried out.

The discussion is not of course exhaustive, and it is confined to factors of tonal structure and technique. A *tonal system* of the sort described and at times charted with reference to earlier works could of course be derived and graphically represented: it would reveal the remarkable extent to which tonicized PCs by which the system is expanded *are diatonically related to A*.

Webern, Four Pieces, Op. 7, for violin and piano, No. 1

An important example from the works of Webern is given next as Ex. 1-49a. It is the first of the pieces for violin and piano, Op. 7.

The tonal structure is of truly compelling effect. There can be no insistent suggestion of conscious creative intent, although Webern is said to have affirmed the importance of tonal relations in his works; the tendencies which seem unequivocal in this piece (and it is representative of many) may well be intuitive. The important concern of analysis is *experiential effect* as plausibly described and underscored in objective evidence. Such evidence of course requires interpretation, and verification in experience (i. e., listening), with such experience conditioned by the understanding which follows from analysis.

Ex. 1-49a. Webern, Four Pieces for violin and piano, Op. 7; No. 1.

Three sketches will illuminate tonal functions of different kinds, all of them oriented toward a primary tonic E♭. The "tonal system" of the piece is simple (suggestive secondary tonicizations of the leading-tone D could be inferred, but the primary E♭ is virtually without enrichment of expanding secondary systems in this very brief, concentrated work). Indeed, there is no significant fluctuation: no real deviation from insistent references to E♭ at a number of levels.

The first sketch (Ex. 1-49b) shows the descent from structural manifestations of e♭³ to e♭² and finally to e♭¹, "root" of the final chord. The first of these pitches is simply held as a violin harmonic, "establishing" the tonic PC. The second is reiterated, and preceded by a succession derived from a chromatic set (illustrated) *which significantly avoids E♭*. The repeated figure containing the e♭² is released, significantly, on c♯² and d², creating an intense expectancy of return of the established E♭.

Ex. 1-49b.   Tonal tendencies in the Webern upper stratum.

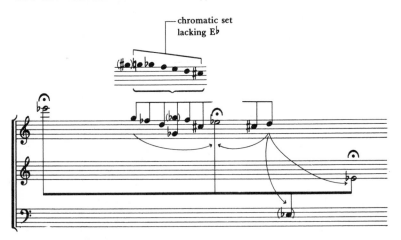

At what might be described as an internal stratum in the piece's spatial field, a quasi-functional harmonic recession takes place, as shown in Ex. 1-49c. A further, implied step in this succession, expressed as a melodic configuration, might well be included; it is represented in the third sketch, Ex. 1-49d. When one *hears* this succession its functional implications are very persuasive. The two neighbors of the "V" are shown by the symbol *N*; one of these is stated in two registers, and is embellished by its own lower

Ex. 1-49c.   Quasi-functional harmonic successions in the Webern.

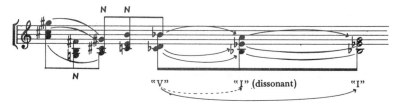

neighbor as indicated in Ex. 1-49c. A dissonant form of "I" precedes the final resolution. Throughout the succession, the importance of voice-leading, its smoothness a result of linear adjacencies, is apparent.

Finally, an ascent in the lower textural stratum (Ex. 1-49d) complements and is a counterpoint to the descent noted earlier (Ex. 1-49b). Again, E♭ is its center; the succession is E♭, e♭, e♭¹. The harmonic succession noted above is included parenthetically, and tendencies of leading-tones and other auxiliaries are indicated by arrows. Particularly effective in function is the penultimate event, F♭ (E♮), which functions (like the d² of the violin, shown in the first sketch) as a leading-tone expecting, and directly antecedent to, the final tonic root.

Ex. 1-49d.   Further (especially lower stratum) tonal expression in the Webern.

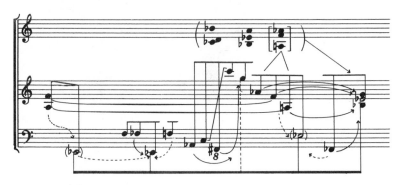

A summary synoptic sketch, superimposing and incorporating principal factors represented in these three, would project a comprehensive image of tonal tendencies and relations in the piece as a whole.

Berg, Four Pieces, Op. 5, for clarinet and piano, No. 4

The works of Berg, strong and resourceful in their expressions of tonality, within both serial and preserial procedures, are greatly rewarding in study of this kind. The following discussion refers to the Four Pieces for clarinet and piano, Op. 5. The reader would do well to study others of these pieces as to manifestations of tonal order; we refer here to No. 4, in C. In this piece, expressions of C are of numerous kinds.

The opening C bass pedal is of course itself highly suggestive and preconditioning, especially as the "root" of a major triad (to which is added two pitches that might be construed as chromatic auxiliaries of the G and E of the triad).

During the statement of this reiterated harmony (consistently of the duration of 3 ♪) the clarinet sounds two motives (one the extension of the other) which tend to "encircle" the C "tonic," one of the motives beginning on B, the other on C♯. This principle of encirclement is made extremely compelling and explicit in the return of the chords at mm. 11–12 (Ex. 1-50a).

Ex. 1-50a.   Berg, Four Pieces for clarinet and piano, Op. 5; No. 4 (clarinet notated at sounding pitch).

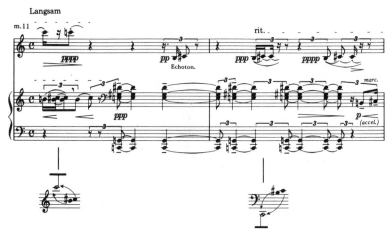

Copyright 1924, Universal Edition. Used by permission of the publisher. Theodore Presser Company, sole representative United States, Canada and Mexico.

In the approach to this reaffirmation of C, there is a strongly suggestive and functional succession which in some ways "expects" C and at the same time powerfully manifests a quasi-dominant sonority in the piano in mm. 9–10. The piano harmony consists of the conventional G and F with the upper and lower chromatic auxiliaries of C—all of this symmetrically disposed around c^2, which appears only fleetingly in the clarinet and is otherwise deliberately withheld, intensifying the expectation of the C "resolution" of m. 11 and its anticipation in the clarinet, as c^3, in m. 10. (See Ex. 1-50b.)

Of major interest in this passage is the motion of the clarinet line toward c^3. In m. 8, the clarinet begins this process with tremolo repetition of two pitches: bb^1 and g^1. Once the line moves, it does so with insistent implications of bileveled (compound) structure functionally directed toward c^3, as summarized in Ex. 1-50b..The lower level of the compound succession moves toward c^2, as does the contraction in the piano, whose chromatic neighbors of C are transferred unresolved to the clarinet in m. 11, at a lower octave. Of

Ex. 1-50b. Berg, Four Pieces for clarinet and piano, No. 4.
Mm. 8–10 and sketch of recessive actions toward C.

Summary of upper
voice "I" preparation:

*Prominent as "V" preparation and auxiliary in concluding measures.

Ex. 1-50b continued.

Copyright 1924, Universal Edition. Used by permission of the publisher. Theodore Presser Company, sole representative United States, Canada and Mexico.

Summary of piano contraction in mm. 9–10:

course, there is tentative resolution in the arrivals on c³ (insistently repeated in slowing tempo in the clarinet's upper stratum), then C in the bass of the piano; the absent c¹ does appear as root of the piece's final sonority.

Other factors of quasi-functional support of the primary C can be noted briefly. For example, the final recession of tonal structure toward C involves an underlying chromatic ascent of the clarinet toward g³ (e-f¹-f♯²-g³) in a progression by which that "dominant" is projected with great emphasis. The progression is opposed to a piano descent to CC in mm. 13–17, after which the C triad (with B) is first outlined in the piano bass, then sustained in a chord of piano harmonics and, subsequently, repeated in unstopped notes over c¹. The function of the piano's gradually accrued penultimate harmony (echoed in the clarinet's final phrase) as a complex of "leading-tone" auxiliaries resolving to the final "tonic" is apparent in the sketch of PC content in the two harmonies (Ex. 1-50c).

Ex. 1-50c.

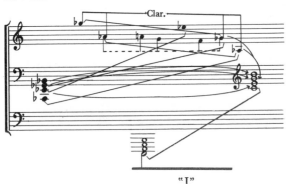

Summary notes on the universality and significance of the principle of hierarchic tonal order

Any analysis of liturgical chant demonstrates, like that of Ex. 1-41, that a critical factor in its structure is the quasi-tonal hierarchy which yields, at points of cadence, to preestablished components of the modal scale as elements of relative finality, the ultimate being the final itself, which is in this sense unmistakably analogous to the tonic of later, formalized tonal functions. Moreover, we have seen that in modal polyphony groups of auxiliaries tend to revolve around notes most basic in the hierarchic, modal or quasi-modal structure, and this too must be recognized as analogous to the systematized tonal functions of later styles. We therefore take the position that modality whether pure or in later evolutionary stages is a manifestation of the fundamental principles essential to tonal organization in music.

Indeed, in much "modal" music the later specific conventions of tonality are in vivid evidence. And while the transition from purely modal to emergent tonal devices is gradual—and overlapping among different coexistent styles, it is clear that the conventions of the tonal period are incipient and sometimes very significantly manifest in applications which long predate their formalization in Baroque and Classical literatures, and that, in modality, *the concept of hierarchic tonal order is truly relevant.*

Along with the wider applications of leading-tone functions by the uses of *musica ficta* in contexts of modal derivatives, one must regard as indicative of later tonal conventions the increasingly supportive role of the bass in early multivoiced compositions—a role characterized more and more by the use of 4ths and 5ths of quasi-dominant-tonic succession, less and less by the intervallic and rhythmic equality between bass and other voices which is a Renaissance ideal.[62] An element in this trend is, of course, the bass line accompanying sixteenth-century vocal declamation in, for example, the practices of lutenist composers; its function is substantially that of defining root progressions of clear tonal purpose, as ultimately is that of the figured bass of the Baroque, an important embodiment of harmonic conventions in the tonal period.

It is primarily the practice of *musica ficta*, of course, with the increasing emergence of leading-tone relations, which contributed in the Renaissance to

---

[62]Of Josquin, Donald Grout writes that "we become aware of a consistent organization of the harmonies along the lines of our own common practice. Though they are still rooted in the modal system, the chord progressions and the general harmonic plan in most of Josquin's works are to a large extent governed by dominant-tonic relationships. One sign of this organization is the conduct of the bass line: more and more it has begun to be distinguished from the primarily melodic nature of the other voices and has begun to assume the function of a harmonic support; consequently it often moves by fourths and fifths. This kind of harmonic organization and this type of bass movement become increasingly prevalent in the course of the sixteenth century." [*A History of Western Music* (New York: W. W. Norton and Company, Inc., 1960), pp. 243–44.]

the gradual dissolution of purely modal conventions, especially in polyphonic music, and to the increasing expansion of "tonal systems" and consolidation of the conventions of the tonal period. At times dense chromaticism is practiced,[63] constituting one of the most intriguing sixteenth-century stylistic currents, to a degree that eventuates in a great flux of tonal reference (Lowinsky's "floating tonality"), presumably as a conscious expressive resource. It is noteworthy that most highly chromatic passages are homorhythmic in texture, to facilitate and focus attention on chromatic successions without competing textural complications.

In other than chromatic styles, too, the increasing use of simpler textures, often in modified polyphonic contexts, is another manifestation of the growing emergence of harmonic formulae of the major-minor system. It is easy to understand that more homorhythmic textures, linked with a bass line less and less independent, increasingly given to defining codified successions in relation to a central tonic function by movement of 4ths and 5ths, would be associated with advanced trends in the rise of major-minor tonality. Moreover, one of the fundamental differences between the polyphony of the Renaissance and that of the Baroque (an issue of style, of course, not of value) is in the latter's firm conditioning of individual lines toward conventional tonal ends and of their confluence in the Baroque to serve prescribed tonal-harmonic functions.

In many transitional works the blends of modality and major-minor tonality are extraordinarily provocative and often of great charm. Where this occurs, modal vestiges should not be regarded as inhibiting tonal order (although many do in the specifics of major-minor terms), but as conditioning the *means* by which tonal order is expressed.

In the Baroque, the use of old melodies—chant, *Lied*, chorale, etc.—as *cantus firmus* in polyphonic compositions or as subjects for variation in compositions of highly provocative ambiguities (markedly in phrygian derivatives) exacerbated the modality-tonality ambivalences and conflicts, the melody imposing upon evolving harmonic conventions of the rising major-minor system vestigial inflections of the past, the harmony increasingly pointed toward the later conventions of the tonal period. Music theory awaits a deeper understanding of this evolutionary process in, for example, seventeenth-century music; at the same time analysis attempts to determine structural consequences of tonal reference *in the individual work*, and seeks to understand how tonality, broadly conceived, functions counteractively and complementarily in its relations with other elements in the musical work. Historical factors of ambivalence and evolution concern the *devices* of tonal affirmation, not the fact of tonality itself.

---

[63]See Lowinsky, *Tonality and Atonality*, for analytical discussion of music of Lasso, Gesualdo, and other sixteenth-century chromaticists.

The technique of juxtaposing tonally fluctuant areas in a musical form with areas of relative stability (or ambiguity with clarity), while dating from very early practices, is fundamental to larger forms of the tonal period. It is of particular importance in the late nineteenth century and in the tonal music of the twentieth century, where fluctuation may be over an extremely wide range. We have noted that in those twentieth-century styles in which the identity of tonic is less explicit, the expression of *relative* repose and *relative* mobility of tonal allusion is a particularly vital, even necessary, and often clearly felt, aspect of musical structure and structural function.

When one or more of the essentials of dominant function are retained in a succession, the sense of that function, as we have seen, with the implication of affirmation of tonic, is likely to be preserved in some degree—whether significantly must, again, be in part a matter of subjective response and judgment. Of importance in such procedures is the expansion of the concept of leading-tone: with the important technique of *tonicizing "encirclement,"* especially potent when the encirclement is by chromatic auxiliaries, the upper leading-tone takes on an importance comparable to that of the traditional lower (as observed, for example, in the Bartók and Berg analyses). Such leading-tones act in encirclement of tonic factors at disparate levels, and in encirclement of the individual factors of quasi-tonic harmony, in practices of voice-leading involving (frequently quasi-dominant) harmonic derivatives comprised of semitonal neighbors to harmonic structures of resolution.

The extent to which such functions denote tonal reference depends, of course, on their relative strength as experienced in a particular context, as established by rhythmic, metric, dynamic, and other means, as well as on *the supportive or contradictory terms of the surrounding particular context.* It is frequently possible in textures of considerable complexity and free chromaticism to establish tonal feeling by such applications of subtle inferences of traditional functions, as we have seen in quotations from relatively recent works.[1]

The question of when tonality is expressed (and functional) and when not—i.e., that of *atonality* (or nontonality), is among many that are probably incapable of insistent verdict. Some theorists insist that any configuration or concurrence of PCs conveys some inevitable tonal sense, especially in cadential actions, while others consider tonal coherence obliterated in contexts of relatively mild complications. Still others regard any consistent application of a twelve-tone set as a kind of "tonality." Perhaps the "truth" is that examples of altered, diminished, possibly extinguished reflections of tonality in recent music are subject to classification into a number of levels of significance of tonal effect and function (Fig. 1-7).

The tonality-atonality question arises particularly with respect to serial music. Tonic function can of course be obscured by contradictory events, but it is clear that serialized associations of PC materials cannot, on the basis of the prescriptive technique of composition in and of itself, be

Fig. 1-7. Conjectural set of classifications of levels of significance of tonal function.

> "Absolute" atonality?
> Atonality as a relative tendency?
> Irrelevant tonality?
> Multitonality? Pantonality?
> Tonal flux extinguishing, or severely
>   attenuating, tonal function?
> Tonal flux within broad, prevailing tonal unity
> Extended (expanded) tonality
> Tonality of quasi-functional manifestations
> Conventional (major-minor) tonality
> Tonality of ambivalent conventions
> Tonality of modal conventions
> Purely melodic tonality
> Primitive ("pedal") tonality

pronounced necessarily "external" or "irrelevant" to the experience of tonality.

In connection with his discussion of cadential functions and other factors which can be interpreted to point to E as a tonal factor in Schoenberg's *Klavierstück*, Op. 33a, Edward Cone makes the following observations, of significance for our consideration of the relevance of tonal allusion (and tonal analysis) in certain twentieth-century styles:

> More controversial is the attempt to find traces of tonal form in avowedly atonal compositions; yet I do not see how music like Schoenberg's, with its usually clear cadential structure, can fail to arouse certain traditional associations and responses.
> To the charge of irrelevancy, I answer that one who cannot indeed hear such cadential phenomena in this music must judge the analysis to be prescriptive and inapplicable. But one who does hear them must admit to that extent the validity of the approach. He may counter that one ought not to hear the music in this way; but he is then criticizing the music, not the analytical method. Unwanted cadential effects would be as great a flaw in atonal music as the chance appearance of a human figure in a nonrepresentational painting.[64]

We would embrace Cone's concept of "relevance" as vital and necessary in analytical discussions of tonality. In serial works, tonal manifestations may well appear (as often in Schoenberg, for example) in the light of techniques already much discussed in examples of preceding pages. In others, "atonality" or "irrelevant tonality" may indeed be found to pertain. But hierarchic tonal order may be implicit too in a twelve-tone set itself (see the following discussion of the Schoenberg song, *Tot*); some specific twelve-

---

[64]Edward T. Cone, "Analysis Today," in *The Musical Quarterly*, XLVI, 2 (1960), p. 185.

tone sets of obvious, potentially functional tonal possibilities are quoted in Ex. 1-51.

Ex. 1-51. Twelve-tone sets: Berg, Violin Concerto; Luigi Nono, *Canto Sospeso* for soprano, alto, and tenor soloists, mixed choir, and orchestra.

Berg Violin Concerto copyright 1936, Universal Edition. Used by permission of the publisher. Theodore Presser Company, sole representative United States, Canada and Mexico. Nono Canto Sospeso *set reprinted by permission of Ars Viva Verlag.*

The tonal implications of the Nono set are especially evident when (as in No. 6b, *Com' è duro dire addio*) the note A is strongly established at beginning and end as a referential PC. The opening of Part 6b has the tenor voice sustaining (*bocca chiusa*) a¹ for two bars, after which the upper and lower "leading-tones" (notes 2 and 3 of the set) enter. The final cadence of the section takes all twelve notes (mm. 407–11) in order from 1 to 12, then returns the first note, now a³, in the first violin. There is, it seems, a firm sense of tonal resolution.

In the song, *Tot*, by Schoenberg, a tonic element

is supported by two "leading-tones" forming the "quasi-dominant" complex

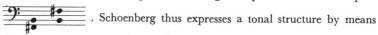 . Schoenberg thus expresses a tonal structure by means

that are free of strict tonal conventions, yet insistent. Examples 1-52a and 1-52b show the composer's applications of the above quasi-tonal functions.

In the excerpts, some suggested primary and secondary tonal implications are indicated. While there are comparable tonal functions at other levels, expressed both melodically and harmonically, those noted are the most vital and pervasive.

In Schoenberg's song, the twelve-tone set is so disposed that when the voice part is based upon the F,C quasi-tonic PCC and its leading-tones, the piano is not, and vice versa. The entire song is an excellent example of quasi-

Ex. 1-52a. Schoenberg, "Tot" ("Lifeless"), from *Drei Lieder*, Op. 48; text by J. Haringer.

Continued allusions to primary F and secondary D by untransposed applications of set in quasi-functional relations; the two "tonics" opposed between voice and piano in mm. 11–13, and between piano strata in mm. 14–16 until cadential "reconciliation:"

Reprinted by permission of Associated Music Publishers, Inc.

tonal functions in a twelve-tone work, and the final cadence significantly realizes tonal expectations, yet is imperfect.[65]

Tonal orientations, which of course would not require realization in actual applications, are potential in the set itself. Schoenberg exploits these particular possibilities (it will be noted that, for example, the final three PCs of the set could have been applied to "tonicize" F♯ as well) in deliberate expression of the primary tonic F and secondary tonic D, in much use of

Ex. 1-52b. Twelve-tone set for the Schoenberg song, "Tot," with potential quasi-tonal affiliations suggested.

[65]Note that the right hand of the piano part in the final two bars, taking the second tetrachord of the row in retrograde order (G, A♭, E, B♭—8, 7, 6, 5), comes out on the low B♭ as final note, lending a functional ambivalence to the F which has been so persistent and nearly constant a tonic center of reference. At the same time, the leading-tones F♯,B and the tritone E,B♭ have in relation to the F,C sonority strongly tonicizing effect.

relevant tetrachordal segments, and in avoidance, although the set is used in retrograde, *of any transpositions.* The second tetrachord has the potential of leaning, dominant-like, toward F, a potential exploited as shown in the quoted excerpts (Ex. 1-52a).

Tonal references may thus, more or less significantly, follow from certain specific properties of the twelve-tone set and its applications, when compositional procedures submit to the implications of such properties: the set fully or partially disposed around a particular axis or axes which, symmetrically applied, may become "spatially" central to the pitch content (as at times in Webern; see Chapter 2, pp. 249–53); intervallic relations implicit or explicit in the set such that potential is established for quasi-functional relations ("dominants," "leading-tones," etc.) supportive of a recurrent PC as "tonic"; such thematic uses of the set as formal "recapitulations" or other recurrences in which a particular variant and transposition of the set takes on quasi-tonal significance in terms of recurrent thematic direction and orientation (e.g., Webern, Op. 22); and the application of the twelve-tone set such that invariant functional relations recur—relations grouping together in disparate set forms invariant adjacencies of two, three, or more PCs having structural predominance; and, of course, rhythmic and other applications in any way lending PC primacy (and, conceivably, hierarchic arrangement centered in that primacy) to a particular element of the set, or elements of the set.

One of the problems in tonal analysis of music in which tonal centers are supported only ambiguously is of course the extent to which analysis should go in the pursuit of and explanation of tonal allusions that are suspected (see p. 171f.). Any music, reduced to its most microcosmic units, obviously has tonal references—i.e., if one considers a work interval by interval nearly any analyst will find in each the experience of one "tonic" (root) or another. Any work, then, can theoretically be regarded as consisting of the constant fluctuation of such "tonics" so that fluctuant tonality is present in every work, even the most "atonal."

The term *pantonal* can refer to a musical situation of the kind suggested above, in which a kind of all-tonality prevails, a constant shifting of tonal reference within the smallest units, and a free combination among textural strata of diverse tonal implications, creating what is analogous to the whiteness of the combination of all colors. In the extreme, such a pantonality must be a *neutralization of tonality*, the extreme spread of tonal reference causing a blurring to the point of extinguishing the effect of any single tonal implication. Pantonality is a concept suggesting a particular perspective for regarding what are also described as "atonal" situations.

This concept may be pertinent to Ex. 1-53, a much-quoted example, in each microcosm of which a tonal center could be said to be implied, but the

Ex. 1-53. Webern, Six Bagatelles for string quartet, Op. 9, first movement.

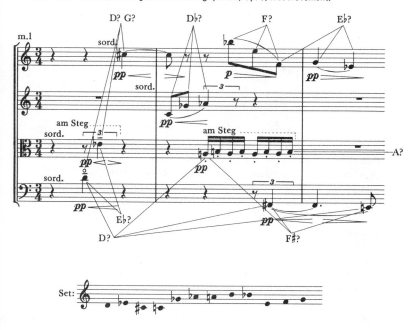

sum of which is so fluctuant as to be a neutralization of tonal feeling. The individual tonal allusions suggested are inherent in Webern's row, which is included in the example.

Whatever results are realized in particular analyses, and these are, again, often in some degree subjectively determined, there is certainly music of the twentieth century in which the aim of the composer is to resist tonal leanings and to achieve what Pousseur calls a "distributive equilibrium—an equilibrium which is directly opposed to that of tonality because its specific harmonic weight is equally distributed at all points" with a resultant "harmonic homogeneity" and "mobility" which, rather than "the thematic rigidity of the series of Schoenberg," are the function of the twelve-tone series.[66] These words seem to state very well the intent and effect of atonality.

[66]Henri Pousseur, "The Question of Order in New Music," in *Perspectives of New Music*, V, 1 (1966), pp. 107–8; translation by David Behrman.

Almost since music began there have been, in given style contexts, complexes of pitches in linear and vertical arrangements by which listeners are conditioned to expect certain responsive succeeding events. These are sometimes conducive to a range of expectations, sometimes very specific in

their implications:

It is thus virtually impossible to exaggerate the significance of tonality in the structure of Western music. Tonal reference and fluctuation are the chief pillars upon which the standard forms of the eighteenth and nineteenth centuries rest, and we have seen that music of the Western tradition before and after what is described as the tonal period is very often dependent on orientation of musical events in relation to a tonic toward which melodic and harmonic elements (perhaps quasi-functional harmonies) are directed. In the vast majority of works of this monumental tradition the language of music is substantially that of dissonance in which cadential and other formal articulative functions are characterized by fulfillment, nonfulfillment, or limited fulfillment of expectations aroused and conditioned by prior assertion of a tonic and its structural, hierarchic system.

Foregoing examples have demonstrated that many twentieth-century composers have sought to achieve new ways of establishing tonal feeling, without altogether dismissing the idea of order around a tonal center, or complex of centers, or tonal axis, with tonal homogeneity a fundamental source of unity and tonal contrast of variety, or with relative stability of tonic opposed in formal delineations to its controlled fluctuation and, at times, relative obscurity.

While the many examples cited in this chapter, diverse as they are in style and historical orientation, give testimony to the vast importance of tonality in the determination of musical structure, our chief purpose has been to show how in various idioms tonality is established and made to fluctuate, and *to demonstrate techniques in the analysis of tonality within a wide gamut of genres and styles.* The analytical techniques incorporated in this study are of an intentionally heterodox scope; their aim is the discovery of tonal structure, range, and system pertinent to the individual work (or at times more broadly to classes of works), and the special means by which tonal structure is expanded and modulated in accord with expressive needs.

When tonality is abandoned, such factors as the recurrence and variation of melodic-rhythmic theme become basic, as do the shaping effects of rhythmic elements, dynamic contrasts, and functional contrasts of texture.

The extent to which tonality is resisted or dismissed in music is thus normally the extent to which other elements—color, texture, rhythm, and others—have ascendant significance, with the controlled distribution of contrasts and affinities among these elements, and among their individual manifestations in progressive and recessive operations, determining structure.

Concluding notes

The foregoing analyses deal with the question of *tonal and linear functions* in melodic and harmonic contexts in which tonality is of essential importance, with a few exceptions in which particular issues are explored apart from such primary concerns. We have seen that in most music linear and tonal functions coincide, and a central point has been that harmonic and melodic analysis is properly viewed from the perspectives of differing structural levels in which events have differing implications.

One of the main points of discussion has thus been that analysis must discover the various *levels* of structural function. The most immediate is that level which is the object of analysis seeking to identify tonal and linear implications of all the notes the composer has written. But an event that is of essential function at a given level, e.g., a cadential note, is often seen to have at other levels auxiliary function in relation to structural factors of higher hierarchic order. It is this kind of consideration that leads to the identification of structural profiles which are more and more fundamental, and which underly that of the harmonic-melodic surface. Still, in the surface reside many, probably most, of the characteristic features by which the uniqueness of expressive power is felt. (It might well be that all the melodies of Mozart, transposed to C and reduced to fundamental structural bases, would look very much alike.)

In some of the foregoing analyses we have been concerned with supplementary, important approaches. Harmonic and tonal rhythms are such a concern, as are considerations of dissonance-consonance fluctuation and of density fluctuation, especially in styles in which tonal implications are obscured. Melodic curve, motivic unities, and rates of eventfulness are other such important supplementary concerns. And in music in which harmonic colors are an important factor in themselves, sometimes independently of tonal function, we have noted that auxiliary chords are often introduced for relatively pure linear function and for their sonorous qualities, even in parallel, nonfunctional streams or complexes of like sonorities in elaborative formulations.

Analysis cannot hope to point to a single, "correct" conception of structural functions. To make this clear and to remind the reader from time to time that in most music a number of analyses can be shown to be admissible, we have repeatedly used the word *interpretation* to describe the results of analysis. The skillful analyst learns, however, to make the most valid possible choices among conceivable suggested interpretations of a given example, on the basis of procedures and criteria of judgment of the most persuasive possible substance.

Chapter 1 will have to be seen, ultimately, in the total context of which it is an aspect. The concerns of the remaining chapters are with texture and rhythm in music; fundamentally, this book regards musical effect and experience as deriving from the complementary and counteractive functional associations of all element-actions. The comprehensive analysis of music must take all into account, and must see, ultimately, their progressive and recessive actions in interrelations by which expressive effect is realized.

NOTES

[a]In the same collection occur many other examples of potential value in these connections, and while space does not permit their investigation here the reader is advised that he will find this basic, rich anthology a fertile ground for study of early tonal structures. For instance, a later Renaissance composition, the delightfully spirited *chanson* of Lasso, *Bon jour mon coeur,* p. 159, might be analyzed from the standpoint of a tonal structure on G which can sound to modern ears ambivalent in its modal F♮ and consequent leaning toward C, and in tonicizations of D and even A in tentative tonal expansions a step beyond that of Ex. 1-7 (foreseeing the later tonal principle of expansion to the level of the dominant beyond the dominant), and relative homorhythm in which the lower voice moves a great deal in 5ths and 4ths. The tonal system of the Lasso example might well be seen to have the following, symmetrical image:

[b]Measures 19–37 of the same piece reveal a comparable expansion of the tonal system in the prolongation of T:I. Secondary tonics b♭ and D♭ (both diatonic factors in t) occur. Moreover, a synoptic sketch of the bass shows a linear expression of t:iv—

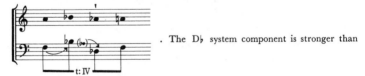

. The D♭ system component is stronger than

any of the fluctuant tonal allusions to this point; it is continued, with its own auxiliary subdominant and dominant functions, for seven measures. The two Liszt examples show tonal expansion in elaboration of harmonic progression (T:I-V) and prolongation (T:I-I).

[c]A comparable example of the principle more broadly applied is Brahms' Intermezzo in A minor, Op. 118, No. 1. In that piece the primary tonic (a) is strongly affirmed at the end, supported by a strong dominant pedal. But the first primary dominant is in m. 11, the first tonic (very brief) in m. 19. Thus, the primary tonic is embellished by fluctuation at the outset, and in a sense the fluctuation is more radical than in Op. 53 since the first measure is itself a secondary tonal reference. There are passing refer-

ences to F, G, and C before the first primary leading-tone appears. Even thereafter the music obscures the primary tonic more than it supports it. The structural importance of the primary tonic is that it draws into focus following the tonal ambiguity which is the chief tonal feature of most of the form. There are, in the fluctuant areas of the Intermezzo, certain hints of the ultimate tonal course: the substitution of a six-four on A in m. 2 for the expected resolution of the F:V₇; the augmented 6th in m. 5, which "expects" A:V but does not produce it; and other abortive references to functions which, in their normal contexts, would be supportive of the primary tonic. Similarly, there are after the final, long dominant pedal, reminiscences of earlier tonal deviations—e.g., the B♭ of m. 35 (part of a dominant of the subdominant), and the F-C appoggiatura over the primary dominant of mm. 37–38. A synopsis of the bass succession might be as follows; it shows again the principle of linear expression of t : i, and the tonal system components are a, F, C—factors in the F:I (F = SD/R/t), F being the system of reference with which the tonal structure sets out. Thus, of the two most fundamental triads of reference, the overall bass line expresses one and a resumé of tonal system components expresses the other:

ᵈA remarkably comparable example for melodic analysis can be found in mm. 12–19 of the first violin part, second movement, of Bartók's Divertimento for string orchestra: its essential course runs from a♭¹ (established and prolonged differently but with comparably strong effect) to d³, again in a tritonal essential movement. The reader will find in the Bartók melody the technique of sequence (repeated motivic units transposed in a conjunct succession of subsidiary high points of largely diatonic relation):

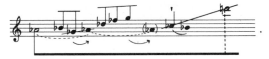

ᵉIn *Accenti*, second piece of the piano set *Quaderno Musicale di Annalibera*, by Luigi Dallapiccola, the single note which emerges out of the harmonically dense motive (the final note of the form of the serial hexachord used in the given instance) often takes on a tonal meaning simply because, in its severe isolation and dynamic stress, it has the effect of "resolving" the preceding, intense dissonance and density. When there are harmonic or melodic elements that support the feeling of tonal resolution at the same time, that feeling is of course enormously strengthened. Thus, at the piece's final cadence a strong sense of tonal fulfillment arises from the quasi-dominant character of the outer voices of the harmony of the final measure (B and D♯) as well as the chromatic succession in "moving" voices: C♯-D-D♯-E. Whether this is the composer's intent cannot be said, but there can be little question that these factors impart tonal impressions and, thereby, stronger impact to the powerful cadential thrust with which the piece ends.

Another example useful for study in the same connection is the first of Webern's Five Pieces for orchestra, Op. 10, in which a concluding, reiterated F, in an atmosphere of severely reduced texture, has the effect of quasi-tonal resolution. The piece should be studied for evidences, of which many could be cited, of quasi-functional projections of (or expectant suggestions of) F, and A and C, in the pitch materials of the piece. [For example, last notes of the trumpet—F, G, A, F; trumpet and trombone of mm. 6–7, centering on F; the "leading-tone" E in the flute motive of mm. 8–9; clarinet phrase of mm. 4–7, centering on F and A; or the succession E (flute)-F-F♯-G(violin)-A-G♯(cello) preceding and supportive of tonal feeling in the final, isolated F.]

ᶠCertainly it must be acknowledged that the analyst will find many instances of apparently arbitrarily and rapidly fluctuant change, or static dissonance effect, in recent styles. The third of Schoenberg's set of piano pieces, Op. 19, is a case in point: dissonance seems relatively fixed in intensity, as is harmonic density (pitch factors of four and five in chords throughout the piece). At the same time, the piece's structure is compellingly shaped by other factors—quasi-tonal function and harmonic rhythm are of particular importance within the harmonic element, not to mention the shaping effects of other element-fluctuations (spatial field, movements of line, rhythms of attack, directions of dynamic intensity, etc.). It must not be assumed, then, that dissonance fluctuation is necessarily a significant factor in the shaping of structure. The discussion of the Op. 23 extract involves only two-note simultaneities; where chords are concerned the evaluation of dissonance quality and process involves appraisal of such quality as the sum of interval properties in chords. This can be calculated in a number of ways, and again a judgment must be made as to significance of dissonance quality in intervallic relations between the lowest in relation to upper voices, the upper in relation to lower voices, or all intervallic relations among all voices in the texture.

ᵍIn the third of Eight Etudes and a Fantasy for woodwind quartet, Elliott Carter develops his form entirely out of coloristic contrasts, since the Etude is entirely an expression of the D major triad without change in its position or distribution and without auxiliary notes or harmonies. Only the assignment of notes of the triad among the four instruments changes. It is perhaps the most elemental expression of tonality that is possible to imagine and it is, in this piece, of striking effectiveness, although it is of course a device that does not bear repetition.

ʰWhen early modal scales are used as resources in melody and diatonic harmony in twentieth-century styles, as they are not infrequently, especially in earlier music of this century, they create the same modal/tonal ambivalences one often associates with works of, say, the sixteenth century, in which, for example, the mixolydian lowered $\hat{7}$ can to modern ears effect a leaning toward the region of the subdominant. For example, the first thirteen measures of Bartók's Divertimento for string orchestra, third movement, sustain, in intense tonal reference, a quasi-augmented-6th harmony of primary dominant function. It is followed by a V-I root succession setting off the principal thematic element, a mixolydian melody which, while on an F tonic, leans toward B♭.

ⁱIn this piece, the reader may wish to evaluate dissonance fluctuation in the light of the composer's own specifications of dissonance in the source cited on p. 110. A number of cadential successions show what appears to be a very purposeful dissonance control: mm. 14–15, in the direction of milder dissonance (note, too, the voice-leading determinants: outer voice contrary motion, and more conjunct inner voice); m. 11, an appoggiatura figure whose pattern of dissonance release is very evident when the tenor and soprano voices are regarded independently; and m. 6, both of whose harmonies contain sharp dissonances, but in which there is nevertheless a sense of release occasioned by the fact that in the first harmony the dissonance occurs between outer voices while in the second it is relegated to an inner position with the consonant major 10th between outer voices—a good example of the *mitigating influence of spacing and distribution* in harmonic dissonance effect. In mm. 18–22, the general increase in dissonance intensity seems to be a compensation for relative rhythmic inertia; and toward m. 30 there is a distinct mounting of dissonance (and steady increase in density) toward climax.

ʲRavel's *Surgi de la croupe et du bond* (No. 3 of *Trois Poèmes de Mallarmé*) might be cited as an example in which tonal structure is *not* confirmed, i.e., is left open, at the conclusion. The early, relatively concise tonal expressions (of D major) deteriorate at its conclusion, where there is only the slightest hint of the original tonic. The final harmony is a combination of dominant on C, to which the bass has progressed in chromatic descent from E, and an A major triad with F♯ added and not resolved. (This latter, if construed as a primary dominant, is the only, faint allusion to the initiating D system.) Tonal clarity thus substantially dissolves in the final cadence. In this sense, the tonal structure is illustrative of opposition of stability and instability (relative clarity and ambiguity) as shaping features. The earlier example from Brahms (1-14) and the Brahms Intermezzo, Op. 118, No. 1, cited in footnote description on pp. 180–81, reveal a pattern in which instability of tonal reference gives way to ultimate, strong clarification; the Ravel does just the opposite:

[k]It was suggested earlier that the two most prominent "tonic" sonorities, harmonically conjoined, provide the intervallic basis for the recurrent motive of superimposed

The collection of these motives at the end of the movement can be seen as a whole-tone series in which, as noted, basic tonal factors are recalled:

The last of the motive statements, that of mm. 138–39, is tonally the most deviant, but it is strongly functional in reemphasizing, at a penultimate point, the B♭ upper leading-tone with which the violin phrase had concluded, at the same time providing a tonally distant perspective against which the ultimate cadential release is strikingly enhanced in effect:

[l]Relatively anomalous techniques of tonal usage like bitonality and polytonality are not treated as such in this study, but in a bitonal situation (e.g., Stravinsky, *Symphonies of Wind Instruments*, 1947 revision, following rehearsal No. 11, where different tonics are actively and deliberately opposed) the expression of tonal center at each stratum is likely to be in accord with techniques and functions like those noted in this chapter. Indeed, it is characteristic of most multitonal usage that each stratum asserts its "independent" tonal center in a very direct, even primitive, manner, as in the Stravinsky example cited.

texture

Introductory notes

Certain of the qualities and classifications of musical texture have been treated abundantly in the work of music theorists; references to relative densities and sparsities of texture, to categories of description such as polyphonic or monophonic, and to many other features and types of musical fabric are common. But adequate formulation has not been given to analytical treatment of processes involving textural events and changes, or to the significances of these in the structure of music.

What *is* musical texture? The texture of music consists of its sounding components; it is conditioned in part by the number of those components sounding in simultaneity or concurrence,[1] its qualities determined by the interactions, interrelations, and relative projections and substances of component lines or other component sounding factors.

Density may be seen as the quantitative aspect of texture—the number of concurrent events (the thickness of the fabric) as well as the degree of "compression" of events within a given intervallic space. There is a vital relation between density and dissonance; the relative intensity of a highly compressed textural complex (say, three components within the range of a minor 3rd) is a product of the severity of dissonance as well as of density.

Furthermore, density clearly has a relation to coloration; thus, two simultaneous pitches sounding in tight compression (say, a major 2nd apart) will project varying degrees of intensity depending on relative homogeneity of coloration (e.g., two clarinets, *forte*) as opposed to dissimilar coloration in which the proximity in musical space seems attenuated by the separation implied in the disparity of color. Similarly, intense dynamic levels exaggerate

---

[1]The term "concurrent" or "concurrence" is used in the sense of "occurring together" —coexisting, intersecting, overlapping in real time. Two lines are in some degree, and *at some specified level,* concurrent if they overlap in any part. Concurrence of individual sounds is only of the moment of sounding together, unless such sounds are parts of concurrent lines.

184

the effect of spatial compression. Relations between coloration and density could be traced far beyond these simple observations.

The nature of interactions and interrelations within the musical fabric, apart from calculable density, might be said to constitute the *qualitative*, as distinct from the purely *quantitative*, aspect of texture. Thus, in conventional broad lines of classification, monophony is a type of texture, and a condition in which certain qualitative features of texture apply. Unlike textures of two or more concurrent components (chordal, polyphonic) monophony is explicit in its condition of minimal density. Examples which follow will be much involved with the demonstration of musical progression and recession as shaped by changes *both in density and in the qualitative interactions of the components of musical texture*. Reference will be made as well to the applications of such changes in the delineation of forms—as, for example, in the emergence of polyphony in developmental contexts, the stabilization of textures in cadential formulations, ·or the common association of relatively uncomplicated texture with thematic statement.

Of necessity in the analysis of textural *qualities* is the evaluation of various kinds of interrelations and interactions among textural components— the degree and nature of interlinear concordance (agreement, lack of conflict) or coincident factors of relative intensity and variance (counterpoint). Changes in relative *independence and interdependence* among concurrent components in a given musical texture will be seen to constitute some of the most decisive (and subtle) factors in the expressive shaping of structure. Much of the attention of this chapter will be devoted to considerations of *textural progression and recession* as shaped by such changes in interlinear relations and in qualitative and quantitative textural conditions, and to the convergence or contrast between a textural structure and those of other elements.

The complementary and compensatory relations of texture with other elements of structure will be evident in examples analyzed in this chapter. A simple instance may be cited: that in which, for example, heavier, greater densities seem frequently to "require" relatively reduced rhythmic activity. Other relations of complementation and counteraction (compensation) between textural and other factors are suggested, for example, in foregoing references to coloration and texture.

If a single pitch is sounded, a texture (here, one of maximal simplicity) is established. If a second pitch is sounded in simultaneity, the texture is altered—its density is increased. If the two pitches are a 2nd apart and they are succeeded by two pitches a 6th apart (the upper moving up a 4th, the lower down a 2nd), a textural "event" takes place—a succession involving not pure quantity (density-number) but involving density-compression and a number of important qualitative factors *in the texture viewed independently of other elements*. (An incipient quality of interlinear independence is asserted in the opposition of direction of movement—a quality subject to enhancement if rhythmic differentiation in the relations is introduced.)

Two lines moving in parallel 3rds may in an important sense be said to constitute a single *real* textural factor consisting of two *components*.[2] At any point at which differentiation is established—in rhythm, in direction of motion, in the distance of motion, or in any other sense—a texture initially consisting of a *single real factor* (of two sounding components) becomes a texture of *two real factors* (or at least progresses in the direction of such differentiation). Progressions and recessions involving changes of these kinds or of analogous effect are decisive in the shaping of musical structure. The foregoing extremely simple illustrations are suggestive of proposed distinctions among implications of factors of quantity and quality in musical texture, both subject to a vast range of subtle and constantly changing features.

The sections immediately following are concerned with the theory and terminology of musical texture, and with further fundamental considerations of the means by which textures undergo quantitative and qualitative modifications in functional events and in the delineation of forms and structures.

Textural progression, recession, and variation as structural factors

Example 2-1a serves as a very simple, but exceedingly vivid, instance of progression and recession within the element of texture.

In the example, there is progressive development of textural complexity toward m. 4 and recessive decline in that complexity (toward textural accord and simplicity) in approach to the cadence at m. 7. The changes in degrees of density and textural diversity—the succession toward maximal interlinear independence and thence toward textural homogeneity—can be traced by evaluation of the numbers of sounding and "real" components at each point of significant change. The exposition of the brief subject, presented in overlapping imitative entries at harmonic intervals of the 4th and 5th, is conventional. Less standard in procedure, but important in the expressive quality as an element of asymmetry, is the variation in *time interval* of imitation: 2♩, 4♩, 2♩. The accrual of voices, their relative independence (in the directly vertical sense) asserted by rhythmic and/or directional differen-

---

[2]The term "component" may refer generically to any textural ingredient or factor as indicated in the immediate context of consideration, and as qualified by such adjectival modifiers as "real" component, "inactive" component, "doubling" component, etc.

Ex. 2-1a. Milhaud, Six Sonnets for mixed chorus ; No. 3, *A peine si le coeur vous a considérées, images et figures* (If the heart has scarcely considered you, images and impressions), on text of J. Cassou.

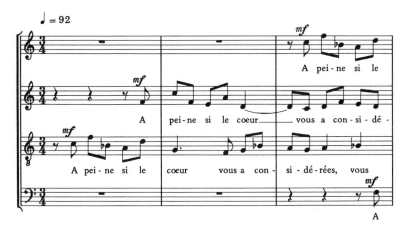

Reprinted by permission of Heugel & Cie., Paris, France.

tiations, can be represented as follows: $1 \ \dfrac{1}{\underline{1}} \ \dfrac{\left(\dfrac{1}{\left(\underline{1}\right)}\right)}{1} \ \dfrac{1}{\dfrac{1}{\underline{1}}}$,[3] the latter condition of

maximal diversity achieved at m. 4, with the entry of the fourth voice. At the end of m. 4 and the beginning of m. 5 the upper two voices become associated in parallel rhythms and directions (we are overlooking minor differentiations in interval of motion at the most foreground level); this condition might be represented by the symbol $\dfrac{2}{\underline{1}}$ —showing three *real* components and four *sounding* components—the first significant decline in the textural diversity. Immediately subsequently the lower voices are disposed in comparable association: $\dfrac{2}{2}$, representing a further decline in textural diversity and complexity (but none in density-number[4]). Finally, at the approach to the cadence, all four voices become strongly *interdependent* in both rhythm and direction of movement (with octave duplications)—a vital factor in the expression of cadence.

Two extremely foreground factors might be noted in extension of the analysis in Ex. 2-1b. First, in the recessive process distinctions of intervallic

Ex. 2-1b. Qualitative and quantitative textural progression and qualitative recession in the Milhaud excerpt.

$$1 \quad \frac{1}{\underline{1}} \quad \frac{\dfrac{1}{\underline{1}}}{\underline{1}} \quad \frac{\dfrac{1}{\underline{1}}}{\underline{1}} \quad \frac{\dfrac{2}{\underline{1}}}{\underline{1}} \quad \frac{2}{\underline{2}} \quad \underline{4}$$

Quality curve (as conditioned by changes in independence-interdependence)

Quantity (density-number) curve

[3]In this symbolization, the actual vertical *alignment* of voices is not necessarily represented. Parentheses may denote a component having independence or substance in some way restricted.

[4]The term "density-number" will be used to distinguish this parameter of density from that of "density-compression," briefly noted earlier. These two aspects of density constitute texture's quantitative dimension; both have further treatment later in this chapter.

content among the various components continue to occasion modest diversity so that, for example, in a situation of almost consistent homogeneity (m. 6) as many as three different ascending leaps are projected.[5] A second very local factor can be seen in the cadence itself, where in one sense there are four components (four different pitches and concluding successions), in another sense one (the agreement of all four voices in rhythm and direction), and in another sense two (octave duplications of soprano-tenor and alto-bass). The analysis suggested in Ex. 2-1b traces the textural process more broadly, omitting any accounting of such local, minor differences, but it is important that they be mentioned as indication of the complexity of even modest textural development and analysis beyond relatively categorical observations.

The foregoing example illustrates very simply the concept of textural progression and recession, *the controlled shaping of textural events* (here, *both quantitative and qualitative*) *in specific structural functions* (here, *of development and cadence*). Changes in texture—surely quantitative changes, but those involving textural qualities as well—*are often among the most readily perceptible and appreciable in the experience of music.*

An example from Josquin is drawn from a setting of the *De profundis* (Ex. 2-2).

The example is a beautiful illustration of the controlled "sloping" of textural structure. The phrase is characterized, in its texture, by significant interdependences of the two lines at the beginning and end, and by significant independences in its central portion. The complementary relation of the textural processes to the melodic structure of the superius is stunningly effective, as is the complementary application of rhythmic technique—syncopation and dotted rhythm at the climactic point.

The association of the two lines at the phrase extremities is not without diversification: at the outset, there is consistent rhythmic identity but oblique, then contrary, motion; and there is some directional opposition within the homorhythmic approach to the cadence. The internal portion is characterized by rhythmic *and* directional differentiation. The phrase is thus an illustration of progressive diversification toward a point of relative intensity, and of the cadential function of increased interlinear interdependence. In the kind of symbology which has begun to emerge in these discussions the example might be said broadly to progress, then recede, from 2 to $\frac{1}{1}$ to 2.

These two examples expose, of course, only some of many parameters of textural shaping; other examples will pose other kinds of issues and reveal other functional, expressive, processive operations.

It seems clear that what we have described as textural "diversity" (complexity, activity—like density an aspect of intensity in the texture) seeks

[5]This textural condition is identified as *heterophony*.

Ex. 2-2. Josquin, *De profundis clamavi* (Motet).

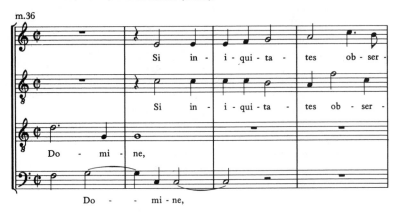

Reprinted from the Smijers edition, published by G. Alsbach and Co., Amsterdam, by permission of Creyghton Musicology-Musica Antiqua, Bilthoven, Netherlands.

release in what we have described as reduced interlinear independence (i.e., textural interdependence, accord, homogeneity, simplicity, inactivity). Thus, progression toward increased levels of diversity and interaction creates the sense of need for reconformity, an expectation that the trend toward complexity will be reversed in cadential expression. Like dissonance, rhythmic acceleration, ascent in pitch, etc., the progressive complication and diversification of musical texture are assumed to be evocative of the impression of rising intensity, an intensity which increases the more the progression is prolonged.

Types of musical texture; problems of classification and terminology

Texture is conceived as that element of musical structure shaped (determined, conditioned) by the voice or number of voices and other components projecting the musical materials in the sounding medium, and (when there are two or more components) by the interrelations and interactions among them.

Except, of course, in monophonic textures, the evaluation of interrelations and comparative substance (of motive, of activity or stasis, etc.) in and among the components of the texture is the all-important problem of analysis both toward the characterization of the textural class and toward the analysis and understanding of functional successions of textural events. Rhythm is surely the most critical factor in interlinear relations; thus, within the independence-interdependence scale of textural "values" it is the most decisive factor in the assertion of interlinear opposition (diversity, resistance, counterpoint). Attention is essential too to interrelations of motivic material (including imitation), intervallic content, directional opposition, and dissonance, as well as number and degrees of proximity in the "vertical" alignment of events, i.e., density.[6]

One is reluctant, as always, to make the problem of terminology a central issue; nevertheless, a part of the business of music theory is lexical, and words (along with some concordance of understanding as to what they signify) are essential to discourse. Complex hyphenated terminological forms which follow from the system outlined here are rarely needed (but are nonetheless logically plausible and fitting); and it is always possible simply to describe events, even though terms denotative of textural conditions and classes are a useful convenience.

If allowance can be understood for the difficulties of firm and arbitrary distinction within any spectrum of textural classifications, and if it can be well understood that any musical instance, seen beyond most local events, is

---

[6]*Density* is defined as that textural parameter, quantitative and measurable, conditioned by the number of simultaneous or concurrent components and by the extent of vertical "space" encompassing them: *density-number* and *density-compression*. It is interesting that the two aspects of texture termed density-compression and *texture-space* (developed later as the overall field or ambitus in which events take place) are necessarily contradictory in progressive or recessive inclinations, assuming a fixed density-number. Thus, the inflation of texture-space is regarded as an intensifying factor ("expecting" recontraction) and increase in density-compression similarly intensifying (cf. dissonance, and the exacerbated interlinear "conflict" of highly "crowded" events). The fact is that cadential processes in music are more often than not operations toward spatial contraction and, consequently, normally increased density-compression in relation to which such recessive factors as consonance and textural simplicity, as well as linear decline and any number of further recessive element-successions, function compensatorily.

likely to represent a mixture of such classifications, there will be value in the statement of proposed terminology.

Certain *widely used terms of relatively firm conventional signification* can be accepted as generally understood.

1. *Polyphonic,* while literally meaning "many-voiced," can serve to denote, as conventionally, multivoiced texture of considerable interlinear independence, often imitative; it is thus generally understood to have qualitative implications beyond its literal, limited meaning.

2. *Homophonic* would literally denote a condition of interdependent voices, but its traditional connotation is that of texture in which a primary voice is accompanied by a subordinate fabric sometimes interactive in tentative ways, the bass normally in a contradirectional or other contrapuntal relation to the primary voice (or voices).

3. *Chordal* is a perfectly acceptable, and very useful, conventional term referring simply to texture consisting essentially of chords, its voices often relatively homorhythmically related.

4. *Doubling* can denote lines homorhythmically-homodirectionally-homointervallically associated (see the following definitions of these terms).

5. *Mirror* association, usually understood as strict, involves a relation that is homorhythmic-homointervallic-*contradirectional*; again, it is a term in common usage.

6. *Heterophonic* is understood to denote a relation that is homodirectional (parallel in contour) but heterointervallic (see below)—having minor diversification of interval content.

7. *Heterorhythmic* is a conventional term adopted in accord with its conventional signification (see below).

8. *Sonority* may be defined as the overall sonorous character determined by texture (including doublings) and coloration (including articulation and intensity of dynamics).

9. *Counterpoint (contrapuntal)* denotes a condition of interlinear interaction involving intervallic content, direction, rhythm, and other qualities or parameters of diversification. (The traditional usage of "contrapuntal" is comparable to that of "polyphonic.")

10. *Monophonic* is taken, as conventionally, to mean single-voiced (monolinear).

Beyond the above, it seems appropriate to formulate certain terms which can be used to apply with some precision to specific conditions of interlinear relation in multivoiced (or two-voiced) and multilinear textures.[7]

---

[7] In this study the term *line* refers to any textural component in which horizontal relation and configuration can plausibly be traced as a logical continuity—an identifiable stratum in the texture at some given level. The term *voice* will normally denote a line having distinct relative independence; it may thus be a complex of doubled lines, but is not itself

A system-scale (spectrum) of textural conditions or "values" from simple (e.g., monophonic) to complex (e.g., ultimately multivoiced, contra-rhythmic-contraintervallic-contradirectional,[8] the highest manifestation of polyphony) can be established as a lexical basis for description of relations among textural components which are concurrent or simultaneous *at some given level.*

In the following system the prefixes *homo-* (*uni-*, or *co-*),[9] *hetero-*, and *contra-*[10] are adopted to refer to conditions of identity, mild and *very local* diversification (as in the conventional "heterophonic"), and more pronounced contrast, respectively. Moreover, three specific parameters (aspects, dimensions, spheres of reference) are adopted as relevant to the evaluation of textural conditions: these are *rhythm* (specifically rhythmic pattern), *direction* (of melodic succession), and *linear intervallic content.*[11]

1. Within the parameter of rhythm, the terms *homorhythmic, heterorhythmic* (both of these in conventional usage), and *contrarhythmic* all emerge as potentially applicable and useful.

2. Within the parameter of direction, the terms *homodirectional, heterodirectional,* and *contradirectional* ("motion" in a straight line exists as a possibility along with motion up and down) all have potential applicability to relations among components of texture.

---

capable of doubling. The term *multilinear* (also bilinear, trilinear, etc.) can thus be used to denote texture of more than one simultaneous or concurrent component. As a rule *multivoiced* (two-voiced, three-voiced, many-voiced) has qualitative implications. (Polyphonic, as noted earlier, strictly means the same thing and has conventional implications of qualitative diversification.) Within these distinctions, which seem necessary and unavoidable in discussion of musical texture, monophonic (single-voiced) texture can of course be multilinear; *line* is the more generic concept.

[8]While such hyphenated terms are rarely needed, they might be used in precise reference to a complex of specific conditions of interlinear relation. It is more usual to refer to single parameters of consideration (e.g., homorhythmic, or heterointervallic), or perhaps to two conjoined parameters of reference in hyphenated terms like contraintervallic-homodirectional.

[9]Applications of the prefix *homo-* are simply an extension of conventional usage, as in "homorhythmic."

[10]While the term "polyrhythmic" (cf. the possible "birhythmic," "triintervallic," "bidirectional," etc.) is a reasonable and perhaps admissible synonym for "contrarhythmic," it is often used in a sense more properly expressed as "polymetric" (a distinction developed in Chapter 3).

[11]Beyond the terminological system outlined here, phrases like "rhythmic contrast," "intervallic conformity," "directional opposition," etc., are freely used to describe particular relations.

An *interval class* (IC) includes any given interval within the octave together with its inversion (complement) and all compound extensions (expansions by one or more octaves) of the given interval or its inversion. If enharmonically equivalent forms are considered of the same class, there are six interval classes (the unison excluded); the issue of enharmonic identity is, of course, one of the appropriateness of functional distinctions among enharmonic equivalents within any given idiom.

3. Within the sphere of intervallic content, the terms *homointervallic* [applicable to IC (interval class), interval complement, specific interval, etc., as are all terms within this group—a distinction to be clarified when appropriate], *heterointervallic* (regarded as synomous with the conventional *heterophonic*), and *contraintervallic* can all be used to describe particular textural situations and relations, usually applying to specific intervals rather than classes.

Of vital, general importance is the need in all analysis or description of musical texture and textural conditions to maintain awareness of the *level of structure* to which reference is made. (Thus, two lines may have contradirectional relation in a local sense but be seen, significantly, to have homodirectional association at a broader level.)

Example 2-3 is a list of very brief, contrived examples in illustration of the foregoing system of terminological classification.

Ex. 2-3.

Relations at the level (within the temporal context) illustrated

homorhythmic

heterorhythmic

contrarhythmic

homodirectional

heterodirectional*

contradirectional

*Applicable at levels of one, two, or three bars.

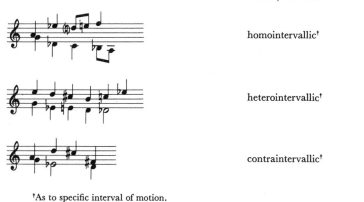

Relations at the level (within the temporal context) illustrated

homointervallic[†]

heterointervallic[†]

contraintervallic[†]

[†]As to specific interval of motion.

Some further considerations of terminology and aspects of texture

Doubling does not result in interlinear interdependence of any certain, absolute degree: the interval of doubling has much to do with the extent of association between two doubled components, even when the doubling is absolutely strict. This fact has to be taken into account in evaluation of a textural situation in which doubling occurs, and it can be appreciated if the differences in degree of interdependence (or "fusion") are considered when doubling is at the octave [duplication of PC (pitch-class)], with texture-space and sonority affected but with the qualitative association of the doubled lines virtually complete, as opposed to a situation in which the interval of doubling is dissonant (e.g., 2nd, or 7th), where individual components assert a greater degree of independence. The factor of interval of doubling and its impact with respect to interlinear independence *is one of dissonance and of size* (or distance between the doubled components). Of course, any doubling at whatever interval greatly compromises the relative independence of lines.[12]

[12]It is not clear whether considerable space between two lines is conducive to greater independence, or whether, on the other hand, a small distance (with dissonance, as in doubling in 2nds) occasions a heightened interlinear resistance (conflict = independence) than does a larger interval. The complexity of this problem is further evident when one considers the impact of specific interval size as opposed to IC in, for example, a relation which is contraintervallic but homodirectional, and when the disparity of interval of motion has one component moving by, say, the compound form of that of the other: a 10th with a 3rd. Presumably, the relative independence manifest in the larger interval of motion is considerable, despite the affinity of IC. No doubt one might go on to hypothesize situations posing

It is noted above that there is one aspect of texture which *is* affected significantly by doubling at octave or compound-octave distances. Attention is given later to the range of the sounding complex (its space, and the profiles delineated in spatial changes) as an aspect of texture particularly important in certain styles. In the analysis of texture-space, and in the evaluation of progressions and recessions formed by its increases and decreases, octave duplications are of course significant. We shall adopt the term *texture-space* (or simply "space") in referring to this aspect (range, field, compass, ambitus) of texture.

Example 2-4 consists of three brief extracts from the Stravinsky Variations for orchestra, a work of importantly texture-conditioning structure. Our concern here is chiefly with illustrating some of the conditions and distinctions of terminology with which we are currently involved; the examples also indicate some complexities of the problem of evaluation of textural relations, and some of the features of textural process to be developed in later analyses.

The initial utterance is homodirectional (resulting in considerable interdependence of component lines) but contraintervallic, a factor to which any degree of interlinear independence is attributable. The subsequent, responsive motive of flutes and strings pits one concurrent choir against the other in a contradirectional relation (denoting a qualitative increase in textural diversity).

The line between heterointervallic (heterophonic) and contraintervallic texture is tenuous but significant: the strings as a group are in heterointervallic association, the flutes contraintervallically related.[13] Within the strings, while celli and violins both have ascending tritonal leaps (a homointervallic relation as to class), they are differentiated in PC—the doubling is in fact at a highly dissonant interval, as well as in typical (for Stravinsky) heterorhythm. The texture of the flutes is homorhythmic and homodirectional, that of the strings heterorhythmic-heterodirectional. That of the entire sounding complex is heterorhythmic-contradirectional-contraintervallic.[14]

---

comparable questions; but the underlying point is that each textural situation will, beyond certain important generalities, pose issues particular to itself.

It is assumed that doubling by perfect intervals, especially the octave, and to a lesser degree consonant 3rds and 6ths, produces a higher degree of interlinear interdependence than other doublings. Doubling at the unison of course does not affect texture at all—not even its spatial aspect, but only sonority.

[13]Within each such relation is likeness (flutes 1–2, and between viola's lower line and cello) involving duplication of IC but disparity of distance—i.e., occurrence of simple with compound forms of the same intervals.

[14]The overall texture of flutes and strings together might be described as of eight *sounding* components (lines), while of the following numbers of *real* components within each of the three parameters of differentiation: in the rhythmic relation, 1; in directional relation, 2; in intervallic relation, 5 (or 4 as to IC).

Ex. 2-4. Stravinsky, Variations for orchestra (Aldous Huxley *in memoriam*).

*All instruments sound as written.

Ex. 2-4 continued.

Both motives of m. 1 are activated by devices of coloration:[15] the articulative doublings of chords in piano, then harp. It is clear that, in summary, the relation between the two utterances of m. 1 is one of progressive tendency toward textural diversification (and expansion of texture-space) in what is perceived as *a textural event of important, although local, structural significance.* The discussion of m. 1 is indicative of the potential complexities of analytical treatment of apparently simple textural conditions, all of them significant factors in textural *effect.*

The second quotation (m. 6) is given in illustration of a *single voice* heavily underscored in coloration and sonority. It is, of course, an extremely potent monophonic statement, with a variety of colors and articulations. In this instance, all doublings but one are unison duplications—of PC *and* pitch *and* interval of motion, as well as of direction; the texture-space is thus affected no more than its monophonic class. (One lower octave doubling does momentarily extend the space, as the double-bass launches the ascending motion with its initiating attack. And there is some heterorhythmic diversification, e.g., in the activating role of the harp.)

The beautiful phrase quoted as the third of the extracts, mm. 20–22, is a further useful illustration. It is strikingly interesting, here, to compare the successions of distinct element-events: that of ascent and descent of melodic line, and that of rhythmic deceleration. But the comparison of textural and color successions affords vivid illustration of necessary distinctions between texture and color or sonority. The texture changes neither in density nor in class. But the coloration is curved in a manner beautifully complementary to the downward-upward curve and rhythmic recession of the line. The distinction—conceptual, terminological, practical—between coloration and texture is very clear in this brief excerpt, as in numerous other passages in the Variations.[16]

---

[15]Concepts and techniques of textural activation, also with reference to Stravinsky, have extensive discussion later in this chapter.

[16]The Variations for orchestra are highly interesting in the study of texture. One avenue of approach would explore the function of texture as thematic, as a prime element by which the form is ordered in lieu of the traditional concept of melodic-rhythmic "theme" and its transformations. Claudio Spies, in an analysis of the Variations ["Notes on Stravinsky's Variations," in *Perspectives of New Music*, IV, 1 (1965)] gives (on p. 63) an outline of the Variations' form with divisions ("variations") marked by changes of tempo, texture, and coloration. Spies writes (pp. 62–63): "Of Variations there are twelve, separated from one another, in most instances, by a measured pause, a fermata or a change of tempo . . . . There is, however, no 'Theme' on whose melodic, rhythmic or phraseological characteristics these variations are constructed. Instead, a sectional design is postulated on varieties of change and contrast, rather than on actual transformation—diversity in phrase-structure, for example—on subtle or abrupt textural shifts, on rhythmic 'variables,' tempo-relations, as well as on a beautifully calibrated system of refrains and a perfect recapitulation.

"Sections II, V, and XI constitute the structural refrain . . . , and the music in these polyphonic measures provides the single most arresting features of the Variations." (Some sentences omitted.)

Texture and style

Characterization and evaluation of the qualities of musical texture are important means to the understanding of styles and style periods. A few parenthetical examples of the kinds of questions having to do with textural phenomena and their relevance to style classification and description will underscore this relation.

1. It is well understood that, for example, the role of the lowest voice is a major consideration of style classification. Thus, a primary distinction between polyphonic textures of the Renaissance and the Baroque is the higher degree of bass equivalence in the former, as compared with its later increasing restriction to intervals of succession which best underlie and support harmonic content within a tonal order.

2. The unique texture of organum, of two or more highly interdependent lines is the feature by which that style is primarily defined. And the evolution of stylistic tendencies within "organum" has to do essentially with the gradual progress toward modest degrees of interlinear diversification.

3. The radical style change which characterizes music history around the beginning of the seventeenth century, the development of monody, is significantly a textural phenomenon characterized by the advent of sung declamation with a subordinate fabric only occasionally vitalized by emergent, briefly competing strands—a development perceived as revolutionary largely because of the prevalence of polyphony of supreme contrapuntal values during the Renaissance.

4. The conceptual attitude termed "pointillism," a dominant feature of some twentieth-century music, is a matter of texture. Such music is stylistically characterized by distinctive, uniquely transparent textures.

5. The evolution of style and craft in the art of many a composer is most comprehensively and revealingly traced in the evaluation of his textures at various points. Beethoven's music is an obvious example.

6. Often the distinction between musical genres is most persuasively drawn on the basis of textural differences. Thus, it is possible to generalize to a remarkable degree concerning textural distinctions between sacred and secular musics of many ages (cf. mass movements and *chansons* of Josquin or Lasso), or in the latter of these categories between dance and other kinds of music.

7. Texture is often (not, of course, invariably) the key to dramatic developments in the resourceful shaping of other elements: thus, for example, it is often in relatively simple textures that the most expansive and adventuresome treatment of harmony is seen, as we have noted. (Or consider the "homophonic" contexts in which highly embellished melody is to be found, as in keyboard music of the Rococo, or the florid operatic styles of the eighteenth and nineteenth centuries.)

8. Any description of the style which we know by the term "impressionism" will necessarily give fundamental attention to texture. An obvious example of this is the technique, in impressionism, of ornamentation of a fundamental harmonic scheme by the idiosyncratic, uniquely characteristic, parallel movement of auxiliary chords within dense textures of interdependent lines.

Textural rhythm

This book suggests that progression and recession within element-structures, events paced and shaped in a way that is interesting and consistent in functional relation to an apparent expressive end, are basic to musical effect. These studies further suggest that a primary facet of rhythm is manifest in the pacing and qualities of the changes constituting successions of events at various hierarchic levels and involving the various elements of structure.[17]

Just as tonal, melodic, and harmonic events (changes) express in qualities (of extent of change) and pacing what we can describe as "tonal rhythm," "melodic rhythm," and "harmonic rhythm," so the changes in texture are expressive, *in timing and in the nature of change,* of what is properly termed *textural rhythm.* (In a logical extension of this idea, reference can be made to "color rhythm" in music—the consequence of the distribution and nature of changes in structure as delineated by coloration, color events.) Naturally, and significantly, the idea of textural rhythm is extensible to that of rhythms of its various aspects (density rhythm, spatial rhythm, etc.).

The importance of textural rhythm, and of other element-rhythms, can hardly be exaggerated. It may be realized, for example, that the rate of accrual of the voices in the imitative exposition of a fugal subject *is a rhythmic phenomenon* (i.e., the pacing and assertiveness of such events in the quantitative-qualitative textural unfolding), this specific aspect of progression a factor of textural change as of no other element and, hence, a fast or slow, strong or weak, succession in "textural rhythm." Within structural segments both large and small, the rate at which texture changes in the course of progression and recession is a vital aspect of expressive effect. Textural rhythm is of most obvious and immediate effect where changes in density are involved, and when the changes are decisive; but subtle qualitative changes are significantly

---

[17]The concept of concurrent element-rhythms, mutually counteractive or coincident in articulation, is pointed out recurrently in this book. The comprehensive treatment of tonal, harmonic, melodic, textural, and metric rhythms (not to mention rhythms of element-parameters—or "subelements"—like density, dissonance, aspects of coloration like dynamics or timbre, etc.) would require a broad context devoted essentially to these problems; but Chapter 3 gives summary emphasis to the concept of element-rhythms and their functional relations, and to the range of issues with which significant development of the concept would have to be involved.

expressive of subtle rhythmic effect. With the concept of textural rhythm we move toward *a comprehensive concept of rhythm as the combination and interaction of all element-rhythms*—indeed, of parametric rhythms of individual tendencies within elements as well (e.g., of texture, but also of its individual aspects).

Example 2-5a is a basis for comment concerning *textural rhythm* as expressed very simply in the recurrence of a significant (characteristic, even motivic) textural event in a Webern song.[18]

The piano part is throughout an alternation between two events sharply distinguished in texture (as in other elements): these appear in Ex. 2-5a— the triplet sixteenth-notes with eighth-note leap (this motive is shortened and varied in its many appearances) and the punctuating chord (sometimes reduced to a single pitch of analogous articulative effect, as in m. 4 or m. 9). Reference in the following comments is to the recurring chord, clearly a motive of primarily textural definition. (Although the evaluation of intervallic content and its changes, as well as functions of such changes, is an intriguing and important problem of study with reference to the recurring chordal motive, and one of relevance to concern with texture, it cannot be undertaken comprehensively here.)[a]

Ex. 2-5a. Webern, "Wie bin ich froh!" (How joyous I am!), No. 1 of *Drei Lieder*, Op. 25, on text of H. Jone.

[18]The song is given in full in Burkhart, *Anthology for Musical Analysis*, 2nd ed. (New York: Holt, Rinehart and Winston, Inc., 1972), pp. 497–99.

© 1956, Universal Edition. Used by permission of the publisher. Theodore Presser Company, sole representative United States, Canada and Mexico.

If the spaces between chord attacks are calculated in ♪ values, we obtain the series of approximate quantities represented in Ex. 2-5b. (The numeral represents the number of ♪ units after the attack and just into the subsequent attack.)

In the linear set of rhythmic values which results from this simple calculation we find relatively short values at the beginning, "middle," and end and relatively long values internal to these key points (note the consequent, broad rhythmic effect), although a pattern of asymmetry is insistent throughout in the failure of any value to recur immediately and of any value to recur at all except for 10, the unit with which each of the song's two major divisions begins.

To the extent that textural rhythm is discernible in occurrences of this fundamental, largely textural event (and, consequently, *in the pacing of textural change*), a textural-rhythmic structure of distinct shape and effect (and unity, within its asymmetrical premises) becomes apparent. The charted

Ex. 2-5b. Representation of temporal distances separating chordal attacks, showing asymmetrical correspondences at various levels.

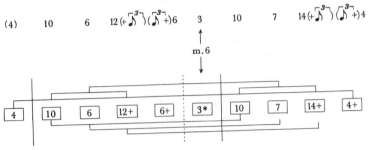

*Most dissonant chord and only instance of two contiguous chords.

representation in Ex. 2-5b is of self-evident basis and import: noted graphically are the (asymmetrical) correspondences among textural-rhythmic "spacings" within the overall time span of the song, and the (again asymmetrically) *analogous resultant (quasi-serialized) structures of the song's two divisions,* indicated by vertical strokes in the diagram. Listening strongly confirms the "rhythm" so articulated as a primary factor in the shape of the piece.

Qualitative and quantitative values

Usage of the term "quantitative" with respect to features of texture, already well established in this study, suggests a reference to the *number of components* (i.e., density-number), a distinctive and vital factor in texture and sonority. The number of components is one aspect of textural density; the degree of compression and volume of texture-space are other quantifiable parameters. Certain other features of texture are *qualitative* (the relative independence-interdependence of its components, the interlinear interactions of dissonance and imitation, etc.). Thus, we speak of *qualitative and quantitative progressions and recessions* as organic, functional, expressive changes in the textural structure.[19]

As suggested in brief excerpts quoted in Ex. 2-6a, the second of the Carter etudes is static in tonal-harmonic content, so that the textural struc-

---

[19]Corresponding classification can be seen to relate in some ways to other elements: in an important sense, the scope or "quantity" of a tonal system is a criterion different in kind from that having to do with the kinds of relations (e. g., distant, diatonic or chromatic) among its various regions; or the number of PC factors in a harmony might be seen as "quantitative" while the relations among them, the intervallic complex formed (the type of harmonic sonority), is a "qualitative" factor.

Ex. 2-6a.   Carter, Eight Etudes and a Fantasy for woodwind quartet, No. 2.

*Sounding as written.

Reprinted by permission of Associated Music Publishers, Inc.

ture (with that of coloration) is largely *the* structure. Textural progression and recession function in a broadly fixed space;[20] texture is accumulative in intensity to m. 12 and subsequently undergoes recessive relaxation to the

---

[20]Despite broadly fixed space, density of course varies, in compression as well as number, at local motivic levels as statements arrive, proceed, exit, reenter, etc.

cadence at mm. 17–18. Following this cadence, there is quick reaccrual of the textural components preceding the final, more abrupt cadence. These are quantitative considerations.

Since the motive is fixed in length, the varied spacings of its entries—that is, the varied distances (or time intervals) of imitation, are crucial in the structure; they constitute the principal qualitative element of textural change.

The control of changes in the distance of imitation (taking into account contiguous entries only, although any entry is in a sense an "imitation" of all preceding entries) can be represented as shown in Ex. 2-6b. The figures represent distances calculated in eighth-note units.

Ex. 2-6b. Analysis of the qualitative textural progressions and recessions (as they concern changing distances of imitation) in the Carter Etude.

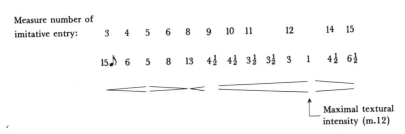

What is striking here is, of course, the progressive complexity of the texture, the progressive "horizontal compression" achieved by the increased *stretto*. This technique is of basic importance in qualitative textural progression in a great deal of music, as subsequent examples will further demonstrate. The progression toward the smallest time interval (m. 12) is, as one would expect in a subtly contrived art form, less than consistent and predictable. Measure 12 is followed by a succession of release in which two subsequent entries follow at increasing distances in preparation of the strongly punctuative cadence of mm. 17–18.

The concluding bars (19–22; see Ex. 2-6a), which are a rapid, intense resumption of the motive, contain imitative entries at extremely close distances—2♪, 1♪, 2♪—in a culminative, sharply progressive operation, followed by relatively abrupt cadential recession.

The Fantasies for strings by Henry Purcell are, as a whole, a truly splendid source for the analysis of texture in *all* its implications.

The quoted excerpt (Ex. 2-7a) is the third of five sections typically

Ex. 2-7a. Purcell, Fantasy in C minor, Z. 738, for strings.

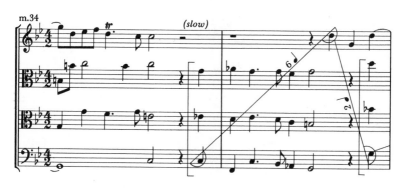

Ex. 2-7a continued.

delineated by changes in tempo and motivic content. The qualitative-quantitative progression is striking.

Ex. 2-7b.

(m. 35)   (mm. 38–39)

| |

3* $\dfrac{3}{1}$ $\left[\dfrac{2}{1}\right]$ $\dfrac{1}{\dfrac{1}{(\overline{1})}}$ 4

*As to rhythmic interdependence.

Following the process symbolized in Ex. 2-7b, involving qualitative progression and recession, a rediversification takes place in resumption of progressive qualitative change as represented in Ex. 2-7c.

Ex. 2-7c.

(mm. 39–40)

4     $\overline{\dfrac{2}{2}}$ $\overparen{\dfrac{1}{\dfrac{1}{\dfrac{1}{1}}}}$

One has only to give attention to these measures as a listening experience to appreciate the persuasive effect, vitally functional, of the textural events represented. Time interval fluctuation is functional too: there is vacillation at first between the intervals of 6 ♩, 2 ♩ (an extreme, early contraction), again 6 ♩, again 2 ♩, and then imitation between voices 2 and 4 at the intermediate distance of 4 ♩. Time intervals of 2 ♩ are associated with tentative stages in the first qualitative progression; that of 4 ♩ is associated with (and somewhat compensatory in relation to) the area of maximal diversification and complexity of interlinear independence. The reader is urged to pursue questions of textural structure and process in other sections of this fantasy, and in other fantasies of Purcell, proceeding to consideration of overall textural shape to which those of individual sections contribute.

Density and dissonance

Density as the number of sounding components is the *density-number*; density as the ratio of the number of sounding components to a given total space is the *density-compression*.

Despite these direct and apparently simple propositions, the question of density is, like those of other aspects of texture, very complex indeed. For example, while there can be no doubt that the proximities by which components are separated in vertical alignment (the degree of compression) constitute an aspect of density (superimposed 2nds make up a "denser" textural complex than superimposed 5ths), the issue of dissonance has to be regarded as a related, conditioning factor.[21] It is reasonable, for instance, to ask whether an harmonic tritone is in some sense more "dense" than a major 3rd. At the same time, it is a convenience to regard the evaluation of dissonance as

[21]Density, in the second sense in which we have defined it (that having to do with the extent of compression of the textural components—i. e., their spatial boundaries in the vertical field and their distribution within such space) can also be seen in its interdependent relation to dissonance in the higher probability of dissonance, and its higher intensity, in contexts of greater density-compression.

It is assumed that dissonance effect can be evaluated and its impact as a textural factor subject therefore to analysis. (On pp. 107–11 there is reference to the problem of classification of dissonance severities.) Whatever scale of dissonance values one chooses to accept, or however it is considered to be modified—as it must be—according to the historical style in question, it is probably true that the minor 2nd and its compounds (m9, etc.) or inversion (M7) are in general expressive of relative dissonance and that of these the smallest interval, the m2 itself, is the dissonance of highest intensity. Texture (density-compression) is clearly a factor in this judgment, and in the subsequent statement that *among the forms within any IC dissonance properties are more severe the smaller the form.* (Whether the M2 is more intense a dissonance than the larger M7 is however problematic; these are distinct classes.) The position of the m2 in the scale of dissonance values, in any style, that is, in which the dissonance-consonance profile is a pertinent structural factor, seems doubtless; what is more significant as a style factor is the manner of its resolution.

a distinct parameter of progressive and recessive inclination, considering density as the simple ratio of number to space.

Some of these issues come into focus when one confronts the question of density in a complex like the one in Ex. 2-8a.

Ex. 2-8a.

What is the "density" of stacked components of a single PC? Should further distinction be made between something like "density-content" and pure "density-number?" (The question is related to, and an extension of, that of the connection between dissonance and density—of the specific intervallic relations, and relatively amalgamative or resistant tendencies pertaining, among the various factors within a textural complex.) Presumably a complex like that of Ex. 2-8a represents a density-number of 3 (or a density-compression of 3:24, where the latter factor is the total space in semitones); but a distinction has to be noted in the relatively greater tendency of "fusion" among components so related, and among components relatively so related (5ths, 4ths, etc.) as opposed to one of more heterogeneous, ultimately dissonant, PC and IC content. All of this concerns the relation of density to dissonance.

The *particular distribution of components* within a given space is a further parameter of consideration within the factor of density-compression. Presumably, the two complexes in Ex. 2-8b are not of equivalent density-compression even though they can both be expressed as 4:24. The point here is a simpler one: we are noting that the evaluation of density-compression may require consideration of simultaneous numbers of sounds *within segments of the total texture-space.*

Ex. 2-8b.

It is suggested earlier that sonority and coloration are further aspects of density—e.g., the extent to which an impression of density is projected is affected by the coloration by which, in part, vertically proximate events are perceived as discrete and "resistant" or "fused."

Figure 2-1 gives the key points in a quantitative progression in the Schoenberg song, *Tot*, in a statement of the density-number curve expressed in numbers of simultaneous pitches. (See Ex. 1-52a, pp. 174–75, which quotes most of the extracts to which reference is made.)

The graphic representation in Fig. 2-1 is explicit in description of the *quantitative progression* of that aspect of texture which we have termed density-number, and its subsequent recession. At the microlevel, of course, there are further gradations; for example, the extreme opening of the song has a density-number 2, and the final sound is of density-number 1.

Fig. 2-1. Functional curve of density-number in Schoenberg, "Tot," from *Three Songs*, Op. 48.

Measure numbers:	1–6	6	9–10	11–12–13	13–14	15–18
Density-number:	4	5–6	7	8	6	3

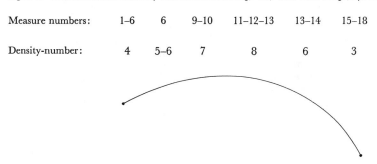

The succession is spaced in a rather common linear ordering in which there is accrual toward a point slightly beyond the temporal "middle" of the song. The high melodic lines of m. 11 are a complementary factor in this progression, as is the striking coloration in that bar, with the voice part heard entirely below the piano. The dynamics, on the other hand, are at times complementary to the density-number curve (m. 6) and at times a compensatory element (m. 11). The foregoing discussion does not (but could be extended to) take up the problem of fluctuation in density-compression.

In the texture of the cadential harmony from the third of Webern's Pieces, Op. 7, for violin and piano (Ex. 2-9), dissonance and density, which are clearly interrelated factors here—one an intensification of the other—are of primary significance in effect. The structure of the piece is, in part, a progression toward increased densities: the opening is relatively dense in compression but not in number—a sustained note in the violin with *staccato*, *ppp*, impulses in the piano a semitone above (never prolonged); but subsequently the textures are relatively open and uncrowded until the conclusion. The piano texture immediately preceding the one quoted is a cluster of three pitches (two semitones, within a diminished 3rd).

Ex. 2-9. Webern, Four Pieces, Op. 7, for violin and piano, No. 3.
(Example 1-28, p. 93, quotes the complete violin part.)

The density of the final sonority, a striking and emphatic contrast to the prevalent textures of the piece, is of course relatively ambiguous in pitch content because of its low register—the register, however, enhancing the richness of overtones and thereby the sense of compression. There are six pitches (and PCs) within the compass of a minor 14th (or augmented 13th). The tritone is the greatest distance separating any two of its components. The sonority is one of severe dissonance (even though use of the pedal and the low register are calculated to counteract any explicitness of pitch), and the dissonance is intensified by the density; the harmony contains tritonal relations (G-c♯ and G♭-C) as well as semitonal relations (or their compound or inverted forms) to each of the three factors in the major triad at its center.[22]

Density-number in the piece as a whole, measured in simultaneities alone, progresses along the following consistent order: *1 – 2 – 3 – 4 – 6*, punctuated of course by reversions to lower orders. It is impossible to escape the conclusion that these element-progressions (aspects of density) are decisive in the structure.

Interlinear independence and interdependence

Much of the concern with texture is directly involved with what is undoubtedly the most fundamental and significant criterion of textural quality—*the relative independence and interdependence of its components.*

Illustration has already been made of essential factors by which interlinear relations of independence or its lack are expressed: *directional, intervallic, and rhythmic conformity or disparity*—all of these of course concerned with relations among concurrent lines further subject to complementary or counteractive factors of dissonance, imitation (motivic parallelism in temporal separation), color, spatial distance and compression, dynamic or articulative distinction, and any of other parameters of projection by which independence is asserted or minimized between two or more components.

Example 2-10 is presented for the reader's consideration at this crucial point. There should be careful scrutiny and evaluation of the various qualitative changes which occur in this beautiful movement, and of the contrapuntal values it embodies without prevalent imitation. Of course, directional contrast is applied in degrees (it cannot exist absolutely!) so that it is compromised as the counterpoint gets underway (note relative intervallic and directional—but not rhythmic—conformity of voices 1, 2, and 4 at the outset,

[22]A symbolization of density-compression in the Webern sonority in question would be 6:22 (6 pitches within the space of 22 semitones). Although compression within a portion of the total spatial field is, as we have noted, often vitally pertinent, distribution is relatively even here.

Ex. 2-10. Corelli, Concerto Grosso in F minor, Op. 6, No. 3, third movement.
(Duplicative *concertino* parts, and continuo figured bass, are omitted.)

or between voices 1 and 2 in mm. 6–7).[23] *Rhythmic homogeneity is studiedly avoided except where functional necessities bring the voices into rhythmic accord in recessive processes.*

The function of dissonance should be examined in the greatest possible detail throughout the movement. The particular value of viewing dissonance as a textural quality is that this view induces one to see *all* dissonance relations. For example, the opening note of the second violin is seen not only as a suspended dissonance against the bass but in its relation (4th) to the upper voice as well. This view of dissonance as a textural quality leads naturally to the conclusion that *the intensity of dissonance effect has to do in part, and significantly, with the number of simultaneous dissonance relations within the texture as well as with their relative severities.* The mere computation of the number of such relations is, therefore, a significant analytical procedure in the evaluation of dissonance effect and fluctuation.

Attention should be given to manipulations of texture in cadential approaches. At m. 9, for example, there is of course increased interlinear accord; but some vitality persists (this is characteristic of internal cadential expression in well-made music) in the "separation" of voice 1 from the others, to all of which it is dissonant, and in the directional opposition of voices 2 and 4. In the final cadence, too, the complementarity of textural recession with those of tonality (left open, one step short of the tonic), harmony, and line is evident and balanced. Along with the tendency toward total interdependence of lines there are compensatory events, again expressing vitality within the cadential process: homorhythm is achieved gradually, preceded by textural grouping of $\frac{2}{2}$; and considerable contrary motion and intervallic

---

[23]In numerous instances in this chapter the textural components will be numbered for convenience of reference; voice number 1 is always the uppermost.

opposition are maintained. Again, dissonance exerts its influence of inter-linear tension and resistance—especially the six-four and the diminished 7th are vital in this regard.[24]

Imitation, a universal feature of many polyphonic styles; multiple counterpoint

The near universality of imitation in polyphonic styles in Western music (and its frequency in homorhythmic, homophonic, and other textures) is evidence enough of its paradoxical value in asserting the individuality of voices. It can be regarded even as the supreme manifestation of interlinear independence, normally complementary to simultaneous rhythmic and, often, directional opposition: *the expression of contrapuntal competition implicit in the enunciation of like motivic material separated in time.*[25]

Two textural components projecting like musical substance at a dis-tance assert their relative independence *by virtue of the separation—and con-sequent diagonal interaction—of clearly identifiable materials in time.* If interlinear interdependence (accord) is the "ideal" of repose toward which textural process ultimately strives, imitation is the most persuasive opposition to that tendency because of the explicit potential for parallelism denied by the imposition of a margin of temporal separation—the distance of imitation, the *time interval.* Thus, the shorter the time interval the more intense the con-flict arising out of the contradiction of motivic affinity and temporal separa-tion.[26] Progressions in adjustment of the time interval are an important technique already demonstrated in the intensity-release curve of textural shaping.[27] (See Ex. 2-6b.)

[24]Actions of dissonance of the sort to which attention is called need not be seen as purely, or even essentially, matters of texture; dissonance is an issue of recurrent concern throughout this book. But viewing dissonant relations as to their impact in textural shaping broadens, and complementarily sharpens, the understanding of this vital aspect of musical effect.

[25]The intensity associated with imitation requires clear distinction between that technique and "dialogue" in which two voices exchange motivic material, the leader dropping out while the follower responds, with no concurrent activity. And the device of melodic sequence, in which motivic recurrence is within a single voice, differs from both imitation and dialogue in that it implies no textural interaction between voices.

[26]The time interval of 0 is of course the ultimate accord, or resolution, of imitative conflict (pursuit). Up to the point of such accord, the association of progressive intensity with contraction of the time interval seems clearly appreciable; any value other than 0 expresses intensity greater than that of wider imitative distance.

[27]Imitation, of course, is very frequently a strict duplication of rhythms *and* intervals *and* directional successions; but every musician will recall instances in which imitative state-ment duplicates intervals only in opposite directions, or rhythms in relative durations but longer or shorter values. (As the time interval changes in imitation in augmentation or diminution, *the angle of diagonal relation changes* in continuing fluctuation of the intensity curve within this particular parameter.)

The distance of imitation, or time interval, is thus seen as a factor in textural intensity in the sense that the more distant the imitation the more "leisurely" the pursuit of one stratum by another; fluctuation in time interval is functional in many more contexts and styles than generally thought. The closer the imitation (the smaller the time interval) the more intense is the "competition"; it is reasonable to assume, and experience confirms, that the awareness of explicit motivic affinity put "out of joint" by temporal discrepancy *must be heightened by a relatively small margin of distance.* This is the basis for the use by composers—demonstrated in countless instances—of stretto, often late in a given form, as part of the expression of intensity toward which textural structure, with other element-structures, progresses.

A mental image of comparative relations can be suggested in this connection. Thus, the following changes are of strikingly different effect in the intensity-relaxation curve, the effect of each readily appreciable: two lines in simultaneity, one doubling the other; a separation of the two such that a diagonal relation, an imitative pursuit of one by the other, is established; a closer imitation, a narrower time interval. It seems impossible to doubt that the most intense of these situations, and the texture of highest urgency of expected resolution, is that in which the temporal disparity is close enough to give stark exposure to the fact of parity temporally denied.[28]

Fluctuations in intensity, occasioned largely by changes in the distances of imitation, are illustrated in graphic style in Exx. 2-11a,b,c, based on three imitative sections from Bartók's Quartet No. 5 for strings; these sections alternate in the first movement with areas of reduced textural complexity.[29]

For an account of many important, prototypical musical forms and procedures in which imitation is of fundamental importance, and for descriptive statements concerning the imitative procedures involved, the reader is referred to the author's *Form in Music: An Examination of Traditional Techniques of Musical Structure and Their Application in Historical and Contemporary Styles*, 2nd ed. (Englewood Cliffs, N.J.: Prentice-Hall, Inc., 1986), Chapter 12.

[28]Although the harmonic interval of imitation, on the other hand, cannot easily be seen as a factor in textural intensity (it in no way determines the harmonic or other interactions at the points of interlinear vertical coincidence), it is of course probably a significant aspect of style; the preponderance, exceptions notwithstanding, of imitative entries at perfect intervals (octave, 4th, 5th) in music up to recent times is evidence of this.

While the memory and effect of, say, dissonant intervals of imitation are perhaps plausible as elements of intensity, the "harmonic" effect of this seems to be "superseded" by that at the point of vertical coincidence—i. e., the intervallic relation between the entering voice (follower) and the leading voice *at the point of entry* is what is decisive, it would seem, for intensity impact of interlinear relation. Furthermore, a "dissonant" harmonic interval of imitation does not find resolution in a "consonant" harmonic interval of imitation in general practice.

[29]The Bartók quartets are extremely fruitful subjects of study in this regard. See, for example, the first movement of the fourth quartet: mm. 8–13 or 14–26 as to progressive interlinear complexity, then release; or mm. 14–22 as to progressive intensification in the shrinking temporal distance of imitation; or mm. 27–37; etc.

Ex. 2-11a. Bartók, Quartet No. 5 for strings, first movement.

Ex. 2-11b. Bartók, Quartet No. 5 for strings, first movement.

.... Resolvent contraction to time interval 0; in m. 16, prepares ostinato; in m. 18, prepares $\frac{1}{2}$ simplification within ostinato. $\frac{2}{1}$

Ex. 2-11c. Bartók, Quartet No. 5 for strings, first movement.

The illustrations show the function in a line of intensity of the degree and rate of change in the time interval (in relation to measure numbers across the top of each graph, and, on the left, a scale of temporal values expressed in note durations). The "intensity line" is of course drawn to connect points of change in the time interval. Most illustrated changes are progressive toward a point of maximal shrinkage of the time interval; at other times there is fluctuation within relative stasis, broadly viewed.[b] (As often in comparable discussions, it is possible to quote only minimal extracts from the work.)

Multiple counterpoint (usually double, triple) is a particular species of imitation in which, if two or more different contrapuntal alignments are contiguous, lines of direct imitative relation intersect, as represented in Fig. 2-2.

Multiple counterpoint in which the treated motive is reduced in size in contrapuntal realignment can be somewhat analogous in effect to the procedures of contracted time interval discussed above. Moreover, a shift in the vertical line of coincidence (e.g., from ⸗⸗⸗ to ⸗ ‒ ‒) along with multiple contrapuntal realignment could have functional consequences analogous to those of time interval change. But variation among appearances of motivic factors in multiple (inverted) counterpoint such that their vertical coincidences are altered is relatively rare. Nevertheless, multiple counterpoint is in the simple fact of contrapuntal realignment in vertical distribution an important technique of textural variation.[30]

Fig. 2-2.

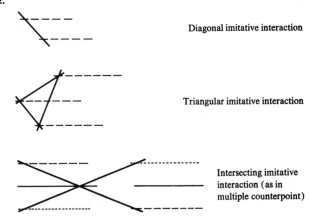

Diagonal imitative interaction

Triangular imitative interaction

Intersecting imitative
interaction (as in
multiple counterpoint)

[30]The interval of inversion is probably a useful criterion of style distinction, but the extent to which this may generally be true is uncertain. Certainly, the preponderance of examples before the twentieth century are at the 15th (or octave), 12th, or 10th—intervals of inversion in which dissonance-consonance relations are relatively (not entirely) stable.

The activation of simple textures

Musical textures are often activated by dynamic, articulative, rhythmic, coloristic, and other means. Techniques of textural activation are applicable, of course, to any circumstances, but they are of special importance in vitalizing relatively simple, fixed textures.

A few examples are given here in illustration of some of the primary techniques of *textural activation*; others will appear in subsequent analyses.[31]

The works of Stravinsky are particularly replete with examples of heterophonic, heterorhythmic, dynamic, articulative, and other types of activation within simpler, often inert, textures. We shall return to some of these questions in analysis of Stravinsky, referring for the moment to an excerpt from one of the symphonies (Ex. 2-12).

This extremely vital passage consists of two major textural complexes in an antiphonal relation, both chordal and considerably homorhythmic. Neither undergoes significant qualitative change: one of them, that in the higher brass and woodwinds, is only moderately progressive in harmonic, melodic, chromatic content; the other, that of the strings, is static (and its influence extends into the wind sonorities, where low brass and horns persist in the pedal A). Within this fundamental context of considerable tonal-textural inertia, an extremely important range of activating devices is interposed.

The *heterophonic* "doubling" (heterointervallic, homodirectional) between, for example, the two bassoons (or cello and viola) in the first quoted bar (B in one, C in the other) gives a momentary, particular thrust to the ostinato pattern. A comparable heterophony occurs in the next bar between double-bass and timpani. The same technique is seen at other points—e.g.,

---

Provocative questions would be concerned with the extent to which general statements might be possible in characterizing practice within given stylistic contexts. It can be suggested that in tonal counterpoint, that of the eighteenth and nineteenth centuries, the intervals of inversion (octave, 15th, 12th, 10th most commonly) are relatively predictable within a given range. To what extent (and how) is this true of earlier styles? To what extent are the resources extended in more recent styles? The answer to the second of these questions would seem perhaps more apparent than it actually is: inversion at the octave and its multiples, and at the 12th and 10th, is surprisingly frequent in many twentieth-century literatures, perhaps for reasons of the relative stability of intervallic relations. The interval of inversion is an important textural factor since it determines the immediate intervallic relations among concurrent voices.

[31]A common device in traditional music, especially that of the eighteenth and nineteenth centuries, is the *local arpeggiation of chordal factors* either in purely chordal textures or in textures in which there is chordal, or partially chordal, accompaniment to a dominant thematic element. The *Alberti* bass, ubiquitous particularly in the later eighteenth and earlier nineteenth centuries, is a characteristic, exceedingly familiar example of this. One might say that rhythmic activation (vitalization) of this and comparable kinds acts toward compensation for the absence of functional textural eventfulness.

Ex. 2-12. Stravinsky, Symphony in Three Movements, first movement.

Reprinted by permission of Belwin-Mills Publishing Corporation.

two bars later between double-bass and cello and in the following bar between the same lines. *Heterorhythmic* relations among piano, timpani, low woodwinds, and strings, in the ostinato texture of which they are components, must also be cited. A further factor in the activation of both textural divisions is the enormously resourceful and potent array of dynamic-articulative emphases (devices of orchestration, of coloration): the frequent, heavy doubling of A in violin and viola, the low octaves of the piano, or frequent marks of articulative stress.

The entire fabric is, then, one of relative textural simplicity, directness, and minimal textural (or tonal, harmonic, or melodic) development—a context in which devices of the sort described function significantly *in compensatory activation* of largely inert textures.[c]

In Ex. 2-13a, also from Stravinsky, a number of points will be seen as of crucial importance and significance in the analysis of texture.

Concern is directed here to identifying and appraising devices by which textures are activated in atmospheres of relative inertia of essential pitch structures.[d] Looking at the example very generally one can see that the texture is "layered" in groups of components differently colored, each qualitatively distinct, so that the entire context can perhaps be said to consist not merely of linear components (i.e., of lines) but of somewhat distinct "subtextures" in a "polytextural" complex.

Tonal relations among these strata should be considered independently —the various implications of the PC materials of separate textural complexes, the essential harmonic structure within each stratum (see for instance Ex. 2-13f), the general C-emphasis of mm. 324–26, and the final harmony as a tonal "synthesis" of the preceding PC elements.[32]

Beyond tonal-harmonic interactions and relations, subtextural complexes are sharply contrasted in rhythmic and articulative character, coloration, and diatonic as opposed to relatively chromatic content; the interaction among these complexes is thus one of vital counterpoint. Activating elements *within each stratum-complex*, especially vital in a context in which tonal-harmonic succession is restricted, are heterorhythmic and heterophonic impulses within bass "doublings" (cf. Ex. 2-12), points of imitation, and various techniques of ornamentation within each stratum. Specific examples of techniques of activation which are of vital effect but which do not materially affect qualitative textural content are given in extensions of Ex. 2-13. All occur in the opening measures of *Canticum*, Part V (Exx. 2-13b, c, d, e).

---

[32]Attention is called to an interesting and insightful discussion of Stravinsky's textures: Edward T. Cone, "Stravinsky: The Progress of a Method," in *Perspectives of New Music*, I (1962), pp. 18–26.

Ex. 2-13a. Stravinsky, *Canticum Sacrum,* Part V (*Illi autem profecti*) ; text from the Vulgate, St. Mark 16 : 20.

*Sounding one octave lower.

Ex. 2-13a continued.

Ex. 2-13b. Activation by articulative differentiation (as to essential linear movements), a species of heterorhythm.

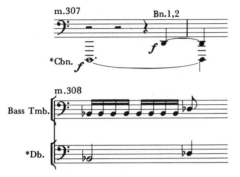

*Sounding pitch.

Ex. 2-13c. Activation by displacements (transferences) of PCs and pitches within a subtextural complex.

*All at sounding pitch.

(Activated chord: ·)

The above techniques (recurrent in a movement of rondo-like restate-ments of thematic material) are motivating in contexts of counteractive forces of inertia, as are those illustrated in Exx. 2-13d and 2-13e.

Ex. 2-13d. Heterorhythmic technique in the Stravinsky (all notation at sounding pitch).

Ex. 2-13e. Heterorhythmic and heterophonic technique in the Stravinsky.

The rhythmic activation of a textural mass of considerable tonal-har-monic inertia is evident as well in the organ solo (Ex. 2-13a, mm. 327–35) by which the *Illi autem profecti* is punctuated. A sketch of its pitch content is given in Ex. 2-13f, one in which its relative tonal stasis is clear. The texture is

Ex. 2-13f. Relative tonal-harmonic inertia of rhythmically activated textural mass in the Stravinsky (summary of structural pitches and neighbor auxiliaries).

"moved" within a limited tonal-harmonic space by devices of rhythm, differences of ornamentation of the fundamentally fixed structure, and the like.

The techniques of controlled textural change and activation of relatively inert textural masses by such devices as those noted are of recurrent importance in Stravinsky, whose works, as suggested in the foregoing references, are invariably rewarding objects of study of shaping aspects of texture. Analysis of the example from *Canticum Sacrum* would ideally go much further than has been possible here, reaching into other areas of inquiry: for instance, the transfer of harmonic elements over boundaries in the form where there is severe and abrupt quantitative change (e.g., between mm. 311 and 312), where polytextural structure gives way to monotexture with corresponding pitch factors "transferred" from soprano and alto voices to the organ, right hand, those of tenor and bass to the organ, left hand, and that of the second trombone to the organ pedal in palpable links of pitch material bridging, in counteractive functions, severe textural and color changes. Throughout the *Canticum* and other works of Stravinsky complementarity of such elements as dynamics and tempo (not to mention others) at points of textural change are of great importance.

*The complementary and compensatory dispositions oг
texture in relation to other element-structures*

Some examples treated earlier have taken up the questions of complementary and compensatory interactions among element-events in functional contexts. For example, Ex. 1-37 is a discussion of cadential process in one of the piano pieces of Schoenberg's Op. 23 (see pp. 107–9). In that analysis a point is made of textural recession as one aspect of that process: texture is reduced in density and qualitatively simplified in the closing bars. The substantial "thickness" accruing in the broad course of the piece (out of the lean two-voice texture of m. 1) is finally reduced to $\frac{1}{1}$, then 1. In the qualitative sense, the insistent imitative interlinear interactions of, for example, mm. 18–19 are slowly relinquished. These interactions among textural components continue into mm. 20–21 but in less explicit forms; and in the final two bars they dissolve almost totally. There is thus a gradual qualitative (as well as quantitative) textural recession. The element-structures involving linear descent, rhythmic deceleration (slowing tempo as well as longer durations), dynamics, articulation (∧ then – , as well as longer *legato* units), and meter (as to recessively longer durations of event groupings) *all function complementarily*. In Chapter 1 it was noted that a compensatory factor in prevailing decline is the maintenance of considerable dissonance in interlinear relations; but here too a recessive curve was noted as a probability.

A choral work of Purcell, a double canon in which there are concurrently two mirror canons (at the ♩) and two strict canons (at the **o**), is helpful in analysis of complementary functions in another instance of cadential process.[33]

Measures 11–13 of the Purcell piece (Ex. 2-14) represent an area of maximal textural vitality[34] in the broad context of the entire work. Progres-

Ex. 2-14. Purcell, *Gloria Patri.*

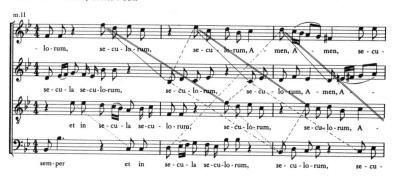

[33]The set of terms adopted for classification of interlinear relations (on the basis of directional, rhythmic, and intervallic aspects) can also be used to denote various kinds of imitative relation, with the term *imitation* understood as generic and subject to modifiers of many kinds. The term *homodirectional imitation* (opposed to *contradirectional*) thus refers to interaction in which leader and follower conform in the direction of motion, a situation for which no generally accepted term is available. (Homodirectional imitation may or may not conform intervallically and rhythmically; hyphenated terms here too are useful in comprehensive denotation.) *Contrarhythmic imitation* can of course be further qualified by common terminology (*in augmentation*—usually understood as homointervallic, *rhythmically free*, etc.) and *contraintervallic imitation* is subject to further, more precise standard classification (*tonal, by complementation, by compound expansion*, etc.). *Free imitation* (or the term *freely imitative*) may denote imitative procedure in which the aspect of relation fluctuates at some stated level. The common term *strict imitation* can denote (like *real imitation*) a follower which conforms in all aspects except, usually, that of PC (e.g., imitation at the 5th). Mirror imitation is homointervallic and homorhythmic, but contradirectional, and the term *rhythmic imitation,* or rhythmic canon, identified by specific reference to a single parameter, is understood to exclude the others (i.e., to pertain to imitation which conforms in rhythm only); this is suggestive of further plausible terms like *contour imitation* (directional conformity only) and *pitch-class imitation* or *interval-class imitation* (as in many serial procedures). One could continue in this process of developing and classifying terms of potential usefulness, incorporating language in common usage wherever it has generally understood meaning. It is unlikely that any set of simple terms can or should be intended as applicable to all situations; descriptive adjectival modifiers are almost invariably useful except in simplest conditions.

[34]The *Gloria* is included in Wallace Berry and Edward Chudacoff, *Eighteenth-Century Imitative Counterpoint* (Englewood Cliffs, N.J.: Prentice-Hall, Inc., 1969), pp. 36–37. The reader is encouraged to trace progressive actions toward mm. 11–13.

Ex. 2-14 continued.

sion to that area is characterized by complementary successions within tonal, linear, and rhythmic structures, and by progressive development within qualitative textural parameters as well, culminating in the complex web of interactions (at highly contracted temporal distances) partly shown in Ex. 2-14.

Following this climactic area a number of recessive tendencies, in complementary function, can be noted immediately: the final dissolution of the canons and of imitative interaction constitutes textural simplification of important consequence, although considerable contrarhythmic activity persists, with voices settling at differing times except for the homorhythmic relation of inner voices; the important rhythmic deceleration can be seen at a glance, as can the recessive, gradual (essentially conjunct) descent of upper voice against modest ascent of the lowest—tendencies in which their canonic followers of course concur. A complementary factor which is less obvious is metric, and can be seen, for example, in the settings of *Amen* in the outer voices: those of the soprano having recessive values of 3, then 5, then 10 ♪, and those of the bass 3, then 5, then 14 ♪.[e]

Example 2-15 is an illustration of quantitative recession in which qualitative factors are only negligibly affected (and in which the sense of decline is extreme). With a situation of tonal stasis, the example shows how persuasive a textural recession, with complementary dynamic and melodic decline, can be.

Of course, with the linear sloping of the upper voice, it is clear that the recession is one of texture-space as well as density. The function of dissonance as a textural factor in interlinear independence is particularly

Ex. 2-15. Bartók, Divertimento for string orchestra, second movement.

apparent: the directional opposition of lines throughout the passage (a determined one, the two essential components in an oblique relation) is intensely complemented by a bitonal situation, the two tonal implications merging at the point of resolution.

The texture is, strictly speaking, only very incidentally of more than two real components, and both remain active until the cadential measure, 49. In that sense the decline is of sonority as well as density and space. Textural *quality* thus remains relatively constant and insistent while the range of doublings is gradually reduced. The disappearance of the lower stratum of the first violin (mm. 44–45) does, however, constitute a true modification in textural quality as distinct from the sonority or density by which the most severe shaping of the succession is carried out. There could scarcely be a more lucid example of the complementarity of elements than this in which density, space, sonority, dynamic coloration, melodic lines, and tonal relations achieve by their confluence a pervasive and determined functional effect.

We are thus cognizant here, as in parallel studies of other element-progressions and element-structures, of the necessity that texture be seen in its relations to other elements. Where such relations are not made explicit, the reader is urged to pose for himself the appropriate questions and to seek their answers to the extent that other elements are functional in the particular processive contexts observed.

Some textural functions in delineation of form

Texture (its class, its qualities, its densities) is of course an essential element by which thematic statement is rendered distinctive and expressive. For example, the stark exposure of a line to be emphasized in and for itself may be in monophonic or very restricted, transparent texture. Or, the contrasts between opposing thematic elements or groups within a sonata or rondo movement are often textural, with textural differences playing a role analogous and complementary to that of changes of tonal reference, dynamic level, and the like. Or controlled textural diversification may be an important variational feature within a single thematic unity, and among its constituent parts. Textural progression and alteration are of course fundamental techniques in thematic development as in any manipulation of motivic materials in a generally unstable context.[f]

Among earlier literatures, one of the most beautiful (and often cited) examples which come to mind in illustration of the principle of textural

change functioning in delineation of form is Josquin's *Tu pauperum refugium,*
subject of extensive earlier comment (see pp. 45–47).[35]

The brief extracts quoted (Ex. 2-16) show the strong textural differences by which, along with contrasts of tonal order and other kinds, sections
in this recapitulative form are contrasted. The first part, only a portion of
which is quoted, is in itself a very expressively disposed textural progression
setting out from a condition of perfect homorhythm which, in the second
phrase, is gradually diversified with tentative imitative interactions, then
largely restored in the brief third and fourth phrases (not quoted). Complementary to change in cadential pitch (upper voice: g^1, a^1, g^1; bass voice:
e, A, e) is this sloped succession shaped by textural diversification and
resolution.

The second part (elided with m. 20) is contrapuntally imitative,
although imitation is not predominant. (Actually, imitation enters very
subtly within the restricted diversification of the fifth phrase, not quoted.)
At the same time that imitative contrapuntal texture emerges, in contrast to
the first part, density is reduced to a consistent two-voice pattern (with
contrasts of coloration). The reduction in density serves the function of
contrast and brings into vivid exposure the interactions of increasingly
independent voices.

The third section is recapitulative, yet a variation (note metric change,
for example), a technique in which Josquin shows admirable inventiveness.
Its beginning is quoted in Ex. 2-16; the homorhythmic condition (and the
thematic material) of the opening return here.

A look into the complete example will reveal subsequent return and
variation of the third and fourth phrases. The section preceding m. 60 is, in
fact, one in which the composer demonstrates a consummate craft of remarkable economy in which the simple motivic substance of the original phrase 3
(mm. 12–13, with anacrusis) is widely extended and developed. Throughout
this process, as in the varied return of the opening two phrases, there prevails
an attitude of essential homorhythm in which there is occasional, restrained
diversification by slight rhythmic differentiations usually productive of
animating dissonance.

The premature cadence on the modal final, E, at m. 60 sets off a closing
section of cadential elaboration again marked by significant qualitative contrast of texture. In opposition to the preceding, there are now once again
points of controlled imitative interplay (on earlier motives) by which the
texture is rendered contrapuntal in modest complexity opposing the stabler,
predominantly chordal textures of Parts I and III.[g]

---

[35]Apel and Davison, eds., *Historical Anthology of Music,* Vol. I (Cambridge: Harvard
University Press, 1949), p. 92.

Ex. 2-16. Josquin, *Tu pauperum refugium,* from Motet, *Magnus es tu, Domine.*

m.27

m.34

m.57

Ex. 2-16 continued.

Dominant textural projection is thus one of chordal homorhythm activated by diversification subtly and often gradually introduced and subsequently relinquished, the overall textural structure marked by the change to imitative counterpoint in mm. 20–33 and, to a lesser extent, in the last nine measures. The manner in which Josquin anticipates the textural quality of the first of these contrasting passages (notably in the second and fifth phrases) is further testimony to the subtlety and control by which his creative procedures are characterized.[h]

Any discussion of texture in the delineation of form (and forms) could of course go on indefinitely. The procedures by which, in so many prototypical designs, formal delineation is one of *relatively* uncomplicated texture in thematic statement set against subsequent relatively diversified, sometimes intense, textural activity in developmental and variational processes, will be recalled by any experienced listener.

And the literature is full of examples of variation forms in which progressions and changes within the textural element are basic techniques.[36] Examples of variation sets are an extremely fertile resource for study of textural progression and recession within individual variations and along the broad lines of overall form encompassing the variation series.

Of course, textural events at all levels of structure are of inestimable significance in the delineation and processive molding of all prototypical forms, and of all forms before and following the tonal period except of course where texture is limited to monophony without even the implications of contrapuntal diversity and interaction in compound melodic line. Textural stasis, progression, recession, and variation are *basic* in the functional processes by which forms are shaped, and by which expressive functional events (climactic, cadential, introductory, expository, etc.) are projected (see Ex. 2-27).

Textural contrasts, more broadly defined, do of course serve as well the function of broad delineation, in complementarity with other relevant elements, in intermovement relations in multimovement forms, and in intersectional relations in highly diversified forms.[i] This factor is perhaps too obvious to require illustration (think, in one of countless manifestations of the principle, of the Baroque suite and the role of texture in the traditional distinctions among dance movements—between, say, the *sarabande* and the *gigue*).

Textural processes in progression toward intensity, in recession toward cadence, and in anticipation of thematic statement

A factor of which a good deal of mention has already been made, that of the shaping of textural change in the direction of increased intensity (in which other element-structures often work complementarily) is carried further in amplification of earlier reference to a Josquin setting of the *De profundis*.

The *De profundis* setting had prior reference (pp. 87–90) in connection with linear melodic and harmonic functions at its outset, as well as limited discussion of textural processes (pp. 189–90) in a different extract. The portion of this magnificent work quoted as Ex. 2-17 is climactic, and its climactic effect might well be said to be *more significantly a product of textural progression*

---

[36]See *cantus firmus, ostinato,* and other textural procedures discussed as variation technique in Robert U. Nelson, *The Technique of Variation* (Los Angeles: University of California Press, 1948), pp. 10ff., 51f., 58–60, etc., and Berry, *Form in Music,* Chapters 8 and 9.

Ex. 2-17. Josquin, *De profundis.*

Reprinted from the Smijers edition, published by G. Alsbach and Co., Amsterdam, by permission of Creyghton Musicology-Musica Antiqua, Bilthoven, Netherlands.

than of any other single factor, although of course complementary rhythmic acceleration and "tonal" progression play important roles.[37]

In mm. 42–54 decisive factors in the texture are noted graphically in the quoted example. The time intervals of imitation are progressively shorter *within the section* as well as between this and earlier sections: the imitative entries of the words *Domine, quis sustinebit?* are initially at 𝅝 , then at 𝅗𝅥 and again at 𝅝 ; and the rising quarter-note motive, 𝄞, the motivic drop of a minor 3rd, , and the cadential drop of a 2nd in half-notes, participate in a number of brief but functionally important imitative interactions in mm. 45–46 at time intervals of 𝅝 , 𝅗𝅥. , and 𝅗𝅥 , as indicated in the example.

Finally, in mm. 51–52, which are highly animated (rhythmically and texturally, but *not harmonically*; note the compensatory stasis of harmonic rhythm), imitative interactions among appearances of the dotted-rhythm motive appear in a number of interlinear relations at the distance 𝅗𝅥 . The textural complexity is enhanced here, moreover, by contradirectional imitation.

This section is the only one to this point in which *four independent voices* emerge in contrarhythmic activity. They do so early in m. 44, two bars after the passage is launched in the imitative entries described above. There is, of course, interim release in, for example, the $\frac{2}{1}$ texture of such a point as m. 49, where the internal voices become interdependent (homorhythmic, homodirectional, almost homointervallic), or even simply in the withdrawal of the tenor at mm. 45–47 or the superius at mm. 48–49. Such factors as the relatively stable bassus at mm. 50–51 (cf. the bass role of later styles, and its restrictive submission to the demands of tonal-harmonic support, cadential definition, etc.), the rhythmic identification (but directional opposition) of tenor and bassus at m. 52, and the ultimate interdependence of voices to which the textural structure finally turns at (not long in advance of) the cadence *are vital factors of recessive process.*

The progression described above, and the larger (higher-level) progression of which it is a culmination, are thus excellently illustrative of a number of the textural factors with which we are concerned. And this highly active, diverse, and complex passage, *the section of greatest vitality in the motet,* is thrown into perfectly calculated perspective by the almost entirely homorhythmic phrases which follow—the only such phrases in the entire piece, significant

---

[37]The section of maximal intensity of textural interaction and diversification (Ex. 2-17) has a near parallel in the final section of the piece, to which the interested reader might refer for comparative study.

in their maintenance of the full density of four components presented in the form's simplest textures.

The reduction in textural quantity (density) as a cadential process is surprisingly rare in music, especially where final cadence is concerned; it is more common in tentative, internal cadence, especially when such internal cadence is preparatory to important events to follow, when such events, as often with thematic exposition, call forth relatively full densities (see the Brahms reference, Ex. 2-20).

The procedure of final cadence, where density of texture is concerned, seems generally to favor the emphatic substance of quantity, as a rule, *while compensatory action of recessive simplification within qualitative textural parameters takes place.* Musical examples show that greater density of compression as well as of number is characteristic of many cadential formulations; relatively ample density-number is, especially in tonal contexts, of value in the *clarity of consonant tonal-harmonic function* at its most crucial point, that of resolution, and increased density-compression is a usual consequence of descent of upper lines. Nevertheless, examples can be found in which dissolution of density is an important aspect of recessive, final cadential process.

A cadence from Sessions' piano work *From My Diary* (Ex. 2-18) shows a functional, comparable density-number recession 4—3—2 as well as a contraction of texture-space from 29 to 13 semitones.

Ex. 2-18. Sessions, *From My Diary*, third movement.

Reprinted by permission of Edward B. Marks Music Corp.

Even where textural qualitative complexity is maintained to a very late point, cadential expression may depend altogether in its preparatory stages, and predominantly in its ultimate formulation, on processes of decline within other elements. In such circumstances cadential feeling is often relatively indecisive.

Example 2-19 is memorable in the twentieth-century concerto literature, and an excellent example for study of the actions of texture in cadence, in this instance the final cadence of a movement. The motive stated twice by

Ex. 2-19. Schoenberg, Concerto, Op. 36, for violin and orchestra, first movement.

*All parts sound as written.

Copyright 1939 by G. Schirmer, Inc. Reprinted by permission.

the solo violin is of primary importance in the entire movement. The "radiation" of its influence throughout the texture is seen in the indications drawn into the example: there are varied imitations of the characteristic semitonal succession in almost every instrumental part. The significant and necessary observation which must follow is that textural complexity, activity, incipient and abortive but impressive interlinear independence, and considerable density are compensated for by the *lack or tight restriction of linear, harmonic, and tonal activity and especially the complementary decline in tempo and dynamics.*

Cadence is often, as we have stated, marked by realization of substantial density, even its full potential in the particular context, with other elements expressive of compensatory recessive stasis and decline. In the Schoenberg this principle goes beyond the accrual of density (useful for emphatic effect) in a texture *active with interlinear, diagonal relations of a considerable number,* while the stasis of relatively "level" lines, dynamic reduction, and gradually slower tempo to the point of fermata are of essential recessive function, dominant in their overall effect even in the atmosphere of a cadence ultimately slightly tentative in feeling. (To the extent that textural activity persists, cadential finality is qualified.)

Of course the deliberate minimizing of the natural tendencies of interlinear interdependence at the point of *internal* cadence (or preliminary stages
in final cadence) is a universal and vital technique of texture for suppressing
too punctuative or conclusive an effect.[38]

And the device of preparation (the process of establishing anticipatory
"atmosphere") can be an important factor in internal cadential process,
usually involving dissonance in a universal technique by which expectation
is heightened. The shaping of texture is requisite and critical to cadential
and anticipatory effect in Ex. 2-20.

The pattern is of course one of decline in density-number, a very common technique by which anticipatory feeling is enhanced (complemented
by the unsettled tonal-harmonic situation) in preparation for resumption
of thematic statement.

Measure 64 is a point of maximal density: the texture is essentially
chordal, strongly activated by heterorhythm and intertransference of chordal
PC factors among very active voices. Dynamic level (*fortissimo*) and extremes
of pitch (texture-space) are of complementary effect. Quantitative release
begins in the following bar; there is some diversification here—a qualitative

Ex. 2-20. Brahms, Quintet in G, Op. 111, for two violins, two violas, and cello, second
movement.

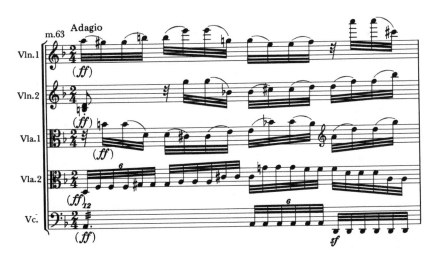

[38]Common modification (density reduction, simplification) of texture *following*
cadential punctuation, one of the devices by which cadence is thrown into relief and resumption "announced," is an omnipresent factor in music.

Ex. 2-20 continued.

m.67

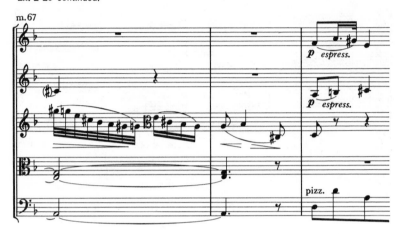

compensation in the quantitative decline—in a limited projection of motivic substance.

The subsequent stage in the process might be symbolized as $(4)\overline{}\text{-}(3)\overline{}^{1}$, with all voices but one now reduced to stasis, and deleted gradually. The surge and accelerated activity of the viola line is compensatory to continued decline, holding the recession in balance, as is the maintenance of dissonance intensity. Other *recessive* factors are the continuing dynamic reduction and the total cessation in harmonic rhythm.

The ultimate cadential measure completes the process, receding from $(\overline{3})^{1}$ to 1, with rhythmic values lengthened gradually as the viola line falls in a complementary gesture, and with harmonic inactivity maintained within the dissonant framework. The entire passage is extremely useful as an example of textural succession calculated in expression of cadential and anticipatory structural function, and of the complementarity and compensation of other, relevant element-events. The manner in which persistent instability of tonal-harmonic content (on the brink of resolution) counteracts all tendencies of recession is typical of tonal contexts.

Texture as space

The following examples show texture in its spatial dimension and indicate particular textural dispositions of very distinctive, even motivic, forms.

There is a sense in which melodic succession in the extremely high or low components expresses an important, functional aspect of texture—a modulating field in which events take place. The *shape and compass* of that field, which we are describing as *texture-space*, a two-dimensioned field setting out "horizontal" and "vertical" boundaries enclosing the element-successions which constitute the musical work, are functionally effective in circumscribing and governing much of structure, and it seems useful to regard this "space" as a distinct aspect of musical texture. The spatial factor (texture-space) might be defined as the field enclosed by "lines" tracing the pitch successions of outer components in addition to the two vertical, or diagonal, "lines" linking these components at "left-right" extremities *at some given level of structure*. All of these references are of course analogous to physical structures on a plane.[39]

One of the examples treated at some length in the discussion of tonality is the first of Webern's Four Pieces, Op. 7, for violin and piano, discussed as Ex. 1-49, pp. 162–65. Let us attempt to see that piece in its spatial texture, as defined, by describing the field within which its pitch events are broadly circumscribed and then by attempting to identify some of the important characteristics of changes in the spatial field as they might constitute an expressive succession within this particular parameter.

In expression and prolongation of its E♭ quasi-tonic the piece sets out with two functionally significant occurrences of this PC four octaves apart (Ex. 2-21). The violin descends thence to a prolongation of activity on e♭² while the bass, first repeating E♭ in m. 4, ascends in the penultimate measure to e♭, after which both recessions converge on e♭¹, the root of the final triad. (Obviously, there are deflections in that spatial field, like the low F♯ of the piano in mm. 6–7, a prominent local expansion of the space; but the foregoing comment describes the essential lines of the spatial contraction as to a marked extent influenced by the tonal centrality of the PC E♭, and the axial centrality of e♭¹.)

Seen in this sense the texture-space succession is one of *recessive contraction*.[j] The resultant focusing on the root of the final, cadential triadic resolution is of course supportive of tonal function, and the analogously "spatial"

[39]It would seem reasonable to extend the concept of two-dimensioned musical space to include a further dimension, that expressed by the hierarchic leveling of element-structures from the "foreground" of the most immediate, detailed successions to the remotest "background"—the structural level at which the broadest, most generalized lines of succession are discerned. Here again, in this reference to a third "dimension" in musical space, terms like "foreground" and "background" are analogous to terms used with reference to the qualities of physical space. (The most vital dimension, time, is symbolized by the "left-right" factor in this image, while the "up-down" factor symbolizes the field of pitch frequencies. The third dimension to which the above reference is made is, then, one of actual "depth" of experience of structure. Other parameters of musical experience—the field of intensity, or that of timbre, for example—can of course be conceived as further dimensions.)

Ex. 2-21. Contraction of texture-space defined by recurrences of tonal PC in Webern, Op. 7, No. 1.

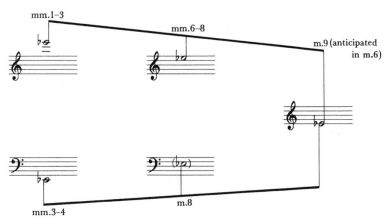

formulation described by these lines of succession from the extremes of the opening to the compression of the final sonority is an important aspect of the piece's structure, constituting a factor significantly complementary in functional effect to that of tonality, to which it is inseparably linked. Concurrently active element-structures (for example, that of rhythmic motion, gently accelerative toward the "middle" and restorative of longer durations toward the end; or upper voice linear descent) are complementarily or counteractively shaped.[40]

The idea of "space" as an aspect of musical texture is especially relevant to the works of Webern. In certain of that composer's works spatial symmetries are formed by the distribution of inversionally-related set-forms in equidistance around a central axis. In Ex. 2-22a, an extracted major segment of the first movement of the Quartet, Op. 22, there can be seen a progressive expansion of the texture-space to an extreme point (m. 22, a critical point in the movement's overall structure), at which the synopsis given in Ex. 2-22b is terminated. The point of extremity to which the spatial progression moves is underscored in a number of ways: there are complementary progressions of qualitative interactions of texture, and color and rhythmic structures are directed intensely to this same point, from which the movement, in a number of complementary element-successions, recedes. The

---

[40]As noted earlier, final increased density-compression is inevitably counteractive, while clearly subordinate, to recessive spatial contraction and, in the Webern, of relatively (and potently) consonant implications.

Ex. 2-22a. Webern, Quartet, Op. 22, for piano, violin, clarinet, and saxophone, first movement.

12−tone set:

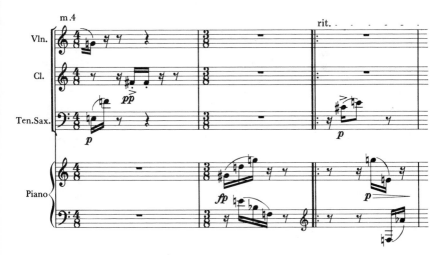

*All pitches sound as notated.

Ex. 2-22a continued.

Ex. 2-22b. Summary diagrammatic representation of the texture-space in the first movement of Webern's Quartet, Op. 22, mm. 1–22.

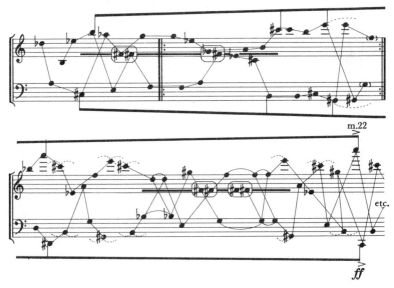

functional actions of all relevant elements to and from m. 22 constitute a fruitful and critical area of study in the movement. (See also Ex. 3-1, p. 307.)

Only the opening bars, and the immediate approach to m. 22, are given in Ex. 2-22a; Ex. 2-22b, however, is a synoptic rendering of the entire passage. It is contrived to show expansions in the texture-space, disposed equidistantly around the $f\sharp^1/g\flat^1$ axis, and maximally inflated at m. 22.

A further example goes back to a far earlier historical reference, the Prelude to a Handel Suite for harpsichord. The shaping of the texture-space is vivid indeed; and this particular kind of configuration of space (cf. the Webern examples), achieved by almost consistent, high-level directional opposition between outer components, projects a characteristic contra-directional counterpoint within an essentially simple textural context. Example 2-23a shows a brief extract and Ex. 2-23b is a condensed represen-

Ex. 2-23a. Handel, Suite No. 3 in D minor for harpsichord, Prelude.

Ex. 2-23b. Synopsis of inflation and contraction in the texture-space as expressed in contradirectional relation of outer components.

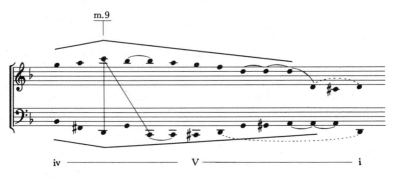

tation; it is evident that there is a single, forcibly directed succession (progressive, then recessive) in which spatial inflation and subsequent contraction must be regarded as most critical elements in the structure.

Motivic texture; the provocative effect of unusual textures

There are many times in music (perhaps especially that of the last hundred years) when materials are of such distinctive textural cast, and when the particular qualities of texture are so vital a factor in the identity and interest of thematic-motivic material, that it seems plausible to think and speak of texture as "motivic"—or of a specific *texture-motive*. A thematic melody in voices interdependently doubled in 3rds, where this textural feature is a necessary and recurrent aspect of the material, would be properly conceived as "thematic texture"[41] in an important sense. In Ex. 2-24, the motive is incapable of adequate characterization without reference to texture *as well as* to rhythmic and linear formulation: one can scarcely imagine representing this material—say, in a thematic index—with one line alone.

A very famous example of motivic texture is the initial sound of the Stravinsky *Symphony of Psalms* (Ex. 2-25; see p. 256); it is a recurrent motivic factor of arresting quality primarily because of its articulation and anomalous, distinctive spacing. It is not significantly defined merely as an E minor triad (as might e:i in a Classical context), nor with respect to its orchestral colora-

---

[41]Consider, for example, the first movement of Stravinsky's Concerto in D for violin and orchestra or the opening thematic statement in Beethoven's Sonata in C, Op. 2, No. 3, for piano.

Ex. 2-24. Debussy, Prelude No. 2 from Book I (*Voiles*).

tion alone. It seems altogether possible that *its most distinctive quality*, in fact, is the anomaly of triadic elements spaced with greatest compression at either end of the vertical space and relative sparsity in the spatial "center." A part of its effect is the doubling of the triad's "middle" factor, a sonority emphasis which seems complementary to the unusual textural disposition.

Of course, texture is—again especially in recent music—sometimes a primary vehicle of arresting effect when it is not, in underlying prevalence, specifically motivic.[k]

Levels of analysis and of hierarchy in the textural structure

The concept of hierarchic levels of structure is not less pertinent to texture than to other elements. For example, a peak of interlinear complexity and intensity, however achieved, will often be seen to be subsidiary and provisional in relation to a subsequent peak of higher intensity; the "goal" of a directed textural progression within a phrase may thus be a point within a broader progression (viewed from a greater "distance") into which its effect is subsumed; or the aim toward which a phrase-level progression is directed may, viewed more broadly, be seen to be as well the goal of directed element-progressions within the scope of an entire structure. Textural structure is thus manifest at various levels, individual shapes falling into a hierarchic order of relatively subordinate relation to functional higher-level successions, with that of the overall structure encompassing and emerging as the fulfillment of all. And a comprehensive, "deep" view of musical structure requires here as elsewhere that observation and analysis be made within formal-structural dimensions of various breadths and depths—at diverse hierarchic levels from that of the smallest formal unit to those of broadly conceived contexts. This aspect of analysis of the texture-structure will be noted further in connection with subsequent analyses, including Ex. 2-26 and Ex. 2-29.

Ex. 2-25. Stravinsky, *Symphony of Psalms*, first movement.

Gesualdo, *Or, che in gioia credea viver contento* (from Madrigals, Book 4)

An example from Gesualdo is given below for relatively comprehensive analysis of texture. Major attention is given to changing interlinear relations within the range from maximal diversity to total accord. Changing, functional patterns of imitation are, however, also of great importance and interest. Thus, while all four sections are imitative (at distances ranging from 1♩ to 15♩), the shortest time interval, briefly suggested in m. 4, becomes appropriately prevalent in the section *Fuggesi* . . . ("flies away"), an area of relative rhythmic and textural animation conditioned by the text; and imitation persists, mostly at 4♩, in the intensely chromatic final section (*Oimè, vien meno*; "alas, it wastes away").

A representation of textural progression and recession (with limited symbolization of qualitative relations as well as density) is given as Ex. 2-26b. Example 2-26a is a quotation of the entire *prima parte* of the madrigal.

Investigation shows that nowhere in this example is a diversity value of

$$\frac{1}{1} \frac{1}{1}$$

achieved. Developing toward points of maximal textural complexity are two progressions of persuasive growth (from one voice alone, or from two lines in interdependence). The intensity profile of the entire structure thus rises quickly within the first several measures, subsequently receding and progressing again to a point of maximal diversity at the immediate outset of the intense final section. Example 2-26b represents the step-by-step processes by which the textural structure is shaped. It is important to note that progression in density-number is significant at more foreground levels (that of the phrase especially, where there is progressive accrual except in the first two units, with the cadence usually formulated in full density) while the progression of textural diversity *significantly features lower degrees of complexity (but not of density-number) in the internal phrases*. It is thus in this second parameter of textural structure that the overall shape at the highest hierarchic level is best seen: the five voices are engaged with considerable consistency throughout the piece while changes in their degrees of interdependence shape the broadly defined textural succession.[1]

Telemann, Fantasy No. 4 for violin alone, first movement

That the study of functional textural events can be critically important even in a medium of inherently limited textural possibilities is evident in Ex.

Ex. 2-26a.　　Gesualdo, *Or, che in gioia credea viver contento* from Madrigals, Book 4 ; first part.

Reprinted from the Ugrino Edition, W. Weismann, ed., by permission of Associated Music Publishers, Inc., as agents of Deutscher Verlag für Musik, Leipzig.

Ex. 2-26b. Textural progression and recession, quantitative and qualitative, represented at phrase and broader levels in the Gesualdo example.

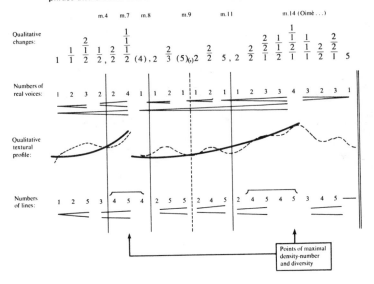

2-27a. We can only scratch the surface here, again; but texture and textural structure in virtually all its aspects could well be the basis of inquiry in comprehensive exploration of this movement.[42]

The movement's form is basically one of recurrent statements of an opening thematic idea separated by episodic digressions of a more fluctuant character. One object of inquiry might therefore concern the applications of textural variation in thematic recurrence. The reader will perceive that the opening material (Ex. 2-27b), like other instances in episodic as well as expository passages, poses a line of compound implications of two strata in oblique relation, with sequential repetition.[m]

The texture of the first appearance of the motive might be symbolized as $\frac{1}{(1)}$, where (1) is an "implied" independent voice. At the second entry, in mm. 34–35, there is variation in the doubling of the lower component in the second part of the sequence but not in the first. (The statement at m. 57 is analogous to that of m. 15 except for restoration of the primary tonic.) These variations, graphically represented in Ex. 2-27c, show texture undergoing transformations complementary to those of fluctuant tonal reference. The

---

[42]The Telemann movement is briefly discussed and quoted in full in Carl Parrish, *A Treasury of Early Music* (New York: W. W. Norton and Co., 1958), pp. 297–301.

Ex. 2-27a.   Telemann, Fantasy No. 4 for violin alone, first movement.

Reprinted from Georg Philipp Telemann, *Musikalische Werke, G. Hausswald, ed., by permission of Bärenreiter-Verlag.*

Ex. 2-27b.   Compound implications in the primary motive, m. 1.

Ex. 2-27c.   Texture in thematic recurrences.

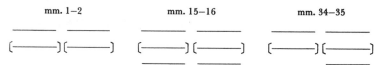

progression constituted by this series of appearances is one in which an initial texture of $\frac{1}{(1)}$ is enhanced in subsequent appearances by a true, sounding doubling component; where this augmentation of density is only partially carried out (mm. 34–35) there is at the same time extension of the unit by repetition of the two-measure pattern.

Most vital to the analysis of texture in this as in any example is again the consideration of the concept of textural progression: the quantitative increase, or the progressive introduction of qualitative changes in the direction of increased complexity and intensity in interlinear relations. It is remarkable, and typical of this movement's unusual interest within the restraints of the medium, that there are qualitative and quantitative textural shapes which constitute an important aspect of its structure in complementarity with other elements.

The obvious but critically expressive profile of the opening phrase, considered in the light of textural change, is an example. The accrual from a condition of two implied voices, one relatively static, to two sounding voices in considerable differentiation, to the four-voice density of the dissonant chord at m. 5, to the release into cadence, with a second sounding voice (inactive) momentarily introduced, is expressive of a persuasive *textural shape* beautifully complementary to that of the line of pitch events, and to that of the occurrence of tonal and implicit dissonance as well.[43]

The textural structure of the digression at mm. 21–34 (Ex. 2-27d) requires special study: it is a crucial element in the climactic, chromatic

Ex. 2-27d.

Reprinted from Georg Philipp Telemann, Musikalische Werke, *G. Hausswald, ed., by permission of Bärenreiter-Verlag.*

[43]The textural structure of the first digression (partially quoted in Ex. 2-27a) is very different from that of the theme: it consists of an *alternation between contrasting textures,* an alternation in which change is variational rather than significantly climactically directed or subsident. (Measures 42–50 of the movement are comparable.) Space does not allow detailed

development preceding the m. 34 cadence. Here are stages very subtly contrasted indeed. Compare, for example, the implied two-voice texture with which it begins, one in which only one of two implied voices is significantly active in pitch-line; from this tentative diversification there is progression reaching a level of determined opposition of the two (albeit still implied) strata after m. 30, and the subsequent, late recession into a condition of relative interlinear accord (m. 33). Further insight into this extraordinary progression can be suggested in the comparison of analogous measures 23, 25, and 29–32. (In what important sense is m. 27 different in textural qualities from m. 23? How, throughout this process, is textural release achieved at punctuating intervals as the directed motion is otherwise continued?) The importance of interlinear independence achieved by the determined, insistent, opposing demands of concurrent textural components is nowhere more potent than at the summit (mm. 30–32) of this progressive shape (an intensity of texture momentarily resumed at m. 41ff.).[44] This fact is critically suggestive with respect to an overall, broadly defined textural progression at the highest architectonic level.

Finally, a spectrum of textural values and conditions might be identified for this piece in a symbolization of content of quantitative and limited qualitative distinctions (Ex. 2-27e).

Ex. 2-27e.

$$ 1 \qquad \frac{1}{(\overline{1})} \qquad \frac{1}{1} \qquad \frac{1}{\dfrac{1}{(\overline{1})}} \qquad 3 \qquad 4 $$

Densities 3 and 4 represent, of course, values of inflated importance in so restricted a medium. Qualitative diversity of three voices, one of them implied, is maximal for this particular context; yet, even the importance of $\frac{1}{(\overline{1})}$, in which there is determined differentiation of components by the means noted above, must be emphasized if Telemann's structure is to be understood. The movement is, in summary, a series of textural progressions and recessions, the former developing (at precadential points) toward maxi-

---

analysis of this passage, nor of the textural structure of the final digression (mm. 63–70)— actually an interruption in the final theme statement, one of subtle, restrained contrasts.

[44]Interlinear intensity in the climactic portion of the movement is suggestive of a textural feature of importance, that in which diversity is achieved by projection of lines whose relative independence is heightened not only by directional and rhythmic opposition but by dramatic contraintervallic relation as well, i.e., by the projection of intervallic features of the *highest possible differentiation*—that of semitonal as opposed to prevalent succession, in the competing stratum, by leaps.

mal quantity and/or maximal diversity and activity in which the texture is significantly complemented by other intensifying factors, *notably tonal fluctuation and dissonance.* Intense qualitative development in the extended digression at mm. 21–34 (Ex. 2-27d) is crucial in textural structure at the broadest hierarchic level.

Bach, "Denn das Gesetz des Geistes," from Motet, *Jesu, meine Freude*

So excellent is Ex. 2-28 for the study of textural structure and process that it is quoted in full.

The opening nine measures are a counterpoint, occasionally imitative: $\frac{2}{1}$,[45] between the alto and soprano components, the latter in a consistent doubling in 3rds; the texture is thus one of two real voices within a density of three lines with restrained imitative interactions and generally contrarhythmic-contradirectional relation between the two essential components. Some imitative interactions are traced as diagonal relations in Ex. 2-28.

Following m. 9 there is a progression in which total interlinear diversification emerges tentatively (m. 11, m. 15ff.) but in which this tendency is restrained by intermittent recession to the textural conditions of the beginning (m. 10, mm. 12–14; note how the textural component consisting of paired interdependent lines undergoes frequent recoloration).

The incipient tendencies in the qualitative progression can be analyzed further in observation of the logical extension of the trends noted above. The consistency of two real voices with occasional imitation in mm. 1–9 thus represents an initial stage; the following bars, with compromising interdependences and consistent imitation, constitute a second stage in the direction of maximal, but not yet achieved, interlinear independence; after m. 15 there is interlinear independence to the end. (In an extreme foreground the rhythmic identification with considerable directional contrast between outer voices in m. 15 is a still intermittent step in the process of diversification, as is that of m. 17.)

Quantitative contrast in the final stage (and momentary relief within the parameter of density-number) is achieved by the opening of the texture to a single voice, with reaccrual of the others, after the m. 19 cadence, the cadential effect of course enhanced by this textural device.

Increasing rhythmic interdependence as well as relative inactivity of the lower voices (especially alto) help to prepare the final cadence, which is nonetheless a relatively sudden cessation of competing contrapuntal activity, enhanced in its provisionally conclusive effect by the fermata and the metric

---

[45]The symbol ⟩ denotes imitative interaction.

Ex. 2-28. Bach, "Denn das Gesetz des Geistes" from Motet, *Jesu, meine Freude.*

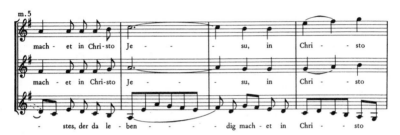

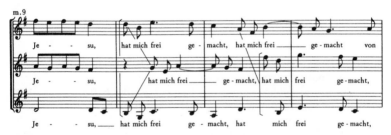

Ex. 2-28 continued.

strength of the final accord. The final phrase, with its stream of imitations at the $d\cdot$, is of course a lower-level textural progression in itself, like the prior section beginning *hat mich frei gemacht.*

The reader will be interested, in further reference to this extraordinary example, to consider the relation of other elements to the textural structure. For example, consider the occurrence of the highest *essential* pitch in conjunction with maximal density and complexity of texture, and the concurrence of the tonal structure, which is modulatory and whose shift of tonal reference also occurs in conjunction with the area of maximal density and intratextural activity. (The persistence of textural complexity, after the noted progressions, to a late point might well be felt as complementary to the open tonal structure.)

Brahms, Symphony No. 1 in C minor, Op. 68, first movement (*Un poco sostenuto*); Introduction

Of necessity, discussion centers here on a portion only of Brahms' first symphony, the introductory first thirty-seven measures of the first movement.[n] It will be possible in this context to consider in an orchestral context a number of features of texture as they pertain to a broad structural function, that of preparation of the main body of the movement. As so often in orchestral symphonic introductions, the tempo is slow in preparation for the *allegro* main body of the movement.

The example is, at the broadest hierarchic level, anacrustic, consisting of a powerful initial attack and subsequent growth and decline to a condition of minimal textural substance, low dynamic level, halted rhythms, relatively settled pitch-lines, and prolongation on the dominant, the most likely harmonic area of anticipatory function. Broadly speaking, there are two textural progressions of compelling spatial and qualitative growth, the second of these having its own, lower-level, progressive anacrustic preparation. There are thus two release areas: the first of these is monophonic, then chordal in texture, the second more active and diverse texturally but with dialogue rather than overlapping interlinear imitation. To a considerable extent, the sense of release is accountable to dynamic reduction and a decrease in sonority, as we shall see, but the resolution of textural complexity is vitally complementary. The entire introduction is quoted in Ex. 2-29a; then the features of texture and textural progression and recession in each of its sections are treated in detail. One striking fact to be emphasized in the analysis is the unmistakable manner in which textural (and complementary) structures are reflected *in analogous shapes at various hierarchic levels* from the broadest, that of the entire introduction, to the most microcosmic, that of a single motive.

It seems desirable to pause briefly to see the introduction as a macro-unit, a broad anticipatory gesture shaped along the lines suggested above and below. These lines represent a path of growth and decline, an intensity curve, as represented in Ex. 2-29b; the graphic treatment includes a summary curve and shows the overall metric function of anacrusis in a discrete symbolization.

Detailed analysis of textural events and processes in the introduction is best treated with reference to its four divisions: mm. 1–9; 9–20; 21–24 and 25–29 (i.e., 21–29); and 29–37. Certain basic factors should be kept in mind: the broad sweep of the introduction at the background level in which its anticipatory function is preeminent and in which it is broadly seen as a I-V progression preparing the *Allegro*; dramatic technique in which element-change is at times violently severe and abrupt, as when texture "explodes" under the pressures of developed intensity; distinctions between "real" voices as opposed to doubling lines, and among textural parameters of density, space, and qualitative interlinear activity; and the operations of complementary forces, to which adequate, consistent attention cannot always be given—events of coloration (dynamics, articulations, orchestration), tonal-harmonic factors such as dissonance and chromaticism, the drive of melodic line (powerfully inflating the texture-space), and rhythm in all its manifestations (e.g., surface accelerations, as of m. 7 or m. 24, metric elongations, like that of m. 8, or the constant use of syncopation and metric displacement, etc.).

Ex. 2-29a.   Brahms, Symphony No. 1 in C minor, Op. 68, first movement.

Ex. 2-29a continued.

Ex. 2-29a continued.

Ex. 2-29b. Intensity curve at two levels, as shaped by textural and other events, in the Brahms introduction.

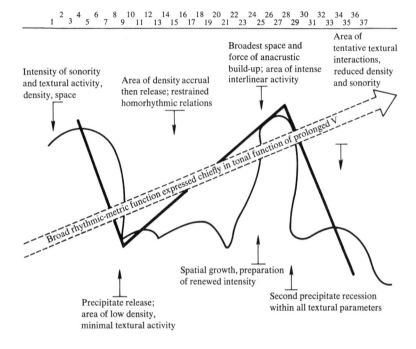

In Section I there are three voices, powerfully stated, each doubled and reinforced. Between voices 1 and 2 there is very little coincidence of movement (i.e., a high degree of rhythmic and metric differentiation); vigorous contrapuntal conflict is apparent too in directional opposition, this factor applied very consistently and fundamentally. Voices 1 and 2 move with great and inexorable drive, intersecting as directions of motion change, dramatically opposed to the rigid insistence of the fixed bass pedal.

Voice 2 (woodwinds, horns 3 and 4, violas) is fortified by doubling in characteristic 3rds (and later 10ths and 6ths), providing increased density with interdependence, a technique largely responsible for the richness of sonority. The sonority of this component (and of the texture as a whole) is of course further enhanced by octave doubling: . The pedal component, too, is enhanced in its sonority by octave doubling: , as is voice 1 (violins and celli):   . The total complex is thus one of three sharply differentiated, heavily doubled components.

The pedal voice is activated powerfully (timpani, double-bass, contrabassoon) by repeated notes in throbbing regularity—a rhythmically insistent factor against the variegated movements of other components— while the first and second horns sustain the tonic PC. The pedal, while a tonally-melodically static component in and of itself, thus constitutes a strong contrapuntal factor against the drive of the other voices, to which it is obliquely related. The sense of rigidity opposed to movement (the latter in surging chromatic successions of great dynamic intensity) implies an impact of severe tension (note such dissonances as C, C♯; C, D; C, B♭; etc.; and finally C, F♯) which builds to a really febrile state, rupturing under its own pressures at m. 9.

The progression, as to texture, maintains and does not compromise the firm independence of the three components; in this sense there is no qualitative change. The vital parameter in which there *is* significant change in the texture *is that of space.* The determined, largely chromatic rise of the upper voice (and subsequently that of the second voice) creates, as against the fixed pedal, *a tense inflation of the texture-space.* (A very acute factor in the increasing space, and increasing conflict of dissonance as well, is the final chromatic movement of voice 1—violins, celli—from F to F♯ against the dissonant pedal.) The texture-space, as to its upward component, is in its foreground a complex interaction of conflicting tendencies: rise of voice 1; rise of (the original) voice 2 against descent of voice 1; final rise of voice 1 against descent of voice 2 into urgently indicated, transitory resolution in m. 9.

The stark contrast of Section II's condition of relative serenity is an aspect of characteristic "romantic" effect. The expression of release is, with the confluence of complementary element-changes, considerably a function of radical change of texture and sonority, but (cf. mm. 29–37) with the all-important, persistent, *compensatory intensity of tonally dissonant prolongation.*

The relative prevalence of homorhythmic texture is an indication of textural recession, and in itself a radical contrast to the texture of the preceding phrase. Actually, of course, chordal texture *accrues*, with sustained woodwinds; and sonority is enhanced, in compensatory relation to the severe dynamic and textural reduction, by such techniques as four-octave duplication in the initiating voice. At phrase level, this initial development has to be seen as a gradually expressed density-number progression preparing the chordal, homorhythmic texture which becomes explicit at mm. 11–12. (The tonally distant harmony of m. 11, derived enharmonically, is of complementary effect in relation to pronounced textural change to explicit homorhythmic conditions.) The only contrarhythmic factor is the continued, residual, now motivic, iteration in the low voice: a subtle activation "spilling over" from the preceding pedal voice.

The accrual represented in Ex. 2-29c is repeated in sequence in mm.

Ex. 2-29c.

13–15. But mm. 15–19, which correspond to but are an extension of mm. 11–12, achieve more substantial progression: texture and sonority develop in complementation to *crescendo*, the pitch-line rises, there is strong chromatic leaning, etc., and the harmony of m. 15 is itself still more distant tonally than that of m. 11. Again, there is doubling in enhancement of sonority, but more significant is the inflation of texture-space (cf. Section I) which is the consequence of pitch rise; tracing the progressively increased distance between upper and lower components reveals an inflation of the spatial field

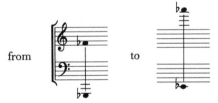

from   to

The abrupt deflation of space (m. 19) is analogous in drastic, summary effect to that of m. 9, although of course within smaller dimensions. The complementarity of linear descent and *diminuendo* are strikingly persuasive. Measures 9–20 are, in summary, a set of lower-level textural progressions and recessions moving, at the level of the section, essentially to and from the syncopated attack at the end of m. 18. As a whole, this section represents a significant contrast to the preceding tumultuous, contrapuntally active conditions; thus, at the hierarchic level of the introduction as a whole, Section II is an area of relative sparsity and inactivity of texture.

Section III serves, in one of its functions, as a return of thematic materials of Section I, but it is condensed from eight to four measures and now is essentially an expression of dominant rather than tonic harmony in keeping with its position in the broad functional tonal-harmonic curve of the introduction as a whole. The anacrustic portion by which it is prepared (mm. 21–24) contains, as do surrounding sections, references to the movement's principal thematic material. Somewhat like Section II, whose materials contrast, it is built texturally of a "compromised monophonic statement" with an accruing chordal background and, *like recurrent patterns in the introduction,* a large spatial inflation by which intensity is mounted and in relation to which dynamic and rhythmically accelerative progressions are again complementary. The main body of Section III (mm. 25–28), to which the preceding four bars are anacrustic, also represents intense spatial expansion, as in Section I, but without the deviating subsidences enroute (hence, the condensation referred to above). The technique of inflation of the texture-space by persistent, determined rise of the upper stratum against a fixed pedal (Ex. 2-29d) *is thus a recurrent technique;* in Section III it is fundamental to the expressive character of both anacrustic and subsequent portions.

Ex. 2-29d.

The development of progressively inflated and expanded texture and sonority in the sustained chordal background against which the ultimately rising and accelerating line of the strings moves is represented in Ex. 2-29e.

Ex. 2-29e.

Here again is a subsidiary progression seen to have important expressive effect within lower-level functional shaping at the level of the phrase. (Once again the complementarity of other elements must be noted; and once again there is the dramatic device of stark contrast of pitch level and range, dynamics, texture, sonority, etc., between Section III and the following. *But note the compensatory continuing stasis of tonal-harmonic condition*—static in its fixed content, but intensifying in the prolongation of dissonant instability.)[46]

With the repeated severe and abrupt change at m. 29 a fourth section emerges, like Section II one of relative tranquillity within all element-structures *except that of tonal function*. Here, for the first time in the introduction, there is significant qualitative (as opposed to quantitative and spatial) textural development. If this is paradoxical, it is not uncommon: at the point of quantitative decline (with complementary reduction of dynamics, deceleration of rhythmic motion, settling of pitch-lines—horn, bassoon, clarinet motive, and final cello line, etc.), Brahms interposes the activating stimulus of interactions among components—the only point in the introduction at which significant imitations arise in a brief, abortive animation of generally declining textural states.

Attention is directed to the individual components of Section IV. *Again there is contradirectional relation*, a characteristic, potent feature of Brahms' counterpoint, between the descending lower motive (derived from the inner voice of the symphony's opening bars) and the ascending *and compound* upper motive (a mirror relation freely derived from Section II?). Texture is again comparable to that of the first section and subsequent manifestations of the same, unifying principle: *that of a fixed element counterpointed against two components forcibly driven in opposing directions*: (⇄). (The "fixed" component is the lower stratum of compound line: texture thus is remarkably analogous to the very different opening of the movement.)[47]

---

[46]It is suggested that further attention be given to comparison between Sections I and III. The main body of Section III (the recapitulative mm. 25–28) is again characterized by determinedly opposed upper voices, severely contradirectional and contrarhythmic in relation, against the fixed pedal beneath. Here, however, the original second voice fails to make ascent subsequent to its initial descent. It levels off; hence, the voices do not intersect as before, because of the formal condensation as well as the higher pitch of the opening (m. 25, violins and flutes) and consequent restrictions of range. In compensation for this restriction, imposed as well on the original upper voice, the illusion of consistent rise is attained by octave transference by doubling violins *at different times*.

[47]Reference has been made to the compound linear structure of the primary motive of Section IV (see the oboe part, mm. 29–32). Here is a fascinating study in texture and textural progression *at a microcosmic level*. For this line is, in its microcosmic projection, a manifestation of the shaping of texture-space "like" that of the monumental Section I and other segments of the introduction as described in these pages. Within that line, and at its lower implied level, a "pedal" is established by the recurring dominant pitch; against this another implied level effects the line's primary rising inflection to a high point from which

A number of imitations should be traced. The motive taken up by the oboe, flute, and cello (imitated at 6 ♩., then twice at 1 ♩.) effects an upward linear projection in the oboe portion and subsequently an implied linear "ascent" of PC, but in descending octave registers, in the succession from

to   to   , a striking

use of compensatory "progression" of "higher" pitch within the opposing context of recessively lower registral placements.

The other motive is taken by horn, then bassoon and clarinet, first at a distance of 3 ♩. (twice), then at a distance of 5 ♩. between the clarinet entry of m. 32 and the final hint of the motive, the viola descent of m. 34. In the progression of imitative interactions noted above (a modest one) it is to be noted that the function of stretto, restrained though it is, in mm. 32–33, is significantly supportive of the achievement at the same time of a peak in the linear rise before the final cadential settling. All of this constitutes a low-level shape of course subsidiary in relation to the ultimate textural-dynamic-pitch release of the introduction broadly heard.

Section IV might, in textural structure, be represented as in Ex. 2-29f.

Ex. 2-29f. A representation of qualitative progression and recession, and the curve of density-number changes, in Section IV.

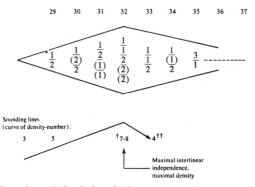

*Symbols not in vertical ordering of voices.

†One unison doubling: a differentiation of sonority and coloration, not of density-number.

‡In m. 34, two unison doublings.

melodic motion (and with it, the spatial relation between the two implied strata) recedes. This is symptomatic of the extent to which analysis can go in consideration of a single element or characteristic of structure at various levels of progression, as well as the remarkable parallels that can pertain among such levels.

There is increased intensity within this subsidiary shape *in density, in space, and in qualitative interlinear interactions*; it is illuminating to "see" this progression-recession in these foreground details and then to stand back to "see" (and hear!) it in its broader context as a release area yet anticipatory of the following *Allegro*, with its vigorous resumption of energy. In Section IV, as throughout the introduction, a basic issue is apparent: the achievement of textural diversity by the rhythmic and especially directional differentiation of lines, an aspect of which is the movement-against-stasis relation of pedal to moving voices. In relation to this fundamental technique, the imitations of Section IV are of ancillary importance, nevertheless significantly functional within the foreground level of that section itself.

Finally, we should recall in broad summary the significance of *all* textural parameters in functional contribution in the expressive effect and character of the introduction as a whole, and in the often strikingly analogous shapes of its parts at various levels. Texture functions in complementary relation to the structures of other elements, in the end achieving the release of spent intensity in a number of aspects, texture included, a release which is compensatory to the persistently static (finally dissonant) tonal condition resolved only in the main body of the movement.

Dallapiccola, *Goethe-Lieder* for soprano and three clarinets (No. 1, "In tausend Formen")

Dallapiccola's *Goethe-Lieder*, like many of his works, are without exception of special interest for the study of textural conditions and processes. Primary attention is given in the present analysis to the first of these songs (Ex. 2-30a). The work's twelve-tone set will be found within a brief supplementary reference at the end of this chapter.°

Brief observation suggests that the song is divisible by cadential punctuation *and by disparity of technique* into three sections: the first, from m. 1 into m. 10, is divisible into two subsections, with the second (after the m. 7 cadence) presenting the voices of mm. 1–4 in mirror variations and with all four forms of the row presented in a context in which imitation is free and occasional;[48] the second section, m. 10 to the upbeat of m. 14, is altogether based on the three-note cellular unit formed by order numbers 1-2-3 (and 6-7-8; see the twelve-tone set), so that there are constant imitative interactions on varied motive forms at close distances; the third section, in which the disposition of the row is entirely linear (m. 13, following the cadence, to

---

[48]The variation in mm. 7–10 is essentially textural, with the voices restating material in multiple counterpoint as well as in mirror relations.

Ex. 2-30a. Dallapiccola, *Goethe-Lieder* (No. 1, "In tausend Formen").

*All notation at sounding pitch.

Ex. 2-30a continued.

the end) features a continual concurrence of inversionally related set-forms (B♭ clarinet with bass clarinet, and voice with E♭ clarinet) producing *two rhythmically free mirror canons* (the relations are contrarhythmic-contradirectional-homointervallic) with a considerable number of imitative relations, those once removed[49] close enough to have significant impact.

There are at various levels important and expressive progressions in the textural structure and these will be summarized. Already clear in the above prefatory comments is the function of texture in delineating the song's three major divisions; naturally other element-changes contribute to this delineation (note rhythmic or dynamic shapes, for example), but the contrasting implications of texture classes and techniques are of great importance in this respect. It is of course generally true in a serial work that where the row is deployed in horizontal distribution, imitation, if the texture is of more than one voice, will result in some way (granted that it can be elusive if rhythmic nonconformity is extreme and persistent); in this sense the first three measures (where the prime form of the set is distributed in vertical and diagonal lines throughout the three-voice texture) contrast with, for example, mm. 14–15 (where each voice presents a given set-form in linear ordering—I[10], P[6], and P[8], then I[5] in the E♭ clarinet).

The functions of textural change in cadential definition are particularly evident in this piece, notably in the final cadence. It is significant that conditions of severe dissonance tend to be maintained at points of cadential resolution; release is critically a consequence of element-changes other than that of harmonic content. To some extent cadential expression is rhythmic (e.g., longer values at even tentative cadences like m. 4, clarinet parts; at m. 7; and at the more decisive cadences of mm. 9–10 and the end). Dynamic change plays a part too: except for the punctuation at m. 13, very much suppressed in the interest of preparation for the climactic section following, cadence is characterized by *diminuendo*—particularly deliberate in the final bars, where there is recessive coloration denoted by such instructions as *p subito, più p, ppp, a bocca semichiusa*,[50] and *perdendosi*.[51] And melodic descent is also palpably functional in cadential expression.

---

[49]If three voices (or more) participate in imitation on a single motive, the earliest follower is in *direct* (or contiguous) imitation while the next follower, in direct imitation with the second entering voice, is at the same time in *imitation once removed* with respect to the original statement. Other voices follow in imitation twice, three times removed, etc., with respect to the original voice and in closer diagonal relations to preceding voices subsequent in entry to the original. This is a significant factor in imitative textures, resulting in *triangular* and *multiangular* relations, because, especially where varied subject forms appear in a single exposition, the lines of significant relation assume very complex patterns in perceptible (not just theoretical) interactions when the distance of imitation is not extreme. When the imitation once removed is closer in shape and intervallic content to the original subject than is the direct imitation, triangular relations are particularly persuasive. (Note the Dallapiccola after m. 13, where imitations once removed are homodirectional, as compared with more proximate contradirectional imitations.)

[50]With half-closed mouth.

[51]Vanishing.

Related to the factor of melodic descent in cadential formulation is that of the *contraction of texture-space* as a device in cadence. The reduction of texture-space to the compass of a minor 6th in the final cadence is an indication of this: in fact, the final chord achieves the work's smallest space.

Comparable recessions in which the contraction of texture-space is an important factor can be seen in the synopsis in Ex. 2-30b; the superimposed pointing bracket is intended to draw attention to composite recessive contraction of the third, fourth, and fifth units at a broad hierarchic level.[52]

Ex. 2-30b. Texture-space contraction in the Dallapiccola phrases and at a broader level.

In other respects too texture functions in the expression of cadence. While the cadences tend to maintain a density of 4 (except for the initial progression fairly constant in the work in general), *they are marked by increased interdependence of component lines*—again with the exception of m. 13, where cadential stability is not appropriate in view of the approaching, climactic progression. The tentative cadence of m. 4 is marked by the accord of all three voices and is prepared by qualitatively recessive rhythmic association between upper voices in mm. 2–3. That of mm. 6–7 is prepared by rhythmic identification between upper clarinets at m. 5 and among all four voices at the start of m. 6. The cadence into m. 10 is of course analogous to that of m. 4, since it concludes the mirror variation of the opening bars, but it is enhanced here by the interdependent bass clarinet and singing voice, each of which pauses on a note of long duration, the voices coincident in attack. And the interlinear interdependence of the final cadence *is the most marked of all*; and its homorhythmic, homointervallic, homodirectional (except for mirrored outer voices—a final surviving factor of textural vitality) conformity is again gradually prepared by qualitative recession. Interlinear interdependence as

[52]The texture-space configuration of the introductory phrase, mm. 1–4, and that of its mirror, mm. 7–10, are of special interest; the spatial shape of the first phrase is one in which the initial compass is that of a major 7th, expanding to the same interval in its compound form, and contracting to the original interval transposed but in a proximate area.

expressed by Dallapiccola is often marked by considerable directional and intervallic conformity as well as rhythmic. In a context of unusual rhythmic diversity, interdependences within the texture (units of 2, 3, 4) have particularly strong effect and are obvious factors of shaping control.

Brief attention should be given to the factor of time interval and to the consideration of possible functions of changes in the distances of imitation.

In m. 10ff., the first section in which imitation is prevalent, indeed constant, the trichordal cellular subset mentioned earlier appears in numerous transformations. If we take its original occurrence as order numbers 1-2-3 as definitive (and take as referential the IC succession 1-2: a rising minor 2nd, then a descending major 2nd), we can note the following specific variations, with rhythmic formulations generally involving two sixteenth-notes with the third tied into a longer note or, later, eighth-notes throughout or triplet sixteenth-notes with the third tied into a longer note: mirror (e.g., E♭ clarinet, m. 11), retrograde (e.g., B♭ clarinet, m. 12), retrograde inversion (e.g., bass clarinet, m. 12), and occurrences in which compound and complementary forms of the intervals are used in expansion of the intervallic content (e.g., bass clarinet in m. 11, or voice setting of *Zauberschleiern*, also a distinct augmentation).

The grouping is easily identified and the interactions among voices unmistakable, although of course those imitations in which two like forms or closely similar rhythmic and intervallic formulations follow directly bring the effect of imitative interaction suddenly into clearest focus: e.g., B♭ clarinet and E♭ clarinet, beginning of m. 13; or the same voices in mm. 11–12. The effect is one of dense entanglement of texture in which four voices, all of them constant in activity, project a single limited idea obsessively in references that relate diagonally to other voices and, if one considers imitations once removed (see dotted lines in Ex. 2-30c), a set of interlinear relations of great complexity. It is in this sense perhaps more than any other that this section is a pronounced contrast to the others.[53]

In mm. 10–13 the distance of imitation does *not* undergo significant change. There is imitation at 4 ♪ (between upper clarinets, m. 10) and at 3 ♪ (between bass and E♭ clarinets, across the bar-line separating mm. 11 and 12), but otherwise *direct imitations* are consistently at a distance of 2 ♪ —in one sense a preparation for the tightest stretto, at m. 13, at 1 ♪. (This does not take into account the augmented forms of the motive in the singing voice, which while involved in the web of interactions seem at the same time somewhat "removed" in relation to the faster-moving clarinets.) Thus, the pro-

---

[53]The line of text set here, *Du magst mit Zauberschleiern dich bedekken* (You may clothe yourself in magic veils), seems a very suggestive basis for the music's texture.

Ex. 2-30c. An incomplete tracing of imitative interactions in the area of greatest textural complexity.

IC sequence 1–2 (m2–M2), in order numbers 1–2–3, the underlying intervallic resource. for mm.10–14:

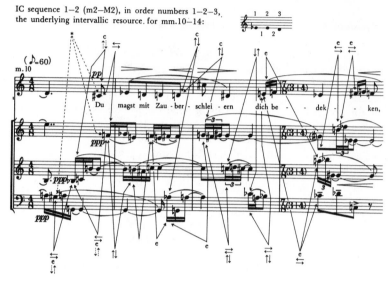

$\uparrow\downarrow$ Only partially applicable.

cBy interval complementation in some degree.

*Instances of imitation once and twice removed, forming multiangular relations.

eIn some degree by interval expansion or contraction involving compound forms (e. g., m9 ⟶ m2).

cedures of imitative distance are of surprising unity, with traces of asymmetry interjected by occasional violations of the normative distance. In this instance *the time interval of imitation functions as a relatively fixed aspect of very active texture, compensatorily stabilizing in its effect* in a context in which there is constant variation of central material in a web of diagonal and multiangular interactions. (Complementary, unifying elements could be noted: the relatively limited *essential* movement of melodic lines, motivic-cellular homogeneity, relative consistency of rhythmic pattern, etc.)

In the climactic section which follows precipitately (note complementary slightly faster tempo, *crescendi*, pitch rise, etc.) we have observed contradirectional canons occasioned by concurrent uses of inversionally related row forms. (Canonic imitations once removed are homodirectional.) Homodirectional canons once removed are at 9 ♪ (B♭ clarinet and singing voice) and 14 ♪ (bass clarinet and E♭ clarinet); those in direct contiguity and in contradirectional relation are at shorter distances: 6 ♪ (voice and E♭ clarinet) and 1 ♪ (B♭ and bass clarinets).[54] In the consideration of time intervals in this section there seem to be three important conclusions to be drawn regarding the functional effect of imitative distance and its changes: (1) there is *constant modification* of the time interval—any regularity of spacing seems insistently avoided in favor of constant flux (cf. the preceding section); (2) the rhythms of the component lines are so contrived that *absolute concurrence (time interval of 0) is achieved only in cadential formulation,* as noted earlier; and (3) the abruptly and maximally *tight stretto with which the section begins* (lower clarinets at 1 ♪) *contributes complementarily to climactic energy,* and is coincident with *forte* and *crescendo,* the performance direction *appassionato,* and other factors.

It is noteworthy in the texture as a whole that density changes are slight; in general the four component voices are rather continually engaged apart from the progressive accrual at the beginning (and the repetition of this pattern in variation a few bars later). A charting of the texture throughout, however, reveals a series of qualitative successions in the direction of maximal diversity and subsequently in the direction of resolution; it reveals maximal textural complexity and interlinear interaction in the song's climactic measures (13–15) and the section approaching these.

With reference to the presentation given in Ex. 2-30d, we can make the following summary observations: at point (a), progression to and through

Ex. 2-30d. A schematic representation of interlinear independence and interdependence throughout the Dallapiccola song.

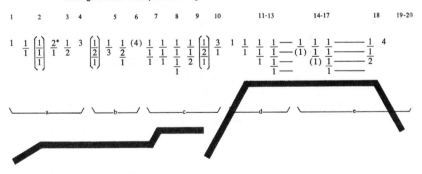

*Symbols of interlinear association—e.g., (2), denote rhythmic interdependence and often directional and intervallic conformity as well.

[54]The time interval of 8 ♪ occurs in direct contradirectional imitation between bass clarinet and singing voice across the bar-line between mm. 13 and 14.

briefly manifest diversity $\frac{1}{\underset{1}{1}}$ (and density 3), recession through diversity $\frac{2}{1}$ to cadential accord; at (b), with density 4 constant, fluctuation between three and two real components to the cadential accord, 4; at (c), density progression from 3 to 4, qualitative progression to maximal diversity-activity in m. 8, then a recession; at (d), quick (but graduated) progression to density 4 and diversity $\frac{1}{\underset{1}{1}}$, maximal diversity continuing into the cadential bar with punctuation a function of rests—i.e., brief opening of texture by the release of the singing voice and bass clarinet; at (e), again, quickly progressive accrual to density 4 and total diversity as above, then a recession to three real components, followed by highest degree of accord at the cadence.

Again, analysis at various structural levels is indicated—e.g., at one level the consideration of the shape within a phrase like that of mm. 7–10, and at a broader level the consideration of the function of this shape and its quantitative and qualitative states in the course of the directed line of intensity reaching its culmination in subsequent sections. *In the broadest view*, the texture is seen to attain through the various stages noted a condition of maximal complexity, vitality, and density in the internal, climactic portions: the diversity $\frac{1}{\underset{1}{1}}$, tentatively developed in m. 8, *is increasingly persistent in mm. 11–16.*

The final cadence is achieved *primarily texturally* despite the actions of complementary element-structures; it is the point of resolution of highly complex and active textures progressively developed, and it is characterized by almost total interdependence of components, an interdependence compromised only by the contradirectional relation of outer voices in a persistent but subordinate manifestation of final textural vitality.

Serialism and texture; texture as a product of chance operations

What might be referred to as "classical" serialism has of course important implications for the content and character of musical texture: the usual avoidance of octave doublings, with consequences for maximal heterogeneity of simultaneous PC content, and the frequency of imitative polyphony induced by twelve-tone procedures are two such implications. A further implication is in the predetermined interlinear heterogeneity of PC content resulting from combinatorial applications of serialism.[55]

Densities and other aspects of texture (registral placement, therefore its spatial configuration) have been prescribed in serialization as extensions of the serial prescription of PC (and other elements). Of course, there can be no general statement about *the* method of serialization of densities and other nonpitch elements; one can only cite this or that method adopted by a particular composer in a given work. The PC set (or derived interval set) can be made to yield a numerical set, of course, by any of a number of means: the set of numbers representing the intervallic distances between the initial pitch of the set and each remaining pitch; the set of numbers derived from such intervallic distances between each pitch of the set and the next; the set of numbers denoting PCs as ordered in the set (usually 0–11, 0 = C and 11 = B) may be used as the set, or basis of derived sets, of densities and durations; or the composer may establish an independent density (or duration) set, or an arbitrary or designed set for any element of his work. (*Texture* in serialism means quantitative aspects susceptible to purely numerical analog.)

One example of specific method is provided by Křenek in discussion of his *Sestina*, a work for soprano, violin, guitar, flute, clarinet, trumpet, piano, and percussion. Křenek's derivation of densities concerns both the original row and the rotational principle of the poetic form, *sestina*.[56]

---

[55]No presentation of combinatoriality is possible here, but the reader is referred to the following sources, especially to Babbitt, who is of preeminent importance in the development of combinatorial principles and applications, and to other sources to which these may lead: George Perle, *Serial Composition and Atonality*, 3rd ed. (Berkeley: University of California Press, 1972), pp. 97–98; Milton Babbitt, "Some Aspects of Twelve-Tone Composition," in *The Score*, 12 (June 1955), pp. 53–61; Babbitt, "Set Structure as a Compositional Determinant," in *Journal of Music Theory*, V, 1 (1961), pp. 72–94. Schoenberg's often quoted statement on inversion of the row transposed a 5th below, combined with the original form so as to avoid PC duplication within each pair of corresponding hexachords, occurs on p. 116 of *Style and Idea* (New York: Philosophical Library, 1950). In contrast to combinatoriality of this kind is procedural fixing or "invariance" of segmental content among set associations; see, for example, Babbitt, "Twelve-tone Invariants as Compositional Determinants," in *The Musical Quarterly*, XLVI, 2 (1960), pp. 246–59.

[56]To quote Křenek ["Extents and Limits of Serial Techniques," in *The Musical Quarterly*, XLVI, 2 (1960), p. 223]: "The *Sestina* is one of the poetic forms developed by the Provençal poets of the twelfth century, its original specimen being ascribed to Arnaut Daniel. It may well be called a serial form of poetry, and its essential formative principle is rotation.

"The poem consists of six stanzas of six blank verses each. It hinges upon six keywords which appear at the endings of the individual lines. If in the first stanza the order of these words is 1 2 3 4 5 6, the words will appear in the second stanza in the order 6 1 5 2 4 3. The principle of rotation which is applied here consists in switching the position of every two keywords equidistant from the center of the series, proceeding from the end toward the middle. According to the same principle, the positions of the keywords in the subsequent stanzas are 3 6 4 1 2 5; 5 3 2 6 1 4; 4 5 1 3 6 2; 2 4 6 5 3 1. The process ends here, since the next rotation would produce the original series. The six stanzas are followed by a *Tornada* of

Křenek's consideration of density as serially determined is that of the number of components vertically coincident; in the following extract from his analysis he cites density-compression (our word) as "another parameter," "the location of the tones within the gamut of six octaves designated as the ambitus of the work," subject to a different governing mode of operation. Křenek's twelve-tone set is given in Ex. 2-31, and below is further quotation of his discussion of *Sestina*. (Křenek's "group A" is the set's first hexachord.)

Ex. 2-31. Twelve-tone set for Křenek's *Sestina*, with derived density series.

Derived density series: 6   3   5   4   1   2

Reprinted by permission of Bärenreiter-Verlag.

three lines in which the keywords, one of each pair in the middle and the other at the end of the line, appear in the order 2, 5, 4, 3, 6, 1." (Reprinted by permission of G. Schirmer, Inc.)

Křenek's self-composed text follows in quotation of the first two stanzas only, the translation as given in the cited source, but with the rotation of keywords indicated. None of *Sestina*'s music can be quoted here; Křenek's article quotes from it only very briefly (p. 227).

Vergangen Klang und Klage, sanfter Strom.	1
Die Schwingung der Sekunde wird zum Mass.	2
Was in Geschichte lebt, war's nur ein Zufall?	3
Verfall, Verhall, zerronnene Gestalt?	4
Die Stunde zeitigt Wandel, wendet Zeit.	5
Das Vorgeschrittne ordnet sich der Zahl.	6
In Schritten vorgeordnet durch die Zahl	6
gestaltet sich Gedanke, doch zum Strom	1
wird strenge Teilung, uhr-genaue Zeit.	5
Ist es vermessen, solches Mass von Mass	2
dem Leben aufzuzwingen, der Gestalt?	4
Der Zwang zerrinnt, erzeugt den neuen Zufall.	3
[Bygone are sound and mourning, tender stream.	1
Vibration of the second becomes the measure.	2
What lives in history, was it only chance?	3
Decline, fading sound, vanished shape?	4
The hour causes change, turns the time.	5
What looks ahead subordinates itself to number.	6
In stages preordained by number	6
thought takes shape, but a stream	1
is (the result of) strict division, of clocklike, precise time.	5
Is it presuming to force such an extent of measure	2
on life, on shape?	4
Force vanishes, brings forth new chance.]	3

Reprinted by permission of Bärenreiter-Verlag.
The composer's English translation, included in the article cited above, reprinted by permission of G. Schirmer, Inc.

"Density" is the next parameter to be determined serially. There are six degrees of density whose succession is determined by the position of the pitches in group A. Again the lowest (C) is called 1, the highest (G♯) 6. Consequently the initial series of densities is 6 3 5 4 1 2. In "density 1" the two tone-groups A and B run off simultaneously in a sort of two-part setting in which the duration of the individual tones is determined by the mechanism described . . . . In "density 2" the first and second time segments of group A run concurrently with the first segment of group B. In "density 3" two segments of each group are developed simultaneously, and so forth, until in "density 6" six segments of each group, i.e. twelve all together, run off at the same time.

Another parameter is the location of the tones within the gamut of six octaves designated as the ambitus of the work. The serial statement adopted for this area reads that the tones of each segment should run through as many octaves as there are tones. The direction of the motion is determined by the direction of the corresponding interval in the original series. Since many segments contain less (sic) than six tones, they cover less than six octaves and therefore could extend over various bands of the complete ambitus. This, too, is regulated by special serial statements. Needless to say that all these serial organisms are subject to rotation according to the sestina pattern, which is the supreme law governing every move of every variable within the whole composition.[57]

In the reference from which the above is taken, Křenek explains further devices of density serialization in his *Sechs Vermessene*, a set of six piano pieces.

A later serial work of mine is a set of six piano pieces, called *Sechs Vermessene*. This German title is a play on words, since *vermessen* in German means "completely measured" as well as "presuming," a pun that cannot be reproduced in English. While the time mechanism is similar to that of the *Sestina*, the construction differs from it in that for the first three pieces a system of five layers is set up in which the first has "density 1" (i.e., one note at a time), the next has two tones together, the third three, the fourth four, and the fifth six tones. The time measurements for the various layers are a result of summing up the interval magnitudes involved in the consecutive tone combinations. For example, the tone series of this composition being:

the first combination of tones in "density 2" is: 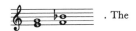 . The

numerical values derived from this progression are 3 (a minor third from G to B♭) and 1 (a half-step from E to F). Consequently the first time segment of the first layer has three units, the first of the second has four (3 + 1). As the density of the layers increases, the number of simultaneously sounding intervals and thus the numerical values of their sums become higher. Therefore *the time segments become longer, which means that the chords, or tone-clusters, with increasing*

---

[57] Ibid., pp. 225–26. (Reprinted by permission of G. Schirmer, Inc.)

thickness are spaced farther apart,[58] *while the single tones of the first layer follow each other more rapidly.* Computations of this kind form the basis of the whole composition.[59]

In illustration of Křenek's basic method of serialization of "layers" and densities in the first three of these pieces, an extract is given from the first (Ex. 2-32). Although the quotation is limited, the density progression is well underway, as is the progression of increasing durations. Identifications of these are included in the example.

Ex. 2-32. Křenek, *Sechs Vermessene*, No. 1.

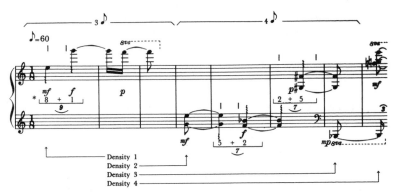

*Notes with wavy stems and numbers indicate subdivisions of the eighth-note. Numbers within slurs show divisions into equal parts, numbers within brackets the groupings of the units of subdivision.

Reprinted by permission of Bärenreiter-Verlag.

In another operation, procedurally opposite yet often paradoxically analogous as to effect,[60] and common in certain contemporary styles, textures are the result of chance by which the performer's "choices" are made within often considerable latitudes.

---

[58]"Spaced farther apart" in attacks, i.e., in relatively longer durations, not in separation by rests.

[59]Ibid., p. 229; emphasis added. (Reprinted by permission of G. Schirmer, Inc.)

[60]While in the Křenek piano piece a contextually functional, palpably significant succession is serially predetermined (the progression of densities having increasing durations), Křenek's method is unusually simple in consequence, with accrual of density (and temporal) values of directly increasing consecutive orders.

Concluding notes

The foregoing analyses and discussions illustrate the modes of textural process as a structure-delineating element in music, and they are a demonstration of the significance and vitality of this element of structure.

Although texture in music is relatively little studied (albeit much referred to), its effect is almost always an important factor in structure and expressive effect in some degree and at some level. Even a slight change— e.g., the abrupt and momentary engagement of the bass or an inner voice in interaction with another melodic entity—can give significant vitality, however abortive, to the texture at the foreground level.

One of the evidences of the significance of textural structure is its immediacy of effect. If this is particularly apparent in quantitative progression (e.g., the graduated accrual of textural components as in so many musical works), it is also true, although subtler in effect, in qualitative changes—for example, the overt passage from homorhythmic to contrarhythmic texture, the fleeting vitalizations of texture by momentary diversification, or the rhythmic and other devices of activation of textures of persistent simplicity of character and content. The textural class of a musical instance is almost certainly one of the first attributes of which we, in listening, become aware; and textural progression or recession (or in static situations the obstinacy of unchanging texture) can be especially compelling and direct in expression of effective, affective musical process.

A specific indication of the significance of musical texture is seen in the apparent fact that complexity or simplicity of texture is important in distinction between what is commonly referred to as "art" music as opposed to "folk," "popular," or "commercial" music. Clearly, one of the primary factors by which art music is, at its best, relatively challenging and interesting is its broad range of textural attitudes and attributes, and modes of textural complexity. The textural uneventfulness which, in part, characterizes so many commercial and popular genres sets them clearly apart from the elaborate, provocative, sometimes monumental processive textures of Western art music. So evident is this that to cite examples seems pointless. It cannot be suggested that this factor is altogether decisive and conclusive in such distinctions ("art music" of small forms, and unpretentious intent, is sometimes relatively, even extremely, uncomplicated in texture), but it may well be that in those instances in which "art" works project little vitality of texture they most approach (in that respect) the realms of popular forms.

Where the range of textural *possibilities* is, in a great art tradition—say, that of liturgical chant—severely limited, it must be said that (1) the limitation *is* that, a boundary which circumscribes the expressive potential of the literature by restricting the parameters within which processive development can take place; and (2) the subtlety of structural delineation, and range of expressive projection, affecting and characterizing *other* element-successions *is significantly compensatory—and probably of magnified value and importance—in relation to the immobility of texture seen as an independent factor*. Both of these observations are valid with respect to liturgical chant, the most obvious instance of highly expressive music in which texture is by definition simple. That great composers in subsequent traditions have so rarely devoted themselves to works of monophonic texture is evidence of the inherent limitations of monophony and the critical importance of textural vitality in highly developed forms of art music.

As this chapter concludes, it should be said again that literatures involved with the study of musical elements other than tonality and harmony (especially those independent of specificity of PC content) leave much yet to be done. Texture and color (timbre, articulation, dynamic intensity, registral coloration, etc.)[61] have been much too little explored in their structural implications. We need especially to understand *process* better, exploring *all* musical events as to their expressions of such fundamental structural functions as progression and recession; this has of course, with respect to the various dimensions of texture, been the concern of this chapter, and if examples to which we have turned have, with accompanying comment, served to point out some approaches to this kind of understanding, they will have served an important purpose.

Rhythm, especially meter, manifest in the functional, proportional interrelations among accentually articulated groups of events, is the concern of the chapter which follows.

---

[61]Unfortunately, references to functional and expressive events and processes of coloration have had, and will have, only tentative exploration in this book. But of all processive functions of element-structures, those of coloration are probably most accessible to analytical identification, even though relative intensity values of timbral differences must be at times the basis for hypothesis of plausible (sometimes seemingly self-evident) but not yet empirically demonstrated function and effect.

NOTES

[a]Study of the varying *specific intervallic content* as to relations between voices 1-2, 2-3, and 3-4 (numbered from top down) in the recurrent chordal factor reveals that the M7 (11 semitones) is always present except at m. 11, whose first chord nevertheless contains overlapping M7s with the m3 the interval of overlapping. Relative dissonance intensities in the chords are complemented by dynamic stress (m. 6) or counteracted by dynamic underemphasis (m. 3) in what can be interpreted as significant functional relations in articulation of structure. Generally high dissonance value in the chords is underscored not only by prevalence of the M7, but by its frequent occurrence between voices 1-2 and 3-4 (it so occurs in half of the chords); the interval between voices 2-3 (P4, m6, m3) is generally relatively consonant, although the crucial *forte* chord of m. 6 projects the M7 between these inner voices as well, standing out as the only exception to a prevalent norm of intervallic content and distribution. The chord of m. 6 is the most dissonant, with three 7ths (2 M7s) superimposed; it has the formal function of launching the song's second part at "midpoint." Measure 6 is unique too as the only point of two consecutive chords (note the dissonance progression between them). Least dissonant chords are probably those of m. 2 (*piano*) and m. 11 (*pianissimo*) at relative extremities in the form. The content of the chords is of course governed in part by the set's three "equal" trichords—

of order numbers 6-7-8 or the ⎹♯♩ ● ♭● configuration of order numbers 9-10-11.

Fluctuations in the space (or density-compression) of chordal events are also of interest in evaluation of function or functional possibilities. Again, the attack at m. 6, *forte,* stands out as *the chord of broadest space* (and necessarily least density-compression) *as well as highest dissonance value*; on the other hand, the *pianissimo* chord of m. 11 has by far the most restricted space (and necessarily greatest density-compression). These two events, of 32-semitone and 19-semitone compasses, respectively, are distinctly anomalous; otherwise spatial fluctuation among chords is limited to the ambitus of (25-26-27-)28 semitones.

The relation of PC content in the chords to that of concurrent vocal phrases is also of interest: the degree to which the chords function responsively (i.e., punctuatively). There is considerable intercomponent interaction of this kind at m. 3, less at m. 5, most of all at m. 11, where the chords do seem responsive-punctuative (especially in a reduced tempo in which such relations are very distinct) in an aspect of the cadential process.

[b]It is interesting to note in the foregoing that where fluctuation is relatively static rather than progressive (e. g., mm. 19–22) complementary effects of ostinato are to be seen. Or, in mm. 21–22, the compensatory effect of motive truncation—analogous to time interval contraction in effect, is a device of progressive rise in the intensity curve while the time interval change is fluctuant between 1, 2, and (once only) 5♪. The device of progression illustrated here, which has important implications for metric structure, is highly characteristic of Bartók (as other passages in the fifth and other quartets will show), as of many other composers of imitative polyphony in all times.

[c]It is noteworthy in the above described circumstances that there is a series of *very locally progressive* accumulations of sonority in the strings, which are chiefly responsible for the ostinato factor. Thus, complementary to local progressions of pitch (and hence of texture-space) within each fragmentary unit, is the growth in sonority as cello and

viola, then violins, enter. The texture cannot be said to be materially affected within these low-level progressions, but sonorous and spatial growth is in the immediate surface a factor in the vitalization of strongly restricted tonal-harmonic content. In the ostinato texture in which the strings prevail the essential PC factors are A and C (occasionally E, and later D is added); of these A has the greater tonal importance, and the horns and tuba, echoing the ostinato, concentrate altogether on A. But (last bar of the quotation) as the two textural complexes become concurrently very active, the A-C distribution is altered in a direction of instability (see the local, tentative, contradirectional relation between double-bass and upper strings—a slight hint of the technique of *displacement* of essentially static PC factors which can contribute to the activation of texture).

ᵈNo impression is intended that Stravinsky's textures are generally qualitatively simple, activated by rhythmic, articulative and other devices, although this is often true. An instance of very complex texture highly diversified qualitatively and quantitatively is found, for example, in the remarkable canons of Part III of the *Canticum*, where the delineation of formal units is very significantly one of differentiation in extent of textural complexity. A case of texture of highly individuated, intensely interactive, voices is the canonic web beginning (*Ego autem humiliatus . . .*) at m. 219 in Part III. The fact that each line is a linear application of the twelve-tone set indicates of course a necessary consequence of interlinear relations; if one considers these relations as extending to, for example, retrograde imitations, and imitations once or twice removed (like that of contrabass trombone and third viola), the entanglement of diagonal, multiangular, and intersecting lines of imitation becomes an intricate maze. Several kinds of canon are in process, including mirror canon (↓ ↑), retrograde canon (⇄), strict canon (↑ ↑), as well as imitations of other kinds (homorhythmic-contraintervallic—first and third violas; cf. mm. 224ff. and 227ff.; homodirectional-homointervallic-contrarhythmic—second viola and contrabass trombone; etc.). Rhythmic differentiation is controlled determinedly in interlinear individuation (as when the viola voices enter at varying metric positions in otherwise strict imitation) as well as by expected, usual nonduplication of PC content in vertical coincidences. In the passage there is progressive accrual of density-number and complexity, with recessive process into the cadence (m. 236) achieved by gradual interlinear rhythmic accord without density reduction. The reader should pursue the analysis of the canons, and of the striking usages of textural contrast in formal delineation throughout Part III (as in the heavily sonorous but monophonic statements which begin and end the movement). The example is one of truly organic textural shape and content, and intense textural energy and motivation.

ᵉComparable examples of complementary element-successions in expression of cadential and other functions will easily be found. The anthology which includes the Purcell *Gloria* (see footnote) contains many excellent objects for study of textural factors in functional processes. For example, the factor of increasingly intense contrapuntal interaction among episodes in fugal and other imitative forms is itself a fruitful area of investigation; this can be evident and unusually accessible in works of even minimal textural complexity, as in the Telemann movement from Sonata in E minor for two flutes, whose imitations are incipient in mm. 5–6 at ♩., then ♩, progressing to extended interaction at ♩ following m. 25 and at the metrically anomalous 2 ♩ (as well as ♩ and 4 ♪) in the final episodic development following m. 33; a number of element-structures function complementarily in these progressive operations.

ᶠSo common is developmental, functional textural process in tonal works that examples for reference seem almost gratuitous. The reader might, however, be referred to the first movement of Haydn's Symphony No. 102 in B♭. One of this movement's most striking passages for study of texture occurs in mm. 122–85 in the development. In a process of powerful density progression out of a single voice, there is elaborate, gradual qualitative progression culminating in an intense canon on one of the basic motives. (Complementary processes of other element-structures are of great interest: tonal flux is the most evident of these, but analysis of concurrent element-actions should include review of changes in the motive itself—e.g., in the size and dissonance of its interval of anacrusis—and consideration of the functions of such changes.) In the canonic segment, voice 3 often functions as a nonconforming, deviant presence, adding density and impact, asserting the contrast of relative unpredictability within the canonic regularity, and maintaining, especially rhythmically, the complete motive truncated in much of the canon. The canon is punctuated, then resumes at mm. 168–69; at m. 176 voice 3 doubles voice 2 in *qualitative recession at the cadential approach*, a recessive event in which sonority is maintained. Considerable canonic energy spills into the c:V cadence ending this section of the development, in striking textural contrast to the extremely simple thematic statement which follows. In studying this example, attention should be directed to analysis of various textural events in these progressive and recessive processes, and perhaps to other passages of functional textural change (sometimes intensely, often abortively, imitative and polyphonic, as at m. 210ff.).

ᵍIn this final textural diversification there are several *degrees* of interlinear independence and interdependence: heterorhythmic-heterointervallic-homodirectional rela-

tion,  , occurring, for example, within a spectrum of

textural conditions extending to true contrarhythmic activity (mm. 62–63) and resolving in final textural accord in which modest diversification (even suggestive, abortive imitation) is maintained to the antepenultimate bar.

ʰMuch further comment might be made: the textural progression and recession partially by which the first four phrases are unified are an instructive object of further study; or, for additional exploration, one might consider the means by which the texture of mm. 27–33 (partially quoted in Ex. 2–16), still strongly imitative, are contrived to produce, within the imitation, a momentary homorhythmic relation between the two voices in preparation for the varied return of Part I.

ⁱAn example of textural structure in this broad sense, sharply delineating severely contrasted sections of a freely structured movement (i.e., highly variegated, non-recapitulative) of broad design, is the Prelude to Bach's Partita No. 2 in C minor. Its first section, slow, is essentially chordal—a largely homorhythmic accompanying texture underlying an upper voice melody sometimes doubled (in 3rds) and occasionally setting off brief imitative responses in other voices. The second section, moderately slow (*andante*), is an embellished upper-voice melody against which the bass voice moves in a relation considerably subservient (and far less intricate) but having contrapuntal value in frequent contradirectional relation to and in occasional imitative interactions with the upper voice. The third section is overtly polyphonic—consistently imitative, a kind of invention, the section of far greatest contrarhythmic and contraintervallic complexity and interlinear independence.

The last section is presumably fast; tempo thus emerges as the most apparent complementary element of delineation. With textural and tempo structures, a palpable tonal structure links the three sections into a broad progression centering on tonic and dominant levels; moreover, the tonal structure is one of progressive degrees of fluctuation through the Prelude's three sections. There is thus complementarity among the various relevant element-structures at the broadest architectonic level, as often at more foreground levels; the various "structures" so projected converge in function to serve parallel ends of formal delineation and progressive intensification and subsequent release.

ʲA further useful example in this connection is the third of Schoenberg's Piano Pieces, Op. 19, in all four phrases of which (although minimally in the second) contraction in space is a significant factor in structure and in cadential formulation *as well as in the piece's overall shape* (smallest spaces occur in the third and fourth phrases). The following shows the spatial configurations of the four phrases with "up-down" distances given in semitones; note recurrences of 37 and 27, as compared with cadential spaces of 14, 12, 11:

ᵏIn the Bartók Divertimento for string orchestra, an instance of striking vertical ordering (at mm. 58–61 of the second movement) is attributable to texture, sonority, and coloration. The accompanying fabric has tight density-compression in close spacing between double-bass and viola; and this thick textural backdrop, given a rumbling activation by rhythmic and articulative diversity, is a striking foil indeed for the void, two-octave doubling of the motive, presented in muted violins. Here, the density-compression can be significantly described only with reference to the *distribution* of events within the texture-space. (Cf. other instances of provocative texture, e.g., mm. 66–68, in the same movement.)

ˡThe madrigal, *Moro, moro*, first part, is suggested for further study of similar questions. Again, form is delineated by lines of text, and the manipulation of textural components in and out of cadential punctuations should be considered. The text induces (at *Corre volando*, literally "runs flying") functional devices of animation and textural intensity comparable to those of *Fuggesi* ("flees", "flies away") in *Or, che in gioia*. A particularly striking feature of the textural structure of *Moro, moro*, perhaps recurrent in Gesualdo, is *the tendency of each phrase to progress (to "evolve") texturally*, both quantitatively and qualitatively, with interdependent relations qualifying these paths of progressive diversification. (At m. 3, for example, voices 3 and 5 start the first process of diversification with homorhythmic but contradirectional relation; voices 2 and 3 are often doubled in restraining the progressive tendencies at phrase level, as at mm. 4–6.) The tendency of each phrase to progress in the direction of textural diversity (nowhere fully contrarhythmic-contraintervallic) is associated with the setting of the intense opening words in typically arresting chromatic manner. These words ("I die, I die . . .") are, with heavy chromaticism, set in restrained and simple texture: they are the focus of anguished feeling out of which the entire poem (and composition) arises. As commonly, the intense chromaticism suggests a texture of relative simplicity—near homorhythmic, chordal succession. This restraint of texture is functional not only in exposing the rich chromatic vocabulary, but in exposing the crucial words of text too; in each phrase, with this initiating precedent, subsequent diversification of texture follows from this condition in a highly important, and intensely perceptible, aspect of shape.

ᵐThe important textural issue of compound line in this movement cannot really be developed in the space available; but ideally this aspect of textural diversity should be pursued independently. (Note, for example, the extraordinary contrapuntal interaction at mm. 40–41, at dramatically opposed registers:

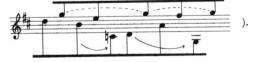

).

In such instances there is true textural diversity within ostensibly monophonic texture, with interactions of vital directional, rhythmic, and intervallic opposition in which dissonance is strongly felt. Understanding of this kind of "concealed" textural diversity and interaction is of course absolutely vital to performance, if dissonant and other interactions of the sort sketched above are to be brought out.

[n]For further study of Brahms in these and related connections attention is drawn, for example, to conditions of texture and textural process in the shaping of phrase structure in the opening of the Quintet in G, Op. 111, for strings. Another example of great interest for the study of texture is the *Adagio* of the Trio in E♭, Op. 40, for piano, violin, and horn. Some factors representative of the extraordinary range of significant textural process and function in this movement can be suggested in hasty summary. The role of textural events in delineation of form is vitally important throughout. (For example, the entry of contrasting thematic material at m. 19 is the subject of startling exposure *by virtue of the change in texture*, quite probably the most arresting of a complex of complementary element-events, and textural change is throughout an important variational device in thematic development and recurrence.) Shaped successions of textural events are of compelling significance: for example, that of the progression from m. 19, which can be traced in various stages, including that of contrapuntal interplay in which a time interval of imitation undergoes contraction from 12 ♪ to 6 ♪; continuation of the process, counteractive to *diminuendo* but complementary to extreme tonal shifts, achieves at m. 30 a time interval of 3 ♪, with the motive undergoing complementary truncation in a manifestation of intensifying metric function. With the time interval fluctuating between 3 ♪ and 4 ♪, the motive is varied in size and in placement in relation to the bar-line: complementary actions are those of rhythmic motion (e.g., *stringendo* and increased activity in the piano), metric instability, intense coloration (e.g., more brilliant violin and horn registers, and *crescendo*), and especially the intense rise in the pitch-line; tonality undergoes compensatory stabilization but with rich chromatic embellishment maintained as in the Neapolitan harmony of m. 35. There is gradual recession into the original theme's restatement eight measures after m. 35, and there are like processes and events of textural, structural significance throughout the movement. (But note, at m. 59ff., the condition of extreme textural stasis—absolute homorhythm and nearly absolute homodirectional association of horn and violin, as well as virtual inactivity of the bass, all complementary to slowed harmonic rhythm, tonal stability, and relaxed dynamic level. Toward m. 74 starkly simple texture is counteractive, on the other hand, in relation to intensifying events of pitch-line, rhythmic acceleration, and especially dynamic level, texture remaining insistently and rigidly uncomplicated.)

[o]No. 2 is a strict canon between the singing voice and the E♭ clarinet at a distance of seven bars; and the continuation of the leader is, from m. 9, a retrograde of the original canonic subject. Thus, simultaneous with strict canon is a retrograde canon between clarinet, as leader, and the singing voice concurrent with it; the retrograde canon is at 3 ♩ .

No. 6 of the *Goethe-Lieder* is basically a mirror canon, the canon in a sense "framed" by the tonally suggestive pitch repetitions of the beginning (singing voice on a) and end (bass clarinet's settling on c). Adjunctive to the canonic procedure are developments of the IC succession 1-2 (as in E♭-E♮-D), twice a trichordal subset of the row:  . The occurrences of this trichordal cellular set will be quickly identified in analysis. With these recurrences, the texture is of greater diversity and greater complexity of interlinear interaction than that of No. 2; the angles of subsidiary diagonal relations change constantly even while the canon is in course. In fact, Dallapiccola concentrates altogether on the three-note subset (order numbers 1-2-3 or 6-7-8) with the result that concurrent with the broader canon is constant imitation on that cellular unit—imitation in mirror and retrograde duplications and in many rhythmic, directional, and intervallic variants. It is striking that only in m. 7 (near the middle) do immediately concurrent intervallic and directional formulations correspond, although in a contrarhythmic relation. The principle of progressive, then recessive process in the "framing" of the very active canon and imitated cellular units, with melodically and tonally more static sections of simpler texture, is functionally important.

rhythm and meter

Introductory notes

All element-processes are rhythmic. In an important sense, the study of rhythm is thus the study of all musical elements, the actions of those elements producing the effects of pace, pattern, and grouping which constitute rhythm.

> To study rhythm is to study all of music. Rhythm both organizes, and is itself organized by, all the elements which create and shape musical processes.[1]

While there are many compelling factors suggesting the critical importance of rhythmic and metric analysis, one of the most persuasive is the fact that metric analysis, in its proper range of implications, *is a vital basis of construction and interpretation of phrasing and articulation* in performance. The study of rhythm, and especially meter, thus proceeds from questions which are truly indispensable to critical, insightful interpretation. Some of these questions can be stated in the following ways: What are the chief events in the hierarchy of musical impulses in a given work, the points of intensity toward which others are oriented? Or, where are the points (and where is *the* point) *to which and from which* musical processes are directed at various levels? A related question which puts the issue of meter in a different way is: Where are the true bar-lines at diverse levels in the musical structure? The present study inquires into many aspects of rhythm beyond that of meter, but questions like the foregoing are a recurrent, underlying preoccupation in the discussions to follow.

It may well be that rhythm and meter, seen as a part of rhythm, constitute the most persuasive and immediately perceptible quality within the range of musical effect. The rates at which events (changes) take place within the various structural parameters, and the patterns into which events group themselves, are of decisive significance in expressive effect in the musical experience.

[1] Grosvenor W. Cooper and Leonard B. Meyer, *The Rhythmic Structure of Music* (© 1960 by The University of Chicago), p. 1; all rights reserved.

The analyses and expository materials which follow will show—beyond somewhat ancillary references made in preceding chapters—how the operations of rhythm and meter permeate and influence the entire range of elements constituting the musical projection.

It has been suggested throughout this book that contrasts in the operations of various structural elements (the element-structures) and the progressive and recessive lines of change in those elements underly morphology and meaning in music in one important sense. Rhythm too undergoes changes with functional consequences for music's intensity scale, playing an essential and telling role in the delineation of processes of growth and decline, climax and subsidence, stability and flux. In this sense, it is no absurdity to speak, for example, of a *metric rhythm* as the rate and pattern of metric change, or a *tempo rhythm* in music. Contrasting rhythmic events function with those of other elements to delineate musical structures at all levels.

A relatively recent effort toward comprehensive theoretical treatment of rhythm gives necessary acknowledgment to the subjectivities and complexities of rhythmic interpretation.

> Rhythmic grouping is a mental fact, not a physical one. There are no hard and fast rules for calculating what in any particular instance the grouping is. Sensitive, well-trained musicians may differ. Indeed, it is this that makes performance an art—that makes different phrasings and different interpretations of a piece of music possible. Furthermore, grouping may at times be purposefully ambiguous and must be thus understood rather than forced into a clear decisive pattern. In brief, the interpretation of music—and this is what analysis should be—is an art requiring experience, understanding, and sensitivity.[2]

> Because *every rhythm is unique*, having its own organization and hence its own particular analytic problems, no selection of examples can possibly cover the rhythmic permutations and analytic problems which may arise.
> The task of organization . . . becomes more difficult once one leaves the "hothouse" variety of example behind and ventures forth into the world of real music. Here, variables do not operate singly. Nor is it generally possible to classify the rhythm of a given example under a single simple category. Not only do groupings vary from one architectonic level to another, but particularly on lower levels changes of grouping are the rule rather than the exception.[3]

We shall have to be continually aware that the importance of a theoretical problem *is not invalidated by the difficulties of approaches to solution*

---

[2]Cooper and Meyer, *The Rhythmic Structure of Music*, p. 9.
[3]Cooper and Meyer, *op. cit.*, p. 60. See also Howard E. Smither, "The Rhythmic Analysis of 20th-Century Music," in *Journal of Music Theory*, VIII, 1 (1964), pp. 69–70.

or by the uncertainties or equivocations of proposed solutions. Indeed, the significance of a question is at times inversely related to its simplicity of treatment. In many instances in prior studies, we have had occasion in analysis to note the factor of interpretive judgment, not of course capricious or arbitrary, citing criteria of analysis in support of such judgment, as opposed to the determination of "right" answers to the questions from which analysis proceeds. The range of significant, plausible interpretations of rhythmic structure is often of particular breadth and diversity; and the possible validity of differing conclusions must be noted as an important object of analysis. The subjective and often elusive criteria at the root of particular rhythmic interpretations are especially evident in the study of accent-delineated metric structure.

The awesome complexity of problems of rhythmic structure and analysis can be seen when one appreciates that *rhythm is a generic factor,* one aspect of which is meter. Yet meter is *only one of numerous manifestations of grouping.* And meter, as conceived here, *is dependent on accent*—a phenomenon whose existence no one would deny, yet in which many qualities of impulse (event, attack) interact variously at different levels of structure. Thus, questions of rhythm lead at some point to questions of grouping, and in turn to questions of meter, which rests upon the difficult questions of accent.

Inevitably, one manifestation of the complexity of rhythmic theory is the problem of terminology, the problem of the medium by which theoretical discourse is carried on in expression of basic concepts. The meanings of such words as "rhythm," "accent," and "meter," not to mention terms like "syncopation" or even "duration" (Does the duration of a rhythmic impulse include surrounding silences?), are variously used in the literature on music. A constant effort is made in the present study to establish fundamental premises linking essential terms and concepts, with terms defined so that their use, if not standard or conventional, will be clear.

The broad basis for the present study might be shown graphically as in Fig. 3-1, in which rhythm is presented as a generic class of *pacing, patterning, and partitioning events in music*; a facet of rhythm is grouping, a subcategory of which is represented as meter.

The position of meter in the graphic representation in Fig. 3-1 must not be misconstrued as indicative of subsidiary importance. The fact is that a very significant, often perceptually immediate, functional grouping is delineated in music by accent, by an event's "superiority" of content and projection in which surrounding (anticipative and reactive) events are "absorbed" into an accent-governed metric unit.

When accent-delineated grouping is firmly established, opposing accents, which are very necessary and usual in interesting music, may be felt as "syncopated" against (counteractive to) a prevailing, precondition-

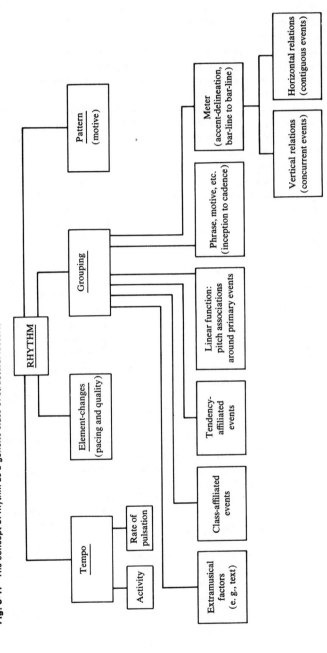

Fig. 3-1. The concept of rhythm as a generic class of structural factors.

ing, still underlying metric basis. Or counteraccent, imposed against a pattern of units not referentially established and preconditioning, may bring about fluctuation in the metric structure: contiguous and concurrent units thus emerge in fluctuant, asymmetrical relations.

Fundamental concepts of rhythm

While it is sometimes broadly described as "ordered time" or narrowly as "meter," it seems essential that rhythm be viewed as both manifold and specific: the sum of a broad range of factors each of which is in some way a manifestation of pace and grouping, the former a product of relative frequencies of events, the latter of their relative qualities and the means by which they are unit-ordered. The factors of rhythm can be detailed as follows.

Rhythm is:

1. *Tempo*, which has two aspects: the eventfulness of music (degree to which the temporal continuity and flow are filled with articulate impulses or related silences) and the frequency of pulsation at some given level.[4] (In the latter aspect, note the recurrent concept of a "norm" of tempo—e.g., that of a physiological manifestation like heartbeat or stride.) We shall refer to these two aspects of tempo as *activity-tempo* and *pulse-tempo* (the degree of eventfulness and the rate of pulse succession,[5] respectively); tempo is thus the quality of rhythmic motion and drive. (As to controlled, functional changes in activity-tempo, see Ex. 2-22, pp. 250–52, one of many extracts cited in which the factor of shaped degrees of "eventfulness" is described as essential in functional effect.)

2. *Pattern or motive* (cf. rhythmic "mode"), as expressed in durational and other strong-weak combinations which have in a given context motivic significance at some level, or characteristics of pattern by which a style, genre, or work can usefully be identified. Rhythmic pattern is explicit

---

[4]*Pulse* will be understood as the felt, underlying, at times regularly recurrent unit by which music's time span is measured and its divisions felt at some specified level—the basis for counting, or conducting, and for metronomic indications of "tempo." Pulses recur regularly only at certain levels in most music, conspicuously at the level of the notated bar; some music however, notably liturgical chant of the Middle Ages, must be regarded as indifferent to regular pulsation.

Impulse is regarded here as the event itself (attack, stimulus, integral silence) superimposed on and related to the stream of pulsation.

[5]As to shaped control of pulse-tempo relations, see Robert Erickson's discussion of his Duo for violin and piano in *Journal of Music Theory*, VII, 2, (1963), pp. 174–92. In this poignant and articulate article, entitled "Time-Relations," Erickson states and enlarges upon his creative interest in the contemporary relevance and usefulness of a concept of a fluid ("incommensurable") time field of which the traditional fermata is representative.

especially in the sequence of attack and change by which the musical "line" is delineated; an important item within this area of rhythmic effect and identity is that in which motivic units become recurrent within broader units and fundamental to the delineation of musical form (e.g., isorhythms, etc.).

3. *The profiles expressed in element-changes* (manifest individually and in confluence) as these changes involve pattern, rate, and degree of change. Thus, melodic rhythm normally seen as the rate and pattern of pitch change (or attack without pitch change) within a line, harmonic rhythm, textural rhythm, and other element- and subelement-rhythms constitute this aspect of rhythmic experience.

4. *Grouping*, or partitioning of music's time span by associations perceived within and among punctuated or articulated unit-orderings of events. One mode of grouping is meter; it is, like tempo, one of rhythm's most telling aspects.

Rhythm as activity and motion

Although it is not to be a subject of extensive attention in this chapter, rhythm as the motor aspect of music (pace, drive, activity-tempo)—the "energy" dispelled in relation to the extent of eventfulness in the succession of impulses—is exceedingly important and fundamental in musical structure and effect.

The control of rhythmic activity is among the most elemental of music's shaping forces, one of the most direct of functional devices, comparable in immediacy to the control of dynamic intensity.[6] The experience of, for example, activity-tempo acceleration in the direction of developmental climax, or deceleration signalling release, is a fact to which everyone conditioned to interesting musical experience will testify.[a]

An example of the shaping power of controlled changes in rhythmic motion (activity-tempo) is afforded by the first movement of Webern's Op. 22, to which reference was made in Chapter 2 (Exx. 2-22, and 3-1). Analyses of other element-progressions toward the climactic mm. 22–23 can be complemented by illustration of composite activity. Pulse-tempo is constant, but there is a distinct progressive curve in activity-tempo mounting toward m. 22 and receding toward the fermata between mm. 27 and 28, the subsident aim of recessive operations following m. 22. In Ex. 3-1

---

[6]The quality of rhythmic motion can be an important and essential factor in the identification and characterization of style. For example, many literatures of the Baroque are marked by relatively constant activity-tempo (as compared with, for example, the more "romantic," changeable impulses of certain other styles).

there are three views of the rhythmic progression. The first of these, perhaps more a representation of significant textural accrual, shows the rate of attack of two- and three-note motives which are a basic unifying material; the second and third portions of the example represent in different ways the composite motion or rate and spacing of attack. The upper line shows this by indicating the frequency of occurrence of rests (separated by ♪ distances of 3, 3, 2, 11, 15, 6, 5, 2, 3, 1, 1) and the lower line by indicating frequencies and durations of notes anywhere in the texture. The example is characteristic.[b]

Ex. 3-1. Representation of activity-tempo curve in a passage from Webern's Quartet, Op. 22, first movement (see Ex. 2-22, pp. 251–52, for extracted quotations).

Recessive and progressive rhythmic actions and relations, tightly controlled and directed to and from relative levels of stability, can be seen in works of Elliott Carter. Carter is known for a procedure of controlled change in tempo described as "metric modulation" by which *pulse and pulse rate* change gradually, often at frequent intervals, in a procedure determining an aspect of tempo-structure at various levels. This method of "covert" tempo change is illustrated in a passage from the String Quartet No. 1 (Ex. 3-2a).

One factor in the quoted passage is *contraction in the low-level metric unit.* (Compare the changes in activity-tempo as well as pulse-tempo; of the two aspects of tempo, it can be seen that first they run parallel, then while there is acceleration in pulse-tempo activity-tempo is held back before the progressive actions of m. 22.) Example 3-2b traces the process toward an accelerated ♩ pulse from 72 MM to 120 MM.

Ex. 3-2a. Carter, String Quartet No. 1, first movement.

Reprinted by permission of Associated Music Publishers, Inc.

Ex. 3-2b. "Metric modulation" in the Carter example.

$$\left(\text{\musicglyph{d}} = \text{\musicglyph{dd.}} \right) \qquad \qquad \left(\text{\musicglyph{d.}} = \text{\musicglyph{d}} \right)$$

5*

♩,   i. e., ♪   or   ♪ ⟶ ♪† , i. e., 3♪ (♪.)   ♩

MM   72   288   360   360   120   120

*In a changed meter signature, $\frac{10}{16}$.

†In $\frac{6}{16}$.

Some composers have used notational spaces between sounds as they are represented on the printed page as imprecise guides to the temporal distances by which they are to be separated in performance. One such example of *proportional notation*, but in which mensural temporal intervals are very specifically indicated, is the Berio *Sequenza II* for harp. Here, durations within notated "measures" are suggested only by relative distances separating the printed notes, but each measure is to correspond to a metronomic pulse at 40MM, so that tempo is rigidly controlled at that level. Metric units at phrase levels are controlled too, in significant degree, by their consequent relative durations, differences of pitch content, differences of intensities, punctuative devices (like specified silences of specific or proportional duration, or abrupt dampening of sound, etc.), and other shaping factors. The element of chance in this work is, then, relatively minimal, amounting to a modest latitude of possibilities in which basic rhythmic structure is relatively inviolate.

In the first phrase (Ex. 3-3a), within a stasis of pitch-line and opposed counterpoint of intensity changes, the rate of attack is one of acceleration, then deceleration in a recessive cadential action of palpable functional effect. This can be expressed very simply (Ex. 3-3b) as a progressive, then

Ex. 3-3a. Berio, *Sequenza II* for harp.

recessive rate of increase and decrease in events per stipulated, regularly recurrent unit of time at 40MM, the distribution of events within the mensural unit suggested by graphic proportioning but not specifically controlled.[7] Comparable processes characterize other phrases.

Ex. 3-3b. Accelerative and decelerative rhythmic changes in the first phrase of the Berio *Sequenza II*.

Number of events per 40 MM unit:		+2	+2	+2		−2	−2	
	1	0	2	4	6	6	4	2	1

Rhythmic pattern as motivic

Especially at more immediate levels of structure it is readily apparent that durational and other weak-strong combinations and distributions have great and constant importance in the projection of distinctive, identifiable, associable motivic and thematic ideas which are exposed and developed in the music of most Western styles.

Rhythmic patterns have in various systems undergone theoretical classification, often as *rhythmic modes* corresponding to and derived from the classes and terminology of standard feet of ancient Greek poetic theory. The most common of these modes are six: trochaic (long-short, or strong-weak: — ◡), iambic (◡ —), dactylic (— ◡ ◡), anapestic (◡ ◡ —), spondaic (— —), and tribrachic (◡ ◡). Other modes (e.g., amphibrach: ◡ — ◡) are noted in some systems.[8]

[7]At the same time, the metric formulation within the phrase clearly has to be seen as one of vertical noncongruity between the two linear components of pitch activity, the lower stratum having accent at its inception, the upper having an extensive anticipative "wind-up" in preparation of its later, noncongruent accent.

[8]For brief discussion of (especially thirteenth-century) rhythmic modal theory, and some bibliographical reference, see Willi Apel, *Harvard Dictionary of Music*, 2nd ed. (Cambridge: The Belknap Press of Harvard University Press, 1969), pp. 535–36. While rhythmic modal theory is of great importance in certain music (for example, in thirteenth-century motets, where the application of such theory is often highly systematized), its applications in music broadly viewed can easily be overemphasized, with a resultant simplistic view of what is commonly highly complex and diversified rhythmic organization. This is not to say that analysis and identification (or conjecture) respecting the substance of rhythmic pattern at various levels has no validity; but it is a crippling preoccupation when it is taken as the end of analysis in which rhythms are considered invariably reducible to one of a few traditional classifications, or modes. Musical situations of real interest pose a complex variability of patterned associations not readily or usefully classified within a limited range of assumed referential norms. Nevertheless, the classifiable "modal" rhythmic pattern may at times be relevant to generic combinations upon which thematic substance and structural principles *are based*; and the traditional terminology and symbology of rhythmic modes are often useful.

There are, as might well be expected, instances of applications of other systemic "modes"—indeed, the theoretical possibilities are without limit. In certain of his works, for example, Olivier Messiaen, a figure of considerable importance in contemporary explorations of rhythmic technique, employs rhythmic patterns derived from exotic systems. In Ex. 3-4 the music is based on three Hindu rhythms two of which undergo prescribed transformations—each attack of the first increased by a ♪ at each repetition, durations of the second decreased by the same value at each repetition, and the third reiterated without change. In the brief extract, the three motives are circled; in their immediate repetitions, prescribed durational modifications are indicated.

Ex. 3-4. Messiaen, *Reprises par interversion* (No. 1 of *Livre d'orgue*).

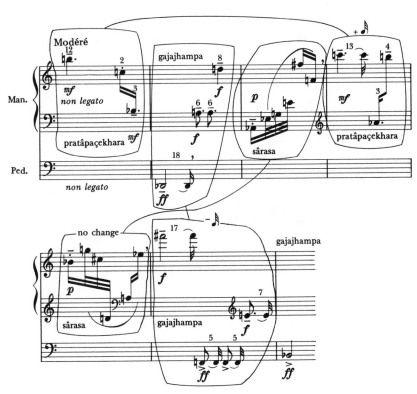

The concepts of *rhythmic ostinato* and *isorhythm* (the latter denoting a recurrent set and ordering of durational values, commonly in tenors of early motets) relate to another practice of rhythm applied motivically. Every student of music is familiar with isorhythmic structures, for example, in many fourteenth-century motets,[9] although more recent applications of analogous techniques are of comparable interest and, perhaps, significance.

The third movement of Webern's Variations, Op. 27, for piano illustrates the isorhythmic principle: thus, the opening four bars plus one 𝅗𝅥 undergo immediate isorhythmic repetition. That is, the initial twelve attacks are duplicated in rhythm by the next twelve (Ex. 3-5). The application of "rhythm as thematic" is again explicit and significant as a parallel to other relations in concurrent effect in the Webern example (e.g., that of the twelve-tone series, occurring as R^{11}—on E♭—in the first twelve attacks, then as RI on E♭ in the next twelve).

Ex. 3-5. Webern, Variations, Op. 27, for piano, third movement.

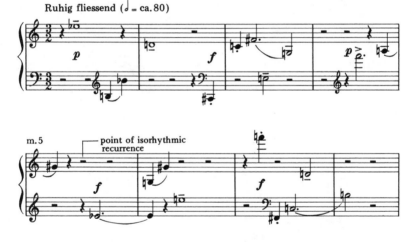

[9]See *Historical Anthology of Music*, Apel and Davison, eds. (Cambridge: Harvard University Press, 1949), Vol. I, Nos. 43 and 44, for examples. A fascinating study of isorhythmic and symmetrical procedures in Machaut's *Messe Notre-Dame*, including discussion of remarkably consistent center-axial "horizontal" symmetries in the work and extending to treatment of comparable technique in other works, is Otto Gombosi, "Machaut's *Messe Notre-Dame*," in *The Musical Quarterly*, XXXVI, 2 (1950), pp. 204–24.

One could of course continue to cite relevant examples of motivic-thematic rhythm at various levels of structure throughout the vast historical span of Western music. Consider, for further reference, the fifth symphony, or the sixth, of Beethoven as to rhythmic motive, in extreme foreground manifestations, having vital and consistent significance. And the entire range of techniques associated with the serialization of rhythms and rhythmic relations is of course related to the principle of motivic rhythm; some of these are noted near the end of this chapter. But concerns of motivic pattern are recurrent too in plentiful studies of thematic process in musical form, especially in literatures dealing with the tonal period. It seems important, then, to move on to more problematic areas of rhythmic theory.[c]

The rhythms of element-successions

We have reiterated the important principle that *every structural element is, in its distributions and qualities of events, expressive of rhythm.* There is thus a rhythm of pitch-line (rhythm seen of course as including meter), a harmonic rhythm, a tonal rhythm, and a rhythm of each of the other elements and parameters of musical events. These rhythms are preeminently: (1) of pacing or tempo—the rate of event articulation and change; (2) of pattern, as manifest in varying durational combinations; (3) of proportions, comparative durational relations among units, or groups of events; and (4) of relative qualities of events and event-successions—degrees (distances) of change, of accent.[d]

The extent to which element-rhythms function concurrently in complementation to or compensation for progressive and recessive, underlying tendencies is invariably striking and illuminating as to function and expressive effect. Take, for example, a brief example from the Diabelli Variations of Beethoven (Ex. 3-6a).

Quickened, sometimes chromatic, *often double-dotted (thus motivic) harmonic rhythm* in the Beethoven example reveals action within this parameter decisively complementary to an overall rise in pitch-line, a tonal progression toward the mediant (typical of much Beethoven, and a variation on progression toward the dominant in the theme), and a driving *crescendo*. Balanced against all of this is the extraordinary poise of constant melodic and iterative motivic rhythms within a slow tempo—the entire complex of element-structures a confluence of deeply affective character. A comparable pattern pertains in the second half of the variation. As to the harmonic-rhythmic parameter, the reader should note in detail the progression out of broad (tonic, dominant) values of the beginning, characteristic of the theme, into controlled acceleration.

Let us focus briefly on mm. 4–8 of the variation. Of harmonic rhythm

Ex. 3-6a. Beethoven, Thirty-three Variations on a Waltz of Diabelli, Op. 120, Variation XIV.

it can be said that all changes are pronounced in degree; roots are usually a 5th apart, once a tritone, once a 2nd (the latter in the cadential iv-V). In the harmonic rhythm the rate of succession accelerates from

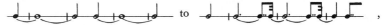

etc. The tonal rhythm is characterized by references to F, and e (the F-e succession relatively strong in distance); a brief reference to a is also crowded into these same bars. Hence, there is tonal-rhythmic eventfulness of strength and frequency. Within the element of coloration, as it concerns dynamic intensity, there is an increased rate of change

(*f*, and *fp* ———— *f* ———— *p*) in mm. 5–8 as compared with the broad pace of dynamic change in mm. 1–4.

Ex. 3-6b.   Representation of various element-rhythms in the Beethoven variation.

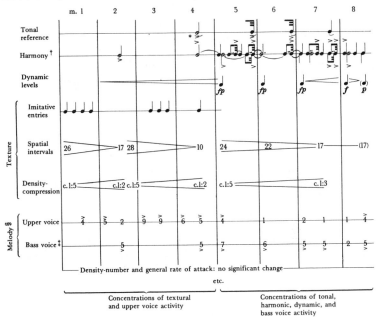

* > denotes a strong event (chromaticism, dissonance, pronounced quantity, etc.).
†In mm. 5–8, the upper line represents more foreground changes.
‡Omitting octave shifts.
§Represented as distances in semitones traversed per $\d$ unit.

What we have referred to as subelements—parameters like dissonance
and chromaticism—have powerful concentration in mm. 4–8, and the rising
melodic inflections of mm. 4–8 (as compared with broad, relatively relaxed,
descending gestures of mm. 1–2 and 3–4) are a further complementary
succession of element-events. We have been concerned in these comments
with complementary *actions* within certain element-structures, and with the
rhythms of those actions—intertwined issues yet capable of discrete analytical
focus. The rhythms of element-actions to which the above analysis calls
attention *are functionally and complementarily accelerative in the second half of the
variation excerpt.*

Texture in the Beethoven functions compensatorily: there are very
modest imitative interactions, unchanging in time interval, slightly animating the relative void of mm. 1–4; but these are abandoned at the area
of acceleration in tonal, harmonic and other rhythms treated above. More-

over, while density undergoes only slight changes, the shape delineated by space (and texture-compression) is demonstrably functional: note, for example, the essential step successions of upper voices in mm. 4–8 as compared with the ascending successions by leap in the bass.

In summary, the general activity profile within various elements *bisects the example* in a manifestation of the role of shaping element-rhythms *to project grouping in a broad sense analogous to those of meter and phraseology.*[6]

The vital importance of study of the conjoined interactions of rhythmic element-structures in music is evident in references to complementary and compensatory relations of concurrent element-successions throughout this book. At the same time, it must be acknowledged that these considerations, and with them the considerations of individual and confluent element- and subelement-rhythms,[10] require exploration far beyond the possibilities of this book.

It is apparent that element-rhythms correspond in diverse ways: some are of course totally or substantially inapplicable in particular situations while others are of primary assertiveness and importance; some may be accelerative and others decelerative (or passive, relatively inactive, or static) in particular contexts, with the weight of movement in one or another of these directions, or in balance, or in inert condition; and some are clearly more applicable at lower levels of structure (e.g., pulse-tempo). It is also apparent that proportional groupings or units manifest in areas within individual element-rhythms, and their interrelations of asymmetry or symmetry and relative strengths of projection, constitute a fundamental aspect of felt rhythmic effect.

Moreover, all element-rhythms are subject to analysis and interpretation at various levels; thus, for example, harmonic rhythm functions at the level of most immediate detail but also at the level of broad changes. For example, the *essential* prolongation of a dominant may represent in one sense broadly inactive harmonic rhythm and in another, more local sense a foreground harmonic rhythm of activating, embellishing changes. An ideal and fully comprehensive analysis, if such were possible, would deal with all element-rhythms individually and collectively, and with their interrelations—all of them projecting (and the analysis of all of them illuminating) that complex, many-faceted, element-structure which is *the rhythm* of the musical example in question.

---

[10]See pp. 78–79 on tonal rhythm; Ex. 1-45, p. 137, on tonal rhythm in the final movement of Beethoven's Symphony No. 2; pp. 201–4 on textural rhythm; Ex. 2-5, p. 202, as to certain aspects of textural rhythm; and other recurrent references to element-structures as rhythmic.

*A theoretical approach to the consideration of meter as
accent-delineated grouping*

An *iterative* (or *neutral*) rhythm pertains among successive, regularly spaced impulses (stimuli) in a series lacking parametric changes of any kind. But functional rhythmic shapes involve grouping occasioned by *differentiations* among contiguous events.

The question of meter is the question of accent, since metric units are initiated by accents, impulses of relatively strong projection. The question of accent is a very complex one indeed; nevertheless, it is an indispensable issue for the analysis of this vital aspect of rhythmic structure in music.[11]

In embarking on a study of meter, we shall make the assumptions (1) that in the vast majority of instances musical effect rests upon the experienced or preconditioned, imagined sensation of a series of pulses punctuating and articulating the time continuum as a psychological fact not necessarily manifest in physical events, such pulses referential as a mental imagery in the musical experience, and a basis for perception of the rhythmic relations of events; (2) that impulses—the actual sounds and silences of which musical projection consists—are superimposed on the established, felt stream of pulsation, and commonly *grouped by distinctions of various kinds*; and (3) that "metric" partitioning is one of several kinds of grouping in music.

Thus, the analysis of meter involves certain primary questions: (1) Which stimuli are perceived as accentual? (2) What is the nature of the structure effected by metric grouping and the interrelations among its units? (3) What is the weak-strong organization by which the metric group is characterized at any given level of structure? (4) What is the relation of metric partitioning to other modes of grouping, and of metric structure to other element-structures? From these difficult but fundamental questions, of course, many highly important subquestions issue; moreover, as implied above, all such questions are subject to diverse implications of different *levels* of structure ranging from the most immediate (apparent in the smallest manifestations of grouping) to the most broad (in which it is at least conceivable that an entire form might usefully be regarded as having a palpable organization—e.g., weak-strong-weak—of significant, essential effect).

---

[11]One trusts, in using the term "accent," that it is clear no suggestion of overt emphasis in performance is necessarily implied; indeed, the properties of accent are generally inherent in the various parameters (pitch, duration, etc.) of the event itself. Sometimes, especially at higher levels of metric structure, subtle and restrained intervention in performance is necessary to bring out important metric functions. But often no intervention is indicated at all, only the avoidance of counterinclinations of timing, articulation, and punctuation. These are vital judgments required in performance; but to say that a particular impulse (event) has "accentual value" is generally to make an observation respecting its inherent properties.

Meter, then, consists of units (large and small at various structural levels) formed by differentiations in the musical events in what we shall describe as diverse "impulse functions." If there is differentiation it is expressed in some parameter or complex of parameters. *Meter is that aspect of structure articulated as accent-delineated groupings within the attack (event) sequence, and the proportional interrelations of such groups at all levels.* Meter may be symmetrically ordered, asymmetrically ordered, or ambiguous in its ordering. Moreover, it may be symmetrical at one level, asymmetrical at another; and of course individual textural components are often of contrasting metric ordering at the same level.

Thus, the analysis of metric structure, whose application in examples in various styles is the principal concern of this chapter, is the evaluation, identification, and/or interpretation of its two primary factors: (1) pattern within the metric unit, its weak-strong components and associations, and (2) the accentual articulation of the units themselves, with consideration of their proportional interrelations. The *functions* of meter in these respects are a necessary, constant concern to which analysis should ideally proceed, involving descriptive conclusion or conjecture respecting the role of meter, and the functions of its varying qualities, in shaping the expressive content as well as the structural unity and diversity of music.

To retrace in summary the broadest steps that have led to this point in the consideration of rhythmic-metric structure, it seems desirable to note again that "rhythm" is regarded as a generic class of techniques affecting pacing, patterning, and grouping of all events at all levels; that "meter" is one of this class of techniques and phenomena, defined as accent-delineated grouping whose structural and expressive functions are manifest in proportional relations of metric units (whether contiguous or concurrent) and the weak-strong associations internal to such units; that meter, like other aspects of rhythm, is felt at various structural levels, perhaps even at the ultimate macrolevel; and that meter is *not* to be equated with regularity, so that metric fluctuation, however extreme, is not "meterlessness."[12]

The concept of meter as, by definition, subject to fluctuation

True metric structure is neither necessarily regular nor necessarily coincident with notated bar-lines at the mensural level.[13] A great deal of

---

[12]It is possible that the term *ametric* has useful applicability analogous to that of the term *atonal*, with reference to structures of relatively extreme instability and ambiguity.

[13]This study will adopt and employ throughout certain terms which refer to classes of structural level in which the notated measure is regarded as a convenient objective point of reference: *mensural* refers to grouping *approximate to, or derived from,* or otherwise demon-

interesting and expressive music is *of irregular accentuation, of irregular metric grouping*.[14] In situations of altered interval of accentuation, meter *fluctuates*, and the idea of fluctuant *as opposed to regular meter* is absolutely necessary to the understanding of music other than that of unequivocally regular proportions. It is on this basis that the assertion is made that in highly fluctuant contexts like those of recent styles meter is not extinguished, but assumes a character more (often far more) fluctuant than those of certain traditions.[15] We shall see as well that even much music commonly regarded, in submission to the deceptive impression of the notated signature and bar-line, as regular in metric grouping *is indeed highly variable at least at certain levels*. We thus avoid any suggestion of a terminological equation in which meter = regularity of unit grouping.

Meter as one manifestation of grouping in music

We have systematically reviewed a number of factors as "rhythm"—aspects of musical structure generically classified as "rhythmic." One of these has to do with relations and interactions among, and weak-strong orderings

strably corresponding in scope to that of the notated measure (without of course necessary conformity of accent to notated bar-line); *intramensural* refers to smaller units and lower levels; *intermensural* refers to broader units and higher levels. There is nothing absolute, as we shall see, in the identification of the "mensural" unit; often, to describe a particular unit (or accent, or level) as of "mensural" significance *is to make a judgment of comparability of relations*. In that judgment, complementary motivic grouping is often relevant, as may be the notated bar-line.

[14]Compare, for example, concepts of meter stated or implied in Edward Cone, *Musical Form and Musical Performance* (New York: W. W. Norton and Company, Inc., 1968), p. 82; Cooper and Meyer, *The Rhythmic Structure of Music*, p. 4; or Smither, "The Rhythmic Analysis of 20th-Century Music," in *Journal of Music Theory*, VIII, pp. 71 and 72. The Smither and Cooper-Meyer comments in this regard describe meter as only primarily, not necessarily, regular; and of course fluctuant meter is at times considered "rhythmic," not "metric."

In an interesting study entitled " 'Extra Measures' and Metrical Ambiguity in Beethoven" [in *Beethoven Studies*, Alan Tyson, ed. (New York: W. W. Norton & Company, Inc., 1973), pp. 44–66], Andrew Imbrie makes (on p. 53) the following statement: "The idea that once an organization in time becomes flexible rather than mechanical it thereby becomes rhythmic rather than metrical stems from the notion that meter has to be absolutely regular." Imbrie's own proposal as to a useful distinction between rhythm and meter proceeds from that important qualification, in which he asserts that meter is not necessarily regular.

The identification of "meter" with recurrent, regular denominators renders extremely problematic the understanding of metric structure in highly fluctuant low-level contexts *before and after the tonal period*; moreover, it induces a simplistic view of interesting tonal music, whose metric structure is so often more varied and fluctuant than meter signatures would suggest, especially at higher levels. It is argued here that a concept of meter is possible (and valid) which is applicable to musical experience in general, even to contexts of highly fluctuant meter such as those of Renaissance polyphony and the present century.

[15]Compare the increased rates and distances of fluctuation in tonal reference, in melodic line, and in other elements.

within, units manifest in grouping of a number of kinds. One of the phenomena by which events are grouped is that of accent, relative impulse superiority, in relation to which surrounding impulses at various levels can be seen as *"reactive," "anticipative"* (anacrustic), and *"conclusive."* Meter is thus an aspect of grouping, or partitioning, which is in turn a vital aspect of rhythm.

We might identify the following as factors *by which, in general, events in music are perceived as grouped into leveled units of structure.*

1. The *grouping of class-affiliated element-events* is one such mode. For example, events subsumed within a particular tonal system, embraced within a given tonal reference, are grouped in this sense, as are, for example, events within a particular kind of textural activity (e.g., imitation), within a particular timbral unity, within a generalized melodic inclination, or within an harmonic complex of associated factors, etc. (In Ex. 3-6, bisection within certain element-structures—e.g., tonality—is on this basis as well as on those of phraseology and other modes of grouping.)

2. The *grouping of tendency-affiliated events* crossing distinctions between elements is another mode of unit delineation. For example, a concentration of events (an element-complex) functioning in the direction of intensity within a given, unified process at some level, is a factor of partitioning. In this sense, the Beethoven excerpt cited earlier (Ex. 3-6) is bisected in the marked acceleration of conjoined, *intensifying* element-eventfulness in its second half. This factor might be characterized as grouping by the delineating effect of the composite profile of change in degrees of activity, in the line of element-rhythms; a segment of that line, where it can be seen to have unity in relation to a given progressive or recessive tendency, is an important area of grouping in this special sense.

3. The most subtle factor of grouping and partitioning, and perhaps the most elusive of perception and penetration, is *the grouping of pitch structures* at various levels *in associations of linear function.* Such grouping is expressed in the orientations of relatively auxiliary pitch events toward and around more essential ones, the sort of association much discussed in Chapter 1. At one level of structure this can be seen as the punctuation of broad time spans as to relative durations of structural prolongations—manifestations (of predominances) of underlying, background events—the areas of hegemony of certain, elaborated events. (This concept is of course closely related in much music to item 1, above, where the specific element of tonality is concerned; but it has to do as well with grouping around structural pitch factors in melody and harmony whether or not such factors are supportive of, and predictable within the norms of, given systems of tonality.) The unit delineated here is one consisting of the essential pitch event (again, at some

given level) together with affiliated events by which it is elaborated, and by which its manifestations are linked in passing motions.

This mode of segmentation is particularly important to distinguish from what we regard as meter: thus, the event which is central to the intrarelated linear complex, like the event central to the set of tonally related events, is often central to a specific tonal system; but that event is by no means necessarily the bearer of accent. We shall find, for example, that the cadence on $\hat{1}$, which has of course that degree as *central to the linear-functional grouping of events preceding it,* is very often nonaccentual—*recessive in the metric sense.* That is to say that the cadential event is always central (within the unit to which the cadence pertains) to the group defined as to functional, linear pitch affiliations (or, in tonal music, to the tonally centered unit); but it is often *not* a point of accent central in delineation of the metric unit (see Exx. 3-7 and 3-8). Ultimately, the tonally-cadentially central event is metrically recessive at pertinent levels, a point on which we shall dwell at a subsequent stage in further theoretical discussion of the distinction between primacy of tonal and linear function as opposed to metric accent.

Within the concepts developed here, an often assumed necessary interdependence, even equivalence, between background tonal and metric structures is sharply denied.

4. *Extramusical factors* may condition, even determine, the grouping of musical events in still another sense. Text is of particularly critical importance in much music in unit delineation at diverse levels. (See Ex. 2-14, where the setting of text is functional in bringing about a recessive succession of units expressed both textually and in musical meters.) The kind of condition shown in Ex. 3-7, in which textual and accentual musical inflections *exactly correspond,* is by no means universal in vocal music. Textual accents on *thou* at the broadest level, on *me* at another level, and on *stole* at the lowest level are in perfectly balanced concordance in relation to musical accents of pitch and duration, as can be seen in the example as represented at three different levels of metric structure. (Other modes of grouping, too, are in correspondence, but the distinction between the primary linear function of G:$\hat{1}$ and I, *as opposed to the metric accent with which the phrase begins,* is clearly evident.)

That the issue of textual influences in grouping is one of substantial complication will be evident in other examples to be cited. One literature in which this issue is of very great (and not well understood) significance might be mentioned in passing—that of Renaissance polyphony, where grouping of all kinds is often of very greatly fluctuant character and complexity, the nature of fluctuation of meter in an important degree the outcome of prosodic inflections which often have to be decided in editing and in performance, and which are commonly (for example in Josquin) in

Ex. 3-7. Dowland, *Come, Heavy Sleep* from First Book of Airs.

till   thou_____   on   me   be   stole.

*See footnote 17, p. 323.

Copyright by Stainer and Bell, Ltd. Reprinted from The English School of Lutenist Song
Writers, *A. Fellowes, ed., by permission of Galaxy Music Corporation, sole U.S. agent.*

conflict with musical accentual inflections, bringing about unit projections
of *great variability and complexity of asymmetrical relations.*

5. *Formal phraseology*—the delineation of such formal units as phrase,
motive, and others purely by cadential, overt punctuation, and by associable recurrence, is of course very important; often unit delineation of this
kind is in effective contrast and functional opposition to other, especially
metric, structures. We shall discuss this question in examples to follow.

6. Finally, we come to *the grouping expressed in accent-delineated meter,*
which depends on the tendency in musical experience to perceive relatively
strong impulse projections as "absorptive" of surrounding, weaker impulses.[16]
Accent-conditioned orderings are hierarchic, their structural relations subject to interpretation *of the extent of prevalence of a given accentual event* over
relatively local or broad areas. Metric grouping, as noted above, may or
may not be in accord with other modes of grouping.

[16]The metric unit is a psychoperceptual *Gestalt,* the nature of whose unity is little
understood; suggested here is the concept of a relatively strong impulse as "absorbing"
(embracing, governing) relatively weak contiguous ones perceived as a "reacting" (dependent)
complex in which the "energy" of the accent runs off, forming in the association of accent and
"reactive" impulses a "metric group" not necessarily punctuated by actual temporal separation. The function of the "anticipative" impulse is treated later as part of the fuller exploration of various "impulse functions."

Ex. 3-8. Haydn, Symphony No. 104 in D, fourth movement.

*See discussion of contrasting grouping of *linear* functions, pp. 320–21, and below.

In the Haydn excerpt (Ex. 3-8), as in the Dowland phrase quoted earlier, *phraseology corresponds to meter*: that is to say that the phrase begins at the same time as the phrase-level metric unit.[17] The initial event is regarded as accentually superior for each phrase—as initiating a metric unit at the same time that it initiates the phrase. (We shall consider other examples in which this correspondence does not pertain.[18])

Group unity, moreover, is simply and clearly evident in the affiliating relations of all events in the Haydn theme to each of several element-classes: tonality, texture, and color.

The metric and phraseological ordering (the metric structure at phrase level evident in the fact that a "bar-line" for each phrase would immediately precede the first impulse) are in opposition to internal ordering of grouping as to linear functions, here of course tonally conditioned. An analysis of the phrases as to orientations of tonally subordinate events to essential ones would regard the cadential note of each phrase as fundamental—points toward which other events incline in underlying stepwise descent. For the entire period, the last note, $\hat{1}$ (or harmony, I) is the essential event toward which all others, at the level of the period, incline, the cadential $\hat{2}$ (V) of the first phrase a broadly viewed auxiliary. But the ultimate cadential event *is recessive at all but the mensural and lower levels of metric structure*.

[17] The symbols used in explication of metric structure at various levels roughly correspond to standard conducting gestures, except that the final impulse of the metric unit is represented differently depending on its function in ending the unit as opposed to function in anticipation of (thrust toward, anacrustic preparation of) the next unit. The symbols are in no way prescriptions for conducting, nor are they considered to have any comparable practical applicability; but they are useful as a way of thinking about relations within the metric unit.

[18] The correspondence of metric structure to phraseology may well be characteristic of Haydn more than, say, Mozart.

A great deal of distortion in musical performance is accountable, we believe, to failure to appreciate this usual metric function of cadential arrival.[19]

Meter as opposed to the notated bar-line

It is fundamental that meter is often independent of the notated bar-line, so that a necessary question in all analysis of meter is: Are the determinants of metric grouping in accord with the notated bar-line, and if not what is the "real" meter? (Or, where is the true bar-line?)

A simple kind of accelerating metric change is illustrated by Ex. 1-3, pp. 35–36, to which reference should be made. Through much of this Chopin prelude the triple division of the notated bar is upheld by accentual mensural factors of various kinds (including the ♩ anacrusis at the outset). But at m. 29 the triple unit yields to a duple division in intensifying contraction of the metric unit complementary to the rise in pitch-line and *crescendo* to m. 34, after which the "normal" situation resumes.[f]

One view of the metric structure might be represented as in Fig. 3-2.

Fig. 3-2.   An interpretation of metric structure in the Chopin (Ex. 1-3).

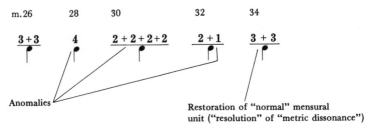

Whether the mensural unit changes (in actual as opposed to incipient metric fluctuation) or simply briefly admits *an acceleration in accent frequency* in relation to which the original $\frac{3}{♩}$ and $\frac{3+3}{♩}$ units *are still felt as prevailing and referential* is a question of perception to be taken up later as to the concept of "preconditioning" metric structure.

A further example (Ex. 3-9) is shared with Cooper and Meyer.[20] (It is necessary that, like many examples in this chapter, it be given in incomplete notation.)

---

[19]"Feminine" cadential arrival is metrically strong at only a still lower level, at the level of some division of the notated bar.

[20]Cooper and Meyer, *The Rhythmic Structure of Music*, p. 90.

Ex. 3-9. Mozart, Symphony No. 41 in C, K. 551 (*Jupiter*), second movement.

What is provocative in the example is of course the *accent given the second beat* in every one of the first six measures: by durational superiority, by dynamic intensity (stress), by texture, by anacrustic support, by superiority of pitch, or by combinations of these factors. Uncertainty, as between the real and notated meters, is at least for a time resolved by the strong affirmation of the downbeat of m. 7 (intensity of dynamic level, duration, harmonic change, initiation of new motivic idea in complementary grouping, changed motion, leaps, etc.), but what of the first six notated measures? Let us assume that the $\frac{3}{4}$ notated meter has no preconditioning effect, forgetting that we know the piece and its notation and ultimate metric order.

Cooper and Meyer insist that the triple meter must be expressed in performance.

> However, the melody is, as Mozart makes clear, definitely in triple, *not* in duple meter. Nor should the theme be thought of or played as metrically ambiguous or vague. There are two reasons for this. From a historical point of view, the rhythm is that of a sarabande, with its typically heavy second beat. Since this rhythm is normally precise, it would be stylistically wrong to perform it ambiguously. From the point of view of internal structure, too, the triple meter should be decisively articulated. For if the latent duple organization is permitted to obscure or dominate the manifest triple meter, the meaning and character, not only of the theme itself but of the whole movement as developing out of the theme, are considerably weakened.[21]

We shall take a very opposite view of the example. Let us argue that the first two notes are anacrustic to the double-dotted a^1, and that Mozart's

[21]Cooper and Meyer, *The Rhythmic Structure of Music*, p. 90. References to examples are omitted.

anomalous accents *do* "shift" the bar-line—i.e., do impose a real meter out
of accord with the notated bar-line. What is expressed is not a "latent
duple meter" but a triple meter which is temporarily displaced in relation
to the notated bar-line. Only harmonic rhythm accords with the notated
bar-line (*establishing a subtle countergrouping*). There is asymmetry in the $\frac{5}{\raisebox{-1pt}{$\bullet$}}$
size of the unit just preceding m. 7; Mozart makes this very persuasive by
continued melodic descent, while faintly recalling the preceding irregular
accent with harmonic rhythmic change under the B♭ of m. 6 (partitioning the
$\frac{5}{\raisebox{-1pt}{$\bullet$}}$ unit as $\frac{3+2}{\raisebox{-1pt}{$\bullet$}}$). The entire point of the metric structure of the passage
seen in this light is as *a succession toward metric resolution*[22] in which the shift in
real bar-line and consequent asymmetry of the unit just described are
stabilized (and brought into accord with the notated bar-line) at m. 7.

Dynamic stress must not be overlooked as contributively meter-
conditioning, nor should the real metric anomaly be thought "weakening."
Mozart has created a provocative structure involving recession out of a
condition of metric ambiguity (dissonance) and it is vital that this be
expressed; m. 7 arrives as a point of emphatic clarification (resolution), not
of course decisive for the entire movement.

Impulses and their functional differentiations

The analysis of meter requires the evaluation of differences among musical
events, the distinctions by which some musical impulses are felt to be strong
and others weak, and by which weaker impulses are grouped in relation to
strong, metrically initiating impulses.[23]

In these connections, questions like the following arise: How do
impulses (events, stimuli) differ in character, strength, and function? Can
such functions apply analogously to silences? How might these functions
be classified and, perhaps, symbolized? Can an impulse have more than one
function—a duality (elision, conjunction) of function?

We shall take a fundamental position that musical events, which include silences through which established pulsation continues and whose
functions are preconditioned by established grouping, are capable of classification on the following exclusive bases of *functional identity and differentiation.*

[22]In the concept of meter developed here, a factor of metric "dissonance" and "resolution" is essential; this concept is perfectly illustrated in the Mozart.
[23]It is now clear that "meter" and "metric" here refer only to accent-delineated grouping, and to no other type. In the unfolding discussion of meter, this essential understanding is
no longer explicit.

1. An impulse may initiate a metric unit (cf. "downbeat"): it is then an *initiative impulse* (accent). The initiative impulse is strong at the level of the initiated unit.

2. An impulse may conclude a metric unit: a *conclusive impulse*. The conclusive impulse, the last in a "reactive" series at a given level, is weak at the level of the unit which it concludes.

3. An impulse may simply carry forward, within the unit, accent-delineated thrust (motion, energy), in a sense absorbing the force of the initiative impulse, reacting to its accentual "energy" and predominance: a *reactive impulse*. Reactive impulses (relatively passive, absorptive) are increasingly weak within the unit.[24]

4. An impulse (cf. "upbeat" or anacrusis) may direct energy toward an initiative: an *anticipative impulse*. The anticipative impulse is weak at the level of the unit initiated by the impulse it prepares, or, put another way, at the level at which it is anticipative.

The meaning, or sense, of the anticipative-initiative (anacrusis-thesis) relation is that the former (weaker) impulse is in some way allied to, thereby supportive of, the latter (stronger): in temporal proximity of attack (cf. ♪ ♪ and ♪♪); in actual articulative affiliation (e.g., ♩♪); in systemic relation— e.g., tonal (𝄞), probably only contributive; or by established precedent (e.g., when a series *begins* ♩ ♪, etc.). Contrarily, the absence of this (anacrustic-thetic) relation means that in some way the two impulses are functionally separate.

The initiative impulse determines the position and occurrence of the metric unit; the nature and number of associated, weaker impulses condition its character. (The presence or absence of anticipative impulse—the question of iamb or trochee, anapest or dactyl—is fundamental in determining the character of the metric unit.)

Whether a particular impulse is seen as weak or strong *greatly depends on the level within which its position is viewed*—its position in the structural hierarchy taken as the context of reference. Think, for example, of the opening two measures of Brahms' third symphony: each of the two chords is metrically strong in the most local sense, yet clearly anacrustic to m. 3.

Essential to the foregoing theory of four impulse functions is the idea that "impulse" at a higher level *is a complex of lower-level events*. The concept of impulse thus expands to the extent that the level of reference is broader.

---

[24]The physical analogy of an object set in motion, impelling another object, which sets in motion another, etc., is tempting; the diminishing force in such a series seems distinctly parallel to that perceived in the relations of impulses within the metric unit.

We can illustrate this very simply by referring to an anticipative impulse beyond the foreground level.

In Ex. 3-10, the initial group of four sixteenth-notes is clearly anticipative to m. 1. At the level of the ♩ , the group forms a low-level (intramensural) metric unit of four events: initiative (┆), reactive (⌐→), reactive (⌐⋯), conclusive (┇). But the entire group is anticipative; thus the "anticipative impulse" at the mensural level consists not of a single event but of a complex of four events. The principle goes further *in the extended anticipative impulse to the phrase-level initiative at m. 4*; here the anticipative impulse is an extended complex of events *consisting of metric units at several levels*. In Ex. 3-10, symbols are varied in representation of impulse functions of such different levels.

Ex. 3-10.   Beethoven, Sonata in B♭, Op. 22, for piano, first movement.

We can see in the foregoing a modest illustration of the *ambivalences of impulse functions at differing levels* of metric structure (i.e., the multiple, or multileveled, functions of impulses). An initiative impulse may initiate more than one unit at different levels (┆). Or an event may be initiative at one level, while subsumed within an anticipative group at another (⌐→), or initiative at one level, while subsumed within a conclusive group at another (⌐┆). There are functional dualities (conjunctions, elisions) of the same level too, as when the final impulse of a metric unit is both conclusive and anticipative at the same level (↗→), or conclusive and initiative at the same level (┆ ; see Ex. 3-17 and others). Conclusive and initiative impulses are thus exactly conjoined in formal elisons, situations in which the inherently weak conclusive assumes vicariously the accentual strength of an imposed initiative (again, Ex. 3-17).

The various impulse functions are, in summary, best described and understood in relation to the governing initiative: the anticipative prepares the initiative and directs "energy" toward it (in a sense "activating" it and contributing to its accentual strength); the reactive departs from (is responsive to) the initiative, absorbing and carrying on the initial thrust in an increasing subsidence of energy;[25] and the conclusive punctuates the motion initiated at the start of the metric unit and is the weakest function within the unit it concludes (bringing the initiating energy to fulfillment and release).

Functions of the cadential (conclusive) impulse

The concept of the conclusive impulse (at certain levels cadential) as weak requires, in view of recurrent interpretation of cadence as emphatic, and as "downbeat," further development and explication.

...I have sometimes been distressed to hear the following passage(s) from Beethoven's Quartets played thus:

instead of thus:

We would argue that any reasonable interpretation of inherent accentual values and relations in the Beethoven motive is just the reverse: the accentual value of the initiating impulse (in pitch superiority and duration especially) lends the motive a clear strong-weak character whose natural tendency is severely distorted in Sessions' interpretation. The f^1 is distinctly the "point from which," its agogic superiority decisive at the foreground and supported at the background, where it is revealed as central to elaboration and prolongation.

---

[25]The "strength" conventionally associated with the impulse on the third beat of the mensural unit of four is a product of the conjoined initiative function *at a lower level*.

[26]Selections from Roger Sessions, *The Musical Experience of Composer, Performer, Listener* (copyright 1950 © renewed 1978 by Princeton University Press; Princeton Paperback, 1971), pp. 13–14. Reprinted by permission of Princeton University Press. The example from Op. 18, No. 1 is only one of the instances to which Sessions refers in the discussion from which the extract is quoted.

Although tonal function can of course *support* metric function (as in the Beethoven motive), it is in and of itself *metrically neutral*:  is not, apart from rise in the upper voice (a discrete parameter), more or less plausible than [music] (cf. [music]). The I (or Î) can be initiative, as when preceded by anacrustic factors or otherwise accentually superior; but it can also be *metrically* weak, as at the end of a metric unit at phrase level (see Exx. 3-7 and 3-8). The *allegro* theme of the Haydn Symphony No. 102 is a useful further case in point (Ex. 3-11).

Ex. 3-11.   Haydn, Symphony No. 102 in B♭, first movement.

The Haydn phrase is a metric unit analogous to that of the level of the notated measure. The phrase begins with a strong anacrustic thrust toward the highest pitch: from that phrase-level metric initiative impulse there is consistent descent (decline within the melodic parameter) in a pattern in which it seems inconceivable to interpret the cadential recession (settling, resolution) as metrically strong, *despite its tonal primacy*. Again, the example suggests that the cadence is metrically recessive except when it has the vicarious accent of elided interjection (i.e., is simultaneous with initiative accent), or is—as rarely—the actual point of superiority within its unit, and except that it commonly occurs within a preconditioned scheme of inter-mensural units so that it initiates a unit *at a lower level* as a means of local enforcement. [The Haydn cadence (Ex. 3-11) is initiative at the local mensural or intramensural level; *more broadly, it is recessive in metric function.*] Central to the concern enunciated here is the concept of "downbeat," of metric accent, as *initiating the metric unit.*

A further way of regarding the cadential arrival as metrically recessive is to consider that it is, after all, the culmination of a process in which element-actions of decline necessarily surpass those of growth; unless this balance is effected in the *sum* of cadential actions, there is composite thrust, which is contradictory. This does not mean that progressive forces do not often attend the cadential process; indeed they do, and they often lend compensatory emphatic affirmative force to cadential resolution, or they convey an active quality in cadential expression—a sense of instability occasional even in final cadences. But it means that in balance, *to the extent that the cadence is stable and conclusive,* recessive tendencies prevail, and caden-tial action is normally strong *at only local levels of metric structure.*

Let us point to one final example in which this principle is manifest (Ex. 3-12), considering the extent to which misconception of the arrival as "metrically strong" *would result in gross interpretive distortion.*

Ex. 3-12. Beethoven, Sonata in C minor, Op. 13, for piano, second movement.

No principle of cadential metric function can be conceived inflexibly, and the foregoing discussion, amply illustrated in accompanying and earlier examples, can perhaps best be further amplified in treatment of a situation which is exceptional to the stated principle. There are times, for example, when the final event in the phrase can plausibly be interpreted as the object of anacrustic thrust on the part of every preceding event (i.e., by the entire complex of preceding events within the phrase). When that situation pertains, it is to be expected that the late phrase-level accent (in an "end-accented" phrase) *sets in motion a balancing metric unit*, often an anticipative group of parallel content in the phrase following. Consider, for illustration, the slow movement of Mendelssohn's Sonata No. 2 for cello and piano (Ex. 3-13a).

Ex. 3-13a.   Mendelssohn, Sonata No. 2 in D, Op. 58, for cello and piano, third movement.

The theme has a guileless quality of great simplicity, and in some respects (e.g., texture) it is simple indeed. In others (e.g., meter) it is intriguingly problematic. That its units at phrase level are asymmetrically related is immediately apparent in their varying lengths, and it will also be noted that apparently like events have varying placement in relation to the notated bar-line.

The basic questions to which, in analysis, a number of possible answers might be suggested are these: Where is the primary initiative accent in the first phrase? (Does the theme phrase recede from an initial accent? Does it advance toward, in an extended anticipative gesture, initiative impulse at its conclusion?) And, what are the relations between metric structure in the first and those of succeeding phrases? An interpretation with respect to these problems is essential to illuminating performance.[27]

Interpretation of the phrase as end-accented is supported by less equivocal structure in the units which immediately follow, especially the third phrase, where the concluding impulse has agogic, *and* pitch, *and* dynamic accent.[28] The entire Part I of the ternary (Ex. 3-13a) could then be viewed in analysis as given in Ex. 3-13b, embracing *a recession in metric unit sizes* (i.e., a broadening) *from 3 to 4 to 5*, the latter quantity maintained to the end of the initial thematic statement.

The anticipative complex can thus be regarded as a strong preconditioning factor throughout the theme, and Mendelssohn brings into increasingly sharp focus its metric function in an end-accented phrase. Its specific form in phrase 3 (where there is a four-note motive repeated in powerful ascent to the high point) has especially determined preconditioning effect in structure of the succeeding phrases.

The accentual value of the concluding attack is of course severely compromised in phrases 4 and 5; phrase 4 undergoes reduction in dynamics

---

[27]Let it be emphasized again that *no* interpretation of metric structure implies gratuitous, brute accentuation of attack, although slight underlining inflection, or underplaying of potential accents not considered metrically valid, might be appropriate. An "underlining inflection" can be in timing as much as, and in place of, articulative emphasis.

In the first phrase of the Mendelssohn (first of four antecedents in an enlarged period), experimentation in varying modes of grouping will render immediately clear the fact that profound differences of structural effect can be effected by even slight differences of intensification and timing; if it is decided that the first beat of the second notated measure is *not* of initiative importance at any level, the performer might have to *underplay* that attack, not merely avoid its intensification. On the other hand, construction of that event as primary would seem to require for its projection some kind of intensification or other deliberate underscoring.

[28]End-accent of the first phrase is also supported by its recurrence at m. 29, which should be consulted. While the first phrase (unlike the others) has a relatively static character, beginning and ending on the same notes throughout the texture, its reprise at m. 29 has the concluding bass moving decisively, the sense of redundancy at the cadence thereby lessened in expansion of the texture-space. At this reprise (m. 29) the final impulse is also longer in duration.

Ex. 3-13b.   Representation of phrase-level meter in the Mendelssohn as end-accented.

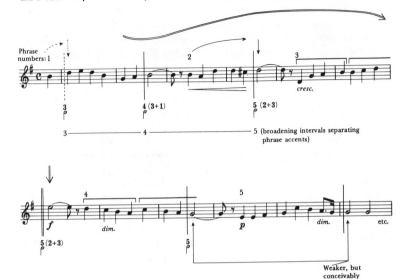

and linear recession, while maintaining the inherent motivic grouping of phrase 3; and phrase 5 assumes a background linear stasis (now on g¹) comparable to that of phrase 1, and it undergoes *diminuendo*. Moreover, its concluding impulse forms a simultaneous initiative for the subsequent unit. End-accent at phrase level may nevertheless be preconditioned in the final two phrases.[29]

The notion of extended anticipative grouping, and a balancing subsequent unit containing the analogous grouping in preparation of the next initiative impulse at the same level, can perhaps best be seen in a notational diminution of representative phrases within appropriately ordered, revised bar-lines.

Ex. 3-13c.   A renotation of the Mendelssohn first phrases.

[29]While the analysis sees phrases 2 and 3 as conditioning others, and confirming tendencies logically deducible in all, an interpretation of *fluctuation* in the locus of phrase-level downbeat cannot be ruled out.

Criteria of accentuation

Accent is a theoretical term denoting the relative projective, qualitative strength of a given impulse as compared with others which precede and follow it and, with it, form a metric unit at a given level.

There are of course times in music when accentual impulses are of relatively unequivocal effect and function; no one, presumably, would dispute or fail to appreciate the mensural metric structure in Ex. 3-14.

Ex. 3-14. Haydn, Sonata in D for piano, third movement (Breitkopf and Härtel No. 37).

The mensural units in the Haydn phrase (in conformity with the notated bar-line) are clearly delineated by relative accentual superiorities at intervals of $\frac{2}{4}$: accent here is expressed in anacrustic thrust, pitch, and duration. (More subtle factors of texture, and such complementary factors as harmonic rhythm, could also be noted.) But music is by no means universally so explicit even at mensural levels, and surely not at higher levels of structure. In fact, the Haydn theme requires some interpretive thought as to the question of metric functions at the level of the phrase: it is not clear, for example, that the initial downbeat a^1 is metrically initiative for the phrase-level unit. Is it, rather, part of an anticipative complex underscoring superior accentual value of a subsequent impulse? The question concerns metric structure internal to the phrase—not formal delineation of the phrase by cadential punctuation at four-measure intervals in another, often counteractive, and in the Haydn probably simpler, mode of grouping.

In some degree, metric structure emerges in a purely "neutral" interpretation in performance—i.e., accents which are the result of such factors as superiority of pitch and duration will, presumably, be felt in some degree in their central referential functions, and there are many instances in which metric grouping, whether in accord with notated bar-lines or not, derives from inherent accentuation of such clarity and decisiveness that a neutral approach is clearly in order. When it seems necessary to "bring out" the metric structure (in instances deemed of relative ambiguity), it is done in a variety of discreet ways: by slight intensification of accentual attack, usually no more than a kind of gentle urgency in projection; by the slightest hurrying of the anticipative impulse toward the subsequent accent; by understating the conclusive impulse, which may be a low-level accent, creating a perspective in exposure of another event; by nearly imperceptible adjustments in timing of attack; and by comparable means which have been implied but which, unfortunately, cannot be explored fully. No meter at any level calls for crude, overt accentuation, unless in parody; at no level is the analysis of metric structure to be understood as suggesting gratuitous intensification of any attack. Although intramensural groupings of particular importance (e.g., asymmetries of necessary vitalizing function) at times require awareness within proper restraint, subtle performed intervention is more likely to be indicated at broader levels of structure.

We are obliged to put aside any extensive investigation of these problems, but it is important that we recognize their ultimate significance and something of their nature, difficulty, and scope. The above comments and questions are indicative simply of the kinds of problems encountered in performance, the kinds of decisions and judgments a performer must make; he must also decide, of course, the extent to which explicitness of metric structure is stylistically appropriate (compare, for example, Wagner and Debussy; or Stravinsky and Webern).

If we accept the Cooper-Meyer definition of accent as "a stimulus . . . which is *marked for consciousness* in some way"[30]—and it is hard to imagine a more suitable one—we must then endeavor to understand the means by which, in music, certain stimuli are so marked or are perceived as emphasized as subjects of accentuation.

It is true that relatively little can be unequivocally known about accent, and that few studies have approached the problem of accent perception in

---

[30]Cooper and Meyer, *The Rhythmic Structure of Music*, p. 8. The authors do not go far in developing the issue of criteria of accent, stating (p. 7) that ". . . since accent appears to be a product of a number of variables whose interaction is not precisely known, it must for our purposes remain a basic, axiomatic concept which is understandable as an experience but undefined in terms of causes." (How much is "precisely known" about interactions of any musical events?)

Peter Westergaard notes that Cooper and Meyer are subject to the related concern that in their analyses "analytic choice at lower levels is evidently largely determined by metric position (even though originally meter was defined as being produced by accent), at higher levels intuitively, by the 'feel' of the harmony." ["Some Problems in Rhythmic Theory and Analysis," in *Perspectives of New Music*, I, 1 (Fall 1962), p. 183, fn. 14.]

laboratory conditions.[31] Those that exist deal with the problem of accent and grouping in only relatively primitive contexts (i.e., in circumstances concerned with rhythmic grouping as conditioned by few parameters of accent usually operating singly). Nor can we with present understanding hope to deal objectively with the question of the influence on these factors of various degrees of *preconditioning*—the preconditioning structure of the musical work as a whole, or the preconditioning understanding most percipients have in some degree of the particular musical rhetoric and its norms.[32]

Accent in real music usually involves many element-actions operating together; and while such actions cannot be objectively measured and comeasured, there is no way out of the need *to evaluate their cofunctioning* if metric

[31]See, for example, James L. Mursell, *The Psychology of Music* (New York: W. W. Norton and Co., Inc., 1937), Chaps. IV, V. Mursell's bibliography on the psychology of rhythmic experience is a useful source of reference, referring back as far as, and in significant degree to, the classic experiments of Herbert W. Woodrow: for example, "A Quantitative Study of Rhythm," in *Archives of Psychology*, No. 14 (1909), and "The Role of Pitch in Rhythm," in *Psychological Review*, XVIII, 6 (1911), pp. 54–77.

Woodrow's studies concern grouping as perceived in series of stimuli variously differentiated in duration, intensity, pitch, and interval of spacing. In exploration of durational and intensity accents, he concluded that a subject interprets the accent of intensity (loudness) as group-beginning and the accent of duration as group-ending, while he concluded that pitch differentiation produces "neither a group-ending nor a group-beginning effect." ("The Role of Pitch in Rhythm," p. 77.) Woodrow's findings are fundamentally qualified and disputed in later research, all of which appears to be comparably far removed from the complexity of real musical conditions. Within the concepts presented in the present study, of course, the question of accent is not one of group-beginning or group-ending, since accent is *defined as metrically initiative*; rather, the issue is one of existence of anticipative impulse or lack of it, in the pattern ♩| ♪ (♩) or (♪)| ♪♪, every metric "group," by definition, beginning with accent. The issue of iamb or trochee is, then, one of the functional affiliation (by temporal proximity, by preconditioning, by articulative relating, etc.) of an impulse to a subsequent, stronger one, as in ♩ |♩ ♪ ♩ |♩ . Or, the trochee differs from the iamb in that its weaker component is somehow functionally discrete in relation to the following accent.

It should be stated, too, that studies of psychoperception of grouping seem often to be impaired by a failure to account for the (perhaps potentially decisive) manner in which a series of differentiated stimuli *begins*.

Sources of relevant bibliography, in addition to Mursell's, are: Woodrow's reference (in the first of the above listings, Chap. I) to still earlier experiments; and M. Schoen, "Bibliography of Experimental Studies in the Psychology of Music," in *Proceedings of the Music Teachers National Association*, Theodore M. Finney, ed., December 1940, pp. 524–27.

[32]"A tone or group of tones may appear to be accented, not because of any particular distinction which it possesses per se, but because a previously established grouping tends to perpetuate itself, making this type of organization the simplest." [Leonard Meyer, *Emotion and Meaning in Music* (© 1956 by The University of Chicago Press), p. 104; all rights reserved.] The notion of preconditioning structure, which has its basis in Gestalt concepts of psychological perception, arises later in the present study; Gestalt approaches are also the basis for the idea that ultimately indivisible metric groups are of only two orders—those of two, and those of three pulses.

analysis is to be carried out. No penetrating approach to the study of rhythmic structure is conceivable without insistent efforts in the direction of a comprehensive statement of criteria by which accent is evaluated. As often in seeking to understand the musical experience, one strives in metric analysis to achieve plausible, reasoned hypothesis on the basis of demonstrable features of the experience in question where empirical verification is unlikely or attainable in only limited degrees.

In approaching such a statement of accentual criteria, it is important to recall the concept of accent (initiative impulse) as *initiating the metric unit* at some level, the energy of the accent *having a kind of "radial" impact of diminishing force through the reactive and conclusive impulses which follow within the metric unit.*

The effort to understand accentual criteria in the experience of music is, apart from the problem of incommensurability, the effort to enumerate *factors which appear to contribute to and condition the perception of grouping by accentuation of certain impulses as metrically "initiative."* It is of course imperative, especially in the listing of abstract criteria, to remember that the necessity of their *contextual evaluation in real musical situations* is ultimately decisive (indeed, criteria can only be seen or expressed as to contextual relations).[33] We must point ultimately too to the necessity of evaluation of accentual impulse *in relation to a given structural level of reference.*

The necessary concern with contextual relativity of accent means, of course, that *any* change within any parameter of musical events can be significant with respect to accent-delineated grouping in an atmosphere of relative parity of events; hence, the list of potential accentual criteria is long and comprehensive.[34] At the same time, the list excludes mention of factors (see pp. 320–22) expressive of other modes of grouping (such "nonmetric" or extramusical factors, noted earlier, as text, cadentially punctuated phrase, etc.); these may be mitigating or counteractive at times in concurrent expressions of grouping not strictly "metric" in nature. Nonmetric factors of grouping (e.g., motivic resumption), when conformant in relation to metric grouping, may give the impression of *fortifying the accentual initiative impulse* and intensifying its quality of accent.

The following list of accentual criteria is punctuated by brief examples which are contrived for the purpose of focus on individual parameters in artificially simple conditions.

---

[33]Within the above two essential concerns, "context" is normally viewed as that of the work in question, but it may also be of style or of genre, etc.

[34]It can be argued that every change within any parameter of structure is metrically initiative (i.e., accentual) *at some level*, although relatively minor changes (i.e., relatively nonaccentual events) can affect meter at only very low levels of structure.

I. *Element-changes toward accentually "superior" values* constitute a primary class of criteria of accent.

1. *Change to faster tempo:* evident, in inumerable examples, in the broad formal pattern with slow introduction; or *a tempo* following *ritardando*, or relatively low-level *più mosso*, or a particular tempo event as the object of accelerative drive, may have metrically initiative effect (Ex. 3-15a). (Less commonly, change to slower tempo may have accentual effect; see Ex. 1-37).

Ex. 3-15a.

2. *Pronounced change of pitch:* high pitch especially is of accentual effect, but the *exposure* of an event—distinctly high or low in pitch—by reason of pitch, in a context of lesser change in pitch-line, must be seen as potentially accentual; "superiority of pitch" denotes the usual accentual factor of higher frequency, but "pitch exposure" is an accentual value involving uncommon projection by reason of pitch, high or low (Ex. 3-15b).

Ex. 3-15b.

3. Related to the above, *approach by leaps in lines*, especially leaps upward: compare the factor of anacrustic approach, most often in a rising inflection; if a leap has accentuating effect, it accents the event following the leap, or contributes to that accent (Ex. 3-15c).

Ex. 3-15c.

4. *Longer duration (agogic accent):* relatively long impulses often have initiating effect (Ex. 3-15d); note, again, that the longer impulse in the iam-

bic foot is regarded as initiative of the metric unit, which contains the impulse anticipative to the next agogic accent.[35]

Ex. 3-15d.

5. *Articulative stress:* e.g., the goal of *crescendo*, or any relatively loud attack, may function initiatively with respect to metric structure (Ex. 3-15e).

Ex. 3-15e.

6. *Change to more intense timbre:* i.e., changes in orchestration from relatively neutral timbre (e.g., clarinet in medium register at moderate dynamic level) to more intense, penetrating timbre (e.g., high, muted trumpet, even moderately loud; Ex. 3-15f).

Ex. 3-15f.

[35]Smither discusses relative agogic values as to particular kinds of contextual associations, treating "absolute" and "relative" agogic values and implications of the position of a note preceded and followed by shorter or longer notes. The perfectly justified qualifications in Smither's appraisal of various kinds of contextual position and relation for agogic accent indicate again the complexity of the problem of analysis of metric structure, even within the concerns of a single parameter (here of duration).

The reader might well refer to Smither's discussion of accentual criteria as a supplement to (in some ways an extension of, and in some conceptually opposed to) that undertaken here. ("The Rhythmic Analysis of 20th-Century Music," in *Journal of Music Theory,* VIII, pp. 61–69.)

In some circumstances, e.g.  , duration of an event

beyond its immediate locus (at a broader level) may have accentual significance; but this factor is of unlikely relevance *as felt accent* (i.e., as a factor in *meter*) where elaborative prolongation is over very broad spans of time. (Compare linear functional association as a nonmetric mode of grouping, noted on pp. 320–21.)

7. *Change to denser or otherwise more intense texture:* thus, accompanying voices or other voices may influence the feeling of accentual impulse in "underscoring" one event over another (Ex. 3-15g).[36]

Ex. 3-15g.

8. *Tonal or harmonic change of unusual degree or distance:* e.g., chromatic progression (Ex. 3-15h) may impart accentual significance to the second event in such succession.

Ex. 3-15h.

9. *Dissonance* in a given harmonic event (Ex. 3-15i) contributes, by virtue of intensity and instability, to its accentual value.[37]

---

[36]Smither (*op. cit.*, p. 66) groups accents of timbre and texture with "dynamic accents."

[37]Specific tonal-harmonic (or scale-degree) content in a harmonic event has been noted as, apart from such qualities as implicit dissonance intensity, a neutral factor with respect to accent. Even where dissonance is involved, its potential for accentual significance is readily submissive to more dominant factors: for example, in the following instances upper voice rise in pitch, a very modest factor, seems clearly of preempting significance:

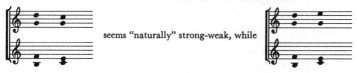

seems "naturally" strong-weak, while

seems weak-strong, both implications subject of course to counteracting or preconditioning opposing forces.

Ex. 3-15i.

II. Certain *associations of impulse functions* constitute a distinguishable class of accentual factors.

1. A metric initiative is significantly enforced in its accentual properties by a *preceding anticipative (anacrustic) impulse* or complex, and by any ornamentation analogous to that of anacrusis (Ex. 3-15j).

Ex. 3-15j.

2. *Temporally very proximate events following the initiative, and elaborating it,* as in certain kinds of ornamentation, contribute to accentual effect (Ex. 3-15k; cf. the possible durational impact of repetition and elaboration of a pitch event near enough its immediate level to be perceived as a factor in its agogic value).

Ex. 3-15k.

III. Accentual factors of *particular conjecture,* but of very probable significance, must be accounted for in any comprehensive listing.

1. One might suppose that, other factors being "equal," primacy of accentual value accrues to the *first in a series* of contiguous events (Ex. 3-15m); thus, the first in a series of identical units (e.g., impulses at whatever level— single attacks, phrases, etc.) is in this sense "superior," and subsequent equal stimuli may thus be perceived as increasingly recessive (redundant). For example, it is unlikely that a percipient would sense an anacrustic (or iambic) pattern in two equal stimuli divorced from any larger context, but he might well perceive the two stimuli as trochaic. Or the perception of ♪ ♪ ♪ ♪ (where the two accents are equal) as a group of four would derive from the sense of the first accent as primary. (Similarly, the second in a pair of identical phrases appears weaker, subordinate in accentual value, because it is second.)

Ex. 3-15m.

2. The *relative proximity of units* may be a factor; for example, accentual force may be mitigated in its effect by the sheer proximity of a preceding unit by which an impulse is "absorbed" in some degree—a question related to that of the delineation and perception of levels of metric structure (Ex. 3-15n).

Ex. 3-15n.

3. Any quality in an event which is in a particular (individual or stylistic) context *unexpected*—the sudden intervention of an event in a context in which it is not likely—may have accentual significance; that is, accentual value presumably accrues to an event which intrudes upon the "normal" or established course of events (Ex. 3-15o).

Ex. 3-15o.

4. An exceedingly difficult but necessary point, one to have further discussion, is the *relation of an event to the preconditioned pulse or metric unit*, especially at lower levels; what is problematic here is the difficulty of

understanding when and whether a given unit is, except in the most blatant cases, preconditioned and/or preconditioning.

5. Finally, whatever the apparent accentual qualities of an event, and however strong and persuasive they appear to be, it would seem that the *position of an event as the object of accelerative progression* is a strengthening factor while the position of an event as object of a decelerative recession mitigates against accentual value. In the illustrated contrived succession (Ex. 3-15p) the loud, long, and relatively high final event is clearly felt as compromised in accentual force by the preceding metric "recession," i.e., succession of units of increasing size, a broadening and thus "decelerative" tendency.

Ex. 3-15p.

No doubt the list of factors contributing, whether decisively or modestly, to accentual inflection in musical successions could be extended and qualified in various ways; such a list of premises is in any case *a necessary basis for the analysis of metric structure*, whether accent is in a given context considered to delineate meter or to function counteractively in relation to somehow otherwise established metric structure.

The problem in the analysis of meter (i.e, the location of real "barlines" at various levels) is of course not merely one of the *identification* of accents. Rather, it is an issue of *evaluation* of usually many coincident factors by which contiguous and concurrent events are differentiated.

The analysis of accentuation must weigh, therefore, and not merely enumerate the various factors as objectively as possible in the terms of context. It is unlikely that *any* accentual factor, even of stress or duration, is necessarily of primary effect, invulnerable to the preemptive (or preconditioning) action of another.

A summary, very brief chart of some of the broad, general characteristics relative to accentual effect might be useful at this point, but it must not be read as in itself a sufficient statement of criteria (see Fig. 3-3).

Fig. 3-3. A brief synopsis of some qualities of accent.

As opposed to

Strong	Weak
Intense	Relaxed
Unresolved	Resolved
Active	Reactive
High	Low
Loud	Soft
Long	Short
Unique, unexpected	Common
Object of acceleration	Object of deceleration
First	Second, third
Preconditioned	Uninfluenced by prior events
Anacrustically underscored (ornamented)	Unsupported by associated impulses
Exposed	Assimilated
Dense	Sparse

Further comment concerning diverse impulse functions

The *anticipative impulse* is the clearest, most unequivocal of all rhythmic-metric functions—weak, tentative, subservient, a ubiquitous device of thrust toward and support of the metric initiative.[g]

The anticipative function extends of course to all levels, so that ultimately an entire form may be seen to have broad anticipative-initiative relations: e.g., the introduction and exposition (taken as wholes) in many works, or the first part of binary design in relation to the second, may exist in this relation very broadly seen. It seems likely, in fact, that the broadest metric shape of many (most?) musical structures is as summarily (and simplistically) represented in Fig. 3-4.

For analysis of anticipative, initiative, reactive, and conclusive impulse functions and determining factors, we take as subject a single phrase from Corelli (Ex. 3-16a), the bass of a portion of the movement quoted in Ex. 2-10, pp. 214–15, noting the accentual criteria which seem applicable.

The first impulse could be seen as initiative for the entire unit: highest pitch *of the essential line*, beginning a descending essential recession from tonic to tonic; contrasting interpretations of the phrase are discussed presently. As to initiative impulses at lower levels, and referring to the numbered events, it can be observed that (1) is strong, entering after rests (see m. 11 of Ex.

Fig. 3-4. Broad, graphic representation of common, overall metric structure in many works; a common musical shape.

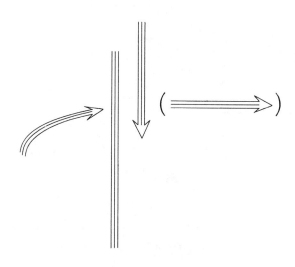

Ex. 3-16a. Corelli, Concerto Grosso, Op. 6, No. 3, in F minor, third movement.

2-10),[38] superior or equal in duration, superior in pitch within its unit; at lower levels (2) is reactive in relation to (1), while initiative of a low-level

[38]It can be stated as a theoretical principle that a silence cannot in itself initiate a metric unit. In a situation of this kind: , the rest can denote an initiative "impulse" only where there are preempting events in other voices whose metric structure is in agreement with that of the voice containing the rest, or where the rest occurs at a point of preconditioned initiative function in a series of related contiguous units,

e. g.,

unit of $\overset{3}{\rho}$ which includes (3). (The first five impulses form subunits of 2 + 3 + 3.) Impulse (4) emerges as a further subsidiary initiative *of plausible higher-level function* (it initiates a final $\overset{3}{\rho}$ subunit of the first $\overset{8}{\rho}$) by virtue of duration and strong approach by dissonant leap; (3) seems distinctly anticipative in its durational inferiority and position prior to leap. Impulse (7) is comparable to (4); and the preconditioning effect of the 3-4-5 grouping is a factor in support of the anticipative function of (6). Impulse (10) is the longest note of the phrase; further, it is supported by a strongly tending anticipative impulse (9); (12) is conditioned as a mensural initiative by the preconditioning precedence of the 9-10 motive, as well as by duration and pitch superiority within the final unit of $\overset{9}{\rho}$.

Proportions in the resultant metric structure might be represented as in Ex. 3-16b.

Ex. 3-16b.   An interpretation of metric proportions in the Corelli phrase.

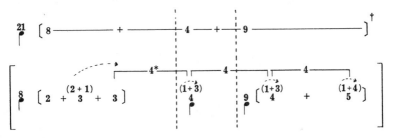

*Accent-to-accent grouping.
†Segments including anticipative impulses.

Asymmetrical features are of great importance in expressive, activating effect; but unifying symmetries and balances should be noted too. Thus, there are several motivically related units of 4 (1 + 3, in which the first impulse is anticipative) and *the outer units of 8 and 9* (from which the internal 4 unit has significant registral separation) *are of important balancing effect* and close interrelation.

Moreover, another way of regarding the asymmetry-symmetry characteristics is to consider the regularly spaced mensural-level accents *following a* $\overset{5}{\rho}$ *anticipative complex* (an interpretation discussed below) as yielding the pattern in Ex. 3-16c.

The question of chief accent ("structural downbeat") at the level of the phrase should be carried further. In connection with this question,

Ex. 3-16c.

$$5 + 4 + 4 + 4 + (5)$$

note the two essential streams of pitch succession (f-F; and the chromatic succession A-Bb-B♮-c) as well as usual criteria of accent.

An essential question for performance follows: Is the first group of anticipative in its functional relation to the first "skip" accent, A? In considering a question of this sort it is sometimes useful to speculate on relative effects of hypothetical varied transformations (Ex. 3-16d) for the light that can be shed on functional relations and actual creative decisions.

Ex. 3-16d.

*Results in total phrase symmetry.

The expressive value of Corelli's solution is evident in its less predictable, less symmetrical result (as compared with No. 1) and in the intensifying 2-2-1, low-level *metric progression within this anticipative group* (as compared with the relative rigidity of all three alternate writings).

In testimony to the range of conclusions to which evidence of accentual criteria and impulse functions may lead, Ex. 3-16e provides a sketch pointing out the two different, reasonable metric interpretations implied in the above discussion, the second of them construing the first five impulses as an anticipative complex at the phrase level. In the second construction, the half-note A, start of the chromatic stratum in the compound line, is interpreted as phrase-level initiative accent, its accentual qualities those of departure from diatonic precedents, dissonance, leap (the first), and agogic value in its immediate context. No doubt other interpretations could be argued. Consequences for correlating tendencies in performance (e.g., treatment of the first note as "up" or "down"?) are crucial indeed.

Ex. 3-16e. Two interpretations of metric structure in the Corelli phrase.

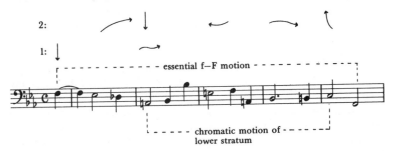

Levels of metric structure and analysis

The concept of levels of structure has been treated at every stage in this book, and it is of great importance in the consideration of meter.

As we proceed, some terminological clarifications should be recalled, and others established. *Metric unit* can refer to the grouping at any level, as indicated in a given context of reference. The *pulse* is the felt unit of counting (as identified); it is a matter of level—i.e., it changes in relation to the level of structure to which reference is made. Pulses are a psychological frame of reference—undifferentiated, and generally of regular, evenly spaced occurrence except in anomalous situations or at higher levels of structure. The *beat* is the pulse of the mensural level—the denominator of the meter signature (admitting $\frac{2}{}\!\!$ as well as $\frac{6}{}$ in compound meters), hence specific as to level; it can change, to be sure, in the course of a piece, but when that is the case a common denominator relating the two beat values can often be identified. The *impulse* is the event itself (attack, or integral silence; stimulus); it is the factor subject, by differentiation and preconditioning, to grouping and weak-strong associations. The impulse at higher levels is an entire formal unit two or three of which constitute the level of reference: these range, in theory, from the phrase to the largest formal divisions.

In determining levels of structure in meter, vital and necessary analytical judgment concerns *the comparability of units, impulses, and accents;* no objective, absolute specification of structural level is possible.

To identify a "higher level of metric structure" is to identify in analysis (1) *a stronger, more fundamental and far-reaching, accentual impulse* and (2) *the accentual initiative of a larger unit* (in which subordinate accents preceding and following are subsumed as anticipative and reactive). Leveled metric structure thus has, like other element-structures, implications both of *breadth* (as to the temporal span over which a given primary accent prevails) and of *depth* (in the penetration of a primary event's metric function through more foreground levels). A higher-level accent conditions and delineates a *broader* unit, and it is initiative as well for all lower levels throughout the structural *depth*.

The principle that a pulse series at a higher level is roughly analogous to the accent series of a lower level is useful in construction of the concept of metric levels.

It is theoretically and experientially valid to refer to an ultimate *primary accent* (primary initiative, structural downbeat) for an entire structure: it is *the point to which energy is directed and from which it recedes* in lines punctuated by lower-level metric initiatives. (See Fig. 3-4.)

Figure 3-5 is a set of symbol distinctions (representing impulse functions and bar-lines) applicable to graphic representation of metric functions and structure at various levels. There is nothing hard and fast about these, and any ordered selection can be applied to analytical representation in a given example. Examples differ, and analytical ranges of inquiry differ, in the number of levels relevant or selected for reference. But such symbolic distinctions are of great usefulness in the analysis of meter, as demonstrated in examples in this chapter.

Fig. 3-5. Symbolic modes of representation of metric functions and structure at hierarchically related levels.

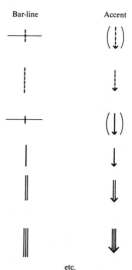

Bar-line   Accent

etc.

The question of a terminology of reference to particular levels of metric structure (as to levels in other element-structures) also arises. Concepts of pulse, or principal subunits of reference, are necessarily subjective and especially difficult beyond low levels. We could in theory refer to a period or other phrase complex as metric "at the level of the phrase," a measure "at the level of the beat," or a phrase "at the level of the measure, or mensural unit"; but this mode of reference is extremely problematic at higher levels, whose units are divisible in various ways at various subordinate levels.

On the other hand, once the scope of the *unit* at the level of reference itself is identified, it becomes possible to refer to that level *by reference to that unit*. This method of terminology yields such references as these, where the term following "of" is the broadest formal unit defining the given level (frame) of reference—the most comprehensive metric unit of reference: level of the phrase, of the notated bar, of three notated bars, of one-half notated bar, of two half-notes, of Part I, of the period, of the motive, of the sequence pattern, of the ostinato, of the talea, of three eighth-notes, of the hemiola, of the whole, and the like.

The Haydn theme used by Brahms for variations will serve as a useful, parenthetical subject of reference (Ex. 3-17a). In the theme, the question of phrase-level initiative is not at all unequivocal, i.e., not immune to alternate interpretations.

Ex. 3-17a. Brahms, Variations, Op. 56A, on a Theme of Haydn; theme.

Two interpretations are suggested in Ex. 3-17a: one of them regards the first impulse, d^2, as initiative for the phrase; the other suggests the possibility of anticipative function for the initial group, in approach to the higher, longer $e\flat^2$ as phrase-level accent. The analysis which follows adopts the first of these interpretations, recognizing the essential structural importance of the d^2 and its validating *immediate* recurrences in prolonga-

tion:

In the following representation of metric levels (intramensural, mensural, intermensural or "hypermetric") the lowest are of course, while theoretically demonstrable and analogous in weak-strong associations even internal to the ♪, of no real experiential or practical significance; they are represented for comprehensiveness (Ex. 3-17b).

Meter at the level of the phrase is revealed as a magnification (amplification) of a five-unit mensural structure, and it is viewed as parallel in weak-strong associations. The renotation in diminution facilitates the apprehension of this idea, and is a recurrent device in this chapter.

The question of the recessive function of cadence arises here, and of the weak-strong relations of impulses at broad levels—a question pursued further as discussion continues. But let it be noted that the consequent phrase in the initial period (represented as one "measure" in the renotation) is

Ex. 3-17b. Renotation of the Haydn-Brahms theme, with impulse functions at various levels symbolically represented.

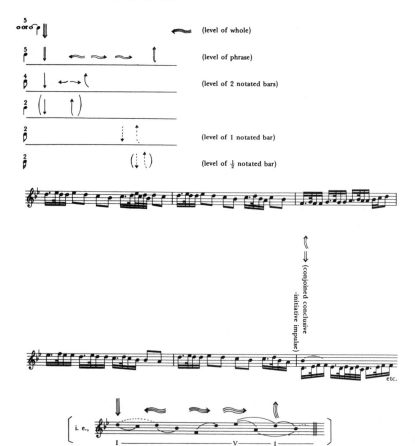

recessive *tonally and melodically* in relation to the antecedent, as is the final phrase, although the latter has an elided interjection of renewed phrase-level initiative lending it vicarious accent.

A chamber work of Brahms (Ex. 3-18a) provides the basis for some extremely absorbing questions of metric structure and process.[h]

Ex. 3-18a. Brahms, Trio in C, Op. 87, for piano, violin, and cello, first movement.

In Ex. 3-18a, intermensural units of $\frac{4}{\rho\cdot}$ are very clearly delineated both in metric ordering and in phraseology. (Against this preconditioning, irregular agogic and registral prominences of violin and cello between mm. 351 and 358 might well be felt as phrase-level syncopations; but the piano at these points maintains, in the bass, the preceding intermensural shape with strong accent at the start of the $\frac{4}{\rho\cdot}$ unit.) A representation of metric structure in the entire cited excerpt is given in Ex. 3-18b.

Ex. 3-18b.

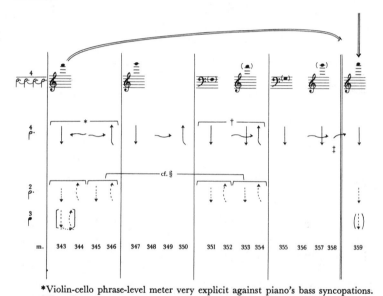

*Violin-cello phrase-level meter very explicit against piano's bass syncopations.

†Piano bass reiterates phrase accents against upper voice syncopations, but with first and third ♩. impulses equal—an accelerative tendency in more frequent "equal" accents.

‡Conclusive impulse now rendered powerfully anticipative at phrase level.

§*Second* unit at half-phrase level accentually equal to first (in piano bass) or *stronger* (in violin, cello) at mm. 351-54 as compared with mm. 343-46.

Example 3-19a is one whose metric structure involves important questions of level beyond the mensural.

In the present example there is (one has only to "conduct" the first five measures at $\frac{4}{\mathbf{o}}$ to sense it) a strong intermensural unity (with acceleration in rhythmic motion) in the first phrase; a second intermensural initiative begins the theme of m. 5. This initial (four-) regularity becomes the

Ex. 3-19a.   Mozart, Concerto in D, K. 218, for violin and orchestra, first movement.

Ex. 3-19a continued.

basis for provocative divergences: the dynamic-texture accent of m. 6, like its counterpart two bars later, heard as syncopation within the established four-measure unit. The initiative accent with which the phrase begins a measure before is, by virtue of higher pitch, anacrusis, and striking exposure as a (*piano*, therefore contrasting) thematic beginning, a strong perspective against which the syncopation of m. 6 is felt, quite apart from the question of preconditioning in mm. 1–4.[39]

[39]It is interesting to note, in looking ahead, that the subsequent theme of m. 19 (it has four-measure intermensural units) features an analogous, syncopated, dynamic-texture accent

Measure 8 poses a more complex question. The extreme thrust of pitch accent, in *tutti*, at the middle of m. 8 is compelling as a new mensural (and intermensural) initiative not only because of the sheer strength of accent and consequent disruption of $\frac{4}{o}$ phrase meter, but because of the strong sense of resumption conveyed by introduction of a new motive, a motive which occupies one "measure" *crossing the notated bar-line.*

This theme unfolds in consistency with its altered intermensural placement: note the corresponding initiative at the half-phrase level at the middle of m. 10, and the recurrence of the irregular m. 8 initiative at its counterpart in m. 12. An asymmetrical horizontal noncongruity of $\frac{4+3\frac{1}{2}+4}{o}$ is so far established.

The restoration of conformity with the notated bar-line (a recession) is of equal interest. Compare, first, the beginning of m. 11 with its counterpart in the repetition, at m. 15. Measure 11 is recessive in relation to the accent at the middle of m. 10; but the variation at m. 15 begins a process of reassertion of the notated bar-line *by accenting* (by upward leap and decisive pitch superiority) *the corresponding motive at that measure's first beat,* leading into a recessive-conclusive intermensural impulse at m. 16. The metric structure of the irregularly placed theme (from m. 8, third ♩) thus turns out to be $\frac{4 \quad 4\frac{1}{2}(2\frac{1}{2} \ 2)}{o}$. The notated bar-line is powerfully reconfirmed at m. 17ff.

The entire passage is outlined in Ex. 3-19b as to primary events in the phrase-level meter. One is inclined to comment again on (sometimes relatively obscure) asymmetries in Classical works, and on techniques of syncopation, and of metric dissonance and resolution, observed at early stages in many movements.[1]

A problem incapable of conclusive objective resolution is the weak-strong relation between antecedent and consequent factors in periodic relations (and extensions of these—e.g., binary, ternary, etc.) having tonal resolution in the second part. We have argued that tonal resolution is, in itself, a recessive process while accentual impact is rather associated with tonal distance and dissonance, and that the factor of specific tonal-melodic-harmonic content is relatively indecisive and submissive as to accent.

Of references cited up to this point, Exx. 3-8, 3-11, 3-12, and 3-17 are clearly of strong-weak ($-\cup$) structure evident in the "weaker"

---

at the point of its second measure (second **o** pulse of the phrase). In each case the anomalous accent is in a context of decline in pitch—a factor which contributes to its perception as syncopation in relation to the phrase-level initiative of the bar preceding. Syncopation as to preconditioning structure is discussed on pp. 372–76.

Ex. 3-19b. A representation of phrase-level fluctuations in the Mozart.

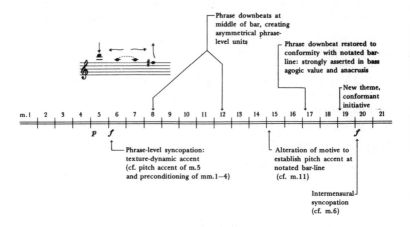

properties of the consequent impulse; Exx. 3-6 and 3-13 appear to project the opposite relation.

The issue of weak-strong association internal to higher-level hyper-metric units in tonal contexts is thus dependent on accentual (intensity, activity) factors largely *extrinsic to that of specific tonal content.* Even in so conventional a procedure as massively amplified V-I, introduction-*allegro* (high-level anacrustic-thetic impulses), the universal downbeat character of the consequent part is a product of accentual conventions beyond the tonal content as such: stress, tempo (!), texture, coloration, etc., rather than the *necessarily resolving, releasing action* of tonal movement toward I.[40]

The concept of the *metric neutrality of tonal content* apart from factors of dissonance, chromaticism, distance, etc., gives rise to important corollary conclusions. The prolonged V of the formal introduction (like its analogs at lower levels) requires for anticipative function such nonaccentual properties as practice demonstrates: textural sparsity and simplicity, slow tempo, lower dynamic levels, etc., or shaping *toward* such conditions, its rhythmic understatement heightened in relation to an accented consequent (see Ex. 2-29).

It must be remembered that in situations of broadly weak-strong or strong-weak relation the conception of "impulse" is that of the entire con-

---

[40]We have stated that, in principle, the accented V is not less plausible or "natural" than the accented I; in fact, given the usual dissonance of V, just the reverse might be demonstrated.

stituent unit: the "accent" is an entire antecedent or consequent segment, not of course its cadence or any other single, subsidiary event.[41]

In discussion of leveled metric structure, we accept and further promulgate the view that even at the broadest levels structural relations (long-short, soft-loud, solo-tutti, thick-thin, low-high, fluctuant-stable, etc.) constitute significant metric order.

> Most of the music with which we shall be concerned is architectonic in its organization. That is, just as letters are combined into words, words into sentences, sentences into paragraphs, and so on, so in music individual tones become grouped into motives, motives into phrases, phrases into periods, etc. This is a familiar concept in the analysis of harmonic and melodic structure. It is equally important in the analysis of rhythm and meter.
> As a piece of music unfolds, its rhythmic structure is perceived not as a series of discrete independent units strung together in a mechanical, additive way like beads, but as an organic process in which smaller rhythmic motives, while possessing a shape and structure of their own, also function as integral parts of a larger rhythmic organization.[42]

In reasserting such a principle, we are in part regarding rhythmic effect apart from the problem of its perceptibility and intelligibility in the musical experience. Far too little is known about the range of musical perception, or the extent to which "macrorhythms" are perceptible and intelligible.

Yet expressed doubts regarding broad rhythmic *experience* apply equally to the question of relations of any kind over the broad expanses of a large work—relations of theme, even, not to mention those of tonality (or tempo, or orchestration). In the following, Sachs' alleged limitation in a twelve-second period of distinct and immediate awareness would in itself preclude

---

[41]In formal relations of two parts (period, binary, etc.) in which stronger metric accent inheres in the second, the appropriateness of the term "initiative accent" might be questioned. (I.e., what does the ultimate "initiative accent" initiate?—a necessary question especially at the highest level.) Yet, as one conceives of "impulses" as of increasing breadth at higher levels one becomes aware of a principle by which the accent (the initiative impulse) with its function over a longer time span *contains the process of its own decline*: it is a "sloped" event within and of itself; moreover, the inherent process of decay has time at higher levels in which to function. Thus, when accentual value resides in the second of two, broad impulses, the process and fact of decline, or recession, is functional *in the course of the impulse*, manifest finally in the recessive cadential action in which initiative energy is ultimately dissipated. The possibility within longer time spans for the impulse to have sloped recession within its own duration is a major and vital distinction in the nature of impulse functions at different levels. Actually, *any impulse*—accentual or not, and at whatever level—*declines within its own duration* except when deliberate progressive intensification is imposed; but this is a perceptually significant feature only at levels in which "impulses" have significant duration.

[42]Cooper and Meyer, *The Rhythmic Structure of Music*, p. 2.

deep assimilation of any temporal work of art; it fails to allow for the capacity of *memory*, memory as it applies even to inarticulate feeling as well as cognition.

> Everybody is entitled to call the ABA of a da capo aria a rhythmic structure or, if he so chooses, even the four movements of a symphony.... But the accessibility to the senses is open to doubt. For any longer piece is very definitely at variance with the findings of modern psychology that "the maximum filled duration of which we can be both distinctly and immediately aware" is twelve seconds, which is the reason why the ancient Greeks limited the length of a verse to twenty-five time units.[43]

There is much testimony to meaningful rhythmic experience even at ultimate structural levels, and the sense of hypermetric structure at intermediate levels can surely not be disputed. Thus, the concept of multidimensional metric structure is developed here as of entirely conceivable practical significance, not as mere theoretical artifice.

To an appreciable extent, of course, intermensural (and intramensural) meters reflect the characters of mensural meters within a given style. That is to say that, in a very general sense, asymmetrical intermensural divisions are more likely in styles in which irregular mensural units are prevalent. But there are important exceptions to this principle: in surfaces of apparent symmetry, critical asymmetries are often imposed within overall metric structures of considerable variation. The principle of the variability of metric content and proportions at different levels of a multileveled structure is, then, of great expressive importance, as in certain of the most stimulating of Classical literatures. (See Ex. 3-19, and others.)

Metric irregularity: horizontal and vertical noncongruity

We shall refer to metric asymmetries as horizontal and vertical *noncongruities* (and to symmetry as *congruity*: conformity, agreement) in precise parallel to the geometric sense having to do with the potential for exact alignment (or nonalignment) of figures in superposition. Noncongruities in metric structure have much to do with musical effect. The present concern is with fluctuation and asymmetries of various kinds, a primary aspect of instability in metric structure.

Examples of asymmetries among contiguous units (*horizontal asymmetry* or *noncongruity*) are evident in some of the preceding citations (Exx. 3-13, 3-16, and others); further illustration will follow.

---

[43]Curt Sachs, *Rhythm and Tempo* (New York: W. W. Norton and Co., Inc., 1953), p. 17.

Disparities among metric units occur not infrequently at simultaneous and overlapping points in the musical texture, creating *polymetric* structures (the opposite might well be termed *homometric*—conditions of parity among concurrent, vertically related metric units at comparable levels).[44] Disparity and affinity of metric unit concerns, of course, not only the size, or duration, of the metric unit but its content as well; thus, for example, a $\frac{6}{8}$ unit in one voice combined with a $\frac{3}{4}$ meter in another would correspond in size (at the mensural level) but not in content; and at a lower level within these units there would be noncongruity of size too. In polymetric situations, there is instability and almost certainly asymmetry as well, manifest at some given level(s) of structure—an effect of *metric dissonance* in many styles.

The nature of noncongruity typically varies in ways that constitute progressive or recessive tendencies of functional significance, a particular aspect of fluctuation which remains to be discussed. At this point it should be noted simply that metric instability, or diversity, can be manifest through the texture or contiguously from unit to unit, or in any combination of these tendencies.

In all of these connections we are, again, talking about real meter which, as we have seen, is frequently not in accord with notated bar-lines and signatures. And again, it is necessary to emphasize that we are treating as "meter" organizations which may be irregular in unit relations and, even, organizations which do not rely upon a constant beat, like the groupings of chant, certain kinds of recitative and declamation, improvisatory passages, and the like.[45]

The nature of relations of proportion among metric units is all-important in the structure and rhythmic life of a musical work. Such pro-portions (relative durations) of metric units can be reckoned in a number of ways: (1) in total real time durations, accounting for tempo changes; (2) in real time durations calculated from initiative to initiative; (3) in the relative numbers of *active* pulses (i.e., pulses marked by events), with reference of course to the same unit of pulse in the units compared, and

---

[44]The terms *polymeter* and *homometer* must apply as extensions of the term *meter* and are generally understood to have to do with texture, that is to concern vertical relations; that is the sense in which they are adopted here. The homometer-polymeter spectrum of possibilities applies to concurrent metric units at various levels, and to their relations of content and size.

[45]Smither makes a number of relevant observations based on the problematic equation of meter with regularity. For example, in discussion of an example from Blacher's *Ornamente für Klavier*, Op. 37, Smither notes Blacher's prefatory reference to "variable meters" and says: "Meter for him evidently means either regular or irregular grouping of a constant unit of measurement, rather than regularity of accentuation." ("The Rhythmic Analysis of 20th-Century Music," in *Journal of Music Theory*, VIII, pp. 80 and 82.)

discounting held as distinct from reiterated impulses—in a sense a measurement of activity-tempo; (4) by comparison of numbers of such pulses whether active or not (cf. 1, above, except for the factor of tempo change); and in other ways. Such disparate modes of calculation of proportional content and relations yield information of different kinds, all of potential significance in metric function and relations.

Fermatas and other phenomena involving indefinite durations are obvious examples of asymmetry among contiguous segments, *assuming they are not interpreted as even multiples of established units*, and the functional meaning of such devices is invariably of interest. Meter's two primary facets (weak-strong associations within the metric unit and relative proportions among units) can be distinctly functional in a context in which the regular pulse succession is interrupted. Of course meter does not cease to exist in such a context. Moreover, in free, cadenza-like situations, it defeats demonstrable functional purpose to project a continuing, regular pulsation and no sensitive performer would do so.

The opening of the second movement of Beethoven's Symphony No. 8 is a celebrated instance of contiguous asymmetry (horizontal noncongruity) in conflict with the notated bar-lines; naturally, it has been approached in analysis in many ways. In view of asymmetrical relation between clearly corresponding events (outset and m. 4, second beat) there is clearly *fluctuation* of some kind in some degree. This movement begins in a situation, then, of *metric dissonance* (cf. Ex. 3-9) subject to later *resolution*.

It is of special interest to carry somewhat further the interpretation of the middle of m. 2 as mensural (and phrase-level) initiative. In that view,

Ex. 3-20a. Beethoven, Symphony No. 8 in F, Op. 93, second movement.

a corresponding initiative is heard at the beginning of m. 6;[46] these two accents are separated by the asymmetrical interval of $\begin{smallmatrix}7.\\ \rlap{\raisebox{0.3ex}{.}}\end{smallmatrix}$, the temporal span by which the beginning iteration is separated from its resumption at the middle of m. 4, and by which the latter is separated from the corresponding event at the start of m. 8 (not shown). Other factors are represented in summary in Ex. 3.20b, including some resultant questions of performance. Of chief importance in the two phrase-level accents are agogic and anacrustic factors.

Ex. 3-20b.   Dissonant, leveled metric structure in the opening of the *Allegretto* of Beethoven's eighth symphony.

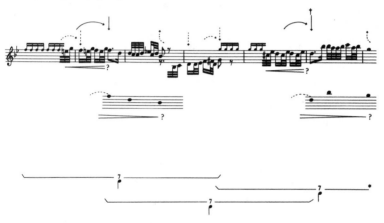

*Extends to event corresponding to that of middle of m. 4.
†Cf. strong accent 7♩ later.

Higher-level horizontal noncongruities (often not immediately apparent) are exceedingly common in music, especially beyond period levels in tonal music, but in general in most music other than of unsophisticated genres.

The concept of vertical noncongruity, in which structure is polymetric, is that of a real bar-line which is *disjunct*, not "perpendicular" to the "line" of temporal succession.

In the extract from Stravinsky's *l'Histoire du Soldat* quoted as Ex. 3-21 the *disjunct* (*nonperpendicular*) *bar-line* can be drawn at a very low level with

[46]Reference to measure numbers is always to notated bars.

relative unambiguity; it reveals a highly diverse, active situation resting on ♩ and ♪ pulses of fixed durations.[47]

Ex. 3-21.   Stravinsky, *l'Histoire du Soldat*; *Petit Concert.*

Restoration of perpendicular
bar-line as at m.66.

*All parts sound as written.

Reprinted by permission of J. W. Chester, Ltd.

The reality of resolution of metric dissonance is also striking in Ex. 3-21, with the nearly *perpendicular bar-line* at which fluctuation converges (there is full convergence at m. 66). The questions of the exact nature of fluctuation, noncongruity, and resolution of metric dissonance, depend on interpretation of the low-level grouping of the double-bass motive; while other motives are relatively unequivocal in metric structure, that of the bass poses possibilities

of  , with interpretive consequences

as to shaping of the motive itself and the precise nature of total polymetric interplay. The foregoing is a very common situation in polyphony, if not often as unambiguous in mensural ordering.

Metric analysis is of particular complexity in music before Baroque instrumental conventions; not only is much unknown about performance

[47]There arises in these connections the intriguing and troubling issue of the significance of the conductor's presence, his gestures an indication of a given (notated) metric structure where fluctuation is an expressive desideratum highly functional in the structure; the conductor often imposes in polymetric situations the *appearance* of conformity and compromises, presumably, the *experience of fluctuation*, or he may in some degree have that effect.

(especially articulative, punctuative practices) of earlier styles, but the metric "meaning" of a musical language in which no norm of bar-line regularity can be assumed is elusive and problematic. Especially in contexts in which preconditioning metric influences are highly unlikely we are often dealing with meter which is *almost constantly noncongruent in all directions*, while cadentially punctuated by areas of relative stability and felt against a perspective of often steady succession at the level of the beat. The frequent presence of text is a complicating factor in metric fluctuation in pre-Baroque polyphonic and other genres. The extraordinary rhythmic fluctuation of this music, assuming expressive, functional significance in relations of fluctuant to more stable areas, explains as much as anything the fascination and arresting power of much of it.

The Josquin *De profundis* setting cited for previous analyses (Exx. 1-26, and 2-17) is of further interest in connection with metric structure.[48]

The analysis of meter in Josquin proceeds from certain basic considerations: (1) the considerable irrelevance of notated bar-line; (2) the decisive importance of text (e.g., metric structure in the initial subject, reproduced in Ex. 1-26, would, presumably, give superior accentual value to the syllable -*fun*- even though the starting note is longer and equivalent in pitch, the *De* in view of its textual subordinacy interpreted as ⨏); (3) a likely, almost constant noncongruity in horizontal and vertical relations—a frequently disjunct real bar-line; (4) the functional resolution in the occasional concurrence of (perpendicular) bar-line; and (5) the crucial implications for performance, in which a discreet, unexaggerated fidelity to accentual values, including those of textual inflection, results in a remarkable *vitality of metric flux*.

Let us, for example, consider metric structure in the initial exposition of the *De profundis* subject in superius and altus (Ex. 3-22).

The agogic value of *De* is suggestive of low-level initiative accent—a manifestation of the work's strongly assertive, decisive beginning—but the textual importance of *profundis*, whose second syllable is the normal recipient of emphasis, lends superiority, at a slightly broader level, to the initiative of the second notated bar. (It has relative agogic accent and pitch accent in its immediate context.) Setting of the following word, *clamavi*, is beautifully

---

[48]A comprehensive analysis of the important, related question of activity-tempo (rhythm as motion) would inquire into the tendency of phrases to begin with relatively longer values, accelerate, and then restore longer values at cadences—a matter closely linked to that of textural function. It would also seek to answer the question of complementarities between faster rhythmic motion (i.e., in shortest durational values) and other forces of intensity (rise in pitch, dissonance, etc.) as well as textural interdependences and other compensating factors of kinds treated in prior discussion. A just consideration of rhythmic motion would consider its role in shaping increasingly large segments and, ultimately, its functions in determining the entire tempo-structure of the work.

Ex. 3-22. Mensural and higher-level accents deriving from musical and textual factors in the Josquin.

Reprinted from the Smijers edition, published by G. Alsbach and Co., Amsterdam, by permission of Creyghton Musicology-Musica Antiqua, Bilthoven, Netherlands.

expressive of normal accent on the second syllable, in relative agogic superiority and in pitch, although the first syllable has agogic value as well, establishing a foreground mensural unit. In a very local sense accent-determining units are as expressed in Ex. 3-22, with typically fluctuant, asymmetrical metric structure; in a broader sense, and at a higher level of metric structure, -*ma*- appears in its purely musical parameters as well as in its textual importance *a central point of initiative orientation* in meter. The extremely fluctuant character of the music is already vividly apparent, and this opening subject exposition is one of relative simplicity.

Assuming the editor's underlay of text, Ex. 3-22 reveals something of an apparent conflict between textual and purely musical influences in the setting of *ad* and *te*; as indicated, it is the former that has musical accent (supported by leap to higher pitch, and in agogic emphasis), while *te* is subordinated musically in every instance except one—that of altus in m. 5, where it is the object of a slight lift in pitch and of melismatic elaboration. There is sudden initiative accent on *Do-* in the upper voices at m. 7, although this prosodically important syllable fails to have emphasis in the tenor of m. 12 (quoted in Ex. 1-26, pp. 88–89). Moreover, *-vi* has emphasis in its musical setting in the upper voices of m. 9 and *cla-* in the tenor of m. 10. These apparent discrepancies in musical realization of "normal" textual inflection can only be discussed as (1) instances in which the composer deliberately subordinates textual to musical impulses, as is sometimes the case (one has only to think, for example, of Stravinsky), or (2) instances in which the underlay of text is subject to question. It is significant that, again given Smijer's underlay, *textual-musical accents are inconsistent through the course of the work* (i.e., in recurrences of words, accents of musical inflection vary; cf. settings of *Domine* in mm. 11–12); that would suggest consciously fluctuant treatment on the composer's part. The problem of metric structure, as it concerns these influences of text, is one of very decisive significance, only suggested here. One imagines that these are issues rarely considered in performance, even though the extent to which performance violates or underscores "natural" textual inflection (or projects words utterly indifferently, if that can be done) critically affects the *experience* of metric structure in such a work, and the experience of complementary and counteractive groupings governed or conditioned by textual accents. In any event, no interpretation could possibly belie the fact of pervasive diversity and vitality in Josquin's metric structures and processes as delineated in textual and musical qualities.[j]

It is important to make an effort to see something of the sources and nature of the inexhaustible rhythmic vitality of Brahms.[k] The slow movement of the Horn Trio (Ex. 3-23) illustrates many highly interesting techniques of metric and rhythmic diversity and controlled fluctuation.[l]

A very visible instance of noncongruity at the level of the notated measure is evident at m. 26; but throughout the first part of the quoted excerpt numerous potent means of mensural variation can be seen even while the notated bar-line retains steadying support: the motivic, articulative (and low-level metric) ♩♪♪♪ grouping of the horn in mm. 23–24; in the violin at m. 25, the irregular five-ordering of eighth-notes (an augmentation of the four- ♪ motive of the horn in the preceding bar); or the further irregularity in ordering of the motive in the $\frac{9}{8}$ bar (see the violin, and piano right hand, with its hemiola); and others. Moreover, there are

Ex. 3-23a. Brahms, Trio in E♭, Op. 40, for violin, piano, and horn, third movement.

instances in which vital interpretive decisions have to be made and worked
out in performance, involving possibilities of underscoring implicit metric
noncongruity—e.g., the same four-note, motivic entity (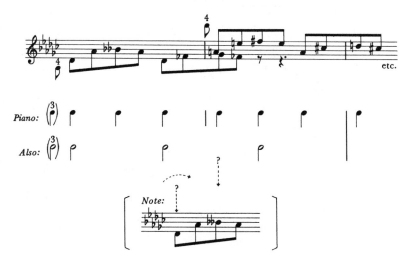)
to which we have called attention often crosses the notated bar-line (see
especially the piano part of mm. 23–24). All of these are matters of significant
potential for diversity in the metric structure and all require careful consideration of structural function and interpretive consequences.

Especially in mm. 27–30 there are many factors of rich interest in the
metric structure. Note, for example, during the piano's hemiola opposition
(manifest at one- and two-measure levels!), Brahms' ingenious exploitation
of the same four-note motive discussed above, with its subtle potential for
a superimposed in an intriguing, vital context of constantly fluctuant
polymetric organization (see Ex. 3-23b). Items of comparable rhythmic-
metric interest arise throughout the movement.

Ex. 3-23b. Potential for superimposed grouping at motive level in the Brahms passage, with
consequent fluctuant, accelerative effect.

The problem of preconditioning metric structure and
syncopation

The concept of *preconditioning* metric structure must now be taken up beyond
its incidental references in foregoing pages. In one sense it is an extremely
simple factor in the determination of accentuation, in another extremely
difficult and complex, like so many problems of rhythmic perception resistant
to comprehensively objective treatment. But it is an essential consideration
in any analysis of meter.

This discussion should take place in two stages: first, let us state some
of the questions involved and some of their implications; then, we shall have
a look at examples in which preconditioning structure (or the lack of it)
would appear to be a factor in the expression and effects of meter, remember-
ing that this issue is of recurrent general importance.

The basic questions are these: With a particular metric structure established, to what extent does it precondition the sense of accent in subsequent
events and their groupings? Does apparent metric divergence in a given
instance—vertical or horizontal—constitute *changed* meter[49] or simply counteraccentuation against a prevailing, persistently manifest, established meter?
Moreover, to what extent does apparent metric opposition in one voice
yield, in fact, in composite metric effect, to the established meter of another?
Or, given two meters in concurrent voices, does one of them, depending in
part perhaps on its position in the texture and other differentiating factors,
"precondition" the perceived grouping in the other?

Suppose a meter, at the mensural level, of $\frac{3}{4}$ is well established and may

be assumed to have preconditioning force. Might (*sarabande*) rhythms like

♩ ♩ | ♩ ♩ then "shift" the real bar-line at some point, in one or more
voices, the longer, agogically stressed half-note taking precedence as the metric
initiator? Presumably, this depends in any given context on the stability of
other voices and of other temporal areas in the preceding or surrounding
preconditioned scheme, and on the applicability of other kinds of accentual
forces—that of pitch, for example, as well as factors of punctuation and
articulation. But the weighing of evidence in particular, complex situations
is a problem of great difficulty and great importance in performance and
critical understanding of structure. Moreover, the question of the presumed
absence of preconditioning regularity is *especially important in situations of
initial metric dissonance and instability* (see Exx. 3-9 and 3-20 in this connection).

---

[49]Useful analogy can be drawn to the problem of the significance (a considerably subjective matter) of tonal fluctuation in traditional music theory; the view of syncopation developed here is of a kind of "incipient" fluctuation-noncongruity of unit not really achieved, not
really eclipsing the established unit, not itself becoming referential.

Throughout these issues the crucial significance of interpretive judgment is evident in the fact that the performer can *fortify or attenuate preconditioning effect* and its functions by even restrained interventions.

These are examples of the kinds of essential questions which involve the issue of preconditioning structure. And the issues are still more complex when cast in other dimensions: what is preconditioning in the particular musical work might be affected by factors of preconditioning in the style, not to mention what is preconditioning in the listener's experience. And what about traditions (e.g., dance), or the possible preconditioning implications of earlier movements in a multimovement work?

As basis for continued discussion, we shall make a number of assumptions.

1. It is very doubtful that there are conditions of preconditioning meter that can be stated as general principles; questions of preconditioning effect must be considered *with respect to the particular context* involved.[50]

2. In many instances there appears to be little or no significance in stated mensural meters as preconditioners; obvious instances of this can be seen in later styles of very fluctuant meters, and in early music in which the bar-line is largely a notational convenience.

3. Where preconditioning is an insistent, effective determinant, opposing accents are commonly asserted in interaction with preconditioned meter; we shall understand these as *syncopation*.

4. Where preconditioning may be of relevance, we shall assume that in some degree an opposing meter (countermeter, or contrameter) is *at least incipiently established* by conflicting accents, its significance (i.e., whether it constitutes syncopation or fluctuation) to be evaluated on the basis of specific conditions of context ultimately a matter for reasoned judgment.

5. The issue of preconditioning, surely applicable to levels of motive and phrase in much music, is probably of diminishing relevance and complexity at higher levels, where *fewer* units over *longer* time spans are less likely to precondition metric experience.

The perception of anacrusis is often significantly, even decisively, governed by preconditioning circumstances (the iambic-trochaic, anapestic-dactylic issue). For example, the theme of the slow movement of Schubert's Quartet in D minor ("Death and the Maiden") is perfectly clear in the function of recurring longer notes as mensural initiatives. But the relation of the half-note to surrounding impulses—the position of the half-note as "end-accent" or "beginning-accent"—would lack its functional ambiguity were

---

[50]One very important factor in that consideration of context is the extent of unanimity throughout the texture at points of change and points of reference (see Ex. 3-9 and others).

Ex. 3-24. Schubert, String Quartet No. 14 in D minor, D. 810 ("Death and the Maiden"), second movement.

there an anticipative approach (cf. the second phrase) at the beginning (Ex. 3-24); normally, it is interpreted as an end-accent, requiring slight punctuating articulation at the middle of the first bar, itself a preconditioning factor.[51] No issue could be of greater moment to the performer in making interpretive decisions of articulation.

The question of preconditioning arises in a different sense in the example from Beethoven (Ex. 3-25). The first note (it begins the movement) can scarcely be heard as an unequivocal initiative impulse, given the B♭'s agogic and intensity values; rather, again dismissing the implications of the listener's prior familiarity (all listening to music that one knows requires an overt submission to its terms), it is conceivable that the initial note of the upper voice has some effect—in the theme melody—as anticipative,[52] while syncopated against the bass regularity and against increasingly prevalent "perpendicularity" of bar-line.

What is especially intriguing in the applications of this theme throughout the movement is the *increasing effect of preconditioning.* Even in the second bar the grace-note anticipative support and the articulation begin to have accord with the notated bar-line, and of course the prevailing mensural structure is quickly established so that subsequent appearances of the theme become "clarified" (cf. the "resolution" of "metric dissonance") as to increasingly distinct syncopation in relation to a preconditioned $\frac{3 \text{ or } 6}{\flat}$. But

it may be that even ultimately a disjunct bar-line is felt in some lingering sense as expressively counteractive to relative regularity in the lower voice. The point of the anomalous accent is its expression of incipient noncongruity.

In the matter of fluctuation or syncopation there is a broad range of possibilities: circumstances in which presumably anyone will feel the precondi-

[51]While it may seem contradictory, it should be noted that the anticipative impulse can on occasion have stress and apparent accentual value superior to that of the initiative to which it relates; *but this can only occur in situations in which a basis for anomaly is laid*—i.e., in situations in which the anticipative-initiative relation is firmly preconditioned.

[52]Compare the Cooper-Meyer discussion in which "stress" on the second note is regarded as distinct from metrically significant "accent" (*The Rhythmic Structure of Music*, p. 30).

Ex. 3-25. Beethoven, Concerto No. 2, Op. 19, for piano and orchestra, third movement.

*Metric dissonance, incipient disjunct bar-line.

†Stabilizing factors: continued conformity of lower voice organization; upper voice ornament; upper voice agogic accent on c^2; upper voice articulation.

tioning effect of established metric grouping, others in which such effect seems doubtful, and of course many in which the effect of preconditioning as a determinant of syncopation seems virtually inconceivable. Throughout this spectrum, one is dealing with real or incipient metric fluctuation in some degree, for while syncopation *is not an independent metric manifestation,* as in polymeter or true noncongruity between contiguous groups, it is functional and expressive as asserting a kind of "shadow" unit challenging the *prevailing metric context.* The question of classification is not idle; it is the question of *effect*: there is a vital functional and expressive distinction between metric opposition felt against a preconditioned, governing basis (with preconditioning meter felt as referential in relation to counteraccentuation) as opposed to one of actual shift of unit size and/or content.[53]

Of examples of syncopation, some illustrate incipient vertical noncongruity, and others incipient horizontal noncongruity; with stronger projection and persistence any could result in true metric shift or fluctuation

---

[53]Terminology here rests upon the idea that where there is syncopation there is relative uniformity of prevailing, preconditioned meter. Thus, in a fluctuant context, where there is frequent change of metric grouping, a consistent frame of reference (i.e., a preconditioning context) is improbable of cognition. (Again, compare the problem of tonal fluctuation.) And, where a pattern initially felt as syncopation within a preconditioned context is highly persistent, the preconditioning meter may ultimately be *disrupted,* not just disturbed, in favor of the syncopated grouping, which then becomes in its turn the prevailing structure.

In a sense, too, the question can be one of *level* of reference where conflict of *contiguous* units is concerned. In, for example, the common hemiola interposed into a prevalent $\begin{smallmatrix}3\\\bullet\end{smallmatrix}$ mensural structure, there is (incipient?) fluctuation at levels of $\begin{smallmatrix}3\\\bullet\end{smallmatrix}$ and $\begin{smallmatrix}2\\\bullet\end{smallmatrix}$, but not at the level of units of $\begin{smallmatrix}6\\\bullet\end{smallmatrix}$, except in the sense of internal ordering involving lower-level groupings.

(change of referential norm), unlikely of course in certain styles. Syncopation is by definition a primarily low-level phenomenon, dependent as it is on steady recurrence of preconditioning, necessarily relatively small and numerous, units.

An instance of phrase-level syncopation is cited in Ex. 3-26. Measure 14 in the Beethoven *allegro* is an instance of conclusive-initiative (⬍) conjunction of impulse functions (there was a metric contraction in mm. 9–10, but a unit of four occurs at mm. 11–14, a further such unit strongly initiated at m. 14). In view of the theme's preconditioned $\frac{4}{8}$ phrase-level meter, it seems likely that the striking event of m. 49 is experienced as a phrase-level syncopation: the *fp* stress, the repeated anacrustic thrust within a contracted frame, the dissonance, all are factors in a startling syncopation and incipient accelerative fluctuation of phrase-level meter, also functional at the mensural level.

Ex. 3-26. Beethoven, Symphony No. 2, Op. 36, in D, first movement.

Stability and flux; metric progression and recession;
compensatory and complementary functions in relation
to other element-structures

To say that a unit of structure is symmetrically ordered is to say that its constituent subunits are at some level (possibly not at others) unvarying, or in some other balanced relation (e.g., 3 2 2 3). To say that there is fluctuation is to observe a relation between a unit and those which follow or are concurrent *at a corresponding level*. The notion of symmetry is, within a given level, associated with the condition of stability, and asymmetry with fluctuation.

Except in random musical situations, changes in meter (like those involving any element) are structurally functional. As with any structural element, there is a vast breadth of possibilities with extremes of metric *stability* on the one hand (constant, unchanging interval of initiative accentuation at all levels in all textural components) and of *instability* on the other (total avoidance of like contiguous or concurrent units in the metric structure, continued fluctuations of meter at all levels). Control of meter within such extremes is a fundamental factor in the articulation of musical structure.

Any given work projects its own norms of metric stability or flux, while usually consistent with, yet at times anomalous in relation to, norms of its style. For most works there is thus a condition of "normalcy" whose characteristics are at a given level referential, some prevailing unit of meter constituting a basis of variation, and some point in the range of possible states between extreme constancy and extreme fluctuation. In many works, the meter signature (or signatures) suggests those conditions of normalcy at the mensural level.

The spacing and frequency, and the quality (i.e., degree or distance) of metric change constitute a rhythm like those of other element-changes, so that it is possible to speak of a "metric rhythm" in music—a rhythm conditioned by the qualities and frequency of changes in metric relations (e.g., temporal distances between points of metric resolution). Metric rhythm in this sense (like tonal rhythm, etc.) is an expressive determinant in music.

As the concept of shaped (and shaping) metric fluctuation—that of recessive and progressive process within the metric structure—is approached, it is vital to keep in mind that any theory of such recessive and progressive operations must have reference, in applications, to *comparable units normally initiated by comparable accents at a given level*, the judgment of comparability in these respects an important part of analysis. There is again no possibility of absolute objective specification within these concerns, but it is clear that any analysis of compared relations and controlled metric change must have reference to units *interpreted as comparable, and uniform in level*. (The potential for shaped rhythms of change in metric relations *between levels*, while not explored here, could well constitute a provocative further area of concern.)[54]

As to unit size, one aspect by which "normalcy" is characterized, it should be noted that variation in unit *ordering* within apparent constancy of *size* would normally denote fluctuation in size at some lower level. Common situations in which meter is functional as a factor of great importance can be listed in the abstract, after which we shall turn our attention to some examples of shaping metric change in works of various styles. Note that reference is always to relation to a norm for a given context of level and temporal span.

1. Relative stability, often a factor in the process of thematic statement (except of course where metric flux is a thematic attribute).

2. Metric instability, often a factor in developmental and transitional processes.

3. Fundamental variational changes in metric unit at mensural and intramensural levels, in such works as "theme with variations" or "rondo" or other recapitulative forms.

4. Metric progression, in direction of (a) shorter unit and (b) increased instability, often significant in a process of mounting intensity; progressive effect is of *acceleration*.

5. Metric recession, in directions of increased stability and longer units (note frequency of tempo retardation and fermata), often a factor in introductory and cadential processes; recessive effect is of *deceleration*.

6. Interesting is the possible relation of metric indecision to states of relative tension; metric indecision may involve uncertainty or suspension of regular beats or pulses (often coincident with dissonance) or a suspension of activity (fermata, or indeterminate pause)[55] in an effect of momentary temporal hiatus (unmarked, unpunctuated or "empty" time; measure-free time) unlike the time of unit measurements (the time of "quanta"—of punctuating events).

The factor of *ambiguity* (uncertainty, indecision) of meter cannot be said

---

[54]Disparities at different levels—e.g., mensural units of four as opposed to phrase-level units of three, constitute asymmetry of an important kind whose significance of effect and function could well be explored; such a relation, crossing structural levels, is one of a dimension of "depth" in the musical experience.

[55]The fermata has two basic functions: it can contribute as the ultimate broadened unit to recessive process (e.g., final cadence), and it can intensify the feeling of instability in fluctuant circumstances by the interjection of a unit of ambiguous length. In the latter function it is often complementary to dissonance. Whether its effect complements finality or intensifies instability seems to depend on other element-characteristics to which it is allied as well as on its position in relation to other units comprising a progressive, recessive, or erratically fluctuant series; in the latter circumstance it seems likely that the fermata is stabilizing in effect. The fermata as emphatic, recessive metric broadening occurs only as a final event.

clearly to contribute to intensification or resolution. Recessive or progressive inclination in metrically ambiguous situations depends on how such situations are perceived as to greater or lesser frequency of accent at a specified level.

Some important progressive and recessive tendencies of metric structure are summarized in Fig. 3-6; in the summary an effort is made to identify parameters of meter subject to processive manipulation in the two broad tendencies noted.

Fig. 3-6. A summary of recessive and progressive tendencies in metric structure.

*Features/objects of recessive change**	*Features/objects of progressive change**
1. Larger units at common level	1. Smaller units at common level
2. Relatively symmetrical unit relations	2. Relatively asymmetrical unit relations
3. Increased constancy of unit size (greater horizontal congruity) at common level	3. Fluctuation in unit size (greater horizontal noncongruity) at common level
4. Increased vertical congruity (homometer, resolution)	4. Increased vertical noncongruity (polymeter, dissonance)
5. Restoration of unit norm (stability)	5. Departure from unit norm (instability)

*Including incipient fluctuation, asymmetry, noncongruity, etc. (syncopation).

Attention is directed to the final cadence of Schoenberg's second of five piano pieces, Op. 23, in study of metric structure as complementary to elements of cadential process already discussed (Ex. 1-37, pp. 107–11). *The recession in composite rhythm*, one of the cadential processes cited earlier, should here be reemphasized; tempo change is a factor within that rhythmic aspect.

In the Schoenberg example, the process by which the metric structure is projected in broadening units, beginning with m. 18, can be expressed as in Ex. 3-27b. In this representation, reference is to the sequential pattern.

The initiative event at m. 17, quoted in Ex. 3-27a, is of broad significance—interpreted as the primary initiative impulse for the entire piece, *one in relation to which all earlier events are broadly anticipative.* In mm. 18–19 (see p. 108), a mensural $\overset{3}{\underset{3}{\text{♩}}}$ group[56] is sharply defined; it has anacrustic and agogic

[56]The symbol ♩ (or ♪, etc.) denotes ♩ (or $\frac{1}{3}$ ♩). Similarly, ♪ = ♪ , or $\frac{1}{5}$ ♩; ♪ = $\frac{1}{5}$ ♩ ; etc.

delineation—strong initiative recurrence and supportive sequential group-ing. The bar-line between mm. 19–20 is denied in one aspect of metric elon-gation, and there is a broadening (decline) in pulse value as suggested in Ex. 3-27b.

Broadly undulating, up-down lines of intensity, marked by recurrent potent initiatives culminating in the powerful impulse of m. 17, yield to a cadential process in which meter is functional *along with other factors of rhythm* (*slowing rate of attack*), *dynamic stress, texture,* and others. Metric process should be regarded not merely as to likely broadened units, but as to the *diminishing decisiveness of initiative accent,*[57] and elongation in the felt pulse (i.e., low-level metric recession), both complementary to deceleration at the mensural level.[m] (The reader should also examine the syncopated thrusts of mm. 18–19, where there can be no question of their submission to prevailing, preconditioned metric grouping.)

Ex. 3-27a.   Schoenberg, Five Piano Pieces, Op. 23; No. 2.

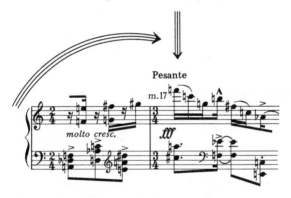

Reprinted by permission of G. Schirmer, Inc., agent for Wilhelm Hansen Edition.

The music of Beethoven is highly rewarding for the study of metric change in its various functions: for example, the technique of progressive contraction of the metric unit in passages—often developmental—of mount-ing intensity.

In the third movement of the second symphony, there is a precursive sign of metrically accelerative tendencies, in development, at m. 29 and the following bars, where progression is evident in insistent, stronger, more

[57]In a context of preceding strong, frequent accents, the relative indecision and ambiguity of accent in the last four bars seem clearly recessive in function; and accentual ambiguity is itself *increasingly* felt after m. 19.

Ex. 3-27b. A representation of metric process in the Schoenberg cadence.

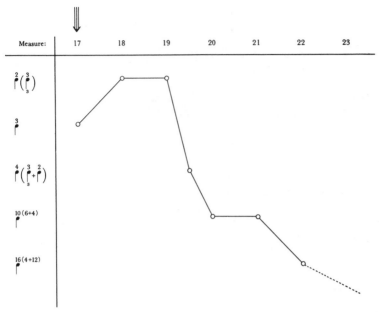

Note: complementary slowing tempo and declining rate of attack; further line of recession in change of pulse in following pattern:

♪ or ♩. (m. 17), ♩ (18-19), ♩ (20), ♩ or ♩. (21), ♩ or 𝅝 (22-23).

frequent low-level accents—a vitalizing factor in comparison with harmonic stasis but in complementation with, for example, dissonance (Ex. 3-28a).

Ex. 3-28a. Beethoven, Symphony No. 2, Op. 36, in D, third movement.

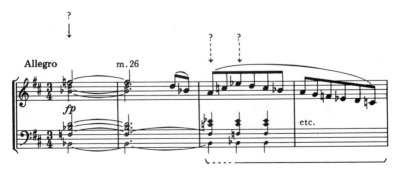

Ex. 3-28a continued.

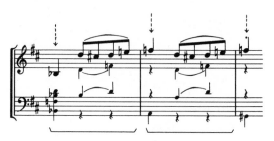

The concluding phrase of the Scherzo portion of this movement departs in variation of the theme at the typical tonal level of the 3rd above, culminating in a tonic cadence eight measures later. This phrase, which first appears in this form at m. 59, is shown as Ex. 3-28b, with three metric levels represented.

Ex. 3-28b.

 ? (The issue is one of agogic as opposed to pitch

accent, and of preconditioning of phrase-level meter.)

In the cadential development of this phrase there is considerable fluctuation in grouping as delineated by phrase repetitions and truncations, as is quickly apparent if one notes that from the point of its inception (m. 59) to the conclusion of the Scherzo there are twenty-six measures.

The stages in metrically progressive cadential approach are the following: (1) repetition of all eight measures; (2) repetition of only the last four measures; (3) repetition of only the last two measures. The horizontal non-congruity at the phrase level is thus immediately visible, with initiative impulses of *increasing* frequency. The pattern is thus one of *metric contraction*, a *progression* lending an activating influence of increasing urgency; compensating recessive tendencies have to be seen in harmonic rhythm and, especially, in predominant movement toward tonal resolution, typically unequivocal.[58] On the other hand, the progressive action of dynamic level is intensifying.

All in all, the cadence is metrically relatively active while emphatic in other parameters; but within the metric process itself, *the steadying function of final metric expansion* (4 out of 2) is highly important. Again, one has only to imagine the cadence without this expansion, i.e., with persistent units of two. Moreover, the effect of ultimate expansion in the phrase-level metric unit *is especially strong in view of the preceding contractive (accelerative) succession*. The process is represented in Ex. 3-28c,d in two distinct modes of graphic illustration.

A composer whose work has been of interest in the direction of particular (very overt) solutions to rhythmic-metric problems is Boris Blacher, who has developed a practice of "variable meters"—the employment of planned sequences of measures of varying lengths.[59]

Blacher's method can be illustrated in brief reference to *Ornamente für Klavier*, Op. 37. The prefatory note identifies the kinds of numerical series

---

[58]A cadence of greater finality—increased recessive tendencies of element-structures in greater accord—could be imagined as a reversed metric process.

[59]Blacher's Piano Concerto No. 2 applies the practice of variable meters extensively.

Ex. 3-28c,d. Representations of metric process in the Beethoven Scherzo.

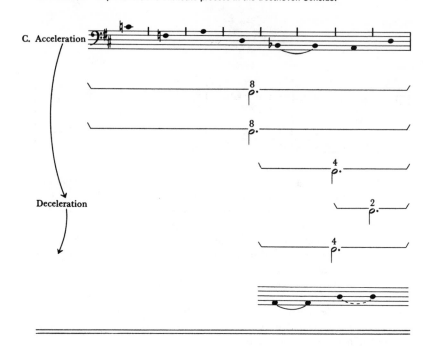

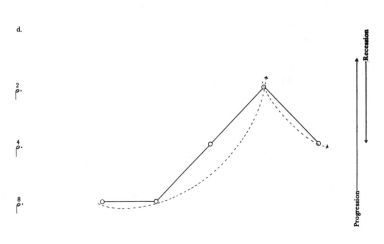

adopted for the pieces in this set, with a basic unit of ♪ for all the pieces. Thus, the first and second employ a simple arithmetical series and its retrograde; No. 3 employs the series 2 3 4, 3 4 5, 4 5 6, etc., and its retrograde; No. 4 employs a "cyclical" or "rotational" series (4 5 6 3 2, 5 6 3 2 4, 6 3 2 4 5, etc.); No. 5 employs an additive series (2 3 5 8 13—the Fibonacci series); No. 6 applies 24 permutations of the four integers 3 4 5 6 (3 4 5 6, 3 4 6 5, 3 6 4 5, etc.); and No. 7 follows the distribution

```
8 7              6 5          4 3
8 7 6          / 6 5 4      / 4 3 2
8 7 6 5        / 6 5 4 3    /
. . . . . . . . . /  6 5 4 3 2 /
8 7 6 5 4 3 2
```

and its retrograde.

Brief extracts from three of the pieces, quoted as Ex. 3-29, illustrate these procedures.

Ex. 3-29. Blacher, *Ornamente für Klavier*, Op. 37 ; Nos. 3, 5, 6.

Allegro ♩ = 96

Allegro ♩ = 92

Ex. 3-29 continued.

Reprinted by permission of Associated Music Publishers, Inc.

Processes of active, static, progressive, recessive, and otherwise shaped fluctuant element-changes thus have in Blacher's methods a strict systematization (at times surely simplistic). Blacher's accents are, in general, expressed unequivocally: textural, articulative, of pitch, of duration, etc., and often underscored in motivic grouping and recurrence of readily identifiable ideas.

An example of minimal difficulty, in which a process of metric progression and recession can be seen in a relatively simple context, comes from a piano piece of Chopin (Ex. 3-30a).

An intensifying progressive process is followed by recession at the mensural level. The example occurs at the conclusion of an active middle section in the parallel minor, where $\overset{6}{\rho}$ motivic units have been prevalent. There is in the quoted excerpt a complementary function of dynamic changes, and in the recession a *ritardando* acts in expansion of the larger, $\overset{4}{\rho}$ unit as the formal

Ex. 3-30a. Chopin, Nocturne in F, Op. 15, No. 1.

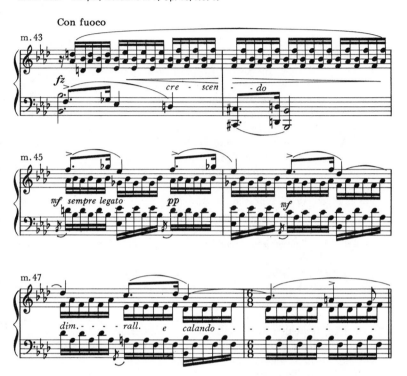

reprise is approached. The metric changes, whether perceived as a shifting interval of real bar-line or as incipient fluctuation against a preconditioned, referential norm, are as summarized in Ex. 3-30b.

Ex. 3-30b. Metric processes in the Chopin example.

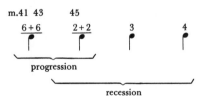

Although the location of initiative accent in the motive might otherwise be subject to debate (in view of the agogic superiority of the arrival note), Chopin's articulation (>) throughout of the first, higher note tends to clarify the issue; the first, accented note is also intensified by dissonance.

Because of the enormous impact of persistently variable, sometimes un-equivocal metric structures often asymmetrical and noncongruent to a degree startling for their time, the earlier works of Stravinsky are a landmark in the evolution of increasing metric flexibility, as are the works of Bartók[n] and Webern in different ways, all of these stimulative of a range of inquiry, resource, and creative impulse by which rhythm and meter have undergone profound transformations in the earlier twentieth century and up to the present. While any of these or comparable literatures could be the basis for extended thesis in itself, we are of course limited to discussion of a few relevant techniques in selected examples, by way of illustration of approaches to metric analysis.[o]

The following references are to Stravinsky's *Canticum Sacrum*, subject of inquiry in earlier connections (see Ex. 2-13, pp. 225–32). In a substantial degree, the impact of textual prosody is here, as in certain prior examples, a factor of difficulty, yet of great (even decisive) importance in metric effect: the extent to which accent is projected in textual inflection as opposed to purely musical factors (where the two are not in consistent accord) depends of course to a great extent on interpretive choice. The metric formulation of the chorus parts is thus subject to textual inflection *as interpreted in performance* (and realized in subtle emphases)—an area of crucial decision making for the performer.

It is apparent that low-level metric structure is one of extreme asym-metry and fluctuation, less pronounced at phrase level, contributing to a general effect of great vigor and mobility. In Part V as a whole, large sections recur in a rondo-like manner; metric (and other aspects of rhythmic, e.g., tempo) change from section to section constitutes a higher level of asym-metrical structure.

Metric noncongruity is of course at times asserted by very conventional means; the hemiola of the organ refrain of Part V (see Ex. 2-13a, p. 226ff., mm. 327–35) is an instance of this; yet it occurs in a context of polymeter of rich polyphonic vitality in which the lowest and highest voices project hemiola *at different times* in a composite structure of disjunct bar-line. Such anomalies as the noncoincident hemiolas, the constantly altered and non-conformant metric grouping of the repeated motive of the third voice, and the $\frac{3}{\text{♩}}$ (or $\frac{2}{\text{♩.}}$) but noncongruent meter of the fourth voice, make for a con-siderable range of metric effect even within the relatively unassuming, recur-rent organ theme.

Metric functions in the final cadence of *Canticum* are chiefly (but not entirely) decelerative in complementation to such other element-recessions as pitch-line descent, slowing of tempo, and total dissipation of contrapuntal textural interactions in the final events. (Example 2-13a, p. 229, includes the cadence.) In one sense, meter is recessive at the mensural level, but only slightly so: that is, the final three, punctuating chords are separated by slightly increasing intervals of time. The attack on the final chord is separated by 11 ♪ from that of the preceding chord, which follows the first of the three by 9 ♩. Even the slight broadening represented in the 9-11 relation is felt as contributive to the more persuasive, functional recessions *in tempo, line, texture, and tonal synthesis.*

An analysis of meter at the mensural level, defined on the basis of attacks initiating the descending motive of m. 341 and the final three chords, is as shown in Fig. 3-7. The example, which interprets the rest which begins

Fig. 3-7. Meter in the final cadence of *Canticum,* represented at mensural level.

$$\frac{11 - 9 - 11 - 9}{\text{♩}}$$

the *adagio* as part of the first *adagio* unit, shows a still fluctuant metric structure. Its vacillation between asymmetrical units explains in part the cadence's active quality, fitting in culmination of the movement's restlessly fluctuant metric structure.[60]

Beethoven, Symphony No. 8 in F, Op. 93, first movement

A further look at Beethoven is afforded by several excerpts from the first movement of the eighth symphony, for each of which unfortunately only brief comment regarding prominent factors—and questions—of metric structure can be given. Let the examples serve as a kind of summary recitation of devices by which Beethoven renders the metric structure expressively variable and of constantly engrossing asymmetries, as well as functional in its controlled changes in the various processes of statement and climactic development. (Example 3-31a poses a question of interpretation comparable to that on p. 329 concerning the Quartet, Op. 18, No. 1, also in F.)

The first twelve measures of the movement fall easily into a 4 + 4 + 4 intermensural grouping (Ex. 3-31b), although the stress at m. 10 (its basis

---

[60]Interpretation of the quarter-rest at the middle of m. 341 as "initiative" is based on considerably preconditioned $\frac{3+3}{\text{♩}}$ units, and the factor of radical tempo change, by which the rest is governed. Inclusion of the final rests as a specific quantity defining the final mensural unit is of course problematic, involving more difficult questions of preconditioned structure.

Ex. 3-31a. Beethoven, Symphony No. 8 in F, Op. 93, first movement.

*Agonic value, but discounting any accentual significance in mere fact of arrival on $\hat{1}$.
†Pitch accent, relative agogic value, feeling of downbeat phrase beginning; but cf. accentual values of impulses at mm. 4, 6, 8, 10 (added dynamic thrust), etc., with implications for the interpretation of m.2.

Ex. 3-31b. A representation of $\overset{4}{\rho}$. phrase-level metric units in the opening of the Beethoven eighth symphony.

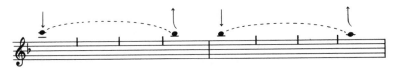

laid in the agogic accent—interpreted as subordinate at phrase level—at mm. 2 and 6) creates a provocative intermensural syncopation.[61]

A continuation of the thematic element maintains this relative symmetry in an eight-measure component of $\overset{2}{\rho}$. units to and beyond m. 20 (Ex. 3-31c).

At m. 21 (see Ex. 3-31d), the two-measure motive continues with its established equilibrium—pitch accent on the higher, initiative note[62]—but soon reaches a stasis of pitch level (after m. 23) and subsequently contracts from $\overset{6}{\rho}$ to $\overset{3}{\rho}$ *in a climactic metric progression.* The initiative higher note has up

---

[61]The interpretation of m. 9 as anticipative to a shifted phrase accent at m. 10 is a question of the preconditioning validity of the $-\smile$ structure of the basic motive (Ex. 3-31a) and that of the $\overset{4}{\rho}$. units (Ex. 3-31b) with which the movement begins.

[62]A syncopating texture accent on the lower of the two notes, having implications short of real fluctuation, occurred at the inception of the motive in mm. 13–14; yet the first note asserts insistent initiative function in significant part because of the preconditioning effect of the original motive (from which it is derived), the precedence of $\overset{4}{\rho}$. units (of which m. 13 is a preconditioned initiative), and the important pitch accent of m. 13.

3-31c.

*An intermensural syncopation of pitch accent unlikely as initiative in the light of preconditioning prior groupings.

to now been in accord with the notated bar-line, while Beethoven gives it dynamic accent (*sf*) at the same time (in confirmation of its accentual significance?). This is no doubt perceived as syncopation in counterpoint to a bar-line preconditioned *in the style as well as in the work itself*, but the effect is nonetheless an acceleration of implied grouping in incipient fluctuation in

the pattern $\frac{6 - 5 - 3}{\rule{0pt}{0pt}}$, from m. 23, the point at which the motive becomes

static in pitch-line. The incipient metric asymmetry of the five-unit is a further jarring event in a climactic progression occurring only twenty-eight measures into the exposition. The entire progression is followed by a measure of silence, after which the motive (now contracted to two impulses) is transposed a 9th below, *piano*, lacking the disruptive accents.

Ex. 3-31d.

The initial impulse of m. 34, following the silence, may well be felt as a downbeat, the motive now clearly transformed from trochee to iamb—its first impulse (upper note) now clearly anticipative; but it is interesting to think about the experience of this passage in the absence of a conductor signalling every notated downbeat (indeed, the sensitive conductor will not do so) and in the absence of gratuitous stresses on the notated downbeats of mm. 34–36. Possibly the metric dissonance is resolved fully, if temporarily, only with the new theme, and its unequivocal, regular texture accents of accompanying chords. (See Ex. 3-31e.)

Ex. 3-31e. Transformations of motive and their metric implications in the Beethoven.

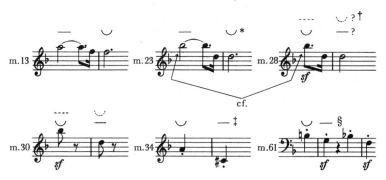

*Relation confirmed by motivic expansion with stronger pitch accent.
†Residual pitch (and now dynamic) accent confused by placement in relation to notated bar-line.
‡Dynamic accent on first impulse abandoned.
§Dynamic accent now occurring in support of transformed metric implication.

At another point, intensifying metric contraction occurs in a context of total textural unanimity (see m. 64ff. in Ex. 3-31f). Horizontal noncongruity grows out of a passage of strong accents in conformity with the notated bar-line—a final step in the transformation of the motive as represented in Ex. 3-31e. At m. 70 a decisive initiative accent in accord with that bar-line launches a $\frac{2}{4}$ motive which is sequentially repeated to form four contracted units, an extremely vitalizing asymmetry before a further thematic entry again restores the bar-line without equivocation.

It is significant that in both of these contractions (mm. 28–32 and 70–72) Beethoven's textural components are in full accord, an indication of the force with which metric process here approaches disruption of the notated

Ex. 3-31f.

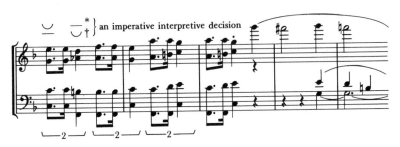

*As to agogic accent and anacrusis.
†As to initial anacrusis, pitch accent, and preconditioned bar-line.

bar-line. The style, of course, does not "permit" maintenance of the fluctuant tendency: invariably, metric dissonance is followed by resolution.

Unfortunately, the movement has to be left with these few suggestions of areas of potential exploration[p] (see also Ex. 3-20, concerning the second movement).

Chopin, Prelude in E, Op. 28, No. 9

The vital theoretical question of the relation between intermensural grouping as manifest in phraseology (cadential punctuation and resumption) and grouping as delineated by metric accent is of recurrent importance, especially since the latter clearly requires the knowing involvement of the performer while the former is more likely to be explicit in the phenomenon of cadential punctuation itself. Such an issue of possible noncorrespondence between phraseology and meter—i.e., of phrase grouping as opposed to accent-to-accent grouping at phrase level—arises in many works of Chopin, including the piece which is now to be fairly comprehensively treated. The Prelude in E is reproduced in part as Ex. 1-18, p. 68, and brief summary extracts given in the following series should make the discussion comprehensible; ideally the reader should have reference to the entire piece.[q]

In instances of *formal* (phraseological) symmetry the problem of organization of higher-level *metric* units can of course be elusive and difficult; yet, the question is inescapable in arriving at interpretive decisions. In the Chopin Prelude in E, twelve notated bars fall into three phrases conspicuously felt in cadential punctuation and resumptions of common initiating material at mm. 5 and 9: the entire form is an enlarged period with two antecedents, each ending on the primary dominant harmony but with some striking tonal diversions in the accelerated tonal rhythms of the second antecedent and in the final, consequent phrase (again, see Ex. 1-18).[63]

It would be easy to assume parallel metric structure in which phrase-level meter corresponds to that of the "normal" four-beat measure, in which phrase-level impulse functions directly reflect those of the mensural unit. Such a view would see the last two phrases as shown in Ex. 3-32a; the quotation is in renotation in diminution.

Ex. 3-32a. Chopin, Prelude in E, Op. 28, No. 9; last two phrases renotated in diminution.

Some hard questions are immediately apparent: (1) Is the *forte* initiative of the first phrase a preconditioning frame of reference in which the *piano*-to-*fortissimo* dynamic progressions of the second and third phrases are understood as resistant syncopations at phrase level? (If so, the representation shown in Ex. 3-32a could have validity.) (2) Should the intermensural "bar-line," on the other hand, be associated with (be thought of as prior to) the climactic *fortissimo*, also a point of powerful pitch-texture accent? If so, *should the metric structure be thought of as beginning with an anticipative unit of three "impulses?"* (See Ex. 3-32b.) (3) Is there, in effect, then, a series of phrase-

level $3 + 1$ groupings creating metric orders counteractively associated with

Ex. 3-32b. The question of anticipative function in phrase beginnings in the Chopin.

[63]We are concerned here not with metric order at the highest level (i.e., whether the three phrases are in a ∪ ∪ — relation), but with metric order internal to phrase-level units.

the symmetries of formal phraseology? (Does not the representation given in Ex. 3-32b bring into focus some kind of "truth" about metric structure in the experience of this piece?) (4) Does phrase-level metric organization (location of phrase-level accent) perhaps fluctuate from phrase to phrase?

If dynamic stress *is* meter-determining accent, associated with *initiative function* in the metric organization or with *syncopation* in resistance to a pre-conditioned organization, such questions are imperative to an understanding of this piece, whose low-level regularities are opposed by higher-level, counteractive metric structure.[r] These questions are reflected in the following sketch (Ex. 3-32c), in which various interpretations of metric structure are represented in addressing the basic question of the location of higher-level accents (ultimately, *the* structural "downbeat"). Although these interpretations embody metric units of largely symmetrical relation, such a relation should of course not be construed as a necessary assumption, as we have seen, despite the symmetry of formal phraseology. And if these interpretations are dismissed in favor of that of metric structure in compliance with phraseology

Ex. 3-32c. A representation of the Chopin as to broad metric structure in which higher-level accents are seen as noncoincident with phrase beginnings.

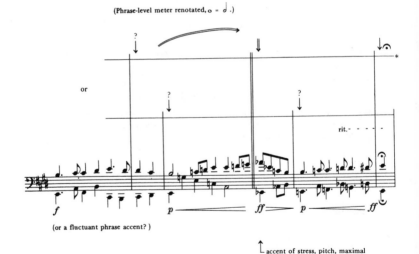

(Phrase-level meter renotated, o = ♩ .)

or

(or a fluctuant phrase accent?)

⌐ accent of stress, pitch, maximal textural expanse, extreme tonal distance, etc.

*Cf. grouping as to phrase punctuation (inception to cadence) and, on the other hand, phrase-level bar-line to bar-line.

(initiative impulses at phrase beginnings), it is impossible to conceive on what basis a broad, primary accent might be deduced.

Although the particular formulations of these questions may have the appearance of unorthodoxy, it is easy to see them, with thought, as very familiar questions, and very constant ones in analysis and performance, couched here in terms that direct attention to musical events *as of metric, thereby rhythmic, significance*. The familiar, analogous questions might appear in discourse about music in forms like these: What are the central points in the piece, the primary events to which successions (lines of intensity, motion, directions of activity) are aimed? What events in the piece are of special moment, of particular centrality of rhythmic function and interpretive projection? Or, what is *the* point in relation to which all others are, ultimately, subsidiary? Comparable questions are the basis for the following inquiry into metric structure in examples from Webern.

Webern: Three Pieces, Op. 11, for cello and piano, No. 3; Five Pieces, Op. 5, for string quartet, fourth movement

Webern's meters are generally thought to be more fluctuant and non-congruent than those of the other two of the three great figures of early twentieth-century serialism, Berg and Schoenberg.[8] And it is very possible that Schoenberg's vast influence with respect to the organization of pitch content in post-Romantic music, an influence reaching dominantly across the century, is equalled by Webern's influence (in certain of his works especially) in the direction of increasing metric flexibility. Moreover, metric functions of the kinds to which we have devoted much attention in these pages—progressive and recessive functional changes, vitalizing noncongruities, motivic meter, and in general the applications of rhythmic factors in the functional and expressive shaping of music—are significantly discernible and important in Webern's music.

The third of the cello-piano pieces of Op. 11 can be seen as an example of what is sometimes termed "nonmeter," "antimeter," "suspended meter," or "ameter" (Ex. 3-33a).

The sense of relative "suspension" of meter is understandable in view of what might be described as very tenuous articulation at a predominantly subdued dynamic level in this very short piece. But, again, no series of differentiated sound events can fail to assert metric grouping, with its inevitable implications for structure of relatively stable or fluctuant orders: in these conditions meter may well assume a very unstable and, at times, ambiguous character. Then, it exists in a particular state; it does not cease to exist. And it would be argued here that in Webern meter is palpably functional (if not immediately apprehensible); metric structure is shaped in telling configura-

Ex. 3-33a.   Webern, Three Pieces for cello and piano, Op. 11; No. 3.

tions far from the erratic, contextually arbitrary, apparently aimless state in which change can cease to have functional effect.

It is true that in a music of severe dynamic restraint and *minimal eventfulness* (with embodied silences of constant relevance) nearly every attack may be felt as initiative of a metric unit at some appreciable level, especially in an atmosphere of slow tempo, with consequent considerable distances between articulate events. This is true in a sense comparable to that in which music of great eventfulness, especially in a texture of constant, complex interactions, conveys an impression of *dense meter of continually variegated and competing implications*, as does the first movement of Webern's Op. 22, cited as Ex. 2-22 and referred to again in the present chapter.

Let us consider the example from Op. 11 as to qualities and implications of many of the attacks, as designated by lowercase letters in the foregoing quotation. In view of its extreme dynamic and pitch inferiority (even considering the limited dynamic potential of the subsequent harmonic), point (a), while initiative at the low level of the $\overset{2}{\text{♩}}$ unit, is anticipative in relation to the more important event (b), "recipient" of the directed thrust of the preceding, anticipative ("wind-up") trill, and strong in its *sf* attack, pitch, striking coloration, and in relation to the subsequent intensity recession and silence. Point (b) embraces the following two notes as a mensural group, recessive in relation to it, these impulses, with subsequent rests, constituting in the cello part itself a $\overset{7}{\text{♩}}\;(\overset{3+5}{\underset{3}{\text{♩}\;\text{♩}}})$ unit. Point (g) is initiative of a further unit. Points (i) are relatively brief; this factor, along with their relative pitch inferiority, seems to convey the sense of function as anticipative impulses in relation to the agogically stronger and higher pitch of the final note, whose metric unit is of course indefinite in length; they at the same time form low-level, subsidiary $\overset{3}{\text{♪}}$ units.

Point (j), initiating a final unit, $\overset{?}{\text{♩}}$, is the highest pitch in the piece, quite possibly the longest in duration, and of striking coloration—a relatively high harmonic on the cello's highest string—and it is not unthinkable that *all preceding events might plausibly be regarded as its anacrustic preparation* (i.e., as having the highest-level function of preparing the final sound).

Point (c) in the piano initiates a noncongruent $\overset{11}{\text{♪}}$ unit since the second component, point (e) and the note following, is clearly anticipative (V-like approach, *crescendo*) in relation to the accent g of the piano's upper voice.[64] The anacrustic preparation of the pitch g, just described, and its pitch superiority throughout the piano part, as well as its position as point of highest dynamic intensity in the piano part, lend this event, labeled (f), a feeling of major initiative function and centrality for the entire piano part. With the recessive (lower pitch, dynamic reduction) harmonic interval (EE, e♭) which follows immediately, and the subsequent silence, point (f) is initiative of another unit (of $\overset{10+1}{\underset{3}{\text{♪}\;\text{♪}}}$) in the piano (cf. the size of the preceding one!). A

---

[64]A number of references to the piano's g of m. 5 must not be confused with the attack labeled (g) in the cello.

final unit is initiated (point h) by an event of maximal density-number and -compression. Point (f) has, with the harmonic interval entering below the attack on g, maximal textural expanse for the entire piece—a factor in its accentual primacy.[65] The final piano event is, broadly, recessive in relation to the initiative accent of m. 5.

Seeing the cello and piano parts as metrically noncongruent, interacting, relatively independent structures, we arrive at the following summary (Ex. 3-33b), taking ♪ (⅓ ♪) as a smallest common denominator.[66] It is a structure of pervasive asymmetry, yet of unmistakable progressive-recessive functions and overall poise, its chief accentual events occurring as *balancing referential points just off center*. There emerges an impression of noncongruent meter in which a high-level bar-line for the two strata of events is disjunct *at an only slight angle near the piece's center*—a circumstance of splendid equilibrium in the structure, with constant asymmetries and fluctuation at the same time.

It is evident that critical interpretive decisions rest upon understanding yielded by the above approaches, or upon some comparable, justifiable understanding. Any interpretation requires, of course, enormous subtlety of projection (but firm awareness) in so tenuous and vulnerable a context of restrained articulation. Again, the questions which are the basis of inquiry in the foregoing analysis are very critical ones, as are the conclusions to which they lead: for example, shaped decline through the b-b♭ of the cello after the accent of m. 2, or treatment of the piano's f♯-G♯ of mm. 3–4 as anticipative preparation of (a leaning toward) m. 5. And the suggested conception of the metric centrality of the cello's f[1] (at point g) points to a delicately recessive, withdrawing articulation of the concluding three attacks.

That Webern's music is a language of subtle metric flux and polymetric structure of often elusive definition is apparent in almost any of his works. (Compare Stravinsky, whose accents are in general so much less equivocal.) At the same time, Webern's meters, and fluid rhythmic surfaces, are too little understood in real depth; grouping influences are often especially interdependent—motive often very influential, even essential, in conditioning meter in atmospheres of considerable equivocation of accent. (In this respect, an occasional work, like the Canons, Op. 16, for soprano and clarinets, is significantly exceptional—not in the common equivalence of motivic with metric unit, but in that work's unusual decisiveness of accent,

---

[65]Study of the piece's structure from the standpoint of textural-spatial shape *illuminates one of its most palpably perceptible aspects*. The pivotal spatial expansion of m. 5 includes, of course, the cello f[1].

[66]The unit taken as denominator has the value of course of avoiding fractional expressions, so that twelve units per notated bar (♩) provide a basis for accommodating in the symbology of Ex. 3-33b divisions of four, three, and six within the notated measure.

Ex. 3-33b. Metric proportions in the Webern piece.

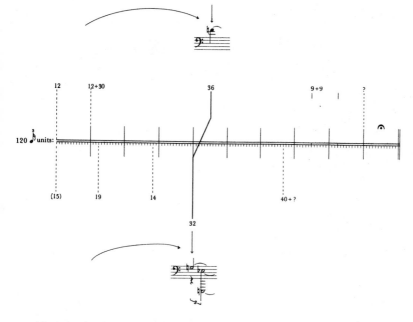

evident in the first piece of the set.) Another Webern excerpt is given as Ex. 3-34a; it is a short movement of much intrinsic interest for the study of meter and other structural elements. Example 3-34b is a sketched representation of implications and questions of metric order and ambiguity at the mensural level in its opening bars.

There are many devices, with typical understatement of coloration and rhythmic nuance, by which events underscore the notated bar-line and the ♩ pulse: on-the-beat attacks of mm. 1–2, with the viola attack of m. 2, third beat, emphasized by anacrustic approach; the overall, general steadiness of articulation of the ♩ , subject to various divisions; initiative attack of the violin 2 in m. 4, part of the clarifying tendency in relation to the relative metric indecision of m. 3; similarly, the initiative attack of the cello in m. 6; in mm. 7–9, the "bracing" effect of viola figuration (the first violin's initiative b² in m. 9 is steadying as the viola rhythm is scattered); all of these are examples of metrically clarifying events relating to the notated bar-line and the beat. Moreover, there is the omnipresent device of anticipative impulse at every level, normally preparing attacks on the beat and/or at the notated bar-line. A few of these clarifying anacrustic events are given in Ex. 3-34c.

Ex. 3-34a.   Webern, Five Pieces, Op. 5, for string quartet, fourth movement.

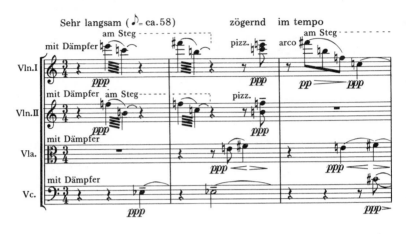

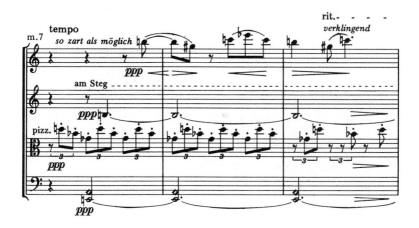

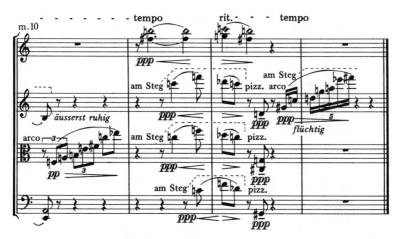

Ex. 3-34b. Implications of $\frac{2}{\text{♩}}$ mensural structure at the beginning of the movement, fluctuating, through ambiguity, toward subsequent affirmation of $\frac{3}{\text{♩}}$.

Ex. 3-34c.

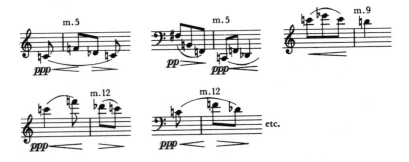

The important rising motives of mm. 6, 10, and 13, related in intervallic content (i.e., one a transposition of the others), are also a manifestation of anacrustic tendency, although not without ambivalence. Of these motives, the following observations concerning rhythmic-metric significance can be made: (1) the obviously conclusive function of the third (m. 13) would presumably have implications for interpretation of the other two, although it is critically different in tempo; (2) the tempo slowing at mm. 5–6 and 9–10 proceeds *through* the motives; (3) the following *a tempo* in each case is a signal of resumption, and rests invariably separate the motive from what follows; (4) the motives are related in important respects—all rise, and all have *diminuendo* (in addition to the noted intervallic identities), while the last is distinct from the others in tempo; and (5) all have in some degree off-the-beat (or off-the-preconditioned-beat) entry and expectations of descent after uninterrupted rise over the distance of a 14th—these factors contributing to persuasive anticipative feeling. There is a suggestion of linking, conjunctive, functionally ambivalent (conclusive-anticipative) tendency one associates *even with the final statement of the motive.*[67]

The general importance of anacrusis in expression of metric structure is thus, with some ambivalences, evident in these motives and in purely specimen extracts quoted in Ex. 3-34c. Additional examples of anticipative impulse can readily be identified.

Let us consider proportional relations in the movement as to *two distinct modes of grouping.* One basis of partitioning is the capacity of the piece to be divided into four, extremely epigrammatic sections on the basis of *ritardando* (*zögernd*, etc.) and *a tempo* delineations. Each of the sections so delineated (mm. 1–2, 3–6, 7–10, 11–13) begins with a rest, and these rests are felt as parts of the sections (II, III, IV) which follow rather than asymmetrical extensions of preceding material in view of (1) relatively consistent preconditioning of the notated bar and (2) the *a tempo* in which each of the rests in question *is included.* The relative proportions (expressed in ♪ values) are shown in Ex. 3-34d.

Ex. 3-34d. Relative proportions among four tempo-delineated units in the Webern.

    I.   10 ♪ + *rit.*   (+ opening rest of 2 ♪ ?)

    II.   24 ♪ + *rit.*

    III.   24 ♪ + *rit.*

    IV.   14 ♪ + 4 of rest + internal *rit.*

Of the outer sections, IV is slightly longer (while both are significantly shorter than the equivalent II and III), although if the opening rest is included as part of I (When does the piece begin?)—which seems more problematic than the concluding rests, more easily felt as incorporated on the

---

[67]These recurrent, unifying motives are thus punctuative (↿) and anticipative (⟋), i.e., ⟋⊢, in feeling, their highly "expectant" qualities looking ahead while other factors (especially tempo affiliations and subsequent rests) seem punctuative of prior events. It is in this perspective that even the final appearance of the motive can be felt as a kind of curiously anomalous "up" impulse (a quasi-anticipative gesture expecting but unfulfilled by thetic response); yet, its more precipitate action (fastest tempo, shortest rhythmic values, marked *flüchtig*) sets it apart, as noted earlier, as a more decisive punctuation subsequent to the cadential broadening consummated just before.

basis of prior structure—we have proportions of I = 12 ♪ and IV = 18 ♪ (in addition to uncertain added quantities occasioned by slowing of tempi). Thus, flanking the symmetrically related internal units are the shorter I and IV, related in the ratio 2:3, the shorter duration of the first section appropriate to its introductory function, and the conclusive function of IV served by its slightly broader length (than I) but compromised by its brevity in relation to II and III, its more active pace of tempo change (accelerated tempo rhythm), and its final *a tempo* motive, a casual, precipitate, punctuative gesture.

The segmentation in the relation 2—4—3 is thus deducible as the numbers of measures in the four tempo-delineated sections (Ex. 3-34e).[68]

Ex. 3-34e. A further expression of relative proportions (numbers of measures in tempo-delineated sections).

$$\overset{\frown}{2} \quad \overset{\frown}{4} \quad \overset{\frown}{4} \quad \overset{\frown}{3}$$

In approaching the issue of broad metric structure, that of accent-delineated grouping, one can plausibly interpret as primary downbeats defining intermensural units the initiative accents of m. 5 (the *crescendo*, extended anacrustic preparation and immediate thrust in complementary outer voices, etc.), m. 9 (expressed in violin 1 only, but dynamically stressed as compared with the c³ following, and of strong anacrustic preparation), and m. 12 (high pitch, some dynamic emphasis, more modest anacrustic approach, but all voices in concurrence). All three of these accents affirm the notated bar-line and emerge in the experience of the movement as points of downbeat "focus" of more than local significance. Proportions, again of

$$\frac{12 \cdot 12 \cdot 9}{\text{♩}}$$ (i.e., 4—4—3), can be seen as *temporal intervals of separation of these important intermensural initiative accents.*[69]

It seems reasonable, too, to interpret mm. 1–4 as of anticipative "impulse" function at the broadest level: consider, for example, the relative ambiguities of these measures coming into relative focus following their

---

[68] It is interesting that this mode of partitioning "agrees" with others: that of articulation by rests (each total silence, except for the anomalous eighth-rest of m. 12, setting off the final motive, begins one of the four sections) and that of relatively fixed registral locus for each section (i.e., the "core" of essential activity for each is a tightly restricted ambitus of pitch events, different for each section).

[69] The issue is again grouping by *accent to accent* (or bar-line to bar-line) as opposed to other modes of grouping noted.

tentative, tenuous, "wrong" metric organization (Ex. 3-34b); the absence of *decisive initiative accent* of more than very local function, e.g., of function comparable to that of m. 5; the registral stasis until the sweeping, broadly anacrustic two-measure descent toward the important downbeat of m. 5; and the striking, relatively affirmative, consequent-feeling concurrence of outer voices at the m. 5 downbeat. The accent of m. 5 comes as a kind of "exhalation," an event which is, within the characteristic atmosphere of restraint, perceived in perspective as a primary release of initiative energy. If that expansively prepared accent is viewed as primary, the movement is seen, at the highest level, as represented in Ex. 3-34f.

Ex. 3-34f. A representation of high-level metric structure extending over the Webern movement.

m. 5   m. 9   m. 12

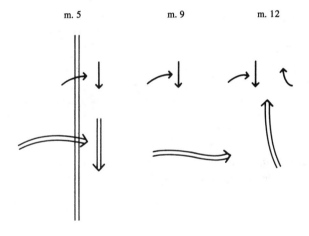

We have considered in the Webern example (1) low-level events of considerable mensural and pulse conformity, (2) the significance of anticipative impulse at all levels, (3) ambivalent functions of the (punctuative, anacrustic) recurring seven-note rising motive, (4) proportional relations manifest in certain modes of grouping—one of them metric, and (5) highest-level metric ordering as expressed *in the distribution and relating of "most important" events*. Related, cofunctional elements of vital reference would include tonal and harmonic rhythms (and relations of PC content—e.g., those of m. 5 and m. 12, key points in the metric structure), as well as motivic-thematic relations beyond their ancillary mention in the foregoing study.

Some twentieth-century problems in rhythm and meter;
recent developments in serialism of durational units—theory
and practice

The severity of change in approaches to and concepts of rhythm in twentieth-century music has provoked a breadth of theoretical concern peculiar to the present time, and one hopes that this concern will eventuate in an accelerating rate and range in the study of rhythm, toward better understanding of rhythmic-metric structure and effect in all music. Certainly rhythm in twentieth-century music is often of particular difficulty.[70]

Problems of meter in the twentieth century center (as with melody, tonality, and other elements) in extremes of fluctuation. The analysis of meter in recent music often reveals (1) an increased asymmetry and noncongruity in both horizontal and vertical dimensions; (2) an increased fragmentation of metric structure resulting from increased tendencies of the motivic surface to relate to and condition meter and grouping; (3) occasional inapplicability of the referential unit of regularly recurrent beat, as in certain contexts of random succession; and in some music (4) the prescribed, predetermining serialization (or other premanipulation) of rhythmic durations and metric grouping, even at all levels.

The field of possible techniques in the serialization of rhythmic elements is of course endless; any factor by which numerical sets are conceived or derived may yield a basis for serialization of durational quantities. The composer's precise techniques in rhythmic (often an aspect of "total") serialization can be a very elusive, sometimes virtually indecipherable, problem, since the composer chooses among an infinite range of possibilities of procedure and permutational principle. Of course, serialization of *any* ele-

---

[70]Nevertheless, the problems of twentieth-century meter are easily (and often) overstated. There is, for example, an enormous volume of significant twentieth-century practice, including some of the important literatures cited in foregoing analyses, in which the notated bar-line has practical importance in representing mensural structure. It is possible that the principle of uncertain significance in notated meter is especially applicable to certain literatures of the present century. But it is also possible that the reverse is sometimes true—that in tradition metric change was conventionally effected in devices of changing patterns of initiative accent without generally altering the standard of notated bar-line consistency, but that in many more recent styles change of notated meter has itself become a convention, more often a significant clue to real structure.

ment has repercussions for meter, since meter is the outcome of variously differentiated element-events and rhythmic durations.

For example, interval content of the twelve-tone set (the IC set) may yield a series of numerical values (Ex. 3-35) as basis for a set of durations.

Ex. 3-35.

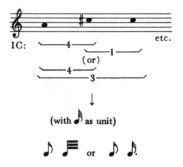

(with ♪ as unit)

Or, a durational set is invented (conceived or derived from some extrinsic source) as a predetermining concept subject to variation (as is a twelve-tone set in classical serialism), employed as a kind of "mode" in permutations analogous to those of classical pitch serialism. Messiaen, for example (in *Mode de valeurs et d'intensités*, one of *Quâtre Etudes* for piano), derives sets of durations simply as twelve even multiples of ♪, then ♪, then ♪. Luigi Nono's *Canto Sospeso* (Ex. 1-51) uses the series 1 2 3 5 8 13 (the so-called Fibonacci series, after its thirteenth-century originator: each integer after the initial consecutive pair the sum of the two preceding); the series is applied to sets of note durations in which it is expressed in various permutations, for example, its retrograde—13 8 5, etc.

Most procedures in rhythmic serialization are based in durations derived *directly from numerical parameters inherent in the PC set itself*; some examples of these are detailed on the following pages.

Of great importance in the evolution of serially-ordered rhythm is the composer Olivier Messiaen, not only because of procedures embraced in his own music but because of his influence on a very great number of younger composers. Messiaen uses a rhythm series in his music as early as 1940, in his *Quatuor pour la fin du temps*.[71]

---

[71] *Quartet for the End of Time*. See Messiaen's own discussion of his rhythmic procedures in the book, *Technique de mon langage musical* (Paris: A. Leduc, 1944).

Messiaen's *Ile de feu 2* (the second of the Four Etudes for piano) employs sets of attack qualities (4), intensities (5), PCs (12), and durations (also 12). The twelve-tone set is shown in Ex. 3-36a; included is its first permutation,

Ex. 3-36a. Set for Messiaen's *Ile de feu 2* and its first, concurrent permutation, with the principle of rotational permutation shown.

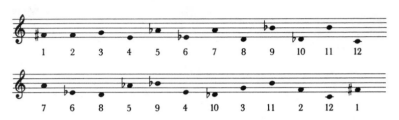

i. e.,

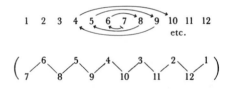

etc.

which appears as a lower-voice counterpoint at the point of initial application of the various sets, the simultaneous statement of *Interversion* (Permutation) *I* and *Interversion II*, quoted in Ex. 3-36b.

The duration series is simply a set of values extending from 1 ♪ to 12 ♪. The permutational principle applied to it is analogous to that on which the twelve-tone set's lower voice variation is based, as shown in Ex. 3-36c, following. At *Interversions I-II* (see Ex. 3-36b), the upper voice has the duration series in the order 6-7-5-8-4-9-3-10-2-11-1-12; the series occurs in the lower voice in the order 3-9-10-4-2-8-11-5-1-7-12-6. This "rotational" principle of ordering durational values is as seen in Ex. 3-36c, in which a graphic representation of pitch ordering is given, followed by similar representations of the ordering of durations in the upper and lower voices. Durational values are *as to spacings of attacks* (i.e., include rests).

There are, in all, ten such permutations punctuated by a recurrent

Ex. 3-36b. Messiaen, *Ile de feu 2* from *Quâtre Etudes* for piano.

"refrain" whose chief melodic voice occurs as a counterpoint to *Interversions IX-X* near the piece's conclusion. As in *Mode de valeurs et d'intensités*, associations of PCs with durational-attack-intensity values are fixed in recurrences. The rotational principle of ordering is a continuation of that established for *Interversions I-II* (as indicated in Ex. 3-36d).

A device for altering the time series on the basis of permutations of the PC set is employed by Boulez in *Structures* for two pianos (cited in Ex. 1-31, where PC and duration sets are given), according to an analysis of the work by György Ligeti.[72] Boulez employs a time set ranging from 1 ♪ to 12 ♪

[72]Herbert Eimert and Karlheinz Stockhausen, eds., "Junge Komponisten," in *Die Reihe*, No. 4 (1958), pp. 38–63. (English edition translated by Leo Black.)

Ex. 3-36c. Rotational principle of ordering PC and duration sets in the Messiaen.

| | 1 | 2 | 3 | 4 | 5 | 6 | 7 | 8 | 9 | 10 | 11 | 12 |

Upper voice pitches:

Lower voice pitches:

etc.

Upper voice durations:
(6 7 5 8 4 9 3 10 2 11 1 12)

etc.

Lower voice durations:

(4 9 3 10 2 etc.)

| | 1 | 2 | 3 | 4 | 5 | 6 | 7 | 8 | 9 | 10 | 11 | 12 |

Ex. 3-36d. Continuation of rotational principle in *Ile de feu 2*.

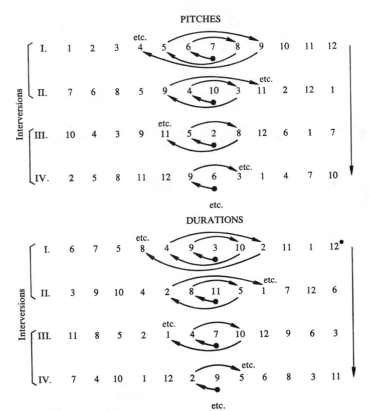

*A rotation from the center of the original row, but beginning with 6 since pitch rotation begins with 7.

(or ♩.). This basic set reacts to modifications in the PC set; for example, if the PC set is transposed up a minor 2nd, a new sequence of order numbers is derived, based on the changed positions of the twelve PCs; this new sequence of order numbers then yields a permutation of the original time set, as shown in Ex. 3-37.

Ex. 3-37. Principle of derived duration set in Boulez *Structures* (see also Ex. 1-31).

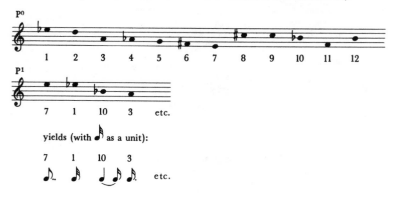

The Boulez is thus an example of a "totally" serialized work in which all elements (pitches, registers, durations, dynamics, etc.) are subject to prescription according to a predetermining system, applied in such a way that for a particular pitch there is *never* a recurrence of the same intensity, duration, etc. This, in contrast to the Messiaen examples, is a procedure of constant "renewal" sought in many works of this kind.

Milton Babbitt, in works as early as 1947–48, has employed pervasive serial operations, presenting in 1955 the following general description of procedures for the serialization of nonpitch components.

The twelve-tone structuralization of non-pitch components can be understood only in terms of a rigorously correct definition of the nature of the operations associated with the system. In characterizing the prime set, it is necessary to associate with each note the ordered number couple—order number, pitch number, measured from the first note as origin—required to define it completely with regard to the set. Then, as transposition is revealed to be mere addition of a constant to the pitch number, inversion—in the twelve-tone sense—is revealed to be complementation mod. 12 of the pitch number. (In other words, pitch number 4 becomes pitch number 8 . . . .) Likewise, retrogression is complementation of the order number, and retrograde inversion is complementation of both order and pitch numbers. Any set of durations—whether the durations be defined in terms of attack, pitch, dynamics, or register—can be, like the pitch set, uniquely permuted by the operations of addition and complementation, with the modulus most logically determined by a factor or a multiple of the metric unit. Thus, the rhythmic component, for example, can be structured in precisely the same way, by the identical operations, as the pitch component; rhythmic inversion, retrogression, and retrograde inversion are uniquely defined, and combinatoriality, derivation, and related properties are analogously applicable to the durational set.[73]

These operations, and consequent associations of order and pitch numbers, are illustrated as Ex. 3-38.

Ex. 3-38. Illustration of permutations by addition and complementation mod. 12 as described by Babbitt.

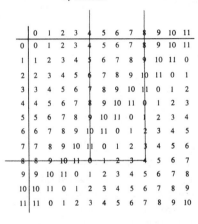

[*Addition and complementation in a mod. 12 system*: lines drawn from two numbers intersect at the number which is their sum (e.g., $8 + 8 = 4$, as indicated); numbers whose lines intersect at—whose sum is—0 (e.g., 8 and 4) are complements.]

0,9 1,11 2,10   9,0 10,2 11,1

[The set (abbreviated); the first number of the pair is the order number (0 to 11); the second is the pitch number (C $= 0$, C♯ $= 1$, etc.).]

0,0 1,2 2,1   9,3 10,5 11,4

[Transposition: a constant (here, 3) is added to each pitch number.]

[73]Milton Babbitt, "Some Aspects of Twelve-Tone Composition," in *The Score and I. M. A. Magazine* (June 1955), p. 60. Peter Westergaard refers to these procedures and discusses their applications in Babbitt's *Composition for 12 Instruments*, in "Some Problems Raised by the Rhythmic Procedures in Milton Babbitt's Composition for Twelve Instruments," in *Perspectives of New Music*, IV, 1 (1965), pp. 109–18.

Ex. 3-38 continued.

0,3 1,1 2,2   9,0 10,10 11,11

[Inversion: transformation of the series of pitch numbers into the series of its complements.]

11,1 10,2 9,0   2,10 1,11 0,9

[Retrograde: complementation of order numbers (plus—i. e., rotated by—a factor of 11).]

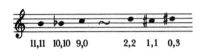

11,11 10,10 9,0   2,2 1,1 0,3

[Retrograde inversion: complementation of pitch numbers of retrograde series (order numbers as in retrograde, above); or complementation of order numbers of inversion, as in deriving retrograde of basic set.]

Procedures for the serialization of nonpitch factors are thus established on the basis of numerical values (paired order and pitch numbers in which $C = 0$) derived entirely from the row and its conventional alterations. By these procedures, all serial operations (permutations of sets, combinatorial applications, etc.) are applicable to the derived set of durations, as to those of all other elements.[74]

Since rhythm and meter are in every sense the consequences of differentiations among the qualities (therefore the functions) of sound events as shaped by all parameters (one of these duration), to the extent that durations, pitches, and other elements are preestablished in serial operations, so is meter significantly predetermined, or totally predetermined where there is total serialism (except when predetermination is precluded within a particular parameter by such practical impediments as limited ranges of instruments). Numerical values, however derived and applied, yield proportional relations among units at all levels; functional interactions of such units are, in many serializations of rhythm, problematic.

Such procedures thus raise the question, one that is reiterated in this book, *of control of the specific qualities of sound events and their interrelations in and*

---

[74]Westergaard ("Some Rhythmic Problems . . . ," p. 115) comments on the problem of control of "interaction of pitch and rhythmic factors" and the question of what "happens to the traditional differential role of rhythm . . . still operative in Webern," noting (p. 114) that "while the precompositional construction of pitch and duration sets is rigorously parallel, their compositional use is highly independent" in view of "the variability of the number of pitches per attack or attacks per pitch." He raises the point that in certain textures the rhythmic ordering *perceived* as a result of these operations may not be that intended.

as to particular contexts and contextual alignments; in serial operations of these kinds, confluences of events are capable of total or nearly total predetermination by systemic procedures which do not foresee, in any functional sense with which these studies have been concerned, particular contextual associations and consequences.

To the extent that serial prescriptions shaping the various parameters of a work set in motion governing, or significantly conditioning, operations that in no way foresee contextual, functional relations and associations, they must be seen as comparable to those of overtly random operations *in consequent effect* of arbitrary affiliations of events. However, as noted in analogous contexts, they are even more random in that the influence of spontaneous, intuitive responses of the performer, usually significantly applicable to chance operations in music, are definitely precluded to the extent that events are predetermined.

The validity of the supposition of blind predetermination of associations of events in total serialism is denied by some composers, while acknowledged by others who consider the consequences of unpredictability a desideratum to be sought. But even to the extent to which contextual associations may be controlled and foreseen in any given procedure, the question must arise as to the nature and depth of functional significances of such associations in the experience of works whose unfolding is prescribed in this sense.

Concluding notes

This study has sought to provide a basis for the consideration and analysis of metric structure, the identification of units at various levels, and the analysis of weak-strong associations and relations internal to those units; it has sought as well to illustrate various kinds and applications of structural techniques—functional and expressive—within the parameters of meter and other aspects of rhythm, seeing meter as the *accent-to-accent grouping of events* delineated around musical projections of relative strength.

We have seen that in dealing with problems of rhythmic analysis, especially in its concern with meter and other manifestations of grouping, one is often led to relatively equivocal conclusions in circumstances of some ambiguity. To some extent this is due to inconclusiveness and uncertainties of knowledge about perceptual responses to musical events which result in groupings at different levels of structure; but the equivocal nature of analytically derived "information" is also to be traced to the fact that rhythmic structure is only rarely, and in situations of least artistic value, unambiguously expressed. Significant ambiguity in metric structure, apart from conditions of gross accentuation and obvious impulse function, is unavoidable, given the extreme *range and complexity of relations* among the many parameters of musical accent. For accentual values are of a scope potentially involving *every element of musical structure*; and the evaluation of relative accentual values is not just a matter of discerning and listing those factors, it is a matter of making difficult *judgments* respecting their relations of effect. It is a question not of simple comeasurement of absolute values, but of evaluating contextual relations *different for every musical situation*. Hence, it is extremely unlikely that a purely objective evaluation of metric structure can be achieved for anything like a comprehensive scope of real musical situations. Moreover, it is for related reasons that the penetrating study of rhythm *engages questions of the nature and functional-expressive consequences of change in all the elements of musical structure.*

The difficulties of rhythmic-metric analysis do not, however, suggest resort to a passive, irrational insistence on purely subjective criteria, or abdication of the effort to understand rhythmic structure according to demonstrable evidence: plausible evidence, in the score and in the experience, can be adduced in support of interpretations of structure, even when the complexity of real music is such that the evaluation of such evidence—the "facts" explicit in the notation of music and in general or particular discernible responses thereto—cannot more than rarely lead to perfectly unambiguous conclusions.

We have sought in this study to identify some of the objective data and circumstances by which rhythmic and metric structures can be understood, and by which such understanding can illuminate the decisions that have to be made in performance (or in critical or stylistic analysis) if interpretation is to be more than mere execution.

Since rhythm is, in a real sense, all of music (i.e., since all musical eventfulness is—usually functionally—rhythmic), a study of rhythm is an appropriate vehicle by which to conclude an exploration into music's structural functions; in rhythmic processes we are reminded powerfully of the interrelations and interactions of element-successions in development and resolution. We see here again that only in simplest situations are element-actions in clear convergence of functional direction; real music bespeaks, in the projection of cooccurring, confluent element-structures, a miraculous and continually absorbing complexity that no musician would deny. That complexity is evident in the breadth and diversity of problems and approaches in music theory, and in the elusiveness of understanding of complex structure and of the relations of structure to experiential effect.

Many of the observations we make in analysis with respect to tonality, harmony, melody, texture, and rhythm (and concerning such further dimensions as color, dissonance, dynamic intensity, articulation, density, space, and so on) are citations of fact, but the farther we move beyond such facts into the evaluation of *interrelations* of events and their *functional-expressive significance*, the more difficult, and the more important, the analysis of music and of the musical experience becomes. Nor do we demean in any way the understanding derived in analysis when we submit demonstrable facts of musical content to varying, plausible interpretations whose relative evaluation is the analyst's further, perhaps most exciting, challenge.

NOTES

[a]The twelfth part of Schoenberg's *Pierrot Lunaire* (*Galgenlied*) is a striking example of the delineation of an entire small structure in significant part by controlled progression in tempo (as to both its parameters) in a line of acceleration qualified only by moderate cadential recession in the ultimate measure. Complementation of this tempo-structure by dynamic changes, texture, and pitch rise is immediately apparent and of potent functional effect.

In a further example, the third of Schoenberg's Piano Pieces, Op. 19, tempo deceleration complements an explicit dynamic succession of release:

$$\frac{f}{p} \longrightarrow \frac{f}{p} \longrightarrow p \longrightarrow pp \longrightarrow ppp$$

[b]Recessive change in rhythmic motion is of course "normal" as a facet of cadential function; this is strikingly evident in composite rhythmic activity in so many examples that further illustration hardly seems indicated. But see Ex. 1-49, p. 163, from Webern's Op. 7, No. 1, an excellent example of activity-tempo curve applicable to the entire piece—progressive, then recessive. Note too the parallel fluctuation in pulse-tempo: the late *ritardando*, and final fermata. Related actions of other element-changes, some of them treated elsewhere in this book, should be considered. The activity curve is instructively seen in arbitrary isolation; that composite (up, down) activity curve is as follows:

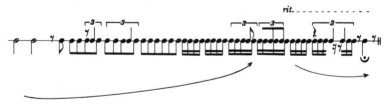

[c]Metric and other types of grouping can in themselves assume motivic significances. An instance of this (at the level of the phrase) may be seen in the final movement of Beethoven's Symphony No. 2. The initial theme ($\frac{2+4}{8}$) is itself a period of six-measure phrases. But what is striking in this movement is Beethoven's employment of six-measure units at crucial points throughout. See, for example, mm. 26 (the theme introduced here), 84–89, 139–43 and the repetition, 151–56, 165–70 (or 166–71), 210–27, 282–93, 290–95, 300–11, 312–21 (a 4 + 6 unit), and other cases. Thus, the character and ordering of grouping (in the above having to do mainly with unit *size* as opposed to internal ordering) may be functionally motivic.

Or, the five-measure unit of the Haydn theme employed by Brahms in orchestral variations is motivic in this important sense, and the "five"-organization is at points in the variations a primary and essential factor of thematic relation, as it is in the concluding ostinato form.

[d]As to all of these factors, regrettably limited reference is afforded by the Beethoven example (Ex. 3-6a). With specific regard to harmonic rhythm it should be reemphasized that the qualitative aspect, as with other element-rhythms, is conditioned by the *nature and degree of change*. Even in situations of relative stasis, a kind of harmonic change (e.g., a rhythm of harmonic inversion) can of course be induced, and it can be delicately moving in functional effect. For example, in the opening phrase of Brahms' Intermezzo in E♭, Op. 117, No. 1, harmonic rhythm is in one sense inert (almost entirely I), in another sense subtly active: the feeling of tightly restrained eventfulness, in varying inverted positions of the prolonged I, is beautifully expressive within a very narrow spectrum of movement.

[e]Element-rhythms can be symbolized and represented by conventional rhythmic notation (as is harmonic rhythm very commonly) or, graphically, as to any number of devices analogous to or extensions of those of Ex. 3-6b—e.g., by numbers of events within any given unit of time (the smaller the unit the more specific the representation). Qualities of events can be symbolized as, for example, p ———— f, ◄ ———— $\frac{1}{2}$, f ———— f♯′, or by numbers representing any quantifiable factor (texture-space, etc.), or by chosen symbols to represent such items as tonal-harmonic events involving strong factors of chromaticism, dissonance, distance, and the like. Representation of proportional relations of event-groups can be shown by any graphic device of measurement—e.g., by lines of varying lengths. Exercises in analytical and graphic illustration of element-rhythms and their interactions can be greatly instructive. Examples for study are of special interest when particular element-rhythmic functions are "concealed" beneath a surface of apparent regularity of (too narrowly conceived) rhythmic eventfulness; consider, for example, Chopin's Etude in E♭ minor, Op. 10, No. 6, as to fluctuations in harmonic and, especially, tonal rhythms.

[f]The question of where the duple division is initiated is more difficult than it may appear, yet an important one for the performer to resolve. In one sense, the first notated beat of m. 29 (included in Ex. 1-3) is the initiator: supporting this view are the preconditioning effect of this point as mensural downbeat in the contextual norm, and the harmonic-rhythmic change; in another sense, the following beat is initiator (consider its approach by leap in both outer voices, and its pitch superiority in relation to the impulse following).

   While this situation is cited as equivocal (many comparable analyses raise questions of this kind) it is clear that the interpretation arrived at will radically govern performance *and affect the nature of the resultant asymmetry*. If the first alternative is regarded as "correct" m. 32, third beat, is considered weak. On the other hand, assumption of the second alternative will render the beginning of m. 29 weak, effecting a $\frac{4}{}$ ♩ unit in the real meter commencing with m. 28, requiring articulation of the second beat of m. 29 as a mensural "downbeat," and causing the entire sequence to end with a stronger impulse, and a resultant strong-strong mensural pattern through the barline separating mm. 32 and 33. The question might be summed up: Do sequential (motivic) and metric units coincide?

[g]See Ex. 3-10, among many. A further example in which a fairly low-level anacrustic complex (cf. Ex. 3-10) has its own distinct lower-level metric structure is the powerful opening gesture of Strauss' *Don Juan*: the accent it prepares (an upper-voice g♯[3]) is strong in pitch, duration, and noncadential tonal change of striking chromatic thrust:

[h]Only one example can be treated in the above discussion, but the entire movement should ideally be explored in all of these connections. Note, in a single limited instance, mensural progressive fluctuation of great intensity at mm. 129–39, a developmental area. The initial attack at m. 139 is a downbeat of broad structural importance; it is approached in a process of metric acceleration in the pattern $\dfrac{3 - 2 - 2 - 1 - 1 - 1}{\text{♩.}}$, and following the peak of this progression (underscored by dynamic and pitch-line changes) there is a recessive $\dfrac{2}{\text{♩.}}$ (actually $\dfrac{3}{\text{♩}}$ —hemiola), complemented by retardation in harmonic rhythm. Do these processes suggest slight, supportive *accelerando* and *trattenuto* in performance? Such interpretive questions are of special relevance in Brahms, as in comparable later styles of greater flexibility.

The question of the accelerative as opposed to decelerative effect of hemiola comes up here—the question as to whether it is perceived as three shorter units of two or one longer unit of six, a matter *subject of course to interpretive control*. One important factor would seem to be the relative accentual forces of low-level impulses initiating the second and third ♩ units: ♩ ♩ ♩ or ♩ ♩ ♩ , again a matter considerably subject to performance control on the basis of analysis of function. In the Brahms example given (Ex. 3-18a), the decisively stronger accent initiating the $\dfrac{3}{\text{♩}}$ unit, and complementary recessions of harmonic rhythm and pitch-line descent, are supportive of broadening effect.

[i]One of the movements cited earlier (Ex. 3-9) in this regard, the *Andante* of Mozart's Symphony No. 41 in C, K. 551 ("Jupiter"), is also a splendid example of intensifying metric progression in the passage following original thematic statement. Beginning at m. 19, there is progression in the pattern (of ♩ beats): 6 – 6 – 2 – 2 – 2 – 2. The unit of $\dfrac{6}{\text{♩}}$, as in mm. 19–20, is established by insistent motivic recurrence; the initiative accentual character of its first impulse is a product of strong factors of pitch—high upper voice, low bass voice, hence broad texture-space; big leaps; *forte* dynamic level; duration; and others. With the metric contractions of such palpable effect in m. 23ff. harmonic rhythm is accelerated. In consulting this passage for supplementary analytical thought, the reader should consider factors of recessive approach to cadence following the progression noted above, and the subsequent increased stability and symmetry (and correspondence to notated bar-line) in accentual patterns of thematic statement after m. 28. There is renewed metric acceleration soon after. The movement is, all in all, a truly rich resource for the study of metric structure and process.

[j]The concluding bars of the motet's first part project one of two highly diversified textures (the other is the approach to the m. 54 cadence) which are focal points for progression of many element-structures of directed intensities. This textural diversity is manifest in part in metric noncongruity in the final bars, where duple and triple units establish divergences throughout the texture and among contiguous segments in an atmosphere of extraordinary flux. The fact that the two most complex segments in the work are at immediate approaches to major cadences (one of them the final cadence) is significant and striking, and it would be a matter of great interest to know the extent to which this is true in works of Josquin.

Josquin's *Sanctus* from the Mass *Faisant Regretz* is a further useful subject of reference: its voices "influence" one another and interact expressively in the extent to which downbeats are felt. Most important in this sense is the steadying influence of the derived phrase in the tenor, whose uninterrupted and unperturbed intermensural

meter ($\overset{4}{\mathbf{o}}\cdot$ —*sanc-tus*) is a foil for the fluctuations of other voices in only relatively

restrained complexity as compared with the *De profundis*. An evidence of beautifully expressive noncongruity, for example, occurs in the conflicting tenor and bassus attacks at m. 5ff. The uniformity of the metric structure in the tenor is compromised

only at the end, where its final unit is broadened into an asymmetrically related $\overset{7}{\mathbf{o}}\cdot$ in recessive action toward the final cadence.

[k]Comparable "displacements" of the bar-line are of great interest in Liszt, as is evident in the quotation from one of the *Transcendental Etudes*, given in Ex. 1-13, p. 57.

[l]The Finale of the Horn Trio is music of supreme rhythmic energy and drive in a context of relative textural simplicity. At the outset the rhythm of *pitch change* brings agogic

emphasis to the half-bar initiative impulses in the rhythm ♪|♩ ♪|♩ ♪|♩ , etc. The bass of the piano carries this out in a different way, with the agogic value of the E♭ expressed as a note followed by rest; but the reader will appreciate, if he listens carefully to the bass, that the same rhythm is there expressed in the underlying pattern of pitch change.

　　Within this apparent regularity (there is regularity at intermensural levels too, as again can be felt with imaginary "conducting" of notated measures as impulses forming groups of two, or four, or eight), there are striking syncopations in the opening bars at intramensural levels. One of these is manifest in the irregular stresses of mm.

3–4, which recur later, in a sense superimposing $\overset{3}{\mathbf{8}}$ units (in trochaic rather than

iambic patterns as to rhythm of pitch change: ♩♩ ♩♩) at points out of joint with the notated, otherwise supported, bar-line. No doubt this is felt as syncopation against a persistent, strongly asserted regularity of mensural order.

[m]The fourth Etude of Elliott Carter's Eight Etudes and a Fantasy for woodwind quartet is excellent for study of opposite, precipitate, progressive metric process. Its opening bars, for example, should be considered as to metric consequences of events *as they take place*, without regard to preconditioned accent and assuming no arbitrary bar-line stresses

in performance. (Is the ♪♩ motive perceived as ⌣ — or — ⌣ ?) In the first five mea-

sures of the Etude, metric acceleration in the series $6 - 4 - 3 - 5 - 2 - 1$ takes place in unmistakable intensification, with counteractive changes in dynamic intensity.

　　For further illustration of metric progression (in which tempo, *crescendo*, and dissonance function complementarily and static harmonic rhythm in counteraction) see Debussy's *l'Après-midi d'un Faune*, mm. 42–46. Immediately following this area in the work there is metric structure of broadened but vertically noncongruent units, and continued recessive process in cadential preparation.

[n]Examples of textural process in Bartók, discussed in Chapter 2, will be found in analysis to have significant correlative features of metric acceleration and deceleration as a fundamental expressive and stylistic trait. The opening of the String Quartet No. 5 (see Ex. 2-11, pp. 218–20) is a case in point, as can be seen in progressively contracted intervals of recurrence of the viola-cello accent of m. 5 in the bars following. Another of many examples in the same movement is the approach to the important hypermetric

accent at m. 170 ($\underset{\frown}{4 - 6 - 2}$　　$\underset{\frown}{11 - 8 - 4 - 8}$), or to the stronger accent

following, or comparable processes involving functional progressive and recessive metric structures.

[o]An interesting application of the principle of rhythmic-metric content as thematic arises in Stravinsky's Variations for orchestra, whose second (m. 23), fifth (m. 47), and eleventh (m. 118) sections are a recurrent "refrain" of contrarhythmic twelve-voice polyphony in which the fact of "thematic" recurrence is chiefly as to rhythmic-metric content. Thus, while there are changes (in viola 4, and in the double-bass) of minor dimensions, the polyphony of Section V is a restatement of the rhythmic-metric content of the lines of Section II, etc. Rhythmic-metric content thus is motivic as a basis for recapitulative form in the Variations. The metric structure of the opening six bars is also the subject of recapitulative procedures; its metric asymmetry is a product of horizontal rather than vertical noncongruity in a context of extreme textural simplicity at the work's inception (see Ex. 2-4, p. 197). Discussion of these elements of rhythmic-metric recapitulation, and of metric "scheme" of the twelve-voice polyphony as indicated in its meter signatures, is included in Spies, "Notes on Stravinsky's Variations," in *Perspectives of New Music,* IV, 1 (Fall-Winter 1965), pp. 62–74.

[p]See, for example, the opening of the development, where a kind of metric acceleration occurs with piled-up elisions of the 2 𝅗𝅥. motive, making for an intense feeling of contraction complemented by pitch rise and prolonged dissonance; in this process there is strong bar-line conformity yielding (at mm. 112–15) to startling ambiguity in acceleration into mensural units of 2 ♩. At mm. 143–52 there is metric progression in relation to which pitch-line descent is counteractive, but in which intensity is again increased by unsettling, syncopated reactive impulses; following m. 164 there is enormous stress on the second beat of every measure to m. 180, a process in which, after m. 167, contradirectional imitations in the bass (at 1♩) are *conflicting in assertion of the notated bar-line.* A further intensifying factor is Beethoven's employment of a three-note fragment of the motive in metric progression in the upper voice after m. 180;

, forming the severest unit contraction of all just before the normal bar-line accent is again decisively restored at m. 184ff. (As to the practice of extreme metric-motivic contractions, compare the Sonata, Op. 53, first movement, mm. 23–28.)

Such matters as the proportional relations of unit segments at higher levels, other instances of progressive contraction, and complementary actions (e.g., dissonance) or counteractive events (e.g., tonal-harmonic stasis) relating to these procedures would be important in continued study.

[q]The matter of correspondence between metric unit and phrase can be explored, too, in others of the Preludes—e.g., the E♭, which is characterized by *phraseological groupings* of eight notated bars throughout while there is great fluctuation in *metric structure* expressed in *shifting points of phrase-level accent.* (Conflict between these two factors, one implying symmetry and the other asymmetry, seems a chief expressive point in this piece.) Consider, for example, the first eight-measure phrase in renotation in diminution—

,

or in relation to the following graphic charting of likely phrase-level and lower-level accents:

The same question can be carried to a higher level: How do the two formally symmetrical and symmetrically related thirty-two-measure sections compare in internal *metric* organization?

ʳThe Prelude in F minor, No. 18, is in a different way a very valuable basis for study of the question of metric structure at the highest level. Such a study would consider (1) the recurrences of ⟋⟍ at many levels, ultimately across the whole expanse in support of the ⸬ at the second beat of m. 17; (2) lower-level progressive and recessive changes as evident in such anacrustic groups (e.g., cf. mm. 1, 3–5, 7–9, 15, 16, etc., in this regard); (3) progressive approach to m. 17 involving the succession 8 - 4 - 3 - 2 ; (4) complementary roles of *crescendo*, pitch rise, chromaticism, tonal flux; (5) the broad, underlying succession V – V/iv – iv – V – i; and (6) background successions involving PCs F-B♭-A♭-C-F and including the horizontal expression of f:i in mm. 9–17, culminating in the m. 17 accent—the highest pitch, a representation of î.

ˢBy no means is this to say that the works of Schoenberg and Berg are not of great interest as to rhythmic structures. The reader is referred, for example, to the Five Orchestra Pieces, Op. 16, of Schoenberg. The first piece of that set, for example, is of constant metric fluctuation, with noncongruities in horizontal and vertical relations manifest in an exceptional clarity of unit delineation by accent and motivic definition. Progressive and recessive tendencies within that structure, and areas of relative resolution, are of important effect in a piece of compellingly active quality from beginning to end, metric diversity an essential aspect of that activity. Such questions as the relations of actual mensural meter to the notated signatures and bar-lines, higher-level tendencies in metric-rhythmic shaping, polymeters (e.g., m. 64ff.), and in general the functional effects of continuous changes in metric structure, are rewarding bases of inquiry in this piece.

editorial notes

Certain editorial and notational practices adopted in this book require brief explanatory comment.

While most footnotes appear on the pages of reference, some (designated by superscript lowercase letters) appear at the ends of chapters. These are of two types: references to supplementary examples within a particular concern, or supplementary comment with respect to cited examples.

Uppercase and lowercase letters denote, as conventionally, major and minor tonics and tonal systems (F, or f) except when the word minor is used as part of the reference, as in F minor. A system conceived bimodally may be referred to by the conjunction of both symbols, as in C,c. The symbols M and m are occasionally used to represent major and minor systems in general (or M,m to denote the bimodal system as a generic concept); thus, m:iv may stand for the subdominant harmony in the minor mode without respect to any individual system. I use the uppercase roman numeral where reference is to the generic, nonparticular, abstracted harmonic element (IV, as a concept apart from any specific tonal identity); otherwise, uppercase and lowercase roman numerals denote major and minor triads, respectively, with the diminished triad represented by the symbol ° (as in ii°) and the augmented by the plus sign (as in III⁺). The major or minor structure of the fundamental triad governs the roman numeral usage with regard to 7th-chords, while I normally rely on the qualifying sense of context in distinction between half-diminished and fully-diminished 7th-chords.

I also use uppercase and lowercase letters to denote *tonicized* degrees or harmonies: T or t for tonic, D for dominant (or D/T where it is necessary to distinguish it from the pitch-class D), sm/T or SM/t for submediant, etc. Secondary relations are expressed as with roman numerals (V/V, IV/ii): for example, SD/SD/T for the harmony on B♭ where it is in the relation subdominant of subdominant in the system on C, and where, as distinct from IV/IV, it is tonicized. Often the term /T is omitted as understood.

The Arabic figure with caret is used to represent the scale degree itself ($\hat{1}$, $\hat{2}$, etc.), and alterations in scale degrees may be shown as $\hat{1}$, $\hat{5}$, and the
♯ ♭

425

like. At times, such symbols as $\hat{2}/\hat{5}$ may denote a particular scale degree as to a secondary system or scale (here, on $\hat{5}$) occurring as referential in some localized sense, as distinct from that on the primary $\hat{1}$ (cf. ii/V).

Pitch-classes are named as uppercase letters. Where specific pitches are cited I use the symbols GG, G, g, g^1 (a 5th above middle C, or c^1), g^2, etc. Enharmonic equivalents are represented as, for example, A♭/G♯. In such expressions as B♭,C♯ the comma stands for the conjunction "and;" in the symbol C-C♯ the hyphen stands for the preposition "to" (C to C♯, a succession). Concepts of pitch-class (abbreviated as PC), pitch-class complex (PCC), and interval-class (IC) are explained at appropriate points. Intervals are identified as to class, or are symbolized as m2, M7, etc.

Where a pitch-class complex (PCC) expresses more than one discernibly functional harmony simultaneously the symbol I+V (or, perhaps, "I+V") is used to denote a kind of "hybrid" function. The symbol "V", or the like, expresses a quasi-functional harmonic element having appreciable "tonal" meaning in some demonstrable sense (as often in modal contexts, or in music of styles more recent than those of tonal conventions, where "V", for example, may be felt as functional despite modifications of interval content and structure). A symbol in parentheses, or accompanied by the ? symbol (as in A?, N?, or iv?) often indicates an uncertain, speculative, item of functional identification, or a factor of questionable significance or other uncertainty.

A symbol such as $\dfrac{\text{I \quad IV \quad V}}{\text{V}}$ denotes fluctuation over a fixed harmony which is concurrent, or over a pedal implying such fixed harmonic function against fluctuation. An underlying bracket or brace (as in $\overbrace{\qquad\text{V}\qquad}$) embraces a succession of local harmonies essentially prolonging and embellishing one of broader significance. There are outlined in Chapter 1 various symbols and techniques for representing pitch structures and affiliations in synoptic sketches of diverse kinds (see pp. 114–16); and many devices for graphic and other representations of textural and rhythmic factors and processes are explained as they occur in Chapters 2 and 3.

In the discussion of rhythm, I adopt the terms *anacrustic* and *thetic*, adjectival forms of *anacrusis* and *thesis* ("upward"-anticipative and "downward" impulses, respectively). And throughout the book I employ such words as *cofunctioning*, *cooccurring*, and *confluent* to describe the interactive relation between discretely identifiable, yet concurrently operative elements in parallel or different ways contributive to structural process.

W.B.

translations[1]

Josquin, *Tu pauperum refugium* from Motet, *Magnus es tu, Domine* (Exx. 1-7, pp. 46–47, and 2-16, pp. 238–40).

Tu pauperum refugium, tu languorum remedium,
    spes exsulum, fortitudo laborantium,
    via errantium, veritas et vita.
Et nunc redemptor Domine, ad te solum confugio,
    te verum Deum adoro, in te spero, in te confido.
Salus mea, Jesu Christe,
    adjuva me, ne unquam obdormiat in morte anima mea.

Thou refuge of the poor, remedy for the weak,
    hope of the exiled, support for the heavy-laden,
    path for the wandering, truth and life.
Now, Lord and redeemer, to thee alone I flee;
    I adore thee, the true God; in thee I hope, in thee I confide.
My salvation, Jesus Christ,
    sustain me, that my soul may never repose in death.

Josquin, *De profundis clamavi* (Exx. 1-26a, pp. 88–89, 2-2, p. 190, and 3-22, p. 368; Psalm 130, quoted only in part; translation as in the King James version).

De profundis clamavi ad te, Domine; Domine, exaudi vocem meam.
Fiant aures tuae intendentes in vocem deprecationis meae.
Si iniquitates observaveris, Domine, Domine, quis sustinebit?

Out of the depths have I cried unto thee, O Lord.
Lord, hear my voice. Let thine ears be attentive to the voice
    of my supplications.
If thou, Lord, shouldest mark iniquities, O Lord, who shall stand?

---

[1]Except where otherwise indicated, translations are by the author. Very brief examples are not included, while those translations given here appear in the order of their occurrence in the book. No effort is made to maintain meter or rhyme in the English renderings.

Gregorian Chant, *Veni creator spiritus* (Ex. 1-41a, p. 121).

> *Veni Creator Spiritus,*
> *Mentes tuorum visita:*
> *Imple superna gratia*
> *Quae tu creasti pectora.*

> Come, Creator Spirit,
> Inhabit the hearts of thine own.
> Pervade with thy supernal grace
> The souls by thee conceived.

Bach, Choral aria, "Drauf schliess ich mich in deine Hände" from Motet, *Komm, Jesu, komm* (Ex. 1-44a, pp. 127–29; poet unknown).

> *Drauf schliess ich mich in deine Hände*
> *und sage, Welt, zu guter Nacht!*
> *Eilt gleich mein Lebenslauf zu Ende,*
> *ist doch der Geist wohl angebracht.*
> *Er soll bei seinem Schöpfer schweben,*
> *weil Jesus ist und bleibt der wahre Weg zum Leben.*

> I yield myself, then, into thy hands,
> and bid the world good night.
> Though my life's course hastens to its end,
> yet is my spirit well prepared.
> It would soar to its creator,
> for Jesus is and remains the true way to life.

Wolf, "Das verlassene Mägdlein" ("The Forsaken Maiden," text by E. Mörike; Ex. 1-46a, pp. 139–40).

> *Früh, wann die Hähne krähn,*
> *eh' die Sternlein schwinden,*
> *muss ich am Herde stehn,*
> *muss Feuer zünden.*

> *Schön ist der Flammen Schein,*
> *es springen die Funken;*
> *ich schaue so darein,*
> *in Leid versunken.*

> *Plötzlich, da kommt es mir,*
> *treuloser Knabe,*
> *dass ich die Nacht von dir*
> *geträumet habe.*

> *Träne auf Träne dann*
> *stürzet hernieder;*
> *so kommt der Tag heran—*
> *o ging' er wieder!*

Early, when roosters crow,
    before the stars disappear,
    I must be at the hearth
    to kindle the fire.

The glow of the flames is beautiful,
    as the sparks fly about;
    I stare into the fire,
    bowed in sadness.

Suddenly, it comes to me,
    unfaithful lad,
    that I have dreamed of you
    in the night.

Tear after tear then
    drops down;
    and so the day begins—
    if only it were ended!

Ravel, "Le Martin-Pêcheur" (from *Histoires Naturelles,* text by Jules Renard; Ex. 1-47a, pp. 143–45).

Ça n'a pas mordu, ce soir, mais je rapporte
    une rare émotion.
Comme je tenais ma perche de ligne tendue,
    un martin-pêcheur est venu s'y poser.
Nous n'avons pas d'oiseau plus éclatant.
Il semblait une grosse fleur bleue au bout
    d'une longue tige. La perche pliait
    sous le poids. Je ne respirais plus,
    tout fier d'être pris pour un arbre
    par un martin-pêcheur.
Et je suis sur qu'il ne s'est pas envolé de peur,
    mais qu'il a cru qu'il ne faisait que passer
    d'une branche à une autre.

Nothing nibbled this evening, yet I take home
    a rare emotion.
As I was holding out my rod,
    a kingfisher appeared and perched on it.
We have no bird more resplendent.
He seemed a great blue flower at the end
    of a long stem. The pole bent
    under his weight. I stopped breathing,
    so proud to be taken for a tree
    by a kingfisher.
And I feel certain it was not fear that made him fly away,
    but that he believed he was only passing
    from one branch to another.

Gesualdo, *Or, che in gioia credea viver contento* (from Madrigals, Book 4 ; text source unknown ; Ex. 2-26a, pp. 258–59).

> *Or, che in gioia credea viver contento,*
> *M'apre la gioia il seno,*
> *Fuggesi l'alma e'l cor, oimè, vien meno.*

> Now that, in happiness, I believe to live content,
> Joy rends my breast,
> My soul flees, and my heart, alas, faints away.

Bach, "Denn das Gesetz des Geistes," from Motet, *Jesu, meine Freude* (Ex. 2-28, pp. 265–66 ; text from Romans 8 :2 ; translation as in the King James version).

> *Denn das Gesetz des Geistes,*
>   *der da lebendig machet in Christo Jesu,*
>   *hat mich frei gemacht von dem Gesetz*
>   *der Sünde und des Todes.*

> For the law of the Spirit of life in Christ Jesus
>   hath made me free from the law
>   of sin and death.

Dallapiccola, *Goethe-Lieder* (No. 1, "In tausend Formen"; Ex. 2-30a, pp. 281–82).

> *In tausend Formen magst du dich verstecken,*
> *Doch, Allerliebste, gleich erkenn ich dich;*
> *Du magst mit Zauberschleiern dich bedecken,*
> *Allgegenwärt'ge, gleich erkenn ich dich.*

> You may conceal yourself in a thousand forms,
> Yet, most beloved, I know you;
> You may clothe yourself in magic veils,
> Omnipresent one, still I know you.

indexes

index of musical examples and citations

Bach, Johann Sebastian (1685–1750):
Motet, *Jesu, meine Freude; Denn das Gesetz des Geistes*, 264–66, 430
Motet, *Komm, Jesu, komm; Drauf schliess ich mich in deine Hände*, 127–34, 428
Partita in C minor; Prelude, 297n
Well-Tempered Clavier, I; Prelude in C, 63–67
Bartók, Béla (1881–1945), 388
Divertimento for string orchestra; second movement, 181n, 234–36, 298n; third movement, 182n
Quartet No. 2 for strings; third movement, 147–62, 183n
Quartet No. 4 for strings; first movement, 217n
Quartet No. 5 for strings; first movement, 217–21, 295n, 422n
Beethoven, Ludwig van (1770–1827), 313, 380
Concerto No. 2 for piano and orchestra; third movement, 374–75
Quartet, Op. 18, No. 1, for strings; first movement, 329, 389
Sonata, Op. 2, No. 3, for piano; first movement, 254n
Sonata, Op. 13, for piano; second movement, 74, 331, 359
Sonata, Op. 22, for piano; first movement, 328, 420n

Sonata, Op. 53, for piano; first movement, 55–57, 423n
Symphony No. 2; first movement, 376; third movement, 380–83; fourth movement, 30–34, 134–38
Symphony No. 3; fourth movement, 34–35
Symphony No. 5, 313
Symphony No. 6, 313
Symphony No. 8; first movement, 389–94, 423n; second movement, 364–65, 372
Variations, Op. 120, on a Waltz of Diabelli; Var. XIV, 313–16, 320, 360, 420n
Berg, Alban (1885–1935), 397, 424n
Concerto for violin and orchestra, 173
Four Pieces, Op. 5, for clarinet and piano; No. 2, 90–93; No. 4, 166–68
Berio, Luciano (b. 1925):
Sequenza II, for harp, 38–40, 309–10
Blacher, Boris (1903–75):
Concerto No. 2 for piano and orchestra, 383n
Ornamente für Klavier, Op. 37; Nos. 3, 5, 6, 363n, 383–86
Boulez, Pierre (b. 1925):
Le Marteau sans Maître; third movement, 102–3

433

index of subjects, names, and terms[1]

Acceleration, 9, 11, 71, 76, 78, 86–87, 136–38, 243, 248, 250, 267, 277, 306–10, 313–16, 324, 339, 344, 355, 367n, 371, 376, 378–83, 392–95, 419n, 421–23n (*see also* Motion; Progression, recession)

Accent, metric initiative impulse, 63n, 66, 90–95, 101n, 123, 126, 134, 149, 154, 303, 310n, 313, 317–61, 364–77, 379–80, 386, 394–97, 418 (*see also* Metric functions)

ambiguity of (*see* Ambiguity, in metric structure)

of associated impulse functions, 342

conjectural factors, 342–44

counter-, 305, 326, 344, 355–59, 372–76, 390–92, 422–23n (*see also*: Metric fluctuation; Metric functions, syncopation)

criteria, 63n, 303, 325, 329, 333–49, 358–61, 365–69, 376, 379–82, 386–95, 399–400, 406, 418, 420–21n

equivalent to higher-level pulse, 350–51, 373

preconditioned (*see* Meter, preconditioned, preconditioning structure)

primary, "structural downbeat" (*see* Metric functions, "structural downbeat")

of superior values, 339–41, 386

textual, 368–69, 388–89

Ambiguity, 10n

in metric structure, 318, 326, 373–79, 380n, 393, 397, 400–406, 417–18, 420n, 423n

of pitch, 213

of tonal orientation, 47, 76, 92, 103–4, 136–40, 150–51, 154–58, 170, 175n, 181n

Ametric structure, 318n, 397

Anacrusis (*see* Metric functions, anacrusis)

Analysis:

as interpretation, 61, 100, 179–80, 302–3, 337–38, 344, 348–51, 377, 418–19

symbols, 44, 48–51, 66, 70n, 114–16, 136, 188, 210, 213n, 215n, 264n, 323n, 328, 334, 350, 352, 379n, 400n, 420n, 425–26

types, 22, 103–14, 178, 350

Apel, W., 120n, 310n

---

[1]The index omits names of some authors and editors of works cited in very minor, passing references. Within items of very broad, recurrent concern, only selected references are given. The symbol *n* is not used where a citation is to a footnote as well as text on the same page. A reference to "individual elements" concerns any or all of the following: color, density, dissonance, harmony, melody, meter, tempo, texture, and tonality.

A CATALOG OF SELECTED
DOVER BOOKS
IN ALL FIELDS OF INTEREST

A CATALOG OF SELECTED DOVER
BOOKS IN ALL FIELDS OF INTEREST

CONCERNING THE SPIRITUAL IN ART, Wassily Kandinsky. Pioneering work by father of abstract art. Thoughts on color theory, nature of art. Analysis of earlier masters. 12 illustrations. 80pp. of text. 5⅜ x 8½. 23411-8 Pa. $4.95

ANIMALS: 1,419 Copyright-Free Illustrations of Mammals, Birds, Fish, Insects, etc., Jim Harter (ed.). Clear wood engravings present, in extremely lifelike poses, over 1,000 species of animals. One of the most extensive pictorial sourcebooks of its kind. Captions. Index. 284pp. 9 x 12. 23766-4 Pa. $14.95

CELTIC ART: The Methods of Construction, George Bain. Simple geometric techniques for making Celtic interlacements, spirals, Kells-type initials, animals, humans, etc. Over 500 illustrations. 160pp. 9 x 12. (USO) 22923-8 Pa. $9.95

AN ATLAS OF ANATOMY FOR ARTISTS, Fritz Schider. Most thorough reference work on art anatomy in the world. Hundreds of illustrations, including selections from works by Vesalius, Leonardo, Goya, Ingres, Michelangelo, others. 593 illustrations. 192pp. 7⅛ x 10¼. 20241-0 Pa. $9.95

CELTIC HAND STROKE-BY-STROKE (Irish Half-Uncial from "The Book of Kells"): An Arthur Baker Calligraphy Manual, Arthur Baker. Complete guide to creating each letter of the alphabet in distinctive Celtic manner. Covers hand position, strokes, pens, inks, paper, more. Illustrated. 48pp. 8¼ x 11. 24336-2 Pa. $3.95

EASY ORIGAMI, John Montroll. Charming collection of 32 projects (hat, cup, pelican, piano, swan, many more) specially designed for the novice origami hobbyist. Clearly illustrated easy-to-follow instructions insure that even beginning papercrafters will achieve successful results. 48pp. 8¼ x 11. 27298-2 Pa. $3.50

THE COMPLETE BOOK OF BIRDHOUSE CONSTRUCTION FOR WOODWORKERS, Scott D. Campbell. Detailed instructions, illustrations, tables. Also data on bird habitat and instinct patterns. Bibliography. 3 tables. 63 illustrations in 15 figures. 48pp. 5¼ x 8½. 24407-5 Pa. $2.50

BLOOMINGDALE'S ILLUSTRATED 1886 CATALOG: Fashions, Dry Goods and Housewares, Bloomingdale Brothers. Famed merchants' extremely rare catalog depicting about 1,700 products: clothing, housewares, firearms, dry goods, jewelry, more. Invaluable for dating, identifying vintage items. Also, copyright-free graphics for artists, designers. Co-published with Henry Ford Museum & Greenfield Village. 160pp. 8¼ x 11. 25780-0 Pa. $10.95

HISTORIC COSTUME IN PICTURES, Braun & Schneider. Over 1,450 costumed figures in clearly detailed engravings–from dawn of civilization to end of 19th century. Captions. Many folk costumes. 256pp. 8⅜ x 11¾. 23150-X Pa. $12.95

STICKLEY CRAFTSMAN FURNITURE CATALOGS, Gustav Stickley and L. & J. G. Stickley. Beautiful, functional furniture in two authentic catalogs from 1910. 594 illustrations, including 277 photos, show settles, rockers, armchairs, reclining chairs, bookcases, desks, tables. 183pp. 6½ x 9¼. 23838-5 Pa. $11.95

AMERICAN LOCOMOTIVES IN HISTORIC PHOTOGRAPHS: 1858 to 1949, Ron Ziel (ed.). A rare collection of 126 meticulously detailed official photographs, called "builder portraits," of American locomotives that majestically chronicle the rise of steam locomotive power in America. Introduction. Detailed captions. xi + 129pp. 9 x 12. 27393-8 Pa. $13.95

AMERICA'S LIGHTHOUSES: An Illustrated History, Francis Ross Holland, Jr. Delightfully written, profusely illustrated fact-filled survey of over 200 American lighthouses since 1716. History, anecdotes, technological advances, more. 240pp. 8 x 10¾. 25576-X Pa. $12.95

TOWARDS A NEW ARCHITECTURE, Le Corbusier. Pioneering manifesto by founder of "International School." Technical and aesthetic theories, views of industry, economics, relation of form to function, "mass-production split" and much more. Profusely illustrated. 320pp. 6⅛ x 9¼. (USO) 25023-7 Pa. $9.95

HOW THE OTHER HALF LIVES, Jacob Riis. Famous journalistic record, exposing poverty and degradation of New York slums around 1900, by major social reformer. 100 striking and influential photographs. 233pp. 10 x 7⅞. 22012-5 Pa. $11.95

FRUIT KEY AND TWIG KEY TO TREES AND SHRUBS, William M. Harlow. One of the handiest and most widely used identification aids. Fruit key covers 120 deciduous and evergreen species; twig key 160 deciduous species. Easily used. Over 300 photographs. 126pp. 5⅜ x 8½. 20511-8 Pa. $3.95

COMMON BIRD SONGS, Dr. Donald J. Borror. Songs of 60 most common U.S. birds: robins, sparrows, cardinals, bluejays, finches, more–arranged in order of increasing complexity. Up to 9 variations of songs of each species. Cassette and manual 99911-4 $8.95

ORCHIDS AS HOUSE PLANTS, Rebecca Tyson Northen. Grow cattleyas and many other kinds of orchids–in a window, in a case, or under artificial light. 63 illustrations. 148pp. 5⅜ x 8½. 23261-1 Pa. $5.95

MONSTER MAZES, Dave Phillips. Masterful mazes at four levels of difficulty. Avoid deadly perils and evil creatures to find magical treasures. Solutions for all 32 exciting illustrated puzzles. 48pp. 8¼ x 11. 26005-4 Pa. $2.95

MOZART'S DON GIOVANNI (DOVER OPERA LIBRETTO SERIES), Wolfgang Amadeus Mozart. Introduced and translated by Ellen H. Bleiler. Standard Italian libretto, with complete English translation. Convenient and thoroughly portable–an ideal companion for reading along with a recording or the performance itself. Introduction. List of characters. Plot summary. 121pp. 5¼ x 8½. 24944-1 Pa. $3.95

TECHNICAL MANUAL AND DICTIONARY OF CLASSICAL BALLET, Gail Grant. Defines, explains, comments on steps, movements, poses and concepts. 15-page pictorial section. Basic book for student, viewer. 127pp. 5⅜ x 8½. 21843-0 Pa. $4.95

BRASS INSTRUMENTS: Their History and Development, Anthony Baines. Authoritative, updated survey of the evolution of trumpets, trombones, bugles, cornets, French horns, tubas and other brass wind instruments. Over 140 illustrations and 48 music examples. Corrected and updated by author. New preface. Bibliography. 320pp. 5⅜ x 8½. 27574-4 Pa. $9.95

HOLLYWOOD GLAMOR PORTRAITS, John Kobal (ed.). 145 photos from 1926-49. Harlow, Gable, Bogart, Bacall; 94 stars in all. Full background on photographers, technical aspects. 160pp. 8⅜ x 11¼. 23352-9 Pa. $12.95

MAX AND MORITZ, Wilhelm Busch. Great humor classic in both German and English. Also 10 other works: "Cat and Mouse," "Plisch and Plumm," etc. 216pp. 5⅜ x 8½. 20181-3 Pa. $6.95

THE RAVEN AND OTHER FAVORITE POEMS, Edgar Allan Poe. Over 40 of the author's most memorable poems: "The Bells," "Ulalume," "Israfel," "To Helen," "The Conqueror Worm," "Eldorado," "Annabel Lee," many more. Alphabetic lists of titles and first lines. 64pp. 5$\frac{3}{16}$ x 8¼. 26685-0 Pa. $1.00

PERSONAL MEMOIRS OF U. S. GRANT, Ulysses Simpson Grant. Intelligent, deeply moving firsthand account of Civil War campaigns, considered by many the finest military memoirs ever written. Includes letters, historic photographs, maps and more. 528pp. 6⅛ x 9¼. 28587-1 Pa. $12.95

AMULETS AND SUPERSTITIONS, E. A. Wallis Budge. Comprehensive discourse on origin, powers of amulets in many ancient cultures: Arab, Persian Babylonian, Assyrian, Egyptian, Gnostic, Hebrew, Phoenician, Syriac, etc. Covers cross, swastika, crucifix, seals, rings, stones, etc. 584pp. 5⅜ x 8½. 23573-4 Pa. $15.95

RUSSIAN STORIES/PYCCKNE PACCKA3bl: A Dual-Language Book, edited by Gleb Struve. Twelve tales by such masters as Chekhov, Tolstoy, Dostoevsky, Pushkin, others. Excellent word-for-word English translations on facing pages, plus teaching and study aids, Russian/English vocabulary, biographical/critical introductions, more. 416pp. 5⅜ x 8½. 26244-8 Pa. $9.95

PHILADELPHIA THEN AND NOW: 60 Sites Photographed in the Past and Present, Kenneth Finkel and Susan Oyama. Rare photographs of City Hall, Logan Square, Independence Hall, Betsy Ross House, other landmarks juxtaposed with contemporary views. Captures changing face of historic city. Introduction. Captions. 128pp. 8¼ x 11. 25790-8 Pa. $9.95

AIA ARCHITECTURAL GUIDE TO NASSAU AND SUFFOLK COUNTIES, LONG ISLAND, The American Institute of Architects, Long Island Chapter, and the Society for the Preservation of Long Island Antiquities. Comprehensive, well-researched and generously illustrated volume brings to life over three centuries of Long Island's great architectural heritage. More than 240 photographs with authoritative, extensively detailed captions. 176pp. 8¼ x 11. 26946-9 Pa. $14.95

NORTH AMERICAN INDIAN LIFE: Customs and Traditions of 23 Tribes, Elsie Clews Parsons (ed.). 27 fictionalized essays by noted anthropologists examine religion, customs, government, additional facets of life among the Winnebago, Crow, Zuni, Eskimo, other tribes. 480pp. 6⅛ x 9¼. 27377-6 Pa. $10.95

FRANK LLOYD WRIGHT'S HOLLYHOCK HOUSE, Donald Hoffmann. Lavishly illustrated, carefully documented study of one of Wright's most controversial residential designs. Over 120 photographs, floor plans, elevations, etc. Detailed perceptive text by noted Wright scholar. Index. 128pp. 9¼ x 10¾. 27133-1 Pa. $11.95

THE MALE AND FEMALE FIGURE IN MOTION: 60 Classic Photographic Sequences, Eadweard Muybridge. 60 true-action photographs of men and women walking, running, climbing, bending, turning, etc., reproduced from rare 19th-century masterpiece. vi + 121pp. 9 x 12. 24745-7 Pa. $10.95

1001 QUESTIONS ANSWERED ABOUT THE SEASHORE, N. J. Berrill and Jacquelyn Berrill. Queries answered about dolphins, sea snails, sponges, starfish, fishes, shore birds, many others. Covers appearance, breeding, growth, feeding, much more. 305pp. 5¼ x 8¼. 23366-9 Pa. $9.95

GUIDE TO OWL WATCHING IN NORTH AMERICA, Donald S. Heintzelman. Superb guide offers complete data and descriptions of 19 species: barn owl, screech owl, snowy owl, many more. Expert coverage of owl-watching equipment, conservation, migrations and invasions, etc. Guide to observing sites. 84 illustrations. xiii + 193pp. 5⅜ x 8½. 27344-X Pa. $8.95

MEDICINAL AND OTHER USES OF NORTH AMERICAN PLANTS: A Historical Survey with Special Reference to the Eastern Indian Tribes, Charlotte Erichsen-Brown. Chronological historical citations document 500 years of usage of plants, trees, shrubs native to eastern Canada, northeastern U.S. Also complete identifying information. 343 illustrations. 544pp. 6½ x 9¼. 25951-X Pa. $12.95

STORYBOOK MAZES, Dave Phillips. 23 stories and mazes on two-page spreads: Wizard of Oz, Treasure Island, Robin Hood, etc. Solutions. 64pp. 8¼ x 11. 23628-5 Pa. $2.95

NEGRO FOLK MUSIC, U.S.A., Harold Courlander. Noted folklorist's scholarly yet readable analysis of rich and varied musical tradition. Includes authentic versions of over 40 folk songs. Valuable bibliography and discography. xi + 324pp. 5⅜ x 8½. 27350-4 Pa. $9.95

MOVIE-STAR PORTRAITS OF THE FORTIES, John Kobal (ed.). 163 glamor, studio photos of 106 stars of the 1940s: Rita Hayworth, Ava Gardner, Marlon Brando, Clark Gable, many more. 176pp. 8⅜ x 11¼. 23546-7 Pa. $14.95

BENCHLEY LOST AND FOUND, Robert Benchley. Finest humor from early 30s, about pet peeves, child psychologists, post office and others. Mostly unavailable elsewhere. 73 illustrations by Peter Arno and others. 183pp. 5⅜ x 8½. 22410-4 Pa. $6.95

YEKL and THE IMPORTED BRIDEGROOM AND OTHER STORIES OF YIDDISH NEW YORK, Abraham Cahan. Film Hester Street based on Yekl (1896). Novel, other stories among first about Jewish immigrants on N.Y.'s East Side. 240pp. 5⅜ x 8½. 22427-9 Pa. $6.95

SELECTED POEMS, Walt Whitman. Generous sampling from *Leaves of Grass*. Twenty-four poems include "I Hear America Singing," "Song of the Open Road," "I Sing the Body Electric," "When Lilacs Last in the Dooryard Bloom'd," "O Captain! My Captain!"–all reprinted from an authoritative edition. Lists of titles and first lines. 128pp. 5³⁄₁₆ x 8¼. 26878-0 Pa. $1.00

THE BEST TALES OF HOFFMANN, E. T. A. Hoffmann. 10 of Hoffmann's most important stories: "Nutcracker and the King of Mice," "The Golden Flowerpot," etc. 458pp. 5⅜ x 8½. 21793-0 Pa. $9.95

FROM FETISH TO GOD IN ANCIENT EGYPT, E. A. Wallis Budge. Rich detailed survey of Egyptian conception of "God" and gods, magic, cult of animals, Osiris, more. Also, superb English translations of hymns and legends. 240 illustrations. 545pp. 5⅜ x 8½. 25803-3 Pa. $13.95

FRENCH STORIES/CONTES FRANÇAIS: A Dual-Language Book, Wallace Fowlie. Ten stories by French masters, Voltaire to Camus: "Micromegas" by Voltaire; "The Atheist's Mass" by Balzac; "Minuet" by de Maupassant; "The Guest" by Camus, six more. Excellent English translations on facing pages. Also French-English vocabulary list, exercises, more. 352pp. 5⅜ x 8½. 26443-2 Pa. $9.95

CHICAGO AT THE TURN OF THE CENTURY IN PHOTOGRAPHS: 122 Historic Views from the Collections of the Chicago Historical Society, Larry A. Viskochil. Rare large-format prints offer detailed views of City Hall, State Street, the Loop, Hull House, Union Station, many other landmarks, circa 1904-1913. Introduction. Captions. Maps. 144pp. 9⅜ x 12¼. 24656-6 Pa. $12.95

OLD BROOKLYN IN EARLY PHOTOGRAPHS, 1865-1929, William Lee Younger. Luna Park, Gravesend race track, construction of Grand Army Plaza, moving of Hotel Brighton, etc. 157 previously unpublished photographs. 165pp. 8⅞ x 11¾. 23587-4 Pa. $13.95

THE MYTHS OF THE NORTH AMERICAN INDIANS, Lewis Spence. Rich anthology of the myths and legends of the Algonquins, Iroquois, Pawnees and Sioux, prefaced by an extensive historical and ethnological commentary. 36 illustrations. 480pp. 5⅜ x 8½. 25967-6 Pa. $10.95

AN ENCYCLOPEDIA OF BATTLES: Accounts of Over 1,560 Battles from 1479 B.C. to the Present, David Eggenberger. Essential details of every major battle in recorded history from the first battle of Megiddo in 1479 B.C. to Grenada in 1984. List of Battle Maps. New Appendix covering the years 1967-1984. Index. 99 illustrations. 544pp. 6½ x 9¼. 24913-1 Pa. $16.95

SAILING ALONE AROUND THE WORLD, Captain Joshua Slocum. First man to sail around the world, alone, in small boat. One of great feats of seamanship told in delightful manner. 67 illustrations. 294pp. 5⅜ x 8½. 20326-3 Pa. $6.95

ANARCHISM AND OTHER ESSAYS, Emma Goldman. Powerful, penetrating, prophetic essays on direct action, role of minorities, prison reform, puritan hypocrisy, violence, etc. 271pp. 5⅜ x 8½. 22484-8 Pa. $7.95

MYTHS OF THE HINDUS AND BUDDHISTS, Ananda K. Coomaraswamy and Sister Nivedita. Great stories of the epics; deeds of Krishna, Shiva, taken from puranas, Vedas, folk tales; etc. 32 illustrations. 400pp. 5⅜ x 8½. 21759-0 Pa. $12.95

BEYOND PSYCHOLOGY, Otto Rank. Fear of death, desire of immortality, nature of sexuality, social organization, creativity, according to Rankian system. 291pp. 5⅜ x 8½. 20485-5 Pa. $8.95

A THEOLOGICO-POLITICAL TREATISE, Benedict Spinoza. Also contains unfinished Political Treatise. Great classic on religious liberty, theory of government on common consent. R. Elwes translation. Total of 421pp. 5⅜ x 8½. 20249-6 Pa. $9.95

MY BONDAGE AND MY FREEDOM, Frederick Douglass. Born a slave, Douglass became outspoken force in antislavery movement. The best of Douglass' autobiographies. Graphic description of slave life. 464pp. 5⅜ x 8½. 22457-0 Pa. $8.95

FOLLOWING THE EQUATOR: A Journey Around the World, Mark Twain. Fascinating humorous account of 1897 voyage to Hawaii, Australia, India, New Zealand, etc. Ironic, bemused reports on peoples, customs, climate, flora and fauna, politics, much more. 197 illustrations. 720pp. 5⅜ x 8½. 26113-1 Pa. $15.95

THE PEOPLE CALLED SHAKERS, Edward D. Andrews. Definitive study of Shakers: origins, beliefs, practices, dances, social organization, furniture and crafts, etc. 33 illustrations. 351pp. 5⅜ x 8½. 21081-2 Pa. $8.95

THE MYTHS OF GREECE AND ROME, H. A. Guerber. A classic of mythology, generously illustrated, long prized for its simple, graphic, accurate retelling of the principal myths of Greece and Rome, and for its commentary on their origins and significance. With 64 illustrations by Michelangelo, Raphael, Titian, Rubens, Canova, Bernini and others. 480pp. 5⅜ x 8½. 27584-1 Pa. $9.95

PSYCHOLOGY OF MUSIC, Carl E. Seashore. Classic work discusses music as a medium from psychological viewpoint. Clear treatment of physical acoustics, auditory apparatus, sound perception, development of musical skills, nature of musical feeling, host of other topics. 88 figures. 408pp. 5⅜ x 8½. 21851-1 Pa. $11.95

THE PHILOSOPHY OF HISTORY, Georg W. Hegel. Great classic of Western thought develops concept that history is not chance but rational process, the evolution of freedom. 457pp. 5⅜ x 8½. 20112-0 Pa. $9.95

THE BOOK OF TEA, Kakuzo Okakura. Minor classic of the Orient: entertaining, charming explanation, interpretation of traditional Japanese culture in terms of tea ceremony. 94pp. 5⅜ x 8½. 20070-1 Pa. $3.95

LIFE IN ANCIENT EGYPT, Adolf Erman. Fullest, most thorough, detailed older account with much not in more recent books, domestic life, religion, magic, medicine, commerce, much more. Many illustrations reproduce tomb paintings, carvings, hieroglyphs, etc. 597pp. 5⅜ x 8½. 22632-8 Pa. $12.95

SUNDIALS, Their Theory and Construction, Albert Waugh. Far and away the best, most thorough coverage of ideas, mathematics concerned, types, construction, adjusting anywhere. Simple, nontechnical treatment allows even children to build several of these dials. Over 100 illustrations. 230pp. 5⅜ x 8½. 22947-5 Pa. $8.95

DYNAMICS OF FLUIDS IN POROUS MEDIA, Jacob Bear. For advanced students of ground water hydrology, soil mechanics and physics, drainage and irrigation engineering, and more. 335 illustrations. Exercises, with answers. 784pp. 6⅛ x 9¼. 65675-6 Pa. $19.95

SONGS OF EXPERIENCE: Facsimile Reproduction with 26 Plates in Full Color, William Blake. 26 full-color plates from a rare 1826 edition. Includes "The Tyger," "London," "Holy Thursday," and other poems. Printed text of poems. 48pp. 5¼ x 7. 24636-1 Pa. $4.95

OLD-TIME VIGNETTES IN FULL COLOR, Carol Belanger Grafton (ed.). Over 390 charming, often sentimental illustrations, selected from archives of Victorian graphics–pretty women posing, children playing, food, flowers, kittens and puppies, smiling cherubs, birds and butterflies, much more. All copyright-free. 48pp. 9¼ x 12¼. 27269-9 Pa. $7.95

PERSPECTIVE FOR ARTISTS, Rex Vicat Cole. Depth, perspective of sky and sea, shadows, much more, not usually covered. 391 diagrams, 81 reproductions of drawings and paintings. 279pp. 5⅜ x 8½. 22487-2 Pa. $7.95

DRAWING THE LIVING FIGURE, Joseph Sheppard. Innovative approach to artistic anatomy focuses on specifics of surface anatomy, rather than muscles and bones. Over 170 drawings of live models in front, back and side views, and in widely varying poses. Accompanying diagrams. 177 illustrations. Introduction. Index. 144pp. 8⅜ x11¼. 26723-7 Pa. $8.95

GOTHIC AND OLD ENGLISH ALPHABETS: 100 Complete Fonts, Dan X. Solo. Add power, elegance to posters, signs, other graphics with 100 stunning copyright-free alphabets: Blackstone, Dolbey, Germania, 97 more—including many lower-case, numerals, punctuation marks. 104pp. 8⅛ x 11. 24695-7 Pa. $8.95

HOW TO DO BEADWORK, Mary White. Fundamental book on craft from simple projects to five-bead chains and woven works. 106 illustrations. 142pp. 5⅜ x 8. 20697-1 Pa. $5.95

THE BOOK OF WOOD CARVING, Charles Marshall Sayers. Finest book for beginners discusses fundamentals and offers 34 designs. "Absolutely first rate . . . well thought out and well executed."–E. J. Tangerman. 118pp. 7¾ x 10⅝. 23654-4 Pa. $7.95

ILLUSTRATED CATALOG OF CIVIL WAR MILITARY GOODS: Union Army Weapons, Insignia, Uniform Accessories, and Other Equipment, Schuyler, Hartley, and Graham. Rare, profusely illustrated 1846 catalog includes Union Army uniform and dress regulations, arms and ammunition, coats, insignia, flags, swords, rifles, etc. 226 illustrations. 160pp. 9 x 12. 24939-5 Pa. $10.95

WOMEN'S FASHIONS OF THE EARLY 1900s: An Unabridged Republication of "New York Fashions, 1909," National Cloak & Suit Co. Rare catalog of mail-order fashions documents women's and children's clothing styles shortly after the turn of the century. Captions offer full descriptions, prices. Invaluable resource for fashion, costume historians. Approximately 725 illustrations. 128pp. 8⅜ x 11¼. 27276-1 Pa. $11.95

THE 1912 AND 1915 GUSTAV STICKLEY FURNITURE CATALOGS, Gustav Stickley. With over 200 detailed illustrations and descriptions, these two catalogs are essential reading and reference materials and identification guides for Stickley furniture. Captions cite materials, dimensions and prices. 112pp. 6½ x 9¼. 26676-1 Pa. $9.95

EARLY AMERICAN LOCOMOTIVES, John H. White, Jr. Finest locomotive engravings from early 19th century: historical (1804–74), main-line (after 1870), special, foreign, etc. 147 plates. 142pp. 11⅜ x 8¼. 22772-3 Pa. $10.95

THE TALL SHIPS OF TODAY IN PHOTOGRAPHS, Frank O. Braynard. Lavishly illustrated tribute to nearly 100 majestic contemporary sailing vessels: Amerigo Vespucci, Clearwater, Constitution, Eagle, Mayflower, Sea Cloud, Victory, many more. Authoritative captions provide statistics, background on each ship. 190 black-and-white photographs and illustrations. Introduction. 128pp. 8⅞ x 11¾. 27163-3 Pa. $14.95

EARLY NINETEENTH-CENTURY CRAFTS AND TRADES, Peter Stockham (ed.). Extremely rare 1807 volume describes to youngsters the crafts and trades of the day: brickmaker, weaver, dressmaker, bookbinder, ropemaker, saddler, many more. Quaint prose, charming illustrations for each craft. 20 black-and-white line illustrations. 192pp. 4⅝ x 6. 27293-1 Pa. $4.95

VICTORIAN FASHIONS AND COSTUMES FROM HARPER'S BAZAR, 1867–1898, Stella Blum (ed.). Day costumes, evening wear, sports clothes, shoes, hats, other accessories in over 1,000 detailed engravings. 320pp. 9⅜ x 12¼. 22990-4 Pa. $15.95

GUSTAV STICKLEY, THE CRAFTSMAN, Mary Ann Smith. Superb study surveys broad scope of Stickley's achievement, especially in architecture. Design philosophy, rise and fall of the Craftsman empire, descriptions and floor plans for many Craftsman houses, more. 86 black-and-white halftones. 31 line illustrations. Introduction 208pp. 6½ x 9¼. 27210-9 Pa. $9.95

THE LONG ISLAND RAIL ROAD IN EARLY PHOTOGRAPHS, Ron Ziel. Over 220 rare photos, informative text document origin (1844) and development of rail service on Long Island. Vintage views of early trains, locomotives, stations, passengers, crews, much more. Captions. 8⅞ x 11¾. 26301-0 Pa. $13.95

THE BOOK OF OLD SHIPS: From Egyptian Galleys to Clipper Ships, Henry B. Culver. Superb, authoritative history of sailing vessels, with 80 magnificent line illustrations. Galley, bark, caravel, longship, whaler, many more. Detailed, informative text on each vessel by noted naval historian. Introduction. 256pp. 5⅜ x 8½. 27332-6 Pa. $7.95

TEN BOOKS ON ARCHITECTURE, Vitruvius. The most important book ever written on architecture. Early Roman aesthetics, technology, classical orders, site selection, all other aspects. Morgan translation. 331pp. 5⅜ x 8½. 20645-9 Pa. $8.95

THE HUMAN FIGURE IN MOTION, Eadweard Muybridge. More than 4,500 stopped-action photos, in action series, showing undraped men, women, children jumping, lying down, throwing, sitting, wrestling, carrying, etc. 390pp. 7⅞ x 10⅝. 20204-6 Clothbd. $27.95

TREES OF THE EASTERN AND CENTRAL UNITED STATES AND CANADA, William M. Harlow. Best one-volume guide to 140 trees. Full descriptions, woodlore, range, etc. Over 600 illustrations. Handy size. 288pp. 4½ x 6⅜. 20395-6 Pa. $6.95

SONGS OF WESTERN BIRDS, Dr. Donald J. Borror. Complete song and call repertoire of 60 western species, including flycatchers, juncoes, cactus wrens, many more–includes fully illustrated booklet. Cassette and manual 99913-0 $8.95

GROWING AND USING HERBS AND SPICES, Milo Miloradovich. Versatile handbook provides all the information needed for cultivation and use of all the herbs and spices available in North America. 4 illustrations. Index. Glossary. 236pp. 5⅜ x 8½. 25058-X Pa. $7.95

BIG BOOK OF MAZES AND LABYRINTHS, Walter Shepherd. 50 mazes and labyrinths in all–classical, solid, ripple, and more–in one great volume. Perfect inexpensive puzzler for clever youngsters. Full solutions. 112pp. 8⅛ x 11. 22951-3 Pa. $4.95

PIANO TUNING, J. Cree Fischer. Clearest, best book for beginner, amateur. Simple repairs, raising dropped notes, tuning by easy method of flattened fifths. No previous skills needed. 4 illustrations. 201pp. 5⅜ x 8½. 23267-0 Pa. $6.95

A SOURCE BOOK IN THEATRICAL HISTORY, A. M. Nagler. Contemporary observers on acting, directing, make-up, costuming, stage props, machinery, scene design, from Ancient Greece to Chekhov. 611pp. 5⅜ x 8½. 20515-0 Pa. $12.95

THE COMPLETE NONSENSE OF EDWARD LEAR, Edward Lear. All nonsense limericks, zany alphabets, Owl and Pussycat, songs, nonsense botany, etc., illustrated by Lear. Total of 320pp. 5⅜ x 8½. (USO) 20167-8 Pa. $7.95

VICTORIAN PARLOUR POETRY: An Annotated Anthology, Michael R. Turner. 117 gems by Longfellow, Tennyson, Browning, many lesser-known poets. "The Village Blacksmith," "Curfew Must Not Ring Tonight," "Only a Baby Small," dozens more, often difficult to find elsewhere. Index of poets, titles, first lines. xxiii + 325pp. 5⅝ x 8¼. 27044-0 Pa. $8.95

DUBLINERS, James Joyce. Fifteen stories offer vivid, tightly focused observations of the lives of Dublin's poorer classes. At least one, "The Dead," is considered a masterpiece. Reprinted complete and unabridged from standard edition. 160pp. 5$\frac{3}{16}$ x 8¼. 26870-5 Pa. $1.00

THE HAUNTED MONASTERY and THE CHINESE MAZE MURDERS, Robert van Gulik. Two full novels by van Gulik, set in 7th-century China, continue adventures of Judge Dee and his companions. An evil Taoist monastery, seemingly supernatural events; overgrown topiary maze hides strange crimes. 27 illustrations. 328pp. 5⅜ x 8½. 23502-5 Pa. $8.95

THE BOOK OF THE SACRED MAGIC OF ABRAMELIN THE MAGE, translated by S. MacGregor Mathers. Medieval manuscript of ceremonial magic. Basic document in Aleister Crowley, Golden Dawn groups. 268pp. 5⅜ x 8½. 23211-5 Pa. $9.95

NEW RUSSIAN-ENGLISH AND ENGLISH-RUSSIAN DICTIONARY, M. A. O'Brien. This is a remarkably handy Russian dictionary, containing a surprising amount of information, including over 70,000 entries. 366pp. 4½ x 6⅛. 20208-9 Pa. $10.95

HISTORIC HOMES OF THE AMERICAN PRESIDENTS, Second, Revised Edition, Irvin Haas. A traveler's guide to American Presidential homes, most open to the public, depicting and describing homes occupied by every American President from George Washington to George Bush. With visiting hours, admission charges, travel routes. 175 photographs. Index. 160pp. 8¼ x 11. 26751-2 Pa. $11.95

NEW YORK IN THE FORTIES, Andreas Feininger. 162 brilliant photographs by the well-known photographer, formerly with *Life* magazine. Commuters, shoppers, Times Square at night, much else from city at its peak. Captions by John von Hartz. 181pp. 9¼ x 10¾. 23585-8 Pa. $13.95

INDIAN SIGN LANGUAGE, William Tomkins. Over 525 signs developed by Sioux and other tribes. Written instructions and diagrams. Also 290 pictographs. 111pp. 6⅛ x 9¼. 22029-X Pa. $3.95

ANATOMY: A Complete Guide for Artists, Joseph Sheppard. A master of figure drawing shows artists how to render human anatomy convincingly. Over 460 illustrations. 224pp. 8⅜ x 11¼. 27279-6 Pa. $11.95

MEDIEVAL CALLIGRAPHY: Its History and Technique, Marc Drogin. Spirited history, comprehensive instruction manual covers 13 styles (ca. 4th century thru 15th). Excellent photographs; directions for duplicating medieval techniques with modern tools. 224pp. 8⅜ x 11¼. 26142-5 Pa. $12.95

DRIED FLOWERS: How to Prepare Them, Sarah Whitlock and Martha Rankin. Complete instructions on how to use silica gel, meal and borax, perlite aggregate, sand and borax, glycerine and water to create attractive permanent flower arrangements. 12 illustrations. 32pp. 5⅜ x 8½. 21802-3 Pa. $1.00

EASY-TO-MAKE BIRD FEEDERS FOR WOODWORKERS, Scott D. Campbell. Detailed, simple-to-use guide for designing, constructing, caring for and using feeders. Text, illustrations for 12 classic and contemporary designs. 96pp. 5⅜ x 8½. 25847-5 Pa. $3.95

SCOTTISH WONDER TALES FROM MYTH AND LEGEND, Donald A. Mackenzie. 16 lively tales tell of giants rumbling down mountainsides, of a magic wand that turns stone pillars into warriors, of gods and goddesses, evil hags, powerful forces and more. 240pp. 5⅜ x 8½. 29677-6 Pa. $6.95

THE HISTORY OF UNDERCLOTHES, C. Willett Cunnington and Phyllis Cunnington. Fascinating, well-documented survey covering six centuries of English undergarments, enhanced with over 100 illustrations: 12th-century laced-up bodice, footed long drawers (1795), 19th-century bustles, 19th-century corsets for men, Victorian "bust improvers," much more. 272pp. 5⅝ x 8¼. 27124-2 Pa. $9.95

ARTS AND CRAFTS FURNITURE: The Complete Brooks Catalog of 1912, Brooks Manufacturing Co. Photos and detailed descriptions of more than 150 now very collectible furniture designs from the Arts and Crafts movement depict davenports, settees, buffets, desks, tables, chairs, bedsteads, dressers and more, all built of solid, quarter-sawed oak. Invaluable for students and enthusiasts of antiques, Americana and the decorative arts. 80pp. 6½ x 9¼. 27471-3 Pa. $8.95

HOW WE INVENTED THE AIRPLANE: An Illustrated History, Orville Wright. Fascinating firsthand account covers early experiments, construction of planes and motors, first flights, much more. Introduction and commentary by Fred C. Kelly. 76 photographs. 96pp. 8¼ x 11. 25662-6 Pa. $8.95

THE ARTS OF THE SAILOR: Knotting, Splicing and Ropework, Hervey Garrett Smith. Indispensable shipboard reference covers tools, basic knots and useful hitches; handsewing and canvas work, more. Over 100 illustrations. Delightful reading for sea lovers. 256pp. 5⅜ x 8½. 26440-8 Pa. $8.95

FRANK LLOYD WRIGHT'S FALLINGWATER: The House and Its History, Second, Revised Edition, Donald Hoffmann. A total revision–both in text and illustrations–of the standard document on Fallingwater, the boldest, most personal architectural statement of Wright's mature years, updated with valuable new material from the recently opened Frank Lloyd Wright Archives. "Fascinating"–*The New York Times.* 116 illustrations. 128pp. 9¼ x 10¾. 27430-6 Pa. $12.95

PHOTOGRAPHIC SKETCHBOOK OF THE CIVIL WAR, Alexander Gardner. 100 photos taken on field during the Civil War. Famous shots of Manassas Harper's Ferry, Lincoln, Richmond, slave pens, etc. 244pp. 10⅝ x 8¼. 22731-6 Pa. $10.95

FIVE ACRES AND INDEPENDENCE, Maurice G. Kains. Great back-to-the-land classic explains basics of self-sufficient farming. The one book to get. 95 illustrations. 397pp. 5⅜ x 8½. 20974-1 Pa. $7.95

SONGS OF EASTERN BIRDS, Dr. Donald J. Borror. Songs and calls of 60 species most common to eastern U.S.: warblers, woodpeckers, flycatchers, thrushes, larks, many more in high-quality recording. Cassette and manual 99912-2 $9.95

A MODERN HERBAL, Margaret Grieve. Much the fullest, most exact, most useful compilation of herbal material. Gigantic alphabetical encyclopedia, from aconite to zedoary, gives botanical information, medical properties, folklore, economic uses, much else. Indispensable to serious reader. 161 illustrations. 888pp. 6½ x 9¼. 2-vol. set. (USO) Vol. I: 22798-7 Pa. $9.95
Vol. II: 22799-5 Pa. $9.95

HIDDEN TREASURE MAZE BOOK, Dave Phillips. Solve 34 challenging mazes accompanied by heroic tales of adventure. Evil dragons, people-eating plants, blood-thirsty giants, many more dangerous adversaries lurk at every twist and turn. 34 mazes, stories, solutions. 48pp. 8¼ x 11. 24566-7 Pa. $2.95

LETTERS OF W. A. MOZART, Wolfgang A. Mozart. Remarkable letters show bawdy wit, humor, imagination, musical insights, contemporary musical world; includes some letters from Leopold Mozart. 276pp. 5⅜ x 8½. 22859-2 Pa. $7.95

BASIC PRINCIPLES OF CLASSICAL BALLET, Agrippina Vaganova. Great Russian theoretician, teacher explains methods for teaching classical ballet. 118 illustrations. 175pp. 5⅜ x 8½. 22036-2 Pa. $5.95

THE JUMPING FROG, Mark Twain. Revenge edition. The original story of The Celebrated Jumping Frog of Calaveras County, a hapless French translation, and Twain's hilarious "retranslation" from the French. 12 illustrations. 66pp. 5⅜ x 8½. 22686-7 Pa. $3.95

BEST REMEMBERED POEMS, Martin Gardner (ed.). The 126 poems in this superb collection of 19th- and 20th-century British and American verse range from Shelley's "To a Skylark" to the impassioned "Renascence" of Edna St. Vincent Millay and to Edward Lear's whimsical "The Owl and the Pussycat." 224pp. 5⅜ x 8½. 27165-X Pa. $5.95

COMPLETE SONNETS, William Shakespeare. Over 150 exquisite poems deal with love, friendship, the tyranny of time, beauty's evanescence, death and other themes in language of remarkable power, precision and beauty. Glossary of archaic terms. 80pp. 5$\frac{3}{16}$ x 8¼. 26686-9 Pa. $1.00

BODIES IN A BOOKSHOP, R. T. Campbell. Challenging mystery of blackmail and murder with ingenious plot and superbly drawn characters. In the best tradition of British suspense fiction. 192pp. 5⅜ x 8½. 24720-1 Pa. $6.95

CATALOG OF DOVER BOOKS

THE INFLUENCE OF SEA POWER UPON HISTORY, 1660–1783, A. T. Mahan. Influential classic of naval history and tactics still used as text in war colleges. First paperback edition. 4 maps. 24 battle plans. 640pp. 5⅜ x 8½. 25509-3 Pa. $14.95

THE STORY OF THE TITANIC AS TOLD BY ITS SURVIVORS, Jack Winocour (ed.). What it was really like. Panic, despair, shocking inefficiency, and a little heroism. More thrilling than any fictional account. 26 illustrations. 320pp. 5⅜ x 8½. 20610-6 Pa. $8.95

FAIRY AND FOLK TALES OF THE IRISH PEASANTRY, William Butler Yeats (ed.). Treasury of 64 tales from the twilight world of Celtic myth and legend: "The Soul Cages," "The Kildare Pooka," "King O'Toole and his Goose," many more. Introduction and Notes by W. B. Yeats. 352pp. 5⅜ x 8½. 26941-8 Pa. $8.95

BUDDHIST MAHAYANA TEXTS, E. B. Cowell and Others (eds.). Superb, accurate translations of basic documents in Mahayana Buddhism, highly important in history of religions. The Buddha-karita of Asvaghosha, Larger Sukhavativyuha, more. 448pp. 5⅜ x 8½. 25552-2 Pa. $12.95

ONE TWO THREE . . . INFINITY: Facts and Speculations of Science, George Gamow. Great physicist's fascinating, readable overview of contemporary science: number theory, relativity, fourth dimension, entropy, genes, atomic structure, much more. 128 illustrations. Index. 352pp. 5⅜ x 8½. 25664-2 Pa. $8.95

ENGINEERING IN HISTORY, Richard Shelton Kirby, et al. Broad, nontechnical survey of history's major technological advances: birth of Greek science, industrial revolution, electricity and applied science, 20th-century automation, much more. 181 illustrations. ". . . excellent . . ."–*Isis.* Bibliography. vii + 530pp. 5⅜ x 8¼. 26412-2 Pa. $14.95

DALÍ ON MODERN ART: The Cuckolds of Antiquated Modern Art, Salvador Dalí. Influential painter skewers modern art and its practitioners. Outrageous evaluations of Picasso, Cézanne, Turner, more. 15 renderings of paintings discussed. 44 calligraphic decorations by Dalí. 96pp. 5⅜ x 8½. (USO) 29220-7 Pa. $4.95

ANTIQUE PLAYING CARDS: A Pictorial History, Henry René D'Allemagne. Over 900 elaborate, decorative images from rare playing cards (14th–20th centuries): Bacchus, death, dancing dogs, hunting scenes, royal coats of arms, players cheating, much more. 96pp. 9¼ x 12¼. 29265-7 Pa. $12.95

MAKING FURNITURE MASTERPIECES: 30 Projects with Measured Drawings, Franklin H. Gottshall. Step-by-step instructions, illustrations for constructing handsome, useful pieces, among them a Sheraton desk, Chippendale chair, Spanish desk, Queen Anne table and a William and Mary dressing mirror. 224pp. 8⅛ x 11¼. 29338-6 Pa. $13.95

THE FOSSIL BOOK: A Record of Prehistoric Life, Patricia V. Rich et al. Profusely illustrated definitive guide covers everything from single-celled organisms and dinosaurs to birds and mammals and the interplay between climate and man. Over 1,500 illustrations. 760pp. 7½ x 10⅛. 29371-8 Pa. $29.95

Prices subject to change without notice.

Available at your book dealer or write for free catalog to Dept. GI, Dover Publications, Inc., 31 East 2nd St., Mineola, N.Y. 11501. Dover publishes more than 500 books each year on science, elementary and advanced mathematics, biology, music, art, literary history, social sciences and other areas.